Anonymous

Message from the President of the United States

Anonymous

Message from the President of the United States

ISBN/EAN: 9783744730938

Printed in Europe, USA, Canada, Australia, Japan

Cover: Foto ©ninafisch / pixelio.de

More available books at **www.hansebooks.com**

MESSAGE

FROM THE

PRESIDENT OF THE UNITED STATES,

TRANSMITTING

THE REPORT OF THE NAVAL COURT OF INQUIRY UPON THE DESTRUCTION OF THE UNITED STATES BATTLE SHIP MAINE IN HAVANA HARBOR, FEBRUARY 15, 1898, TOGETHER WITH THE TESTIMONY TAKEN BEFORE THE COURT.

WASHINGTON:
GOVERNMENT PRINTING OFFICE
1898.

MESSAGE.

To the Congress of the United States:

For some time prior to the visit of the *Maine* to Havana Harbor our consular representatives pointed out the advantages to flow from the visit of national ships to the Cuban waters, in accustoming the people to the presence of our flag as the symbol of good will and of our ships in the fulfillment of the mission of protection to American interests, even though no immediate need therefor might exist.

Accordingly on the 24th of January last, after conference with the Spanish minister in which the renewal of visits of our war vessels to Spanish waters was discussed and accepted, the peninsular authorities at Madrid and Havana were advised of the purpose of this Government to resume friendly naval visits at Cuban ports, and that in that view the *Maine* would forthwith call at the port of Havana.

This announcement was received by the Spanish Government with appreciation of the friendly character of the visit of the *Maine*, and with notification of intention to return the courtesy by sending Spanish ships to the principal ports of the United States. Meanwhile the *Maine* entered the port of Havana on the 25th of January, her arrival being marked with no special incident besides the exchange of customary salutes and ceremonial visits.

The *Maine* continued in the harbor of Havana during the three weeks following her arrival. No appreciable excitement attended her stay; on the contrary, a feeling of relief and confidence followed the resumption of the long interrupted friendly intercourse. So noticeable was this immediate effect of her visit that the consul-general strongly urged that the presence of our ships in Cuban waters should be kept up by retaining the *Maine* at Havana or, in the event of her recall, by sending another vessel there to take her place.

At forty minutes past 9 in the evening of the 15th of February the *Maine* was destroyed by an explosion, by which the entire forward part of the ship was utterly wrecked. In this catastrophe two officers and two hundred and sixty-four of her crew perished, those who were not killed outright by her explosion being penned between decks by the tangle of wreckage and drowned by the immediate sinking of the hull.

Prompt assistance was rendered by the neighboring vessels anchored in the harbor, aid being especially given by the boats of the Spanish cruiser *Alfonso XII* and the Ward Line steamer *City of Washington*, which lay not far distant. The wounded were generously cared for by the authorities of Havana, the hospitals being freely opened to them, while the earliest recovered bodies of the dead were interred by the municipality in a public cemetery in the city. Tributes of grief and sympathy were offered from all official quarters of the island.

The appalling calamity fell upon the people of our country with crushing force, and for a brief time an intense excitement prevailed, which in a community less just and self-controlled than ours might have led to hasty acts of blind resentment. This spirit, however, soon gave way to the calmer processes of reason and to the resolve to investigate the facts and await material proof before forming a judgment as to the cause, the responsibility, and, if the facts warranted, the remedy due. This course necessarily recommended itself from the outset to the Executive, for only in the light of a dispassionately ascertained certainty could it determine the nature and measure of its full duty in the matter.

The usual procedure was followed, as in all cases of casualty or disaster to national vessels of any maritime State. A naval court of inquiry was at once organized, composed of officers well qualified by rank and practical experience to discharge the onerous duty imposed upon them. Aided by a strong force of wreckers and divers, the court proceeded to make a thorough investigation on the spot, employing every available means for the impartial and exact determination of the causes of the explosion. Its operations have been conducted with the utmost deliberation and judgment, and while independently pursued no attainable source of information was neglected, and the fullest opportunity was allowed for a simultaneous investigation by the Spanish authorities.

The finding of the court of inquiry was reached, after twenty-three days of continuous labor, on the 21st of March, instant, and, having been approved on the 22d by the commander in chief of the United States naval force on the North Atlantic Station, was transmitted to the Executive.

It is herewith laid before the Congress, together with the voluminous testimony taken before the court.

Its purport is, in brief, as follows:

When the *Maine* arrived at Havana she was conducted by the regular Government pilot to buoy No. 4, to which she was moored in from 5½ to 6 fathoms of water.

The state of discipline on board, and the condition of her magazines, boilers, coal bunkers, and storage compartments, are passed in review, with the conclusion that excellent order prevailed, and that no indication of any cause for an internal explosion existed in any quarter.

At 8 o'clock in the evening of February 15 everything had been reported secure, and all was quiet.

At forty minutes past 9 o'clock the vessel was suddenly destroyed.

There were two distinct explosions, with a brief interval between them.

The first lifted the forward part of the ship very perceptibly; the second, which was more open, prolonged, and of greater volume, is attributed by the court to the partial explosion of two or more of the forward magazines.

The evidence of the divers establishes that the after part of the ship was practically intact and sank in that condition a very few moments after the explosion. The forward part was completely demolished.

Upon the evidence of a concurrent external cause the finding of the court is as follows:

At frame 17 the outer shell of the ship, from a point 11½ feet from the middle line of the ship and 6 feet above the keel when in its normal position, has been forced up so as to be now about 4 feet above the surface of the water, therefore about 34 feet above where it would be had the ship sunk uninjured.

The outside bottom plating is bent into a reversed V shape (Λ), the after wing of which, about 15 feet broad and 32 feet in length (from frame 17 to frame 25), is doubled back upon itself against the continuation of the same plating, extending forward.

At frame 18 the vertical keel is broken in two and the flat keel bent into an angle similar to the angle formed by the outside bottom plates. This break is now about 6 feet below the surface of the water and about 30 feet above its normal position.

In the opinion of the court this effect could have been produced only by the explosion of a mine situated under the bottom of the ship at about frame 18 and somewhat on the port side of the ship.

The conclusions of the court are:

That the loss of the *Maine* was not in any respect due to fault or negligence on the part of any of the officers or members of her crew;

That the ship was destroyed by the explosion of a submarine mine, which caused the partial explosion of two or more of her forward magazines; and

That no evidence has been obtainable fixing the responsibility for the destruction of the *Maine* upon any person or persons.

I have directed that the finding of the court of inquiry and the views of this Government thereon be communicated to the Government of Her Majesty the Queen Regent, and I do not permit myself to doubt that the sense of justice of the Spanish nation will dictate a course of action suggested by honor and the friendly relations of the two Governments.

It will be the duty of the Executive to advise the Congress of the result, and in the meantime deliberate consideration is invoked.

WILLIAM MCKINLEY.

EXECUTIVE MANSION,
March 28, 1898.

RECORD

OF THE

PROCEEDINGS OF A COURT OF INQUIRY

CONVENED

ON BOARD THE UNITED STATES LIGHT-HOUSE TENDER MANGROVE BY VIRTUE OF A PRECEPT SIGNED BY REAR-ADMIRAL MONTGOMERY SICARD, U. S. NAVY, COMMANDER IN CHIEF, UNITED STATES NAVAL FORCE ON NORTH ATLANTIC STATION,

TO

INQUIRE INTO THE LOSS OF THE U. S. B. S. MAINE, IN THE HARBOR OF HAVANA, CUBA,

ON THE

NIGHT OF FEBRUARY FIFTEENTH, EIGHTEEN HUNDRED AND NINETY-EIGHT.

PROCEEDINGS

OF A

Court of inquiry convened on board the United States light-house tender Mangrove, by virtue of a precept signed by Rear-Admiral Montgomery Sicard, United States Navy, commander in chief United States naval force on North Atlantic Station.

FIRST DAY.

U. S. LIGHT-HOUSE TENDER MANGROVE,
Harbor of Havana, Monday, February 21, 1898—10 a. m.

The court met pursuant to the above-mentioned precept.

Present: Capt. William T. Sampson, United States Navy, president; Capt. French E. Chadwick, United States Navy, and Lieut. Commander William P. Potter, United States Navy, members; and Lieut. Commander Adolph Marix, United States Navy, judge advocate.

The court was cleared and the orders constituting it, together with all the accompanying instructions, were read aloud and appended, marked as follows:

Precept, together with two accompanying telegrams forming a part of it, marked "A."

Letter from the convening authority to the president of the court, giving certain officers the right to be present at the investigation, marked "B."

Second letter from the convening authority to the president of the court, allowing any other persons to be present during the investigation should the evidence develop any facts which might implicate such persons, marked "C." All other matters preliminary to the inquiry were determined, and, after deciding to sit with closed doors, the court was opened.

The judge-advocate, having requested and received permission, introduced as stenographer Frederick J. Buenzle, chief yeoman, United States Navy.

Captain Sigsbee, United States Navy, commanding the U. S. battle ship *Maine*, whom the convening authority had notified of his right to be present during the investigation, appeared and requested permission to be present at such times during the investigation as he might desire, but did not want any counsel.

The judge-advocate read aloud the precept and accompanying instructions heretofore referred to.

Captain Sigsbee was asked if he objected to any member of the court, to which he replied in the negative.

The members were severally duly sworn by the judge advocate, and the judge-advocate was duly sworn by the president, all of which oaths were administered according to law.

Chief Yeoman Frederick J. Buenzle, United States Navy, was duly sworn as stenographer by the judge-advocate.

All witnesses were directed to withdraw.

The court being duly organized, the inquiry proceeded as follows:

Capt. CHARLES D. SIGSBEE, United States Navy, a witness called by the judge-advocate, was duly sworn by the president.

EXAMINATION IN CHIEF.

By the JUDGE-ADVOCATE:

Q. What is your name, rank, and present station?
A. Charles D. Sigsbee; captain, United States Navy; commanding U. S. S. *Maine*.
Q. When did you take command of the *Maine?*
A. On the 10th day of April, 1897.
Q. When did the *Maine* arrive at Havana the last time?
A. On the 24th day of January, 1898.
Q. About what time?
A. About half past 9 in the morning.
Q. Do you know, or have you any reason to believe, that the authorities of Havana knew of the *Maine's* coming?
A. Yes; I understand that they were notified by the United States consul-general.
Q. Upon your arrival, did you take a pilot?
A. I did; I took an official pilot sent off by the captain of the port of Havana.
Q. Did he berth the *Maine?*
A. He did.
Q. Where?
A. The berth is in the man-of-war anchorage off the Machina, or the Shears. It is to all appearances one of the regular mooring buoys of the place. My recollection is that the pilot said that it was buoy No. 4. Our bearings, taken soon after mooring, did not place it exactly according to the charted position of buoy No. 4, but no note was taken of this because it was assumed that the charted position might represent former positions, and the buoys might have been changed somewhat in the examinations of the moorings.
Q. Have you been to Havana before frequently or recently?
A. I was here about 1872, and again about 1878.
Q. Do you know if you were placed in the usual berth for men-of-war?
A. No. I can only state that by remarks I have heard since the explosion.
Q. State what you heard.
A. I have been informed, since the explosion on board the *Maine*, by Captain Stevens, who is temporarily in command of the steamer *City of Washington*, of the Ward Line of steamers, that he had never known in all his experience, which covers visits to Havana for five or six years, a man-of-war to be anchored at that buoy, and that he had rarely known merchant vessels to be anchored there, and that it was the least used buoy in the harbor.
Q. Will you please describe the surroundings when first moored to this buoy?

A. The Spanish man-of-war *Alfonso XII* was moored in the position now occupied by the *Fern*—about 250 yards to the northward and westward of the *Maine*. The German ship *Gniesenau* was anchored at the berth now occupied by the Spanish man-of-war *Segaspe*, which is about 400 yards about due north from the *Maine*. A day or two after the arrival of the *Maine* the German man-of-war *Charlotte* came in and was anchored about four or five hundred yards to the southward of the *Maine's* berth. Other vessels, merchant vessels, came and went, anchored and moored in localities more or less remote, from 200 yards upward.

Q. Will you please describe your surroundings at the time of the explosion?

A. It was a calm and still night. At the time of the accident the Spanish man-of-war *Alfonso XII* was at the berth, as before stated. The small Spanish dispatch boat *Segaspe* had come out, I think, the day before and taken the berth occupied by the Spanish man-of-war, the *Gniesenau* having left. The steamer *City of Washington* was anchored about two hundred yards to the southward and eastward of the *Maine's* stern, slightly on the port quarter. That is as much as I can give. Other vessels were remote, so far as my recollection goes.

Q. When did you coal before the last coaling?

A. We coaled at Key West within a week of the time of our arrival.

Q. How much coal did you take at that time, if you remember?

A. I think about one hundred and fifty tons.

Q. Was the coal regularly inspected?

A. My recollection is that it was. It was from the Government coal pile, and we had the usual men on shore; and while I can not now state specifically, it was our invariable custom on board the *Maine* to inspect all coal before it was brought on board.

Q. How much coal did you take in the last coaling previous to this, and where?

A. It was at Key West, and I think in the neighborhood of 300 tons.

Q. Into what bunkers was the coal placed at these coalings?

A. Generally in the forward bunkers, because it was customary to use coal from the forward bunkers first. These bunkers naturally, therefore, were replenished with new coal.

Q. There is a peculiar bunker under the forward turret, abreast the 10-inch magazine. Do you know when that was last emptied?

A. I can not personally recollect that particular bunker.

Q. Did you ever receive any report from the chief engineer of your ship that any coal had been too long in any bunker?

A. Never that I can recollect.

Q. Did the fire-alarms in the bunkers work?

A. They were sensitive. They worked occasionally when there was no undue heat in the bunkers, on which occasions we invariably examined the bunkers and got a report.

Q. Regarding inflammables and paints on board the *Maine*, were the regulations strictly carried out in regard to the stowage?

A. Strictly, so far as my knowledge and my orders were concerned. I was very particular on points of that kind. I was especially particular in my directions to the chief engineer concerning the disposition of waste which had been used. He had informed me that it was always kept in a covered metal bucket until thrown overboard with the ashes. He has since informed me that it was habitual to throw it overboard every day with the ashes.

Q. How often did you discharge ashes in Havana?

A. I can not now recollect; but I remember giving certain directions in connection with hired lighters and not dumping in the harbor. The chief engineer was generally very solicitous about getting ashes out of the ship promptly.

Q. Where were ashes kept until discharged?

A. Those that I saw were dumped about the region of the bulkhead between the two fire rooms. There was a passage out of the forward part of the forward fire room which would have been blocked by ashes.

Q. Regarding paints and inflammables, was there not a paint room well forward below the berth deck?

A. The paint room was in what is called the eyes of the ship, just below the berth deck, the extreme forward compartment.

Q. What were the regulations in regard to that paint room? Was the painter allowed to stow any inflammables there?

A. He was not. The inflammables were stowed in chests aft, according to regulations, and when inflammables were in excess of our chest capacity they were allowed to be kept in the bathroom of the port or admiral's cabin.

Q. I believe Japan dryers, turpentine, and such were kept forward inside the superstructure. Am I not correct?

A. That is my recollection.

Q. Regarding the electric plant of the *Maine*, have you any reason to believe, from your observation of the lights or from any reports that may have been made to you, that there had been serious grounding?

A. None whatever; and there was no sudden flaring up of the lights before the explosion.

Q. No perceptible disturbance of the lights?

A. None whatever; there was a total and sudden eclipse.

Q. What were the regulations of the ship in regard to taking the temperature of the magazines, etc.?

A. There were no special regulations other than those that were regulations. The magazines were examined according to regulations, and reports made accordingly and sent to the Department. I always examined the temperature myself and conversed with the ordnance officer as to the effect of various temperatures on the contents of the magazines, and in his opinion, and my own, the temperatures were never near the danger point. I do not think there was any laxity in this direction. I can not recollect any. When I joined the ship I found it was considered unnecessary to use slippers in the magazine, and I directed that they should be used.

Q. Do you recollect any work going on in the magazine or shell rooms on the day of the disaster?

A. My recollection is that the keys were called for that morning at quarters in the usual way. I can not recollect any other call for the keys on that day.

Q. Were the keys properly returned after quarters?

A. Yes; so far as I can recollect. The regulation reports were made at 8 o'clock by the executive officer. The keys of all the shell rooms and magazines, and the spare keys, have been recovered by the diver in my stateroom, where they were always kept.

Q. At the time of the disaster what boilers were being used?

A. The two after boilers in the after fire room. More than one boiler was in use, for the reason that our hydraulic system was somewhat leaky.

Q. Please inform the court in a general way, giving any particulars you wish to give, in regard to your relations to the Spanish authorities and native authorities or people, from the time of the arrival of the *Maine* until the time of your disaster.

A. My relations with the officials were outwardly cordial, and I have no ground for assuming that they were not really cordial. The members of the autonomistic council of the Government, however, seemed to have brought to the attention of the Navy Department the fact that I did not visit them. They made me no suggestions to visit them. From the letters and telegrams received from the Navy Department there seems to have been some embarrassment caused the Government at Washington by the fact that I made them no visit. I took the ground to the department that it was unknown etiquette to call on the civil members of the colonial government other than the governor, but that I would have exceeded etiquette at any time on suggestion from the council. Without waiting for orders I made a visit afterwards. My visit was pleasantly received, and promptly returned by certain members of the council. They sent on board a large party of ladies a day or two afterwards. The president of the council, on board the *Maine*, made me a very cordial address, which I could not understand, and which was interpreted to me briefly. I replied briefly, expressing kind sentiments and a hope for the continuance of cordial relations between Spain and the United States. Fancying that some expression cordial to the colonial or autonomistic government might be expected of me, I evaded the point, and used only this expression: "I beg to express my admiration for the high purpose of your honorable body." My reply was afterwards printed in at least two papers in Havana, but the terms made me favor autonomistic government in the Island. I am informed that the autonomistic government in Havana is unpopular among a large class of Spanish and Cuban residents. I have no means of knowing whether my apparent interference in the political concerns of the island had any relation to the destruction of the *Maine*.

Q. Was there ever any demonstration of animosity by people afloat?

A. Never on shore, so far as I am informed; but afloat there was a demonstration. It was the first Sunday after our arrival, on board a ferryboat, densely crowded with people, both civil and military, who were returning to Havana from a bull fight in Regla. The demonstration consisted of yells, whistles, and apparently derisive calls emanating from about thirty or forty people at most. It was not general.

Q. During the stay of the *Maine* at Havana did you take other than the ordinary precautions which are usually taken on every man-of-war for her protection?

A. I did.

Q. Please state them fully.

A. I had sentries on the forecastle and poop, quartermaster and signal boy on the bridge, signal boy on the poop; the corporal of the guard especially instructed to look out for the port gangway; the officer of the deck and quartermaster especially instructed to look out for the starboard gangway; a quarter watch was kept on deck all night; sentries' cartridge boxes were filled, their arms kept loaded, a number of rounds of rapid-firing ammunition kept in the pilot house, and, in the spare captain's pantry, under the after superstructure, additional charges of shell close at hand for the secondary battery; steam kept up in two boilers instead of one; especial instructions given to watch carefully all the hydraulic gear and report defects; the officer of the deck charged with the necessity for making detailed reports to me, even in minor matters. I had personally instructed the master at arms and the orderly sergeant to keep a careful eye on everybody that came on board, and to charge all their subordinates to the same purpose. I instructed them that, when any persons came on board to go below, they were to go with them, and carefully observe any packages that might be held, on the supposition that dynamite or other high explosive might be employed; and to afterwards inspect the routes these people had taken, and never to lose sight of the importance of my order. I further instructed the marine officer to make at least two visits during the night to the posts of the vessel. The whole purport of my orders and directions was that we should consider the *Maine* in a position demanding extreme vigilance. Doubtless I gave many other detailed orders of a minor character that I can not now recall.

Q. Regarding strangers being in the ship, at what time were they compelled to leave the ship?

A. I think Lieutenant-Commander Wainwright was rather severe on desultory visitors. Very few visited the ship, except people of the highest social standing in the city. They came commonly from 2 to say 5 o'clock. They were always accompanied about the ship by officers, and of course under the supervisory orders of the master at arms and sergeant of marines. People were allowed to visit the ship from about 10 to 12, and about 1 to 4. I think there were but two visits of Spanish military officers. Once, about two weeks ago, a party of five or six Spanish officers came on board during my absence. They were reported to me as having been constrained, and not desirous to accept much courtesy. They accepted no refreshments, but I afterwards learned that it is Spanish custom not to accept refreshments unless they are at hand at the time the offer is made. On another occasion, about the same time, a Spanish officer came off with his wife. He made a visit to my cabin, and was shown about the ship by an officer under my direction. I invited Spanish officers to visit the ship; in fact, I made considerable effort to get them on board socially in order to show good will according to the spirit of the *Maine's* visit to Havana; but with the exceptions noted, no military officer of Spain visited the ship socially, so far as I can remember. I know that the purser of the *Alfonso XII* made a social visit; but I can not recollect a purely social visit from other Spanish officers. The ward-room officers of the *Maine*, perhaps, have further information on this point.

Q. Among the precautions which you took was the fact of having extra lookouts on the deck. Was there ever any report of any unauthorized boats attempting to approach the ship and being ordered off?

A. Never, to my knowledge.

Q. On the night of the disaster, were all your extra precautions in force? I mean, in regard to quarter watches?

A. I assume that they were; they were never rescinded, and up to the night of the explosion, as far as my observation could go, my knowledge is that they were carried out. I was especially impressed during the whole visit here by the prompt tendency of the sentries to report any infractions of orders on the part of the crew.

Q. At the time of the accident, do you know what boats were down, and where?

A. I assume that one of the cutters was down, and one of the steam launches. I think the first steam launch was down. The steam launch, I have since been informed, was riding at the starboard boom, and that one of her crew was saved. He is now in the hospital at Havana.

Q. What kind of a night was it at the time of the explosion?

A. It was a very quiet and warm night, and I remember distinctly that the echoes of the bugle at tattoo were singularly distinct and pleasant. A little rain fell after the explosion, which may have been precipitated by the concussion of the explosion.

Q. Was it a dry night?

A. There were stars, but I think it was somewhat overcast. I think I saw several stars after the accident, but it was somewhat overcast according to my recollection.

Q. How was the *Maine* heading at the time of the explosion?

A. Approximately northwest. She pointed toward the shears—somewhat to the right of the shears, near the admiral's residence.

Q. Where were you at the time?

A. I was writing at my port-cabin table, after side. I was dressed.

Q. Please give your experience in full?

A. I was just closing a letter to my family when I felt the crash of the explosion. It was a bursting, rending, and crashing sound or roar of immense volume, largely metallic in its character. It was succeeded by a metallic sound—probably of falling débris—a trembling and lurching motion of the vessel, then an impression of subsidence, attended by an eclipse of the electric lights and intense darkness within the cabin. I knew immediately that the *Maine* had been blown up and that she was sinking. I hurried to the starboard cabin ports, thinking it might be necessary for me to make my exit in that way. Upon looking out I decided that I could go by the passage leading to the superstructure. I therefore took the latter route, feeling my way along and steadying myself by the bulkheads. The superstructure was filled with smoke, and it was dark. Nearing the outer entrance I met Private Anthony, the orderly at the cabin door at the time. He ran into me and, as I remember, apologized in some fashion, and reported to me that the ship had been blown up and was sinking.

I reached the quarter-deck, asked a few questions of those standing about me—Lieutenant Commander Wainwright, I think, for one—then I asked the orderly for the time. He said that the exact time of the explosion was 9.40 p. m. I proceeded to the poop deck, stood on the side rail, and held on to the main rigging in order to see over the poop awning, which was baggy and covered with débris; also in order that I might observe details in the black mass ahead. I directed the executive officer to post sentries all around the ship, but soon saw that there were no marines available, and no place forward to post them. Not being quite clear as to the condition of things forward, I next directed the forward magazine to be flooded if practicable, and about the same time shouted out myself for perfect silence everywhere. This was, I think, repeated by the executive officer. The surviving officers were about me at the time on the poop. I was informed that the forward magazine was already under water, and after inquiring about the after magazine was told that it was also under water, as shown by the condition below reported by those coming from the wardroom and steerage.

About this time fire broke out in the mass forward, over the central superstructure, and I inquired as to the spare ammunition in the captain's pantry. That region was found to be subsiding very fast. At this time I observed, among the shouts or noises apparently on shore, that faint cries were coming from the water, and I could see dimly white, floating bodies, which gave me a better knowledge of the real situation than anything else. I at once ordered all boats to be lowered, when it was reported that there were only two boats available, namely, the gig and whaleboat. Both were lowered and manned by officers and men, and by my direction they left the ship and assisted in saving the wounded jointly with other boats that had arrived on the scene from the Spanish man-of-war, from the steamer *City of Washington*, and from other sources. Later—I can not state precisely how long—these two boats of the *Maine* returned to the starboard quarter alongside, and reported that they had gathered in from the wreck all the wounded that could be found and had transferred them to the other boats—to the *Alfonso XII* or to the *City of Washington*.

The poop deck of the *Maine*, the highest point, was by that time level with the gig's gunwale while she was afloat in the water alongside. The fire amidships was burning more fiercely and the spare ammunition in the pilot-house was exploding in detail. We had done everything that could be done so far as I could see. Lieutenant Commander Wainwright whispered to me that he thought the 10-inch magazine forward had been thrown up into the burning mass, and might explode in time. I directed him then to get everybody into the boats over the stern, and this was done, although there was some little delay in curbing the extreme politeness of the officers, who wanted to help me into the boat. I directed them to go first, as a matter of course, and I followed and got into the gig. We proceeded to the steamer *City of Washington*, and on the way I shouted to the boats to leave the vicinity of the wreck, and that there might be an explosion. I got Mr. Sylvester Scovell to translate my desire to one or two boats which were at that time somewhat nearer the fire than we ourselves were.

Having succeeded in this, I went on board the *City of Washington*, where I found our wounded all below in the dining saloon on mattresses, covered up, and being carefully attended by the officers and crew of that vessel. Every attention that the resources of the vessel admitted was being rapidly brought into use. I then went on deck and observed the wreck for a few minutes, and gave directions to have a muster taken on board the *City of Washington* and other vessels, and sat down in the captain's cabin and dictated a telegram to the Navy Department. At this time various Spanish officers—civil, military, and naval—appeared on board, in their own behalf and in representative capacity, expressing sympathy and sorrow for the accident. The representatives of General Blanco and of the admiral of the station came on board, and the civil governor of the province was on board in person. I asked them to excuse me for a few minutes, until I completed my telegram to the Navy Department.

After finishing the telegram and putting it in the hands of a messenger to be taken on shore, I conversed for a few minutes with the various Spanish gentlemen around me, thanking them for the visit and their sympathy. I was asked by many of them the cause of the explosion, and I invariably answered that I must await further investigation. For a long time the rapid-fire ammunition continued to explode in detail. The number of the wounded was reported to me later. I have some difficulty in remembering figures. I think we found about 84 or 85 men that night who survived. It was also reported to me that the wounded on board Spanish vessels had been taken to the hospitals on shore, as were also the survivors who had reached the machina, in the neighborhood of the shears on shore. To keep a clear head for the emergency I turned in about 2 o'clock, getting little sleep that night, owing to the distressing groans of the wounded.

Q. By the time you reached the quarter-deck, were all the large explosions over?

A. So far as my experience is concerned there was simply one impression of an overwhelming explosion. I do not recollect details. I have already stated the explosions of minor character.

Q. But you yourself saw no large upshoot of flame?

A. When I came from the cabin, I was practically blinded for a few seconds. I thought only of the vessel, and took no note of the phenomena of explosion. It is probable that the explosive column had subsided wholly or practically by the time I reached the deck. I am not sure, because of the intense blackness.

Q. You state in your story that the *City of Washington* attended to the wounded. Did not the Spanish man-of-war also do the same?

A. I am not very sure personally, but the reports were that they were doing all that was possible. There was no reference to me on the part of the Spanish officers for sending the wounded on shore. I assume and believe that they did everything in their power to care for the wounded, and have continued to do so most conscientiously ever since.

Q. How many were wounded; how many killed; and how many were saved not wounded?

A. I would have to refer to my figures for that, and they are not now at hand. The muster, I think, shows 101 saved, including the wounded, and 253 lost. Some of the wounded have since died. My duties have been too complex since the explosion to enable me to memorize all the figures.

Q. From your examination of the wreck, as far as you have been able to make, what magazines or shell rooms, if any, should you say were blown up?

A. From the appearance of things about the wreck it is extremely difficult to come to any conclusion. The center of the explosion appears to have been beneath and a little forward of the conning tower, and on the port side. The forward part of the superstructure has been thrown upward backward over the after part and toward the starboard side, indicating an explosion on the port side of the ship. In the region of the center or axis of explosion was the 6 inch reserve magazine, which contained very little powder—probably, I am informed, about 300 pounds. The 10 inch magazine is in the general region, but it is on the starboard side, under the forward turret, which is well out on the starboard side. Over the 10-inch magazine in the loading room of the turret, and in the adjoining passage, and well on the starboard side, were a number of 10-inch shell, permanently placed. There were also several additional shell in the loading room. It is difficult, therefore, to conceive that the explosion involved the 10-inch magazine, because of the location of the explosion, and because I have had no reports that any 10-inch shell were hurled into the air by the explosion. The violence of the explosion, although not its immediate locality, indicates that the 10-inch magazine may have been involved.

Q. Where was the 10-inch shell room?

A. The 10-inch shell room was abreast the 10-inch magazine on the port side. It opened on the port side of the vessel.

Q. Was it not between the reserve 6-inch and 10-inch magazines?

A. It was.

Q. Do you know the thickness of the bulkhead between those three divisions?

A. I can not recollect. I should say that it was of ordinary metal, the thickness of a bulkhead of similar construction in other parts of the ship.

Q. Do you know what was between the coal bunker and the magazine?

A. I think nothing but the ordinary steel plate. It is so aft.

Q. Where was the small-arm ammunition locker forward, and what was in it?

A. We had received a new supply of ammunition, and this was kept forward of the thwartship armor bulkhead. I mean the small-arm and rapid-fire ammunition.

Q. Was there any smokeless powder?

A. There was no great gun smokeless powder ammunition. All the great gun ammunition was the ordinary brown powder.

Q. Was there not a 6-inch ammunition room forward of the small-arm ammunition rooms?

A. There was; supply for the forward 6-inch guns.

Q. On what side was the powder stowed in that one?

A. I have visited it, but I can not now exactly recall the exact position of the stowage. I know the powder chute is on the starboard side.

Q. Do you think that the forward 6-inch magazine blew up?

A. I do not think so. I can not find reason to suppose so. One man at least was blown out of the forward superstructure into the water. It is more than probable that he would have been blown to atoms if that magazine had exploded.

Q. Where did you keep your gun cotton?

A. Aft, under the cabin. The war heads were all stowed in that part of the ship which was not affected by the explosion. It was away aft.

Q. Where were the gun-cotton primers and detonators kept?

A. They were always kept in my cabin.

Q. Was any torpedo of the *Maine* fitted with its war head at the time of the explosion?

A. It was not. They were put in especially good condition, but none were fitted with war heads.

Q. Please state all the steps you have taken since the accident to ascertain its cause, and any results you may have obtained.

A. I have examined the wreck myself, conversed with other officers and men, and to some slight extent, in a categorical way, with the Spanish admiral. I have had a board of three officers make inquiries throughout the bay, but I have not yet received the reports from all the officers; nor have I had time to read the preliminary reports now in hand. I have not sent down any divers until this morning, not having had the necessary facilities. The best divers here are apparently in the employ of private parties, and since the Spanish authorities are very much averse to an investigation except officially, on the ground, as stated by the Spanish admiral, that the honor of Spain is involved, I have foreborne to examine the submarine portion of the wreck for the cause of the explosion until this morning. The divers of the fleet are now at work. I have had divers down in the cabin, and have recovered by that means the cipher code and magazine keys.

Q. What was the state or the condition of the *Maine* as far as discipline was concerned?

A. It was excellent. This is attested by the fact that the *Maine* was chosen for the duty on which she was engaged. She would not have been chosen had she been in any other than good discipline. The marine guard was in excellent condition. The medical reports from the medical department will show, I think, that about one man and one-quarter per diem were on the sick list during the past year. In the paymaster's department I think I am justified in saying that none of the reports of the paymaster to the Government at Washington were returned to the vessel for correction during my period of command. In the engineer's department the vessel was always ready and always responsive. I can recollect no letter from any source relating to the engineer's department which could be considered in the least of an adverse nature, except that the bureau once objected to a boiler being used in any degree as a tank. I think the punishment reports of the *Maine* are as small as those of any other vessel of the Navy in proportion to complement. They were uncommonly small. A quieter, better-natured, well-ordered, and apparently satisfied crew I have never known on board any vessel in which I have served.

Q. Have you any fault to find with the behavior of any officer or man at the time of the disaster?

A. None. I consider that the conduct of all was admirable. The behavior of the officers toward me personally and the prompt and responsive recognition of my authority was admirable, and instances of bravery are known both among the officers and crew in the direction of rescuing shipmates.

(The judge-advocate announced that at present he had no further questions to ask Captain Sigsbee.)

Examination by the COURT:

Q. What is the highest temperature you remember to have been reported in the forward magazines?

A. The highest temperature that I remember—and I think I can recall the figures—was 112°; but that was in the after magazine, where the temperatures were higher than in the forward magazines. I do not recollect the temperature in the forward magazine, because they were not so high as in the after magazine.

Q. Was any loose powder kept in the magazines, or was it all stowed in the usual air or water-tight cylinders, which each contains a charge?

A. I never permitted any to be kept loose, and do not believe that any was so kept.

Q. What was the status of the coal bunkers next to the forward magazines? Were they full, or had there been any coal used out?

A. All the bunkers were ventilated through air tubes, examined weekly by the chief engineer, and otherwise as was necessary, and they were connected electrically to the annunciator near my cabin door. The forward coal bunker on the port side was full, so I understand; the forward coal bunker on the starboard side adjoining the magazine has been reported to me as being one-half full, and it was in use at the time of the explosion.

(The judge advocate here informed Captain Sigsbee that no further testimony would be taken from him at present, and that he should appear to-morrow, Tuesday, at 10 a. m., when the testimony given by him to-day will be submitted to him for his approval.)

The court then, at 1 p. m., adjourned to meet to-morrow, Tuesday, the 22d instant, on board the United States light-house tender *Mangrove*, at 10 o'clock a. m.

SECOND DAY.

U. S. LIGHT-HOUSE TENDER MANGROVE,
HARBOR OF HAVANA,
Tuesday, February 22, 1898—11 o'clock a. m.

The court met pursuant to adjournment of yesterday, but was one hour late on account of official visits to the captain-general and the admiral commanding the naval forces.

Present: All the members of the court, the judge-advocate, and Capt. Charles D. Sigsbee, U. S. Navy.

The record of the proceedings of yesterday was read and approved.

Lieut. G. F. M. Holman, U. S. Navy, appeared as a witness, and was sworn by the president.

Examination by the judge-advocate:

Q. Please state your name, rank, and present station.

A. George F. M. Holman, Lieutenant, U. S. Navy, stationed on board the U. S. S. *Maine*.

Q. When did you join the *Maine?*

A. When she went into commission, on the 17th day of September, 1895.

Q. What duty have you performed on board the *Maine* during that time?

A. The duty of navigator and ordnance officer.

Q. Did this duty also put you in charge of the electric plant?

A. Yes.

Q. Were you on board the *Maine* when she last came into the harbor of Havana, Cuba?

A. I was.

Q. Upon what day was that?

A. The date of arrival—January 24, 1898, this year.

Q. You have been on duty on board the *Maine* ever since?

A. Yes.

Q. In what depth of water was the *Maine* moored?

A. Five and a half fathoms. Around the mooring buoy the water varied in depth from 5½ to 6 fathoms.

Q. What kind of bottom?

A. Very soft, muddy bottom.

Q. Were you on duty on board the *Maine* from the time she arrived here up to the present?

A. Yes.

Q. Regarding the magazines of the *Maine*, what precautions do you know were taken for safety whenever the magazines were opened?

A. The usual precautions were taken with regard to all lights, if any were burning, and to stop smoking. The police, the master at arms, and others were always notified, and word sent, in fact, all over the ship. The galley was screened and the flag was hoisted in receiving ammunition on board, or putting it out. On all occasions, when magazines were opened, word was sent, as already said, all over the ship.

Q. What precautions were taken by the men in entering the magazines or shell rooms?

A. The question came up some time ago as to putting on the magazine shoes, that is, a short time after Captain Sigsbee took command. Prior to that time the order had not been enforced in regard to magazine shoes and slippers. Captain Sigsbee gave the order to make them wear their magazine shoes when they went down.

Q. Were all other precautions taken described by regulations?

A. Yes; so far as I know.

Q. Please state whether any work had been going on in the magazine or shell rooms, or in the small-arm ammunition rooms, within a day or so of the explosion?

A. On Monday we had our usual drills, and part of it being a drill of the powder division at their stations. I do not know of any work going on around the magazines. I would, no doubt, have known if any had been undertaken.

Q. Was Monday the day of the explosion?

A. No; Tuesday was the day of the explosion.

Q. On the night of the explosion, at 8 o'clock in the evening, when the reports are usually made, were the magazines and shell rooms reported secure?

A. That I do not know. The reports were not made to me.

Q. But you have no reason to believe that any of them were opened?

A. No, sir.

Q. Who was in charge of the gunner's work at that time?

A. Chief Gunner's Mate Brofeld; the gunner had not been on duty for something like three weeks.

Q. Had Brofeld been chief gunner's mate of the *Maine* during her whole commission?

A. Yes.

Q. Did you consider him a thoroughly reliable man?

A. Yes.

Q. Do you consider the individual members of the gunner's gang reliable?

A. Yes.

Q. How many of the gunner's gang were saved?

A. I have not seen the list.

Q. Please state to the court how the orders in regard to the taking of the temperatures of the magazines and shell rooms were carried out on board the *Maine*.

A. The temperature was taken daily of the magazines and shell rooms and ammunition rooms, and recorded in monthly reports to the Bureau.

Q. Was this fully carried out up to the time of the explosion?

A. I have no doubt that it was. I know of its having been carried out to within at least two or three days previous. I presume that it was carried out the remaining part of the time.

Q. Who took this temperature?

A. The chief gunner's mate; previously the gunner.

Q. How high did the temperature reach during your experience on board the *Maine*?

A. The hottest magazine was the 10-inch after magazine, where it reached as high as one hundred and ten in hot weather, remaining there for some time.

Q. Can you state to the court how much ammunition was stowed in the 6-inch reserve magazine which was on the port side of the ship abreast of the 10-inch shell room?

A. I think there were about 200 pounds of saluting powder in tanks. If there was any other powder there, it was of small amount. I am not sure.

Q. Were there any 6-inch charges stowed there?

A. I think not. We had room for all our 6-inch powder in the regular 6-inch magazines. I know of no 6-inch charges.

Q. How are the magazines and shell rooms on board the *Maine* constructed? Are they lined with wood?

A. No; the bulkheads are iron and not lined with wood. They are floored with gratings—a wooden flooring; the powder is kept on wooden racks. The shells are stowed in chocks.

Q. Do you know the thickness of the bulkhead between the reserve magazine and the 10-inch shell room?

A. No; I do not.

Q. There is, I believe, a steel bulkhead between the two?

A. Yes; I think so.

Q. How much powder was stowed in the forward 10-inch magazine?

A. I think there were about 150 or 160 tanks, representing seventy-five or eighty charges, say, approximately, some of these being full and others reduced charges, some 125 pounds to the tank, that being the weight of one of the tanks of a full charge. These figures I give I can not be exact in.

Q. I suppose there were about as many shell in the shell rooms as there were full charges in the magazine?

A. Yes, probably the same number.

Q. How was the fixed ammunition room forward located?

A. Over near the midship line of the vessel, abaft the 6-inch magazine.

Q. Can you state approximately what that contained at the time of the explosion?

A. That contained 6-pounder and 1-pounder shell and small-arm—that is, rifle and 6-millimeter—ammunition. I can not say how much.

Q. What was in the forward 6-inch magazine?

A. About two hundred or more 6-inch charges and a corresponding number of shell in the shell room adjoining.

Q. On which side was the powder stowed?

A. A little over to the port side of the midship line.

Q. In the 10-inch magazine forward the powder was to starboard of the shell, was it not?

A. Yes.

Q. Do you know what there was between the coal bunkers and the reserve magazine—how thick a partition, and of what material?

A. I do not know positively.

Q. You have stated that you were also the electric officer of the ship. Will you please state what wiring went down into the magazines and shell rooms? I mean the forward one.

A. None. There were electric lamps in the light boxes, and wires leading to these lamps, but they were separated from the magazine by a double plating of glass.

Q. Were there any steam pipes in dangerous proximity to the magazine or shell room?

A. No.

Q. Were you on board at the time of the explosion?

A. Yes.

Q. Did you notice any serious action of the electric light which would indicate grounding just previous to the explosion?

A. No.

Q. Where were you at the time of the explosion?

A. In the after part of the wardroom mess room.

Q. With whom?

A. With Lieutenants Jungen and Jenkins and with Chief Engineer Howell.

Q. Please describe your experience in full.

A. While conversing with Mr. Jungen and Jenkins, a heavy explosion occurred, which was evidently in the forward part of the ship. This explosion shook the ship violently, and the noise it made consisted of a low grumbling, comparatively speaking, a low and heavy grumbling, followed by a heavy booming explosion. It was precisely similar to many other submarine explosions I have heard, except that it was on a much larger scale. A submarine explosion always gives two shocks—one transmitted by the water, the other immediately following—the atmospheric shock. The lights went out at once, and we were left in darkness. My first impression was that the ship had been attacked. I called to the rest, "We have been torpedoed. Get up on deck." In the darkness I could not see whether the others were ahead of me or following me. I made my way to the wardroom ladder, and found the ladder intact, so far as I could judge by feeling, and went up this ladder and out through the door in the after superstructure to the main deck. I found the ship settling very fast, and a great deal of wreckage about, so I went up on the poop, where I found Captain Sigsbee and a number of officers and a few of the men.

The quarter boats that were in condition were lowered at once and sent to pick up men who were around the ship in the water crying for help. Efforts were made to extinguish the fire, which had broken out in the wreck of the middle superstructure. These efforts were unavailing, and there was little that could be done beyond rescuing a few people who could be gotten at forward. The ship settled slowly, and careened slightly to port. After everything had been done that could be done the ship was abandoned, Captain Sigsbee being the last one to leave. The condition of the wreck was practically the same as now, except that the ship has settled lower in the water since we left her. When we got into the boats the poop deck was dry, and, I should judge, about 2 feet above the water. The condition of the forward part I do not know. I did not know the state of the tide at the time.

Q. When you first heard the rumbling noise you spoke of, did the ship list either way?

A. Not so far as I observed. I observed a heavy shaking of the ship. If there was any lifting either way, it was not perceptible to me.

Q. When the heavy explosion took place which followed it, had you reached the upper deck?

A. No. The first part of this explosion I have spoken of and the second part, the heavy one, succeeded each other almost simultaneously, and a very short interval of time separated the two features.

Q. Did the second explosion list the ship, as far as you can recollect?

A. No; not as far as I can recollect or observed.

Q. You have had considerable experience at Newport in matters of explosives, I believe. What was your impression of the whole affair?

A. My impression, not verified yet by what the divers are finding, is that a very heavy mine went off under the *Maine's* bottom.

Q. Did you think that the explosion of this mine—remember I am only speaking of your impression—was followed by the blowing up of any of the *Maine's* magazines?

A. The noise produced by a heavy mine would be great in itself, and adding this noise to it would probably be coincident, practically forming one and the same explosion. From the noise alone I can hardly form an opinion whether the magazine went off also.

Q. During the stay of the *Maine* at Havana were you executive officer at times?

A. No.

Q. Were you acquainted with the special orders issued by your commanding officer in regard to extra lookouts at night and the quarter watches on deck?

A. I heard them spoken of officially.

Q. Did you ever hear of any unfriendly demonstration being made at night, or any unauthorized boats attempting to approach the ship and being ordered off?

A. No.

By Capt. CHARLES D. SIGSBEE:

Q. What was the state of discipline on board the *Maine* just following the disaster?

A. Remarkably excellent, every one doing his duty with coolness.

By the COURT:

Q. Would, in your opinion, the noise produced by the explosion of her magazine so low in the water as those of the *Maine* be very similar to an explosion of a mine from the outside of the ship?

A. I think it might be.

Q. Was there any private ammunition or loose ammunition stowed in the forward magazine?

A. No.

Q. Was there any other ammunition other than the ordinary powder used on board?

A. No; none that I know of. I am sure there was none.

By the JUDGE-ADVOCATE:

Q. Where were the fixed torpedo charges stowed?

A. We had only a few filled ready for use in the torpedoes, and they were kept by the officer of the powder division, Mr. Hood. I think that he had them in the supply boxes of the torpedoes, together with the other accessories.

Q. Where was the gun cotton stowed?

A. The wet gun cotton in the war heads was stowed in the torpedo-head room, which was aft, under the forward part of the steering-engine room. The dry gun cotton for the torpedo primers and the exploders were stowed in lockers in the cabin.

By the COURT:

Q. At what times were the temperatures of the magazines taken, and was it necessary to open the magazines and shell rooms to do so?

A. The order which I gave for taking the temperatures of the magazines and shell rooms, and which, I believe, was generally carried out, was to take the temperatures after quarters, or as near quarters as may be convenient. It was not necessary to open them to take the temperature—not to open them completely—a small plate, ordinarily closed, being removable from the hole through which the thermometer could be reached.

Q. In describing the manner in which the magazines were fitted, you say the floor of the steel deck of the magazine was covered with a grating. Was there any grating on the sides of the magazines?

A. No.

Q. Did the tanks stow against the steel bulkheads?

A. No, they were not stowed to touch the steel bulkheads, as I recollect; the uprights and the framework for holding the tanks were set a little ways from the bulkhead. I do not think that it would have been possible to stow the powder tanks to touch the side. They rested in chocks and did not touch the sides.

There being no further questions to ask this witness, he was notified to appear to-morrow morning at 10 o'clock to read over his testimony, and after having been cautioned by the president of the court not to converse in regard to matters of the inquiry, he withdrew.

The court here took a recess until 1.45 p. m.

The court reassembled at 1.45 p. m.
Present: All the members of the court, the judge-advocate, and Capt. Charles D. Sigsbee, U. S. Navy.

Lieut. Commander RICHARD WAINWRIGHT, U. S. Navy, appeared as a witness and was duly sworn by the president.

Examined by the JUDGE-ADVOCATE:

Q. What is your name, rank, and present station?

A. Richard Wainwright, lieutenant-commander, U. S. Navy, executive officer of the United States battle ship *Maine*.

Q. Since when have you been executive officer of the *Maine*?

A. I relieved Lieut. Commander A. Marix at Norfolk on the 7th day of December, 1897.

Q. Have you been on board the *Maine* ever since then?

A. Every day; until February 15.

Q. Will you please tell the court how the regulations in regard to paints and inflammables were carried out on board the *Maine*?

A. Strictly carried out. None below.

Q. What were the regulations on board the *Maine* about closing the doors and everything below decks at 8 p. m., when holds and storerooms were reported?

A. Not only the holds and storerooms were closed, but all the watertight doors, excepting those absolutely needed for communication. All the hatches from the protective deck up, excepting those over the dynamo room, and those two that communicate through over the evaporators and allow the heat to come up.

Q. Was the usual report made by you to the commanding officer at 8 p. m., on the night of the disaster?

A. It was. I can state here in special connection that the captain instructed me on Saturday to be particular to see if the inner passages were closed. Yes, it was about Saturday. We had a board with hooks on it, and tallies for all the doors that were not regularly closed, but only closed for collision, or for night, or for guard quarters, etc. I made an examination myself of that, and found some of the tallies missing about the same time, and gave special instructions to Mr. Cluverius to go through the inner passages prior to the time of closing, and see all the tallies in place, and to afterwards examine the board so as to see if they had been closed; and I had also the intention on Tuesday night in my mind to examine the board, but I did not get around.

Q. Were the regular reports made to you at 8 o'clock that night?

A. They were.

Q. Had the magazines been opened that day?

A. Not to my recollection.

Q. What were the orders in regard to visitors and people not belonging to the ship while you were in Havana?

A. All visitors were scrutinized by the officer of the deck before coming on board, and only those that were thought desirable were allowed to come on board. Unless a special party belonging to the officers, only a few at a time were allowed on board. All the masters-at-arms and sentries had special orders to allow nobody below unaccompanied. When there were people not taken around by officers, but who the officer of the deck thought desirable to be shown around, they were always accompanied by a reliable member of the crew, and at such times they were not to take them into intricate parts of the ship, and they were confined to the berth deck.

Q. Captain Sigsbee, of the *Maine*, issued certain orders and instructions in regard to special lookouts at night and a quarter watch to be kept on deck. Did you take steps to see this order carried out?

A. I did.

Q. Were they in force and being carried out at the time of the disaster?

A. They were. I heard the quarter watch mustered, and the officer inquiring whether they all understood their stations, where their stations were at the guns, etc. The men had been standing quarter watches for some time, knew their stations, and therefore the officer of the deck merely questioned those he was doubtful about as to whether they knew their stations. I saw the sentry from the poop after the disaster. He came on board the *City of Washington* and brought his belt and rifle. None of the other lookouts were saved that I know of.

Q. Who was the officer of the deck at the time of the disaster?

A. Mr. Blandin.

Q. During the stay of the *Maine* at Havana, did any hostile demonstration afloat ever come to your notice?

A. No, sir.

Q. Do you know of any case, either reported to you or from your personal observation, of an unauthorized boat attempting to approach the ship and being warned off?

A. Not warned off; but frequently these small boats were hailed and came very close. The hail was answered and they went on.

Q. Did you have confidence in the police force of the *Maine*?

A. The utmost confidence.

Q. Did you have confidence in the marine guard of the *Maine*?

A. Yes; a good marine guard and under good discipline.

Q. What is your opinion of the discipline and the character of the crew of the *Maine*?

A. Fine discipline; the crew were very obedient, very quiet men. They needed a little more exercise, that was the only fault that I could find.

Q. Do you know what boats were down at the time of the explosion?

A. I know that the first steam cutter was down. I believe that to be the only boat.

Q. Where was she at the time?

A. At the starboard boom.

Q. Where were you at the time of the disaster?

A. When the explosion took place I was in what is used as the captain's office, called on the plan the admiral's office.

Q. Will you please state your experience at the time of the explosion?

A. I was standing in the office with Mr. Holden, who was in there at the time. I felt a very heavy shock, and heard the noise of objects falling on deck. I was under the impression, from the character of the noises, that we were being fired upon. I moved out and came on the main deck through the starboard door, and passed up on the after-superstructure deck by the ladder on the starboard forward corner. I then recognized the captain's voice. As near as I can recollect the course of events, the captain told me to see the boats ready to be lowered, and I gave the order to clear away the boats. I saw very few men coming, and I went from davit to davit to see someone ready to cast off the falls. I found generally that they were all officers. Most of the officers I recognized from time to time right on the poop. I then noticed indications of fire forward. This all occurred very quickly together. I spoke to the captain about flooding the magazines, or he spoke to me about it. Someone then pointed down the hatch, where the water was coming up, and of course there could be no reason to flood the magazines. I then called someone to help me to go forward and see if we could get the fire out.

I remember Mr. Hood and Mr. Boyd started with me, and we succeeded together by going over the awning to what was apparently the break of the central superstructure—the afterpart. As soon as I got there it was evident from the mass of what appeared to be burning cellulose there was no chance of fighting the fire. Mr. Boyd got upon the superstructure and passed two men who were crying out very loudly—one had his arm broken, I think—and got them both in the gig. They were both able to help themselves after they recovered from the shock. Before going forward I gave the order to lower the gig, the captain acquiescing to this order, and when I returned lowered the two remaining boats—the second whale boat and the barge. The three boats had different officers in them that I had detailed to go into this boat or that. We pulled about the afterpart of the ship and picked people out of the water. By that time the ship was crowded with boats. The first one that I noticed was from the *City of Washington.* I noticed a number of Spanish boats. I suggested to the captain that there might be danger from the mass that was burning of further explosion. I was equally confident that there was no one left in the water, and that we had better get the crowd of boats out of the way. He authorized me to shove the boats off.

I ordered the gig to back in, and ordered the other boats off. The captain did not want to go. I pressed him finally, and the only way to get rid of the men was to shove off ourselves. When the captain followed me into the gig, we pushed in among the boats and induced them to go off, taking the wounded to different vessels. The captain then took the gig to the *City of Washington,* lying on our port quarter, say between three and four hundred yards distant. I then ordered an officer to commence taking a list of the saved and wounded of the *Maine's* crew. I sent Mr. Blandin in the gig to pull around the ship, and sent Mr. Holman over to the Spanish flagship to get our well men, if there were any, and take a list of the wounded. Not having sufficient men to keep up the patrol, I called the gig in by the captain's direction. That was some considerable time after the disaster, when there was no chance of any wounded being left.

Q. What was the discipline on the part of the officers and men immediately following the explosion?

A. I consider it excellent. All orders were obeyed with the promptness of a drill. The captain told me what orders he wished me to give, and the only order not promptly obeyed was the final order to leave the ship, and the officers hesitated until it was given in an imperative manner.

Q. Please state your experience of the shocks and noises you heard during the explosion.

A. I only remember one very heavy shock. I was so much shaken up that it took me an appreciable time to find the handle of the door, the door having been closed by the shock, and pull it open.

Q. Did the ship list any at this time?

A. The first list I noticed was after we commenced lowering the boats—a list to port.

Q. When did you first see and examine the wreck after the disaster?

A. At daylight the following morning I took the gig and Lieutenant Hood and a few of the men and attempted to board the wreck. I was warned off by an armed boat's crew—Spaniards. I then pulled around the wreck. It was not fully daylight enough to make my impression at that time valuable. There were still some burning fragments. I know that parts of the wreck which I thought I recognized then I found I was mistaken in when I had a chance to examine it in daylight.

Q. Will you please describe the wreck as you found it after you had a full chance to examine it by daylight?

A. The after part of the ship appeared to be intact from the crane aft, with a heavy list to port, the port turret being about 2 feet under water. The main deck was folded back, carrying the central superstructure with it at a line between the two cranes and about the line between the two fire rooms. It was folded in a direction from port to starboard, so that the port 6-inch gun was lying nearly over the starboard 6-inch gun, the conning tower pointing downward about where the armory was—that is, the starboard after corner of the superstructure. The forward smokestack was lying abreast and partly over where the first whaleboat hung; the siren was on the starboard side of the after superstructure. The after smokestack was lying on the port side abreast of the fore-and-aft bridge, between the after and central superstructure. At the lowest tide we had I stood on the port waterways, and could see nothing that I could recognize as any part of the ship forward of the crane on the port side of the main deck.

There were some portions of the wreck forward of this line mentioned on the starboard side. By looking in underneath it I saw a torpedo port, apparently of the starboard forward torpedo. I recognized part of the washroom—I believe it was part of the foremen's washroom—immediately abaft the starboard turret having a small scupper with a lip, a hold-down valve, and also a half round bulkhead separating portions of the washroom. Forward of that again I recognized pieces of bottom plating with anchor scars. They had a triangular piece that led me to believe it to have been under the starboard anchor. Forward of that was some wreckage with old rope, which I think had been where the anchor gear was stowed. Forward of that one of the fore yardarms was sticking up. As far as I can tell from the above water view, there is an angle between the after body of the ship and the forward, with an apex to starboard.

Q. You have had charge since then of the wreck?

A. With Captain Sigsbee's orders, I have had general charge.

Q. Have divers been at work? If so, since when?

A. Since about the 17th.

Q. Will you please describe any discoveries of importance that have been made by any of these divers, and, if it is a matter of importance, give the name of the diver, if you can?

A. The first thing of importance that I know of having been found was the finding yesterday of two powder tanks, one 6-inch and one 10-inch. They were crushed together and flattened in. The divers could report very little that day. That diver was Chief Gunner's Mate A. Olsen. I will bring those tanks to the court to-morrow. These cases did not contain any powder. The 6-inch case, while ruptured and torn, did not appear to me as if it had been injured by an explosion of powder within it. The 10-inch case I thought to have been ruptured by the powder within it when I examined it, but I was far from certain. I could not understand its not being more seriously torn apart. If I had seen the case without any knowledge of an explosion, I should have said it was not an exploded case. These were found in the forward body of the ship, and I now believe them to have been found in the reserve magazine.

This morning a 10-inch tank was recovered full of powder, with the cover slightly opened. That gave me the impression that the tank had been forced open by weights or pressure without flame or heat, as there was sufficient opening, had there been flame or excessive heat, to reach the powder, and as I carried it in my mind, with pressure in there it would have been fired before any water could have possibly reached and drowned it. Ensign Bromby is looking out for the divers forward and Naval Cadet Cluverius for the divers aft. The divers tell me that they can find nothing of the port side of the ship forward of this general line that I have mentioned. They find the cellulose belt, I am not certain on which side. They also think they have been in the coal bunkers. They found one shell fused for 6-pounder near where they found the full case, or somewhere in that vicinity, only approximately.

Q. I forgot to ask you in speaking of the crew, to give me the record of Chief Gunner's Mate Brofeld, as far as you know?

A. He was the most painstaking, obedient, hard-working man. I have known him to be working in the turrets most of the night.

Q. Do you know anything about his good-conduct medals and continuous-service certificate?

A. No.

Q. But you do know that he had a permanent appointment?

A. I do. I can say that he was well acquainted with all the work of the ship, and while he was acting gunner things went in a very satisfactory manner, whereas they had not done so before.

Witness desired to state the following:

I saw in the chief engineer's room of the *City of Washington* a large piece of cement heavily coated with oil. I then thought it was a piece of bottom cement. I now am inclined to believe it came from the forward blower on the port side.

There being no further questions to ask this witness, he was notified to appear before the court to-morrow at 10 a. m. and read over his testimony; and he was furthermore informed that it was the wish of the court that at any time any important discoveries were made in the wreck he should at once appear and notify the court.

The witness having been cautioned by the president not to converse on matters relating to the inquiry, he withdrew.

Naval Cadet W. T. CLUVERIUS, U. S. Navy, appeared as a witness before the court and was sworn by the president.

Examined by the JUDGE-ADVOCATE:

Q. What is your name, rank, and present station?

A. Wat Tyler Cluverius; cadet U. S. Navy; attached to the U. S. battle ship *Maine*.

Q. How long have you been attached to the *Maine*?

A. Ever since the 15th day of May, 1897.

Q. Have you, during that time, ever been assistant navigator?

A. About four months of that time.

Q. Do you know all about the electric wiring of the ship?

A. A great portion of it, sir.

Q. Is there any electric wire on board the *Maine* so laid as to endanger the magazines or shell rooms?

A. To my knowledge there is not.
Q. Were you on board the *Maine* on the night of the explosion?
A. I was, sir.
Q. Where were you?
A. I was in room 3 of the junior officers' quarters.
Q. Will you please state to the court what shocks you experienced and what next you heard?
A. My first knowledge of anything occurring was a slight shock as if a 6-pounder gun had been fired somewhere about the deck. After that a very great vibration in my room, which was then followed by a very heavy shock, and still continued vibration and rushing of water through the junior officers' mess room, and the sound as if something breaking up all the time.
Q. Were you asleep when you felt the first shock?
A. I was not, sir.
Q. What work have you been engaged on since the disaster?
A. I have been engaged in working with the divers.
Q. Will you please state to the court any important discovery or discoveries made by the divers? Give the name of the diver or any important reports made to you which might give us some information as to the state of the wreck and the cause of the explosion.
A. I was in charge of the diving aft, from the after part of the ship, when we found several important papers, which were turned in to the commanding officer. I was present this forenoon on the float forward where they had gotten up a 10-inch powder tank intact. That is about all of importance that I know of in connection with this. My work has been wholly aft.
Q. What is the situation of the junior officers' mess room?
A. The junior officers' mess room is in the same compartment as the wardroom officers' mess room, directly forward of it.

There being no further questions to ask this witness, he was notified to appear before the court to-morrow morning at 10 o'clock and read over his testimony; and, after being cautioned by the president not to converse on matters relating to the inquiry, the witness withdrew.

Naval Cadet J. H. HOLDEN, U. S. Navy, appeared as a witness before the court, and was sworn by the president.

Examined by the JUDGE-ADVOCATE:
Q. What is your name, rank, and present station?
A. Jonas Hannibal Holden, naval cadet, U. S. Navy, attached to and recently serving on board the U. S. S. *Maine*, now wrecked in the harbor of Havana, Cuba.
Q. How long have you been attached to the *Maine*?
A. Since the 15th day of May, 1897.
Q. How much of that time have you been assistant navigator?
A. About four or five months.
Q. Do you know of any electric wiring on board the *Maine* that would endanger the magazines or shell rooms?
A. I do not.
Q. Where were you at the time of the explosion?
A. I was in the captain's office with Lieut. Commander Wainwright, the executive officer of the *Maine*.
Q. By the captain's office you mean, I suppose, the one marked as the admiral's office on the plan?
A. Yes, sir.

Q. Will you please state to the court what shocks you experienced and what noises you heard at the time of the explosion?
A. At the time of the explosion, first, there was an explosion of considerable force, and about three or four seconds afterwards there was another explosion of far greater force, and a terrible shaking; then we rushed up on deck.
Q. Did the ship list any during either of these explosions?
A. She seemed to be picked up and listed slightly to starboard.
Q. Was that the first or second explosion, this list to starboard?
A. It seemed to me to be the first.
Q. What duty have you been on since the explosion?
A. On duty as aide to the captain.
Q. Have you had anything to do with the divers?
A. No, sir.

Examined by the COURT:

Q. Where would you locate either of these two explosions—on the starboard or on the port side?
A. The first explosion, my impression is, occurred on the port side. I saw a shoot of flame, which seemed to be on the port side.
Q. How about the next and larger explosion?
A. I could not distinguish anything at the second explosion.
Q. Was there any water?
A. All I saw was a column of flame.
Q. Did this column of flame seem to come up through the ship or up through the decks?
A. I could not tell. It seemed to be well to port. It was well over to port.

There being no further questions to ask this witness, he was notified to return to-morrow morning at 10 o'clock and read over his testimony when convenient.

The court then adjourned to meet to-morrow, Wednesday, February 23, 1898, at 10 o'clock a. m.

The court then proceeded to make a personal examination of the wreck.

THIRD DAY.

U. S. L. H. TENDER MANGROVE,
Harbor of Havana, Wednesday, February 23, 1898—10 a. m.

The court met pursuant to adjournment of yesterday.

Present: All the members of the court, the Judge-Advocate, and Capt. Charles D. Sigsbee.

The record of the proceedings of yesterday, the second day of the inquiry, was read and approved.

Lieutenant HOLMAN was called before the court and handed so much of the record of yesterday as contained his testimony, whereupon he withdrew, after being directed to read over his testimony and indicate any corrections he desired to make.

The JUDGE-ADVOCATE. I now ask the permission of the court to introduce as stenographer Mr. John W. Hulse, and Mr. H. L. Bisselle, assistant to the stenographer. I should like to have them sworn, and assist me in preparing the record of the court.

Permission being granted, the stenographer, John W. Hulse, was duly sworn by the judge-advocate, in accordance with U. S. Navy regulations, and took his seat as stenographer of the court. Mr H. L. Bisselle was also sworn as assistant to the stenographer.

Chief Engineer CHARLES P. HOWELL, U. S. Navy, appeared as a witness for the prosecution, and was duly sworn by the president.

Examined by the JUDGE-ADVOCATE:

Q. What is your name, rank, and present station?
A. Charles P. Howell, chief engineer, U. S. Navy, stationed on the *Maine*.
Q. When did you join the *Maine*?
A. The 21st day of December, 1895, to the best of my recollection. It was either the 19th or 21st, I have forgotten which—about the 21st.
Q. You have been chief engineer of the *Maine* ever since?
A. Yes, sir.
Q. What coal bunkers on board the *Maine* are adjacent to the magazines in the forward half of the ship; I mean magazines and shell rooms?
A. If I could refer to the blue print I could tell you the numbers of them. A15 is on the forward starboard side under the forward turret. That is adjacent to the 10-inch magazine. A16 is similarly situated on the port side, and that is adjacent to the 6-inch reserve magazine, I think they call it. B3 is on the starboard side, and B5 is also on the starboard side. They are adjacent to the magazine. B4 and B6 are on the port side, also adjacent to the 6-inch reserve magazine.

Examined by the COURT:

Q. The first two are adjacent to the 10-inch magazine?
A. Yes, sir. Perhaps I could state that a little better now, as I first went from the starboard side to the port side and back again.

Examined by the JUDGE-ADVOCATE:

Q. Go ahead in your own way. Make it as plain as you can.
A. On the starboard side, adjacent to the 10-inch magazine, are coal bunkers A15, B3, and B5. On the port side, adjacent to the 6-inch reserve magazine, are coal bunkers A16, B4, and B6.
Q. Please state to the court, as near as you can recollect, the history of coal bunker A15, from the time you joined the ship up to the time of the explosion?
A. A15 is a bunker which it is difficult to put coal in or to take coal out of, and, besides, you have to go through B4 and B5. To take coal out of A15 you first have to empty B3 and B5, and to put coal in A15 you have to partially fill B5, and then fill from B5 into A15. As I say, it is a difficult bunker to put coal in and take coal out. Those bunkers forward have been emptied as frequently as possible in order to lighten the ship forward. We have always tried to take coal out of the forward bunkers as much as possible, because when they are full the ship has a tendency to go down forward. It was the same way on the port side. A16 is a difficult bunker to fill, and is the last one that is emptied on the port side, because we have to take coal out of B4 and B6 before we can take any out of A16.
Q. Have you always inspected coal on board the *Maine* before receiving it?
A. Yes, sir.
Q. Have you, during the time you have been chief engineer of the

Maine, had any signs of any kind of spontaneous combustion in the coal bunkers?

A. No, sir; none whatever. In connection with that I have frequently examined the different bunkers all around everywhere, and the different kinds of coal. I have never seen any signs whatever of any bunker heating. I have examined them from the outside, and when they have taken coal out of them; also particularly when we have taken in coal that I thought was more liable to spontaneous combustion than other coal. I have never seen any signs of heating.

Q. When did you make your last examination of these bunkers, previous to the explosion?

A. Bunkers B3, B5, B4, and B6—unless you want to consider some others, I will not mention any others—are emptied, and they have been emptied about two weeks.

Q. That is, previous to the explosion?

A. Yes, sir; B3, B5, B4, and B6.

Q. Those have been empty?

A. They have been empty ten days or two weeks. All of those have been entirely empty. In that time we have painted all those bunkers and we have scaled them. Also we have scaled the chutes that led down to them, and painted them. A15 was about half empty until the day of this explosion. On that day, at 4 o'clock, we began taking coal from A15, to keep the ship on an even trim. I have not been in that bunker personally since they began taking coal out of it, though I have passed around these bunkers, and I felt of them within a week on both sides. I have been to the wing passages, and every time I go through there I can feel those bunkers. I pass right by the bunkers. It is a quarter of an inch thick, and I put my hand on them. I never have gone through there without putting my hand on them to feel the temperature.

Q. You never found any signs of heating?

A. I never found any signs of heating—any variation.

Q. At the time of the explosion what was the condition of bunker A16?

A. It was full of coal.

Q. Is it easy of access for the purpose of feeling the temperature?

A. Yes, sir; on all four sides.

Q. Do you mean that it can be easily felt for temperature on all four sides?

A. Outside; yes, sir, for temperature.

Q. How close is this bunker to the magazine itself?

A. Personally I do not know what is between the bunker and the magazine. I know there is sheet iron, but whether that is lined with wood on the magazine side I do not know.

Q. The inboard bulkhead of the bunker is against the magazine, is it not?

A. Yes, sir.

Q. Is not a portion of the inboard bulkhead of this bunker easily accessible without going into the magazine?

A. Yes, sir.

Q. The escape hole is there, I believe?

A. Yes, sir.

Q. Leading into the loading room?

A. Yes, sir.

Q. Then, in case there should be any spontaneous combustion in

S. Doc. 207——3

bunker A16, would it not be likely that it would be felt by people going to and fro in the passing room?
A. Yes, sir; decidedly so.
Q. What kind of coal was in bunker A16?
A. To the best of my recollection, it was New River coal. I have a memorandum of that in my notebook, but I haven't it here. It is lost.
Q. Where do you receive New River coal?
A. At Newport News.
Q. Regarding the steam piping of the *Maine*, was there any piping in dangerous proximity to the forward magazines or shell rooms?
A. No, sir.
Q. Did any steam pipes lead through bunker A16?
A. No, sir.
Q. What boilers were in use at the time of the explosion?
A. The two aftermost boilers in the ship, one on each side.
Q. What was the condition of those boilers?
A. In good condition. We were in the habit of carrying about 80 to 100 pounds of steam in port.
Q. For auxiliary purposes?
A. For auxiliary purposes, in port.
Q. How much did you carry in those same boilers when steaming at sea?
A. One hundred and twenty pounds.
Q. Who was the engineer of the watch at the time of the explosion?
A. Assistant Engineer Merritt.
Q. I believe he was lost?
A. Excuse me; I made a mistake. It was Mr. Morris—Assistant Engineer Morris.
Q. Did you have what you consider a competent watch on duty for two boilers?
A. Yes, sir.
Q. A watch of reliable men?
A. Yes, sir.
Q. In your opinion it would have been impossible for those two boilers to explode with the pressure they were carrying?
A. Yes, sir; the explosion would not have done much damage under ordinary circumstances.
Q. What is the approximate length of the two fire rooms?
A. Each fire room is about 48 feet long.
Q. Where were you at the time of the explosion?
A. In the ward-room mess room.
Q. Will you please state to the court what noises you heard and what shocks you felt at the time of the explosion?
A. I was suddenly startled with an unusual shock. There was then a continued series of convulsions and a noise like the tearing of the ship to pieces, then a tremendous crash, then apparently the sound of falling débris. Then the ship felt as if it was waving and unsteady on the deck.
Q. Did you notice any list of the ship at the first explosion or the first shock?
A. No, sir; I did not notice it until after this series of shocks, when I started to go on deck. Then the ship appeared to be listed over about 10°.

Examined by the COURT:

Q. Which way?
A. To port.

Q. That is a great list, you know.
A. Let me modify that. I should say it was listed over about 5° to port.

Examined by the JUDGE-ADVOCATE:

Q. After you reached the deck, did you see any upshoot of flame, or anything of that kind?
A. No; none to any extent. Now and then there would be a small explosion, like the explosion of a 6-inch shell, perhaps.

Examined by Captain SIGSBEE:

Q. You have said that bunker A16 was full of coal?
A. Yes, sir.
Q. Was that bunker not exposed on two sides on the deck immediately above the 6-inch reserve magazine?
A. It was.
Q. Was not the immediate vicinity used by the men employed in the hydraulic room as a sleeping place or loafing place?
A. There was a storeroom——
Q. I mean on the inboard side?
A. Yes, sir; there was a storeroom on the port side of the hydraulic room. One side of it was up to the bunker, and that room was much frequented.
Q. But was there not another side of that bunker in the hydraulic room itself—the inboard side of the bunker?
A. No, sir; there was a storeroom between the hydraulic room and the bunker.

Examined by the COURT:

Q. It was the electric storeroom?
A. The electric storeroom.

Examined by Captain SIGSBEE:

Q. What I am trying to get at is that the men used to habitually lie in that corner—the port forward corner in the hydraulic room—with their heads right against what must have been that bunker?
A. There is a storeroom between the hydraulic room and the bunker.
Q. There was?
A. Yes, sir; on the same level.
Q. Was not that bunker exposed on three sides at the forward entrance of the port-wing passage?
A. Yes, sir; that bunker was exposed on three sides, which was much frequented. It was exposed on the fourth side by an empty bunker at this time, and we had had men in there painting.
Q. It is not likely that the hands of the crew must have rested on that bunker many times a day through the use of that wing passage?
A. Yes, sir.
Q. In traversing the passage?
A. Yes, sir.

Examined by the COURT:

Q. Could the entire length of the bunker A16, abutting against the 6-inch reserve magazine, be examined from the outside of the bunker?
A. Not from the magazine itself.
Q. That is, from the outside of the coal bunker?
A. Allow me to explain that. I have never been in that magazine, but I do not see any reason why the temperature could not be found from the magazine as well as any other place.

Q. How could you examine the temperature of that coal bunker on the outside where it abutted against the top of the magazine?

A. We did not examine it from the magazine; we examined it from aft and outboard.

Q. This coal bunker is represented on the same deck as this magazine. How could you get at the outside of that coal bunker on this deck?

A. Not on the deck shown here, but on another deck.

Q. But the magazine is not on another deck.

(Captain Sigsbee here made a rough drawing of the bunkers and explained it to the court.)

Examined by the COURT:

Q. Would the heating of coal in the bottom of such a bunker cause such a heat two decks above as to be very noticeable?

A. I should say yes, sir.

Q. That is, no heating could take place in one part of the coal bunker which would not diffuse itself through the mass?

A. Without rising up to the highest point of the bunker.

Chief Engineer HOWELL desired to add the following testimony:

The dynamo room also goes out of that bunker, in addition to what has been brought up.

The judge-advocate requested that the testimony given by the witness be not read to him by the stenographer, but that he be directed to report to-morrow morning at 10 o'clock, when he will be furnished with so much of the record as contains his testimony and asked to withdraw for the consideration of the same, upon the completion of which he will be again called before the court and be given an opportunity to amend his testimony as recorded or pronounce it correct. The request was granted and the witness was instructed accordingly, whereupon he withdrew, after being cautioned by the president not to discuss matters pertaining to the inquiry.

Lieutenant HOLMAN appeared before the court.

The JUDGE-ADVOCATE. If the court please, I request that the witness be cautioned that the oath previously taken by him is still binding.

The witness was duly cautioned as requested by the judge-advocate.

The JUDGE-ADVOCATE. Lieutenant Holman, you have read over the testimony given by you on yesterday. As it it now recorded, is it correct?

Lieutenant HOLMAN. It is correct, as now recorded, with one exception.

The JUDGE-ADVOCATE. Sit down, please, and make that correction.

Lieutenant HOLMAN. I would like to change my evidence with regard to the amount of saluting powder that was on board.

The JUDGE-ADVOCATE. Make your statement.

Lieutenant HOLMAN. I stated 200 pounds. It must have been considerably more than that, but how much more I do not know. On reflection, thinking of the amount that we used for one salute, and the saluting powder not being down so as to require a new supply or a new requisition, we must have had very much more than 200 pounds.

The JUDGE-ADVOCATE. You can not give us approximately how much was in that magazine?

Lieutenant HOLMAN. No; I can not.

Examined by the COURT:

Q. What was the ordinary temperature of the dynamo room?

A. The temperature of the dynamo room in weather such as exists at present was about 90°—not far from 90°.

Q. If there had been a serious rise of temperature in bunker A16, which abuts on the port side of the dynamo room, do you think it would have been quickly noticed in the dynamo room?

A. No; not unless it were such a rise in temperature as to set fire to woodwork—such as to manifest itself in that way, setting fire to the woodwork in that bulkhead.

Q. Would not the men naturally frequently come in contact with that bulkhead?

A. No.

Q. It was the port side, and it formed in that way [indicating]?

A. In the port side dynamo room, aft, between the entrance to the central station and the side of the ship, was a desk and several searchlight ammeters.

(A blue print was here shown to the witness.)

Q. What I wish to know is whether in case of a serious rise of temperature in the bunker would it not have been noticed in the dynamo room?

A. I do not think it would.

Q. You said, in answer to a question, that a rise in temperature would not be noticed unless it were such a rise as would set fire to the woodwork on that bulkhead. There was woodwork on that bulkhead, was there?

A. Yes.

Q. Was that in such close contact with the bulkhead that in case that bulkhead had become very hot, or heated to a heat which would have ignited wood, it probably would have ignited that switchboard or caused it to char?

A. Yes; if the heat had been maintained for some time. The woodwork, as I recollect, was not in immediate contact with the bulkhead, but set off a little way from it.

Q. But would not a serious rise of temperature in that bulkhead have made itself felt in the general temperature of the dynamo room to such a degree as to be very noticeable; because a temperature which will ignite anything like coal or wood is a very high one?

A. Yes; I can conceive that there might be such a temperature as to manifest itself in that way.

There being no further questions to ask this witness, his testimony was read aloud to him, and by him pronounced to be correct; and, having been cautioned by the president not to discuss matters pertaining to the trial, he withdrew.

Lieutenant-Commander WAINWRIGHT here appeared before the court.

The JUDGE-ADVOCATE. Lieutenant-Commander Wainwright, I now hand you so much of the record of the proceedings of yesterday as contains your testimony before the court of inquiry. I ask you to withdraw, read it over, and make any corrections you desire, after which you will please return and inform the court of those corrections.

Paymaster CHARLES M. RAY, U. S. Navy, appeared as a witness and was duly sworn by the president.

Examined by the JUDGE-ADVOCATE:

Q. What is your name, rank, and present station?
A. Charles M. Ray, paymaster, U. S. Navy, attached to the U. S. S. *Maine*.

Q. How long have you been attached to the *Maine*?
A. I joined her on the 2d of February last.

Q. Referring to your storerooms in the forward part of the *Maine*, was there any inflammable or dangerous matter stowed in any of those storerooms?
A. Not to my knowledge and belief, sir.

Q. What was stowed forward belonging to your department, and where was it stowed?
A. I think these are the only two rooms I had [indicating on blue print]. There was stored in them preserved meats, small stores, and some clothing.

Q. Where were you at the time of the explosion?
A. I was in my own room, sir.

Q. In the wardroom?
A. In the wardroom.

Q. Will you please state to the court what shocks you experienced, and what noises you heard?
A. My first impression, my first shock, you might say, was a sort of an upheaval. My impression then was, from the downward tendency, that the ship had been broken in half, and that she was sinking. I immediately got out of my chair and stood under the lintel of the door. There were small pieces falling from above—small pieces of the deck, I suppose. I gathered myself together from that, and heard the water rushing in from forward, and then I made my way on the superstructure. After that, the only explosions I heard were from the *City of Washington*, of the small arms.

Q. At the first shock you felt, did you notice any perceptible list of the ship?
A. No, sir.

Q. After you reached the deck, did you notice any upshoot of flame, or anything of that kind?
A. No, sir; not except the ordinary burning of fire.

Examined by the COURT:

Q. What was the usual temperature of your storerooms just forward of that magazine?
A. That I can not say. I am not familiar enough with the storerooms.

Q. You had not been in the ship long?
A. No, sir; just two weeks, and I had not settled down, in fact.

Examined by the JUDGE-ADVOCATE:

Q. Was your jack-of-the-dust saved?
A. No, sir.

Q. Was your yeoman saved?
A. No, sir; their names are not on the list.

There being no further questions to ask this witness his testimony was read aloud to him and by him pronounced to be correct; and, having been cautioned by the president not to discuss matters pertaining to the trial, he withdrew.

Surg. LUCIEN G. HENNEBERGER, U. S. Navy, appeared as a witness and was duly sworn by the president.

Examined by the JUDGE-ADVOCATE:

Q. What is your name, rank, and present station?
A. Lucien G. Henneberger, surgeon U. S. Navy, attached to the *Maine*.
Q. How long have you been attached to the *Maine*?
A. Since November 10, 1896.
Q. Where did you stow inflammable matters belonging to your department?
A. We had alcohol, whiskies, and brandies in the medical storeroom, and a few bottles of each for immediate use in the dispensary.
Q. Where was the medical storeroom you speak of situated?
A. Beneath the wardroom.
Q. Did the dispensary lead into the sick bay?
A. It did.
Q. Were there any sick at the time of the explosion?
A. There were three or four on the sick list at the time of the explosion.
Q. Were there any attendants to the sick?
A. Three.
Q. Did the apothecary sleep in the dispensary?
A. He did.
Q. Then you feel reasonably certain that if there had been any explosion of any kind there it would have been noticed at once?
A. At once.
Q. Where were you at the time of the explosion?
A. In my bunk.
Q. Will you please state to the court what shocks you felt and what noises you heard at the time of the explosion?
A. I was lying in my bunk reading, and I felt a sudden upheaving of the ship. The lights were extinguished, and this was followed immediately by a deep boom, as of an explosion. That was all I heard.
Q. Did you notice any list of the ship at the first shock?
A. A list to port. As I went up the ladders the ladders inclined toward the port side.
Q. That was after you had felt the first shock—this list?
A. Yes, sir. I felt the shock before getting out of my bunk; but just as I got out of my bunk I made my way forward to the wardroom door and began to climb the ladders.
Q. What I wish to know is whether, at the very first shock you felt, there was a perceptible list?
A. No.
Q. After you reached the upper deck did you notice any upshoot of flame or anything of that kind—any more than the ordinary burning of fire?
A. No.
Q. Can you give the number of the wounded that were sent to the hospital at Havana?
A. There were 29 sent to the San Ambrosia—approximately 29; I do not know whether that is the exact number—and 6 to the Alphonso Treize.
Q. How many of these patients have since died?
A. Six.
Q. How many of the wounded were sent to Key West?

A. I do not know how many went by the *Olivette* the first trip. She left in such a hurry that it was almost impossible to tell. There were 10 sent by the *Mangrove* the following day but one.

Q. You are not able to give this court the number of killed, are you?

A. No, sir.

There being no further questions to ask this witness, his testimony was read aloud to him and by him pronounced to be correct; and, having been cautioned by the president not to discuss matters pertaining to the trial, he withdrew.

Private WILLIAM ANTHONY, U. S. Marine Corps, appeared as a witness, and was duly sworn by the president.

Examined by the JUDGE-ADVOCATE:

Q. What is your name, rank, and present station?

A. William Anthony, private, U. S. Marine Corps, U. S. S. *Maine*.

Q. Were you one of the marine guard of the *Maine* during her last stay at Havana?

A. Yes, sir.

Q. Were you on board the day of the explosion?

A. Yes, sir.

Q. On what duty?

A. On orderly duty, aft.

Q. What watches had you had that day?

A. I had the 8 to 12 p. m. watch—the first watch, sir.

Q. Had you had any watch during the daytime?

A. Yes, sir; from 8 to 12 in the forenoon. I had both watches, 8 to 12 p. m. and 8 to 12 a. m.

Q. During the forenoon watch had the magazine keys been taken out of the cabin?

A. Not by me, sir; not by anybody, to my recollection. The drill was that day, and it did not necessitate opening the magazine.

Q. Do you know whether the keys of the magazine and shell rooms were in their proper place in the cabin at 8 p. m. that night?

A. No, sir; my business did not call me as far as the captain's stateroom.

Q. You made the usual reports to the captain that the magazines were in proper condition that night?

A. Yes, sir.

Q. Where were you at the time of the explosion?

A. I was standing on the main deck, just outside of the door, on the starboard side.

Q. Please tell the court what you felt and what you saw.

A. I first noticed a trembling and buckling of the decks, and then this prolonged roar—not a short report, but a prolonged roar. The awnings were spread, and where the wing awning and the quarter-deck awning should join there was a space of at least 18 inches. I looked out and saw an immense sheet of flame, and then I started in to warn the captain.

Q. Did you notice any perceptible list to the ship at the first shock?

A. At the first shock the ship instantly—that is, the quarter deck, where I was standing—dipped forward and to port, just like that [indicating]. It apparently broke in the middle like that [indicating] and surged forward, and then canted over to port.

Q. Canted over to port after the first shock?

A. Yes; it was continually settling more to port while I was on board.

Examined by the COURT:

Q. I would like to have you describe a little more particularly where you saw this upshoot of flame.

A. It was well forward. It must have been forward of the superstructure. I could see the débris going up with it. I do not know what it was, but I saw firebrands going up.

Q. Was it on the port side or the starboard side?

A. It looked more to port than it did on the midship line. It looked like it covered the whole ship. It was an immense glare that illumined the whole heavens for the moment, as much as I could see for the awnings.

Q. Did you see any water with it?

A. I didn't notice that, sir. I started in the cabin at once.

The court had no further questions to ask the witness.
There were no further questions to ask the witness.

The judge-advocate requested that the testimony given by the witness be not read to him by the stenographer, but that he be directed to report to-morrow morning at 10 o'clock, when he will be furnished with so much of the record as contains his testimony, and asked to withdraw for the consideration of the same, upon the completion of which he will be again called before the court and be given an opportunity to amend his testimony as recorded, or pronounce it correct.

The request was granted, and the witness was instructed accordingly; whereupon he withdrew, after being cautioned by the president not to discuss matters pertaining to the trial.

The JUDGE-ADVOCATE. I would like to state to the court that there are three gentlemen of whom I have knowledge not belonging to the Government who, I believe, saw the explosion from outside the ship, and if the court wishes their testimony, I think I can produce them to-morrow morning. One of them is Captain Teasdale, of the British bark *Deva*; another one is the engineer of the floating dock, Mr. Rolfe, and the third one is the manager of the oil works at Regla, Mr. Van Sickle.

The PRESIDENT. We should have them.

The JUDGE-ADVOCATE. I think they are willing to come to-morrow morning. I only got this information over night.

Lieutenant Commander WAINWRIGHT here appeared before the court.

The JUDGE-ADVOCATE. You have read over your testimony given before the court on yesterday. Is your testimony as recorded correct?

Lieutenant Commander WAINWRIGHT. It is.

The witness then withdrew, after being cautioned by the president not to discuss matters pertaining to the inquiry.

Capt. CHARLES D. SIGSBEE was then called upon by the judge-advocate to state whether his testimony as given to the court in the first day's proceedings was correct as recorded, and he announced that it was correct as recorded.

Captain Sigsbee was then requested to take the stand and did so, being cautioned by the president that the oath previously taken by him was still binding.

Examined by the JUDGE-ADVOCATE:

Q. What officers have been detailed by you to obtain information in regard to any outsiders who may have seen the explosion of the *Maine*?

A. Lieutenant-Commander Wainwright, Lieutenant Holman, and Chief Engineer Howell, all of the *Maine*.

Q. Have any of those officers made any report to you as to obtaining my information?

A. I have had no report made to me yet, but I know that Mr. Holman has some notes.

Q. I have Mr. Holman's notes before me, and I know the witnesses he has found.

A. I submitted to the board, especially to Mr. Holman, whose time was available when I made out the order, a series of questions relating to the phenomena of the explosion, and I gave him directions to interview persons about the bay and in the city, in order to gather information relative to these questions.

Q. Mr. Holman's notes are the only reports that have been made?

A. That is all I have now.

Q. He is one of the members of that board?

A. He is one of the members of that board.

Q. Do you wish to give any further testimony in regard to coal bunker A16? You informed me that you did.

A. Is that the one on the port side?

Q. Yes.

A. It is my opinion that if the interior of coal bunker A16 had been so hot as to be dangerous to the 6-inch reserve magazine that this heat would have shown itself in the outside plating of the bunker, in the passing room of the forward turret, in the wing passage connecting therewith, and in the passage communicating with these two apartments. In passing from the passing room into the wing passage there was a turn to the left. On three sides of this turn the plating of the bunker was exposed. The passage was narrow. The tendency, therefore, of a person in passing and in turning to the left would have been to place the left hand on the plating. I went through this intermediate passage, I think, the day before, and observing that one of the logs of the manhole escape from that bunker was not tightly wedged in place, I gave directions to see that it was always kept tightly closed, except when intended to be opened altogether. I put my hand on the log and there was then no appearance of undue heat. This was either the day before or two days before—I think the day before the explosion. Also, there were electric leaves on the outside of this bunker, in the wing passage, and it is probable that undue heat would have interfered with the insulation, and have given warning somewhere. That is all I desire to say on that.

Q. Do you also wish to testify in regard to the record and character of Chief Gunner's Mate Brofeldt?

A. Yes, sir; I had occasion to send Brofeldt's record to the Navy Department two or three weeks ago. His record was a very fine one. He had three good-conduct medals on his present enlistment record, covering about two years. According to my recollection, every mark under every heading was a maximum. He had received no punishment whatever. His record was absolutely perfect, and he would have gained on it, had he continued in the same course, another good-conduct medal.

The court had no further questions to ask this witness.

The judge-advocate requested that the testimony given by the witness be not read to him by the stenographer, but that he be furnished with as much of the record as contains his testimony upon the meeting of the court to-morrow morning at 10 o'clock; that he be directed to examine the same, upon the completion of which he will be given an opportunity to amend his testimony as recorded, or pronounce it correct.

The court then (at 12 o'clock noon) took a recess until 1.30 o'clock p.m.

The court reassembled at the expiration of the recess.

Present: All the members of the court, the judge-advocate, the stenographer, and Capt. Charles D. Sigsbee.

Ensign W. V. N. POWELSON, U. S. Navy, appeared as a witness, and was duly sworn by the president.

Examined by the JUDGE-ADVOCATE:

Q. What is your name, rank, and present station?
A. W. V. N. Powelson; ensign, U. S. Navy; serving on board the U. S. S. *Fern*.
Q. Were you on board the *Fern* when she arrived at Havana shortly after the explosion of the *Maine*?
A. Yes, sir.
Q. How long after the explosion did you arrive? The explosion took place at 9.40 p. m.
A. We arrived on Wednesday at about 3 p. m.
Q. What duty have you been engaged on since you have been in Havana, regarding the wreck of the *Maine*?
A. I have not been on any official duty in connection with the *Maine*.
Q. What duty have you done with regard to the wreck of the *Maine*? Have you not been present a great deal during the diving?
A. Yes, sir; I have been on the *Maine* every day since the *Fern* has been here, and have been present most all day.
Q. Will you please tell the court, as far as you can, the condition of the wreck, and also of any important discoveries made by any of the divers, giving the name of the diver, if you can?
A. The forward part of the ship, forward of the after smoke pipe, has been completely destroyed, as far as all appearances go. The conning tower now lies in a position opposite the door leading into the superstructure aft, and to starboard. The conning tower is inclined at about 110 degrees to the vertical, with the top of the conning tower inboard. The forward 6-inch superstructure gun now lies completely turned upside down over the after starboard 6-inch superstructure gun. The frames which supported the deck plating and planking of the port gangway forward of the main deck are bent upward and against the superstructure, the angle of bend decreasing as you go aft. The fixtures underneath the main deck on the port side, consisting of pipes, wood casing for the electric wires, standing lights, etc., have been completely wrecked, while on the starboard side these fixtures, occupying a similar position, are in some cases almost intact.

This is especially so under the conning tower at the starboard side, where the woodwork of the electric wires is scarcely burned at all. The port bulkhead, between the main deck and the berth deck at the conning-tower support, has been blown aft on both sides, but a great deal more on the port side than on the starboard. The fire-room hatch immediately abaft the conning-tower support, between the main and the berth deck, has been blown open in three directions, aft, to starboard, and to port. The forward side of the hatch, being stronger, forming the support of the conning tower, was not much injured. The pipes in this hatch were very little injured. The protective deck under the conning-tower supports, where it is secured to the armor tube from the conning tower is bent in two directions. The plates on the port side are bent up and the plate on the starboard side is bent down.

By the Court:

Q. Do you mean with reference to their original positions?

A. With reference to their original positions. There is a beam supporting the protective deck a few inches abaft the armored tube. This beam, to port of the midship line, was bent up to starboard of the midship line. The rivets were sheared. The beam broke at the midship line, due to weakening at this point by pipes passing through it. These rivets, holding the beam to the deck, were sheared almost at right angles to the fore-and-aft line. The starboard crane was broken completely off, due to the superstructure falling upon it. The port crane supports are bent, but the crane itself seems intact. The forward smokestack now lies forward side up along the starboard quarter-deck, about the position of the waterways, and almost clear of the awnings stanchions. The after smokepipe lies with its forward side uppermost, just inboard of the port turret. The main masthead was broken at a point about 4 feet from the lantern. The foremast fell forward and a little to port. The break just forward of the port crane at the main deck is a very clean one, the wood still remaining fastened to the deck plating at the edge of the break.

Just foward of the conning tower, underneath the main deck, two beams meet at right angles, one fore and aft, and the other athwart ships. The fore-and aft beam is broken at the point where it touches the athwartship beam. Both parts of the broken beam are pushed from port to starboard. A grating was found on the poop awning, just foward of the after search light. A piece of the side plating, just abaft the starboard turret, between the torpedo tube and the turret, is now visible, about 15 feet forward of the starboard crane, and about at the position of the ship's side. This plate was bent outward, and then the forward end bent upward and folded backward upon itself. This plate was sheared from the rest of the plating below the water line. This plating below the water line has been pushed out to starboard. The gratings from the engine room hatch were blown off.

Q. Those were the unarmored gratings?

A. Yes, sir; the superstructure gratings. In hauling in some wires a strainer was picked up from the bottom at a point about opposite the poop capstan and 70 feet from it—a composition strainer.

Q. The composition strainer, you say, was picked up where?

A. It was picked up on the starboard quarter. I was hauling in the electric wires yesterday and hooked on to it, and picked it up at that point.

Q. Is there anything to show where the strainer came from?

A. The chief engineer thinks it was a strainer from the firemen's washroom.

Q. It was not an exterior strainer?

A. No, sir; it was not a strainer in the ship's side. The athwartship beam, at the point where the break occurs on the port side, is pushed a little forward at the point where it joined the outside plating.

Q. When you speak of the break, you mean the break in the main deck?

A. Yes, sir; the break in the main deck. Near the piece of outside plating, near the turret to which I have just referred, and just inboard of it are some pieces of red shellacked planks. On these planks is bolted a composition track about 2 inches wide and an inch thick. At the ceiling of the central station a standing light on the port side was found completely blown from its supports, only three screws remaining in the protective deck to mark its position. On the starboard side, about 5 feet from this light, was another deck light, fastened to the protective deck, and nothing in this light was destroyed except the glass globe protecting the light and the glass of the incandescent light itself. The woodwork and wires were intact. Did you mean for me to say anything about what the divers reported, or just what I saw?

By the JUDGE-ADVOCATE:

Q. I would like to have you state any important discoveries which might lead us to draw some conclusion as to the cause, and if the discovery of a diver gave you the information, state the name of the diver; but before you do that, I would like to ask you whether the forward and after parts of the ship were in line.

A. As far as I could judge, the forward and after parts of the ship were not in line. The ends, where the explosion occurred, seemed to have been pushed from port to starboard, I should judge from 5 to 10 degrees.

Q. That makes an angle of the ship with the apex to starboard?

A. With the apex to starboard; yes, sir.

Q. Will you please go ahead with the discoveries of the divers?

A. The divers reported to me that at a point where the 10-inch shell room should be they discovered 10-inch shell, regularly arranged, but the ship had sunk down so much that some of the shell were in the mud.

By the COURT:

Q. That mud was inside the ship, of course?

A. Yes, sir. They were not able to determine that exactly. The name of one diver was Olsen, I think. The diver Smith reported that he saw a number of broken 10-inch powder tanks. He secured a 10-inch powder tank that still contained powder, and it was hoisted to the surface, and is now on board the *Fern*. He also secured some tanks in a better condition, one 6-inch and one 10-inch tank that I saw. This diver reported that he had found more full tanks, but a diver who went down next after Smith was unable to secure any. At a place where the paymaster's storeroom should be we found a great many vegetable cans. Gunner Morgan reported that in walking on the bottom he fell into a hole on the port side and went down in the mud. He also reported that, as far as he could judge, everything seemed to be bent upward in the vicinity of this hole. He also reported that the plates seemed to have been pushed over to starboard and bent down over the top of the 10-inch magazine, from which he reasoned that he would be able to find, perhaps intact, powder tanks farther down; that the broken ones on top had been broken up by these plates. The one 6-inch tank that I saw appeared to me to have been an empty tank, broken by the explosion, as it was not badly dented, and merely ripped the length of the seam.

By the JUDGE-ADVOCATE:

Q. How did the empty 10-inch tank appear to you?

A. The empty 10-inch tank was badly battered. When I saw it it had been already dipped in a sterilizing solution, and I could see no evidences of powder upon it.

Q. Was it ruptured, as if a charge had exploded inside of it?

A. It was flattened out and battered out of all conceivable shape. I could not say.

By the COURT:

Q. Have either of the divers been on what you consider the outside of the ship?

A. They had not up to last night. They report that the mud is so deep that it will be impossible for them to walk on the bottom, and they wish some large scow moored over that part, so that they can be supported from the scow, and that, I believe, is being done to-day. I requested the diver to go aft and see if he could see the condition of the port forward boiler. He started aft and found coal, and discontinued his work before he got as far aft as the boiler.

Q. What is the condition of the starboard turret?
A. To my knowledge it has not been found, sir.
Q. That is, the place where it belongs has been examined, and you think it is not there?
A. I understand that something was found at or about the place under which the turret formerly was, but they have not been able to determine exactly what it was. I have had no information from the wreck to-day. I have not been there.
Q. What impression is produced upon your mind by the reports, so far as you have quoted them?
A. From reports alone, or from the appearance of the wreck?
Q. I mean either the reports that have been made to you, or the conditions which you believe to exist.
A. The impression produced upon me is that an explosion took place well to port of the midship line and at a point in the length about opposite the conning tower.
Q. What weight are you giving now to the statement made by the gunner, Mr. Morgan?
A. That opinion is based entirely upon the observation of things above water. The fact that a full powder case was found and the fact that empty powder cases were found does not, in my mind, admit of an expression of opinion until something further is produced.
Q. You do not see anything upon which to base an opinion?
A. No reports so far from the divers upon which to base an opinion.
Q. I say again, what weight do you give to the statement made by Mr. Morgan as to his falling into a hole on the port side?
A. No weight, sir.
Q. You give no weight to that?
A. No, sir; because I think he may be mistaken about it.

By the JUDGE-ADVOCATE:

Q. You have stated all that you know about it, have you?
A. I think I have, sir. I have a little notebook in my pocket, in which I made notes of things at the time.
Q. Please refer to that and see if there is anything else?
A. The arc of the engine-room telegraph and the shaft of the steering gear, coming down through the armored tube (turret), was bent from port to starboard underneath the protective deck, and the port side of the protective deck under the conning-tower supports was covered with a greasy sort of deposit, while the starboard side was comparatively free from it.

(At this point Naval Cadet Holden entered the court and was handed so much of the record of the court as contained his testimony. He was then directed to retire, examine it, and return and state whether or not his testimony as recorded was correct.)

Ensign POWELSON then resumed his testimony.

The WITNESS. The forward smoke-pipe hatch, between the main and the superstructure decks, while it is dented, does not show signs of internal pressure of gases. I said that the fire-room hatch did; that it was blown out in all directions, and the hatch at the engine room where the funnel came through was not exploded. It is dented. The fire main running along under the main deck had its asbestos covering and canvas burned much more on the port than on the starboard side.

On the main deck, just forward of the conning tower, where the fore-and-aft angle bulb beam to which I have referred was located, the planking was blown off on the only remaining plate of the main deck on the port side, while the wood was still attached to that part on the starboard side between the base of the conning tower and the turrets. The wood planking there on the plating was still fast to that, while on the port side it had blown off the plating. All the wood-deck planking and the plating was blown off the main-deck beams of the port gangway forward of the break. On the starboard side of the conning-tower support the protective deck is pulled away from the support about 5 inches. On the port side it is not.

By the COURT:

Q. Would that show a pressure from port to starboard?

A. That would indicate that the pressure lifted the protective deck up on the port side, and the protective deck on the starboard side held fast and bent that deck downward, away from the conning-tower support, broke that one end of that beam off, and sheared it right straight across. I have a little sketch here, which the court might look at, to make clear what I have said.

(Witness here exhibited to the court two sketches, showing diagram of various parts of the sunken ship, and explained them to the court.)

Q. Mr. Powelson, you spoke of that strip which is on the starboard side of the outside plating of the ship, which was folded and rolled back?

A. Yes, sir.

Q. And you gave it as your opinion that the portion of the outer plating underneath that, from which that was torn, was bent outward?

A. Yes, sir; I can see that. That is about 2 feet under water, where that shear occurs.

Q. Can you see the outside plating on the opposite side?

A. No, sir.

Q. You can not?

A. I took some soundings. I forgot to tell you about that. I found about 5 fathoms of water all along the ship, on both sides, down to the mud. I took a 14-pound lead line, 4½ fathoms, and I dragged with a wherry along on the port side for obstructions. I dragged right close to where I imagined the waterways on the port side of the ship had been, judging from the position of the ship, and I found no obstructions at all. With 4½ fathoms of line out, going along slowly on the starboard side, I did find obstructions for a distance of 20 feet from where I had reason to suppose the waterways had originally been.

Q. That is to say, the fact that there were obstructions on the starboard side and not on the port side would indicate that while the port side was not ruptured, if it was ruptured, the burr was on the inside?

A. I do not think you understood me exactly. There is nothing left of the port plating at all. As you go right in across the ship there is nothing. I dragged along the outside to see if there had been anything that had fallen out, and I could find nothing. As I came in, taking soundings right along from the port side, after I got inside a few feet, or nearly under the waterway, then I began to find obstructions in about 3½ fathoms of water. I dragged right along here [indicating] on the port side, and I found nothing along in there; but over on this side [indicating] I did find things all along here; and I found something hard right in here, just abaft that crane [indicating].

Q. Which may be the turret?

A. It was hard for about 15 or 16 feet along there, as near as I could judge, and not much out of mud; probably only 4 feet out of mud; but the lead had a different feel there from what it had anywhere else. That is what I thought was the turret. Of course, I could not be certain, and there is not enough evidence to state that opinion absolutely.

Q. Have you ever been attached to the *Maine?*

A. No, sir; I have never been attached to the *Maine.*

Q. How have you become so well acquainted with the *Maine?*

A. I thought I was going to the *Maine* when she went in commission. I was on the *Vermont* at that time, and I used to go over to the ship frequently and go through her, with an idea of learning. Then I was on the staff of Admiral Bunce, and made an inspection of the *Maine* and learned more at that time.

Q. You think the ship on the port side opposite that support is entirely gone?

A. Yes, sir.

Q. Entirely blown out?

A. Yes, sir; because I could get nothing less inside, I think, than three fathoms and a half of water; but from the break itself it goes right down standing here over the waterway [indicating]. You can go down there about 4 fathoms with the lead line, but there does not seem to be anything out here [indicating]. That little plate to which Captain Chadwick referred is exactly in line with the mainmast.

Q. That protective deck?

A. The protective deck of which you speak. It is on a line with the mainmast at the port crane, and goes to this plate [indicating]. That is the reason I thought that, whether it was the starboard or the port plate, there would not be much difference, except as to the angle, because that was so far over from the side, coming from the mainmast [witness indicates on diagram].

Q. It is an important thing to know. That [indicating] is a piece of the quarter deck. If that had been broken off the ship's side, and was thrown up in here [indicating], that is very material.

A. It is over to port. You can not tell exactly where that place was in the beginning.

Q. Could you not tell by very careful soundings around that or by the divers? You see the divers are even now down at the floor of that [pointing out of the window at the wreck].

A. The divers do not seem to be able to express themselves as to what they see down below. I have talked to them and have not been able to learn very much.

Q. That is the difficulty; they do not know what they find.

A. They see things there, but they do not know exactly what they are or what the conditions are.

Q. How often were you on duty over there at the wreck?

A. As I said, we are not detailed for the duty over there. We have days duty on the *Fern*, but of course Mr. Bookwalter and myself attend to the work on the ship, or on the wreck, or anything Lieutenant Wainwright wants us to do.

There being no further questions to ask the witness, the judge-advocate requested that the testimony given by the witness be not read to him by the stenographer, but that he be directed to report to-morrow morning at 10 o'clock, bringing with him an ink sketch similar to the one shown to the court to-day, lettering the different parts, and also an ink sketch of that piece of protective deck referred to in the testimony, the sketches to be on foolscap paper, either on separate sheets or on the same sheet, when he will be furnished with so much of the record as contains his testimony and asked to withdraw for the consideration of the same, upon the completion of which he will be again called before the court and be given an opportunity to amend his testimony as recorded, or pronounce it correct.

The request was granted and the witness was instructed accordingly, whereupon he withdrew, after being cautioned by the president not to discuss matters pertaining to the inquiry.

Naval Cadet HOLDEN here appeared before the court.

The JUDGE-ADVOCATE. Naval Cadet Holden, is the testimony given by you before the court on yesterday correct as recorded?

Naval Cadet HOLDEN. It is.

The witness then withdrew, after being cautioned by the president not to discuss matters pertaining to the inquiry.

The court then (at 2.30 p. m.) adjourned to meet to-morrow, the 24th instant, at 10 o'clock a. m.

FOURTH DAY.

U. S. L. H. TENDER MANGROVE,
Havana Harbor, 10 a. m., Thursday, February 24, 1898.

The court met pursuant to adjournment of yesterday (Wednesday).

Present: All the members of the court, the Judge-Advocate, the stenographer, and Captain Sigsbee.

Previous to the meeting of the court the members were engaged in making an examination of the wreck.

The record of the proceedings of yesterday was read and approved.

Chief Engineer HOWELL appeared before the court.

The JUDGE-ADVOCATE. Chief Engineer Howell, I now hand you so much of the record of the proceedings of yesterday as contains the testimony given by you before the court. Please withdraw, read it over, and then return to the court and state whether you desire to make any corrections in the testimony, or whether it is correct as recorded.

The witness then withdrew.

Naval Cadet CLUVERIUS appeared before the court.

The JUDGE-ADVOCATE. Naval Cadet Cluverius, I now hand you so much of the record of the second day's proceedings as contains the testimony given by you before this court. Please withdraw, read it over, and return to the court and state whether you desire to make any corrections in the testimony, or whether it is correct as recorded.

The witness then withdrew.

Mr. WILLIAM H. VAN SYCKEL appeared as a witness, and was duly sworn by the president of the court.

Examined by the JUDGE-ADVOCATE:

Q. Please state your full name, your residence, and what business you are engaged in.

A. My name is William H. Van Syckel. My business is superintendent of the West India Oil Refining Company.

Q. Are you a resident of Havana?

A. No; I am a resident of what would be a part of Reglas.

Q. Were you in either Havana or Reglas on the night of February 15, when the *Maine* exploded?

A. I am in a part of the Province of Reglas, but my situation is in the building which they called formerly Billott's Hospital, now the petroleum works; but we belong in part to Reglas. I was in the house, answering your question, at the time of the explosion.

Q. Will you please state to the court all you saw and heard in regard to that explosion?

A. I was inside at the time of the explosion, and immediately went outside. What I saw was a bad sight. Everything was flying in the air. There were columns of black smoke, and pieces and parts of the ship.

Q. Was there any flame flying up into the air?

A. Yes; all those pieces of timber were aflame. It was like pieces of rag and pieces of timber.

Q. You saw no solid upshoot of flame?

A. No; that had passed. There were particles. When I saw it, there were still particles arising.

Q. Please state to the court what sound you first heard which made you leave your house and go out. What was the nature of it?

A. First a rumble. Then the terrific explosion. That rumble startled us, and then the explosion was almost instantaneous. That is, no quicker had we heard the rumble than the shot came.

Q. How long a time elapsed from the time you first started until you came out and saw these pieces in the air?

A. That is hard to state. If you are sitting here at the table and run right to the door when you hear a concussion, it is perhaps one or two seconds.

By Captain SIGSBEE:

Q. Did you see anything like shooting or falling stars or fireworks?

A. Yes; apparently. Those pieces afterwards came down. We stood and saw them come down. There were different colors amongst them, apparently different kinds of timber or different pieces of coal or ash. Some fell very slowly. Others came down more rapidly.

By the COURT:

Q. Were there many small pieces that were on fire?

A. Seemingly, yes: thousands of them.

Q. I mean pieces——

A. They were all sizes from what I should judge from where I stood. My position was about a mile and three-quarters from here.

Q. In sight of the ship?

A. In sight of the ship; yes, sir.

Q. Did you notice whether there were a great many of these what Captain Sigsbee describes as stars, all of one size?

A. No; I could not say that. I couldn't say there were. They appeared to be all of different sizes, going in all directions.

By Captain SIGSBEE:

Q. Did you see any bursting shell?

A. That was afterwards; but they all appeared to be aboard.

Q. There were no bursting shell in the air?

A. No; no bursting shells in the air. I saw nothing that appeared to be bursting in the air, any place.

Q. Did any stuff fall in Reglas, near you?

A. No.

Q. Have you heard of any shell or pieces of shell being picked up on shore?

A. No; I have not.

By the COURT:

Q. Was your view such that you could tell from which part of the ship this explosion took place?

A. No; not at the moment. We were not in a position—that is, we knew that the forward funnel had gone immediately after the explosion. That we could see by the glasses.

Q. That the forward funnel had gone?

A. Had gone. In fact, both funnels had gone, but we could see afterwards with the light that the forward funnel appeared to be lost—thrown overboard—and of course the forward mast also. We could see these things from there.

There being no further questions to ask this witness, his testimony was read aloud to him by the stenographer, and by him pronounced to be correct; and, after being cautioned by the president not to converse about matters pertaining to the inquiry, he withdrew.

The witness then added the following testimony:

The people who would be able to give more exact information, and who were at the time looking at it, were aboard the bark *Matanzas*. They are on their way to New York. They were there in that vessel, and they could see if there was any water column or anything of that description. Of course they were closer by, and would be better judges, and could give better ideas than we could from shore.

The COURT. But they, you say, are on their way to New York?

A. They are on their way to New York.

There being no further questions to ask this witness, his additional testimony was read over to him by the stenographer, and by him pronounced correct. The witness then withdrew, after being cautioned by the president not to converse about the matters pertaining to inquiry.

Chief Engineer HOWELL here appeared before the court.

The JUDGE-ADVOCATE. Mr. Howell, you have read over your testimony?

Mr. HOWELL. I have.

The JUDGE-ADVOCATE. Is it correct as recorded?

Mr. HOWELL. It is.

Chief Engineer Howell then resumed the witness chair, and gave the following additional testimony:

Examined by the JUDGE-ADVOCATE:

Q. After the explosion, Captain Sigsbee appointed you a member of the board to make certain inquiries and get certain information. Is there any information which you have obtained which would be useful to this court?

A. No, sir; I have heard a number of versions of the explosion. I do not see how they could be of particular use to the court, unless it be with one exception. If you would like to have that man come aboard, he was on the *City of Washington*.

Q. Do you refer to Mr. Rothschild?
A. Yes, sir.
Q. Will you send him over, if you can?
A. I will do the best I can.
Q. Are there any combustibles of any kind stored below decks belonging to your department? If so, please state what and where.
A. Cotton waste is the only one I think of at this moment. That is stowed in the storeroom abaft of the engine room.

By the COURT:

Q. Clean cotton waste?
A. Clean cotton waste, stowed in a storeroom abaft of the engine room.
Q. Did you have no driers or anything of that sort belonging to your department?
A. They are kept on deck in proper tanks, with wooden boxes outside the tanks.

By the JUDGE-ADVOCATE:

Q. What instructions did you have from your commanding officer in regard to old cotton waste that had been used?
A. We have a number of copper tanks in the engine room and fire room, about 22 inches high and 15 inches in diameter, with covers on them. They are kept there for the purpose of putting old refuse in them, and oil waste and anything of that style that has been used. Every day they are carried away, thrown in the ash pile and thrown overboard.

There being no further questions to ask this witness, his testimony was read over to him by the stenographer, and by him pronounced correct.

After being cautioned by the president not to converse about matters pertaining to the inquiry, he withdrew.

Naval Cadet CLUVERIUS appeared before the court.

The JUDGE-ADVOCATE. Mr. Cluverius, is your testimony as recorded correct?

Mr. CLUVERIUS. It is correct, sir.

The witness then withdrew, after being cautioned by the president not to converse about matters pertaining to the inquiry.

Capt. FREDERICK G. TEASDALE appeared before the court as a witness, and was sworn by the president of the court:

Examined by the JUDGE ADVOCATE:

Q. Please state your full name, residence, and profession.
A. Capt. Frederick G. Teasdale, Walker Hall, Winston, Darlington, County of Durham, England. I am master of the *Deva*.
Q. What is the *Deva*?
A. It is a bark.
Q. Where is the bark *Deva* now?
A. Lying at the Reglas wharf.
Q. How far from the place where the *Maine* was anchored on the 15th of February?
A. Nearly half a mile; between quarter and half a mile.
Q. Were you on board the *Deva* when the *Maine* exploded?
A. I was on board, writing my mail, getting ready for the next day.
Q. Where were you?

A. Sitting at the cabin table writing when I heard the explosion. I thought the ship had been collided with. I ran on deck when I heard the explosion. I felt a very severe shock in my head also. I seized my head this way [indicating]. I thought I was shot, or something. The transoms of the doors of the cabin are fitted in the studs on the side, and they were knocked out of place with the shock. The first seemed to be a shot, and then a second, or probably two seconds, after the first report that I heard, I heard a tremendous explosion; but as soon as I heard the first report—it was a very small one—thinking something had happened to the ship, I rushed on deck, and was on deck just in time to see the whole débris going up in the air.

Q. Please describe, as graphically as you can, how this appeared to you—what you saw.

A. The stuff ascended, I should say, 150 or 160 feet up in the air. It seemed to go comparatively straight until it reached its highest point of ascent. Then it divided and passed off in kinds of rolls or clouds. Then I saw a series of lights flying from it again. Some of them were lights—incandescent lights. Sometimes they appeared to be brighter, and sometimes they appeared to be dim, as they passed through the smoke, I should presume. The color of the smoke, I should say, was very dark slate color. There were fifteen to twenty of those lights that looked like incandescent lights. The smoke did not seem to be black, as you would imagine from an explosion like that. It seemed to be more a slate color.

Q. Was there anything that appeared to you to be shooting stars or anything like that?

A. No; I never saw anything like that; only a series of smaller explosions, after the first one, you know. That occurred at stated intervals, probably twenty minutes or half an hour each. You would hear small reports from the deck, as if they were scattered shells about the deck which were going off, but they would not do any harm; some going in one direction and some in another.

Q. When you first saw this thing, was there a large batch of solid flame?

A. No; I didn't see any flame whatever. There never was any flame whatever.

Q. You are sure you reached the deck in time to see the large explosion?

A. I was on deck in time to see everything. I could bring forward evidence by bringing my mate or any of my officers. I was the first one on deck, and they came up afterwards. The stuff had not reached its final ascent when they came up, and I was up two or three seconds before they were. The stuff was still ascending when they came up.

Q. Could you see whether water was thrown up?

A. No; I was too far away to testify whether there was water or not.

By the COURT:

Q. Could you tell from where you were at what part of the ship this explosion took place?

A. Oh, yes; I could see the ship distinctly from stem to stern. They were working a search light from the shore, and they threw the search light on the ship, and that is the first time I knew it was the American man-of-war had blown up. We were under the impression before that that it was one of these large Spanish steamers that had blown up. They put the search light on the vessel, and the first thing I saw about her was the davit for lifting the steam launch out with. Then I saw the fighting top on the mizzenmast, or the mainmast, as we call it. I could distinctly see the stem of the vessel, and I could see this patch of debris right in the light. I could see that the funnel was lying at an angle of about 35 degrees, I should say, on the top of the debris, but it seems to have altered its position during the night. I suppose when the stuff finally got settled it changed its position somewhat.

Q. What I refer to particularly was, when you saw this column of smoke and debris ascending, could you tell then what part of the ship it was coming from?

A. No; I could not see anything then. It was too dark then. I don't suppose we noticed very particularly for that, because we were so much interested in seeing the stuff going up that we couldn't see anything of that sort, I suppose. I should say it was somewhere about the middle of the vessel from the appearance of other craft about there at that time. I passed the ship the afternoon before, about 7 o'clock, in a boat.

Q. How many explosions did you hear?

A. I heard two distinct explosions. The first one was a very sharp one, and when that explosion took place it was as though some steamer had collided, and the shock was something tremendous.

Q. That is to your own ship?

A. Yes; I am alluding to our own vessel at the present time. Then there was a tremendous explosion after that, but before the second explosion took place I rushed out of the cabin on deck, thinking something was the matter with our vessel; that she had collided, or something. I rushed up on deck to see what was the matter, and I do not suppose I was more than a second from the time I heard the first explosion until I was on deck. The sound was not fully gone from the second explosion when I reached the deck.

By Captain SIGSBEE:

Q. Did you see the vessel lift in the water at all?

A. No, sir; I can't say that I saw that, but I could distinctly see the vessel from the fore end to the after end—the whole of the stem and stern and everything. I mentioned something to my officers then. There was something on the forecastle head. I think they appeared like two men standing there. I was looking at the ship with a long telescope. It may have been a gun or something of that sort. I do not see how a man could have been standing there, the state the ship was in. I could distinctly see the guns on the foredeck, but there was nothing surrounding them. It seemed as if the protections of the guns had been blown away. The ship was lying with the deck over toward me, from the position we were in at that time, and I could see one gun distinctly there and another one up here again [indicating]. Then on the forward deck I could see two objects. They appeared to me, with a glass, in the dark, like two men standing there; but, of course, it may have been something else.

Q. How much of a wave was thrown over in your direction?

A. There didn't seem to be much of a wave with us, but there was a decided movement of the vessel shortly afterwards. My mate remarked to me afterwards—he said: "Do you feel the vessel rolling now?" And that was my first mate remarked that to me.

Q. Was the vessel heading as she is now?

A. No; we were lying at anchor.

Q. I mean the *Maine.*

A. No; I think the wind was northwest at the time.

Q. I mean the *Maine.* Was she heading practically as she is now?

A. Yes; practically as she is now; but she seems to have moved her position somewhat from what I saw her the afternoon before.

Q. I am speaking now of the time of the explosion.

A. Yes; she is lying much in the same position as she was at the time of the explosions. She did not seem to have altered her position in any way since that night—not the slightest.

Q. Did you see any dead fish around the bay?

A. I never saw any; no, sir.

Q. Have you ever heard that fish leave this harbor at night and go outside?

A. I never heard any remark about that. I have seen a good many fish here, but they were very small fish, just spluttering about on the top of the water. I have never seen any in the night time, but any time when there is any spluttering among the fish it generally occurs in the daytime, so far as my observation has gone. The wind coming in that direction carried a lot of light material over our vessel that night. Quantities of paper and small fragments fell over our ship, and for some time after. I picked up some boiler coating or coating from steam pipes the next morning. There also seemed to be felt and hair. I also picked up an envelope addressed to Mr. Silley, United States ship *Maine*. The stamp was gone from the envelope. The envelope was somewhat charred, and showed as though it had been in the midst of an explosion, or something like that, and where the stamp came off the place underneath was perfectly clean. I gave it to the officer who came aboard our vessel.

Q. You gave it to Mr. Holman?

A. Yes, sir.

Q. To whom was that addressed?

A. I think Silley or Seller. The writing was rather bad and hard to make out.

Q. Is that all, Captain?

A. I think that is all, sir. If you wish to ask me any questions, I will be glad to answer them.

There being no further questions to ask this witness, his testimony was read over to him by the stenographer and by him pronounced correct.

The witness then withdrew, after being cautioned by the president not to converse about matters pertaining to the inquiry.

Private ANTHONY here appeared before the court.

The JUDGE-ADVOCATE. Private Anthony, I hand you so much of the record of the proceedings of this court as contains the testimony given by you. Please withdraw, read it over, and then return to the court and state whether you desire to make any corrections, or whether the testimony is correct.

The witness then withdrew.

Chaplain JOHN P. CHIDWICK, U. S. Navy, appeared before the court as a witness, and was sworn by the president.

Examined by the JUDGE-ADVOCATE:

Q. Please state your full name, rank, and present duty.

A. John Patrick Chidwick, chaplain, U. S. Navy. I have no relative rank.

Q. You are attached to the *Maine*?

A. Attached to the *Maine*.

Q. Where were you on the night of the 15th of February, when the *Maine* was blown up?

A. In my room, aboard the ship.

Q. Please state to the court what shocks you felt, what noises you heard, and what you saw in regard to the explosion.

A. I heard a loud report, and everything became dark as soon as I heard the report. The lights were out, and there was a crashing sound of things falling. I then rushed on deck. I got on the captain's poop and saw the captain there giving his orders. After trying to cheer up the men who were crying out in the water for help, I was ordered by Lieutenant Jungen to go into a boat, which I did. We rowed around the ship and picked up one man. Then, at the orders of the captain, we pulled off for the *City of Washington*.

Q. How many shocks did you feel?

A. I remember only one.

Q. Did you notice any list to the ship when that shock was experienced?

A. It struck me that I did, to the port side. I am not positive about that.

Q. Port down?

A. Port down; yes, sir.

Q. But you are not positive?

A. No, sir.

Q. At the time you reached the deck had the large explosion taken place and was it over?

A. Yes; it was over and the forward part was then aflame.

By the COURT:

Q. From what direction did this first explosion or shock seem to proceed?

A. The impression on my mind can not very well verify anything I would say. It was like a loud report; everything became dark, and then the noise of falling things. As I say, I have an indistinct remembrance of the ship falling toward the port.

Q. Afterwards or at the same time?

A. Yes, sir; when I was in the room; when I heard the report.

There being no further questions to ask this witness, his testimony was read over to him by the stenographer and by him pronounced correct. The witness then withdrew.

Private ANTHONY here appeared before the court.

The JUDGE-ADVOCATE. Is your testimony as recorded correct?

Mr. ANTHONY. Yes, sir.

The witness then withdrew, after being cautioned by the president not to converse about matters pertaining to the inquiry.

Ensign POWELSON then appeared before the court.

The JUDGE-ADVOCATE. Mr. Powelson, have you brought the drawings you were instructed to make?

Ensign POWELSON. I have one. I have not quite finished the other.

The JUDGE-ADVOCATE. You can bring that later.

Ensign POWELSON. Yes, sir.

The JUDGE-ADVOCATE. If the court please, Mr. Powelson has brought with him one of the drawings he was instructed to make, which I request may be appended to the record.

(Said drawing is hereto appended, marked B.)

The JUDGE-ADVOCATE. Mr. Powelson, I now hand you so much of the record of the proceedings of this court on yesterday as contains your testimony. Please withdraw, read it over, and then return to the court and state whether you desire to make any corrections, or whether the testimony as recorded is correct.

The witness then withdrew.

The JUDGE-ADVOCATE. I ask that the court be cleared.

The court was cleared, all persons except the members of the court and the judge-advocate withdrawing.

The court was opened, and the stenographer and Captain Sigsbee entered.

The JUDGE-ADVOCATE. Captain Sigsbee, the court was cleared in order to permit me to tell the court what steps I had taken to ascertain what mining had been done in the harbor of Havana, and the difficulty experienced in obtaining any testimony on that subject; also to submit to the court certain letters, which can not be used as evidence, but which also bear on the same subject, and to receive instructions of the court in regard to this matter.

The court (at 12 o'clock noon) took a recess until 1.30 o'clock p. m.

The court reassembled at the expiration of the recess.

Present: All the members, the judge-advocate, the stenographer, and Captain Sigsbee.

Ensign POWELSON appeared before the court.

The JUDGE-ADVOCATE. Mr. Powelson, is the testimony given by you as recorded correct?

Ensign POWELSON. I wish to make the following corrections in the testimony:

On page 27 insert the words "top of the" before "conning tower."

On page 28, in the fifth line, strike out the word "port." In the fifth line from the bottom, the sentence should end with "up." In the fourth line from the bottom add: "From port to starboard," after the word "sheared."

On page 30, third line, change "the" to "a."

On page 32, first line, change "one" to "the," making it read "name of the diver."

On page 33, sixth line, "better" should read "battered."

On page 35, the first one in the first line, "turret," should be erased. In the seventeenth line "exploded" should be "burst."

On page 36, fifth line, "five inches" should be "twenty inches." In the twelfth line the words "with one end of" should be erased.

On page 39, fourth line, change the phrase "at port crane" to "and port crane." In the fourteenth line, change "quarter" to "protective."

The JUDGE-ADVOCATE. Is your testimony as now changed correct as recorded?

Ensign POWELSON. Yes, sir. I have with me now the other sketch which I was directed by the court to make.

The JUDGE-ADVOCATE. If the court please, I ask permission to append the sketch produced by the witness to the record.

(Said sketch is appended hereto, marked E.)

SIGMOND ROTHSCHILD appeared as a witness before the court and was sworn by the president.

Examined by the JUDGE-ADVOCATE:

Q. Please state your full name, residence, and business.

A. My full name is Sigmund Rothschild. My residence is in Detroit,

Mich. My business is packing tobacco on the Island of Cuba, being here since 1871.

Q. Were you in Havana on the 15th day of February when the *Maine* was blown up?

A. I was.

Q. Where were you?

A. On the *City of Washington*, coming that evening.

Q. How far was the *City of Washington* from the *Maine* at the time of the explosion?

A. I can not give the exact distance, but I asked Captain Stevens, captain of the *Washington*, what distance he would call it, and he said about 300 feet.

Q. Where were you at the time it happened?

A. Right on the stern of the boat, and for the following reasons: Let me explain, gentlemen. We were only 17 passengers, and after the *Washington*, which came in about 8.30, had received her place, all the other passengers went down to take beer. They invited me and I said I wouldn't drink any, and my friend who is upstairs, Mr. Wertheimer, also said he would not drink any. We were sitting then in the smoking room. This was about 9.30. I said, "Let us go to the stern of the boat and watch the *Maine*." I made a joke about it. I said, "We are under the guns of the United States; we are well protected, and we can sit here." The chairs were sitting in the center of the open place aft, and we wanted to pull the chairs toward the bench, toward the railing. In doing so, I had brought my chair just about in this condition [indicating], and had not sat down when I heard a shot, the noise of a shot. I looked around and I saw the bow of the *Maine* rise a little, go a little out of the water. It couldn't have been more than a few seconds after that noise, that shot, that there came in the center of the ship a terrible mass of fire and explosion, and everything went over our heads, a black mass. We could not tell what it was. It was all black. Then we heard a noise of falling material on the place where we had been, right near the smoking room.

One of the lifeboats which was hanging had a piece go through it and make a big hole in it. After we seen that mast go up, the whole boat lifted out, I should judge, about 2 feet. As she lifted out, the bow went right down. It didn't take a minute after the lifting of the boat until the bow went down. We stood spellbound, and cried to the captain. The captain gave orders to lower the boats, and two of the boats which were partly lowered were found broken through with big holes. Some iron pieces had fallen through them. Naturally, that made a delay, and they had to run for the other boats, or else we would have been a few minutes sooner in the water. Then the stern stood out like this, in this direction [indicating], and there was a cry from the people "Help," and "Lord God help us," and "Help! Help!" The noise of the cry from the mass of human voices in the boat did not last but a minute or two. When the ship was going down, there was the cry of a mass of people, but that was a murmur. That was not so loud as the single voices which were in the water. That did not last but a minute, and by that time we saw somebody on the deck in the stern of the ship, and it took about a few minutes when the boats commenced to bring in the officers. We took them to our rooms. A great many of them came without anything on but a pair of pants and nothing else. That is about the whole story in regard to the shot.

To prove to you, gentlemen, about that shot which was heard, the gentlemen who have gone on to Mexico in the same steamer, they were drinking beer, and they were about as far from the portholes as this would be [indicating]. They heard the shot first, and the shot brought the gentlemen sitting on this side of the table immediately to the port-hole. Then the fire came out of the center. So the shot was heard by everyone, as we stated that night in the papers. It was a shot similar to a cannon shot. I do not know what it was, because I am used to this island, and I know at 8 o'clock they fire a shot. This was about 9.35 or 9.40, and it was an unusual time for hearing a shot. If it had been about 8, I would not have been looking around, because every night we hear that here; but being an unusual hour I looked around, and I saw the upheaving bow of the *Maine*, just a little, not very much; but the next minute the middle section commenced to go up. She commenced to go down, and in less than a minute after the upheaving she was down in the water.

Q. Which side of the *Maine* was toward you?

A. We were lying in the same direction; that is to say, when we sat on the stern we looked at the stern of the *Maine*. Our boat lay pretty near in the same direction. I looked out from the stern to my right side.

Q. You mean the *Maine* was pointing right toward you—the stern of you?

A. No.

Q. Which side of the *Maine* was toward your vessel?

A. The right.

Q. The starboard side?

A. Yes, sir.

By the COURT:

Q. You were lying here somewhere [indicating]?

A. Yes; just like looking in this direction, on this side [indicating].

Q. You were looking toward the port side of the *Maine* then. Were you on the Morro Castle side of the *Maine* or on the other side of the *Maine*?

A. We were on the side away from Havana. If this is the bow [indicating] this is our boat. I was looking from here to here.

Q. Then you were looking at the port side of the *Maine*?

A. Whatever you call it. I am not a good sailor. I must make that confession. I was looking from this stern to this stern [indicating]. Here is where our stern was, and I was standing about here [indicating]. Here is the place where I stood. That is the smoking room, and this is where all that stuff fell down, the iron; and here, a little nearer the engine room, was where the engineer was sitting when that cement fell. Have you seen that?

Q. We have heard of it.

A. It is kept by the engineer for me. He says he will bring it back from Mexico. It broke a chair and made a large hole through the deck. It is a large piece. I think it must weigh about 30 pounds.

Q. How thick was the cement?

A. The cement was about 2 inches in thickness.

By the JUDGE ADVOCATE:

Q. When you heard that first explosion, did you feel any vibration on board of your own vessel?

A. No, sir; none—nothing but hearing it. There was no feeling at all.

Q. Did you feel any vibration when the *Maine* blew up?

A. I did.

Q. You are certain there was a distinct interval between the first shot and the blowing up?

A. Sure, because it was the shot which made me look first in that direction.

Q. Which side of the *Maine* did the explosion seem to come out of?

A. This we will call the *Maine* [indicating]. The explosion came about here. Take that as the entire boat. There is where it came [pointing at about the middle of the *Maine*]. I am positive, because I saw the whole width of it.

Q. Was it on the side toward you or away from you?

A. On our side. The whole mass came over our heads.

Q. On your side?

A. Yes, sir.

Q. Will you tell us whether you saw anything going up in the air which exploded after it got there, like rockets?

A. No, sir; nothing exploded in the air, because we would have seen everything. Nothing exploded. It was merely a dropping against our boat. It came over our boat and on our boat, but nothing exploded after it went in the air.

Q. At the time of the first report, or at the time of the second explosion, did you see any water flying up?

A. From the boat, nothing, except when the *Maine* went down. Then there was a splurge of water from the lurch of the boat.

Q. You saw no great upshoot of flame at the second explosion, either?

A. No; the flame came after, more like a burning fire flame. It was an explosion which showed that it was fire, you know, but not that flame which we seen afterwards, burning for hours—what we call a flame. It was an explosion, and it ended with that and set it on fire afterwards. This ship was burning until 2 o'clock in the morning.

Q. That is, the explosion made no great illumination?

A. No, sir.

Q. This upheaval caused by the second explosion was limited, you say, to that portion of the ship which you have marked out there?

A. No; the first shot I heard I saw the upheaval here at the bow—not a great deal. When the second explosion came the whole of it was raised, only less from the stern, and immediately she went down just as fast as she could.

The JUDGE-ADVOCATE. The forward half of the ship?

A. Yes, sir.

By the COURT:

Q. Did that extend clear across the ship?

A. Naturally, we couldn't tell from the masses and from the fire how far it extended on the other side, because we were on one side of it; but it looked as if that whole center here was torn out, from the place where I looked at it. Whether there was anything untouched here [indicating] we couldn't see it from this end. It was impossible, because on this end everything came out clean, so that the whole surface was taken out. We couldn't tell from our side exactly how much it took out.

Q. In regard to the interval of time between the first explosion and the second, did you do anything which would enable you to make a measure of that time?

A. No; and I will tell you why. When that shot, or that noise, was heard, it gave me merely time to look around to see where it came from. It was night on the water, and I couldn't tell. I just turned my eye around, and by the time I turned my eye around this explosion commenced to come.

Q. One or two seconds only?

A. Not more than few seconds, just as a man could look around. It would only take a few seconds.

Q. A second is a long time under such circumstances.

A. I know what seconds are since that time, when we were getting our boats down to help the people that were drowning. I know what seconds are since that time. I never knew it before. The noises of these two explosions had no connection, but they were two distinct things. That is to say, the noise and the fire did not come together. First was the noise, the shot, and when the shot was over, then this explosion took place.

Q. You saw the ship move at each one of these explosions?

A. At the first shot the bow of the boat just lifted about that much [indicating]. At the second one it was more of an upheaval of the hull, with the exception of less here at the stern. Then the bow went straight down like this in this direction [indicating].

Q. The people on board the *Maine* were quiet before this?

A. They were all down stairs, with the exception of Mr. Wertheimer and myself, only two.

Q. I mean on board the *Maine?*

A. Perfectly quiet. We even made the remark how quiet everything looked on board of that vessel.

Q. You saw no strange boats about her?

A. Not from our side, and it was pretty well lit up, if everything could have been seen. We were interested because we had just arrived, and having read so much in America about the *Maine*. We were interested to inspect the boat, not to look for any strange thing; but we saw nothing under the boat or near the boat. When we came in, all these harbor boats were on the other side of the *Maine*, up toward this part of the city [indicating]. The ferry which runs from here to here [indicating] was taking her regular course amidst all the cry. She was right here then and she did not come to help. The ferry runs across from here to here [indicating]. I went to Captain Stevens and I said: "For God's sake, can't you holler to that boat to go nearer?" Naturally, being in midstream, I did not expect she would with a lot of passengers, because it looked threatening with that stern part out, as if another explosion might happen; but after she had taken her passengers off she had ample time to go to their assistance before we could get there. She was under steam and she ran steady. Those boats run steady.

Q. The Spanish man-of-war in the harbor did send boats?

A. Oh, yes. By the time our boats were in the water we saw the flash light coming toward the *Maine* and their boats were ahead of the light, so they came immediately. They also got a big piece of iron, which fell on our boat, which was used for binding the boat together on both sides.

Q. An angle iron?

A. An angle iron. That also fell on our deck.

Q. Did you notice any very large pieces of iron plate that were torn off or thrown up?

A. No, I did not see any large pieces. I saw a big bulk flying. It didn't look like heavy pieces. It might have been a human body, because everything that came over us looked dark. We saw large pieces of timber in front of our vessel which flew against it, but nothing you could see with your eyes, because it was so glaring on account of this explosion when it went up that you could see nothing until it went over, and then you could see it as a mass and not as an article which was lit up. You could see it as a dark mass.

Q. Some of the pieces, you think, went over the *Washington*?

A. I am sure they went over our heads. You see, this stern of the *Washington* is pretty clear. Everything would go over, while here in front they would fall against something. We were sitting back of the cabins, which was a large space free from the deck, and everything went over us; some of them went not more than about 10 or 12 feet over us; the others went very high, but you could not tell what it was, except it was a dark matter. There was afterwards many single shots going off; that kept on for hours afterwards until about 2.15 in the morning, but it was nothing like an explosion. It was single pieces of something going off, that stopped right there.

Q. Did you notice anything flying aloft when the first shock was heard?

A. No.

Q. Nothing flew up in the air?

A. Nothing flew up in the air. I looked around. I thought the shot may have come from something else. If anything flew up I would have seen it; but my eye went not alone to the boat but went all over, to see where that shot could have come from. Nothing went up, because my eye was directed the moment the shot was heard. I saw no commotion, no lurch, like this [indicating]; just a little lift. Then came the explosion, which gave the whole mass a lift.

There being no further questions to ask this witness, his testimony was read over to him by the stenographer and by him pronounced correct.

The witness then withdrew, after being cautioned by the president of the court not to converse about matters pertaining to the inquiry.

LOUIS WERTHEIMER appeared before the court as a witness and was duly sworn by the president.

Examined by the JUDGE-ADVOCATE:

Q. Will you please give your full name, residence, and what business you are in?

A. Louis Wertheimer; business address, 148 Water street, New York; private address, 133 West Ninety-third street, New York City.

Q. What business are you engaged in?

A. Dealer in leaf tobacco.

Q. Were you in the harbor of Havana on the 15th day of February when the *Maine* exploded?

A. I was a passenger on the *City of Washington*.

Q. How far was the *City of Washington* from the *Maine* at the time?

A. I should judge between 100 and 125 yards.

Q. Where were you at the time of the explosion?

A. At the actual moment of the explosion I was in the stern of the *Washington*, having left about halfway between the smokestack and the chief engineer's cabin, where I was standing talking with Mr. Rothschild, to take a seat on the chairs which were on the stern of the *Washington*. We left our post because there were no chairs there, and when we reached the stern of the boat and had just taken hold of the chairs to move them out from the center of the vessel the explosion occurred.

Q. Then the *Maine* was in full view of you at the time.

A. We were looking directly at her at the time.

Q. On which side of the *Maine* were you looking?

A. We were on the starboard side of our boat—the stern starboard side—and we were looking at the *Maine*.

Q. The *Maine* was abreast of you?

A. I should judge she was parallel to us. The same tide must have put her in the same position we were in.

Q. Please tell us what you felt and saw.

A. We heard a report.

Q. You?

A. I heard a report, a minor report, minor in comparison with the greater report which immediately followed, and at an interval of anywhere from five to fifteen seconds following this first minor report came a great explosion. We saw an upheaval, and the air was black with flying objects which we could not distinguish, but there were sufficient of them to blacken the sky. In the same burst of flame which followed this immense upheaval I saw, clearly and plainly, the vessel rise in the water a distance which apparently was 3 yards, but which in reality must have been greater, and then settle down before the light of the explosion went out. The whole thing was over so quickly that I could not hazard a guess at the time, but suffice it to say that in the burst of flame which followed the upheaval of this flying mass I saw the vessel settle in the water.

Q. Do you say you noticed an upheaval at the first explosion or first shock—an upheaval of the vessel?

A. As closely as I can say, I should say the upheaval followed the flying objects—either that or simultaneously. The time was so very, very short between them, if there was a difference between the rising of the vessel, the upheaval of the vessel and the upheaval of the objects flying in the air, that it would be difficult to mark it.

Q. I am now referring to the first shot you heard. Did you notice any movement of the *Maine* together with that?

A. No; not at all; and bear in mind that the interval was very, very short between the first and the great explosion.

Q. You probably meant, when you said from five to fifteen seconds, less time than that, if you count in your own mind how long five seconds would take.

A. Let me see how long five seconds actually took and I can judge better. [Witness examines his watch.] It certainly was less.

Q. Less than five seconds?

A. Yes, sir; it certainly was less.

Q. Did you feel any shock aboard the *Washington* at the first explosion that you heard?

A. No, sir.

Q. Did you at the second?

A. Yes, sir; decidedly—a strong tremor running through the vessel.

Q. Did you see any shell explode in the air at this second upheaval?

A. No; nor was I looking upward at the time. My eyes were fixed then on what was left of the *Maine*—the deck—settling in the water. I didn't look in the air at all. I have heard it said here that people in the city saw a great burst of colored lights in the sky, as though signal rockets were exploding there. I saw nothing of that from the *Washington*, because my sight was not fixed in the sky. It was fixed on the vessel itself—the hull.

Q. Had you been looking at the *Maine* for some little time previous to this?

A. Fully ten minutes.
Q. Did you see any boats around her?
A. Nothing; but the night was very dark. Between the time that the cornet—I took it to be the cornet—sounded on the *Maine* and the extinguishing of lights at the explosion there was very little light in the bay. It was a very, very dark night, so much so that Mr. Rothschild, myself, and another passenger were discussing the color of the *Maine*, whether she were white or gray.
Q. There were some electric lights showing on board the *Maine*, though, were there not?
A. When we entered, yes; as we came up to our buoy there was a great deal of light. There seemed to be a good deal of moving about. We heard a concertina playing when we moored, which was all previous to the cornet sounding.

By the COURT:

Q. I would like to ask if, on thinking it over, there is in your mind any confusion between the upheaval of the ship following the principal explosion and the fact that she immediately went down?
A. Will you repeat that question, please. I didn't quite catch it.
Q. You say when this explosion took place, either simultaneously or instantly after, you saw the vessel rise in the water?
A. Yes, sir.
Q. You should say at least 5 feet?
A. Yes, sir.
Q. Of course she immediately stopped and went down entirely under the water?
A. Yes, sir.
Q. Do you suppose that if she had simply gone back to the position from which she started, it would appear in your mind to be as much as 5 feet that she rose out of the water?
A. I think she raised more than 5 feet. I say it was what appeared to me to be 3 yards—9 feet—but I think in reality it must have been more, judging from the size of the vessel. She certainly settled deeper when she came down after being heaved up than she had been originally.
Q. Yes; she went entirely under the water then.
A. Yes; she settled immediately in the water.
Q. You think it was as much as 9 feet that she was raised?
A. I should estimate it at that; yes, sir.
Q. What part of the ship was it that was lifted so much?
A. The part that was nearest to us, which was the part we were looking at. It must have been her stern, because her stern was probably parallel with our own.
Q. Whereabouts did this explosion occur with reference to the *Maine*?
A. In what part of the *Maine*?
Q. Yes.
A. That would be very difficult for me to say, because I am not familiar enough with the ship. It looked to be rather more forward than the middle of the ship.
Q. Was it that part of the ship that was lifted out of the water?
A. No; not the part that I refer to as being lifted out of the water, because what I saw lifted out of the water must have been her stern, being the nearest to us, while the part that exploded was farther away from us.
Q. Was not this lifting of the stern due to the fact that the bow was depressed?

A. That I couldn't say.

Q. Just as if this [indicating] was the bow of the ship, and the explosion took place here forward of the center, could the raising of the stern be due to the fact that this end went down?

A. No, sir; it was too quick for that. It was too sudden a lift. It must have been an independent force that lifted that hull as I saw it lifted. It could not possibly be the depression of the forward end raising the hind end, because that would result in a gradual motion, and this was a decided lifting up.

Q. Could not that [indicating] have been the portion of the ship where the explosion took place?

A. No; the explosion was forward of the stern which I speak of seeing raised from the water.

Q. That part which was raised was to your right hand as you looked, was it, or to your left hand?

A. To the right. We were lying reversed from this, were we not, with the stern to the mouth of the bay?

Q. The *Maine* is lying now just as she was on that occasion. You were on that side of her, looking this way, and the stern was to your right hand.

A. Yes, sir; the stern was to our right hand.

Q. It would depend on how you were facing, yourself; but the explosion was to your left, if you were not looking directly at it?

A. We were looking directly at her, though.

Q. Then the explosion was to the left end of the part you saw raised?

A. I really can not agree with you on that, because I take it that we were looking immediately at her. She was in front of us. We were facing the vessel directly. Supposing that she was lying parallel to us—yes, you would be right, it would be to the left then. I should prefer, as a layman, to omit the words "bow" and "stern" because I distinctly say that part of the vessel nearest to us. I was standing on the stern of the *Washington*. That I can say positively, but I can not say positively which was the stern or bow of the *Maine*. I simply take it for granted that she was lying parallel to us, and that the same tide that swung us swung her.

Q. Suppose this is the *Maine* [illustrating]. Instead of lying in that position, she might have been lying in that position [indicating]?

A. We looked to that part of the *Maine* which was nearest to us, and we were on the stern of the *Washington*.

Q. If you were looking right opposite you, and she was in that position, then it was the part you were looking at that was raised?

A. Yes, sir; decidedly and emphatically.

Q. That is the bow of your ship [indicating]. Did the *Maine* appear in that direction or in that direction [indicating]?

A. That I didn't notice.

Q. For instance, as you stood on the deck of the *Washington*, was your head turned somewhat toward the bow of the *Washington*, or were you looking over the stern somewhat?

A. Somewhat astern; yes, sir.

Q. In other words, there would be the *Maine* and here would be the *Washington* [indicating].

A. If this was our ship, my line of vision, more or less, was directed in this direction [indicating]. The *Maine* was to the right of us. That part I am reasonably positive of.

There being no further questions to ask this witness, his testimony was read over to him by the stenographer, and by him pronounced correct.

Lieutenant-Commander Wainwright asked permission at this point to be present, and permission was granted.

Gunner CHARLES MORGAN, U. S. Navy, appeared as a witness and was duly sworn by the president.

Examined by the JUDGE-ADVOCATE:

Q. Please state your name, rank, and present duty.
A. Gunner Charles Morgan, serving on board the U. S. S. *New York*, of Key West, Fla. I am on duty here, diving.
Q. Have you personally done any diving about the wreck of the *Maine?*
A. Yes, sir.
Q. How often have you been down?
A. I was down once.
Q. How long did you remain down?
A. An hour and twenty-five minutes.
Q. Will you describe to the court, from your own knowledge, what you yourself saw and felt, the condition of the wreck of the *Maine*, and anything you may have discovered down there of importance.
A. On being dressed and going down the ladder and lowered down to the bottom, I was landed among a lot of tanks, some being 6-inch and some being 10-inch powder tanks, all being empty and broken up. I also found what I supposed to be the ceiling and the linings of the magazine woodwork. Then walking around a little way from the tanks, I fell off. I landed down in soft mud. I tried to pick my way back again and I came across what I supposed to be the bulkhead. Placing my hands upon it, I found it went in, and overhauling it a little more, coming up higher on it all the time until I got to the top, I found myself back among the tanks again. Then moving away from there a little way, I found that I got among a lot of wires, which I supposed to be in the dynamo room, and also among some accumulators; and everything in the line of bulkheads and frames had a tendency of showing from port to starboard. After overhauling these frames, I started to walk away from that direction, going along a little way to the left, as I supposed it to be, and there I came across a lot of frames, as they seemed to be. They were turned up and over. A little way from there I got among the paymaster's stores, canned wet provisions. In turning around again, I began going back toward the same amount of powder tanks—the empty tanks. Being satisfied I was around the 10 and 6 inch tanks, I had the signal to be called up.
Q. You say the tanks were empty and broken. Broken in what way?
A. Some were just split open and others had their heads off, and others were just simply pressed down; some had the impression of the powder showing on them.
Q. Did many tanks appear to have been burst open by the charge inside of them having been exploded?
A. Not so many as those which appeared to be just split open.
Q. Would the brown powder, exposed to constant weather, like the powder aboard the *Maine* has been exposed in an open tank, be likely to melt out?
A. Yes, sir.
Q. Dissolved?
A. Yes, sir.

Q. And some of these tanks might have been full at the time of the sinking, and the powder has since been dissolved and leaked out?
A. Yes, sir.
Q. Will you explain what you mean by saying the frames went from port to starboard?
A. I would say that the edges of what I supposed to be frames that held the bulkheads and things of that kind had a tendency of being turned over from port, facing down to starboard, from left to right. They had a curve.
Q. Are you fairly well acquainted with the construction of the *Maine?*
A. Not very well. I have been on board of her two or three times.
Q. You have looked at the plans since you commenced diving?
A. Yes, sir.
Q. Where do you think you were when you struck all these tanks?
A. I thought I was forward of the boilers and in around the hydraulic pumps. I ought to have been.
Q. Did you ever explore what you consider to be the outside of the ship?
A. I was down in the soft mud there, but I suppose I was on the outside.
Q. What is the condition of the port side of the ship?
A. The place I was at was all gone.
Q. Perfectly open to port?
A. Perfectly open, except little ragged edges from the pieces there on the bottom?
Q. Did you touch the starboard side of the ship at all; did you reach that?
A. Just on the starboard side, over the 10-inch magazine. That was all.
Q. Did you touch the starboard side?
A. No, sir.
Q. It has been stated in this court by another witness that you fell into a hole. What about that?
A. There is a space there where it is deeper than any other place. That is where the soft mud is.
Q. You could find no bottom to that hole at all?
A. Yes; there is bottom there.
Q. How far did you get in?
A. About half waist. Near the armpits.
Q. What was the nature of the hole? Did you find the boundaries of the hole at all?
A. No; it is an open space, very soft, slushy mud.
Q. But you did not touch the edges of this hole?
A. It is simply an incline, but nothing to make a round hole.
Q. You do not know how big the hole was then?
A. No, sir.
Q. You do not know how the metal was bent at the hole?
A. There was no metal at the hole.

By Captain SIGSBEE:

Q. Do you know whether you reached the outside shell of the ship anywhere?
A. I couldn't say, sir.

By the COURT:

Q. You spoke of being among the 6 and 10 inch powder tanks when you first went down. How many powder tanks do you estimate you found?

A. I would say there were at least from 20 to 25 there, sir.

Q. If the powder had dissolved and leaked out of the tanks, would not the powder bag have been left intact in the tank?

A. It would depend if they were cut and jammed in the tank. We found pieces and brought them up to the surface. If they were not cut, they would be found in the tank.

Q. Where would they go?

A. Down there among the wreckage.

Q. Do you think powder would dissolve sufficiently to entirely leak out through the cartridge bag?

A. If it was broken and crushed—yes, sir.

Q. But if the cartridge bag were not broken?

A. It would stay in the tank, just the same as the 10-inch, if it was not broken, but it would dissolve.

Q. Did you find any powder cases that were full and closed tight?

A. At the time I was down?

Q. Yes.

A. No, sir.

Q. You said in answer to a question as to where you were when you found these powder tanks, that you thought you were in the hydraulic room?

A. Because the accumulators were there, and also the position of the accumulators, and the magazine would make it around that room, near the 10-inch magazine.

Q. But the hydraulic room is over the magazine?

A. Yes, sir; but the lining of the top floor and the magazine all being broken open, just as though it had been crushed up to the woodwork and sticking out, the woodwork being tongued and grooved, and the woodwork leaving an open space there, showed the accumulators lying around.

Q. I am referring to the powder tanks. I asked you where you were when you found these tanks. You said you were in the hydraulic pump room. Is it possible that during all the time you were down you had not been as low as the magazine?

A. I am quite sure I was as low as the magazine, because no wood of that kind would be down there below that deck.

Q. Were you ever in her magazines when she was in order, before this occurrence?

A. No, sir; I never was in her magazines. I took special notice of it when I struck it, knowing that that was something strange to be down there. I put my hands over it and noticed it particularly, and found it was an inch thick. Then I put my hand right along and noticed it was a part of the flooring. Then when I came across these other things together it led me to understand I was at the magazine.

Q. How could these powder tanks have been in the hydraulic room?

A. There probably being no solid deck there, probably they got down in below there. The accumulators were right around in that surface, and they were secured to that after bulkhead above the magazine.

Q. But they were not in the hydraulic room?

A. No, sir; they were all around the magazine at that time.

Q. They just dropped down into the magazine. Is that it?

A. Yes, sir; they just dropped down in there.

By Captain SIGSBEE:

Q. Do you find any 10 or 6 inch shell below?

A. There were four 6-inch shell lying there. The man wanted to hook them up, and I told him not to, because we didn't have men to haul them up. He also put a 10-inch shell on.
Q. Was this your own experience when you went down under the water?
A. No, sir.
Q. You did not find any shell yourself, individually?
A. No, sir.

There being no further questions to ask this witness, his testimony was read aloud to him, and by him pronounced to be correct, and having been cautioned by the president not to discuss matters pertaining to the trial, he withdrew.

Chief Gunner's Mate ANDREW OLSEN, U. S. Navy, appeared as a witness and was duly sworn by the president.

Examined by the JUDGE-ADVOCATE:
Q. What is your name, rate, and to what ship are you attached?
A. My name is Andrew Olsen, chief gunner's mate, U. S. S. *Iowa*.
Q. Have you been sent over here for the purpose of doing diving duty on the wreck of the *Maine?*
A. Yes, sir.
Q. How many times have you been down?
A. I have been down four times.
Q. About how many hours in all?
A. About eight or nine hours, I guess—around there. I couldn't say exactly how many.
Q. State to the court your own experience while under water, as far as the condition of the *Maine* is concerned, and any discoveries of any importance that you may have made while under water yourself.
A. The first time I went down, I went right down over the forward part where she was blown up, seemingly over some fire rooms. I found the wreck all blowed up. I found a lot of grate bars down there. The second time I went down, I went down farther forward. I struck a lot of 10-inch shells. Forward of the 10-inch shell, the plates were bent right inboard over them.

By the COURT:
Q. Forward of the shell?
A. Yes, sir; forward and outside of the 10-inch shells. Some of the shells are laid with the point of the shell pointing up. Some are armor-piercing shell and some are common shell. The points of some are standing up and some are lying down. Right forward and to the left of them, and seemingly on the left side of the shells, there are plates bent inboard over the shells.
Q. You imagine yourself looking forward?
A. Yes, sir. Going over them plates, I struck into a lot of 6-inch shells with their slings on them. Then going to the right from there over in that direction [indicating], I found a lot of wreckage over that way. It seemed blown over to starboard. I put my hand in some of the cracks and pulled out some 6-pounder shells. I pulled out one complete 6-pounder cartridge, shell, and all, and one shell that was all blown up—all of them 6-pounder cartridges.

The next time I went down I went right down outside the ship, right forward of the crane on the port side. I followed the bottom along. The ship's side was blown outward, and right alongside the crane you can walk on it. Following the ship's side from there forward, the ship's side seemingly goes into shape again. You come to the part where she is blown up completely. Then part of her bottom plates are turned up. Then you follow the bottom from there up and the plates are blown outward. At the top and underneath the bottom they are blown inboard like that [indicating]—bent in. About 3 feet forward of that there is a piece of iron laid along, seemingly the bulkhead. The skin of the inside of the double bottoms is curled over like a sheet of paper inboard, from stem to stern. Right in amidships on the same place there is an armor plate, one plate complete, the top of the plate standing up.

The plate is inclined over to starboard. It is laid over to starboard completely. It stands up with the thick part of the plate down. It is inclined forward, like that [indicating], and over to starboard—one whole, complete plate. The thickness of the plate on top is 7 inches exactly. I measured it. On the forward part of that plate is wooden backing, and forward of that wooden backing there is a thin sheet of steel, and the bolts holding the armor plate into the backing are there, two of them. I felt them. I could feel the hexagonal ends, with washers. Whether they are rubber or leather washers I couldn't say. I couldn't see them. I could feel them underneath those ends; and that place extends over to starboard about the midship line of the ship. Inside the 10-inch shell room, seemingly, where all those shells are, I found a lot of empty tanks. Some of them were small pieces—three or four small pieces there which I couldn't get hold of. Most of the tanks are cracked right in the seam, and there are some 10-inch leaves or parts of tanks in there in amongst the shells. Right over this place that is bent in by the 10-inch shell room there seemed to be the frame of the ship, standing up and bent inboard on the port side.

On the edge of this armor plate, on this thin sheet of steel that is inside of the backing, you can see the rivet holes, and seemingly some kind of an angle iron inside this steel. You can feel the rivet holes on the edge of it. If you follow this armor plate you do not strike anything at all. Everything is completely blown away. There is nothing but the bare bottom, mud. If there is anything in the mud I can not find it, because it is so deep down; but I have been trying to dig down as far as I could. I have been down about five feet in the mud, digging and scraping.

By the JUDGE-ADVOCATE:

Q. Whereabouts on this plan would you put that armor plate? Here is the shell room, you see. There is the 6-inch spare magazine and here is the 10-inch powder magazine.

A. This plate would be around here [indicating].

Q. At the after end of that shell room?

A. Yes, sir.

Q. To the port of the midship line?

A. Yes, sir; port of the midship line. May be it might be a little over on the midship line; but if it is, it is not much.

Q. Near frame 30?

A. Yes, sir.

Q. Where did you find the skin of the double bottom turned up and in?

A. A little abaft here, seemingly.

Q. A little abaft of frame 30?

A. Yes, sir; a little abaft this armor plate—a few feet abaft it.

Q. How far out from the middle line of the ship would you estimate it to be—half way, or two-thirds of the way to the side?
A. I should judge it was about here [indicating].
Q. About two-thirds of the way from the middle line of the ship?
A. Yes, sir.
Q. At frame 30?
A. Yes, sir.
Q. Where did you find the bottom entirely blown away?
A. Right about here [indicating].
Q. Between frames 24 and 28?
A. Yes, sir. This armor plate, I should judge, would be about here [indicating]. The bottom seems to be gone there.
Q. How about these shell? Are those shell there still?
A. Yes, sir; there are some shells right in the after end of it, I judge, right here [indicating].
Q. There are no shell in the forward end?
A. No, sir; not there, but right over here, seemingly. At those shells the plates are bent in over them.
Q. That is on the port side of the shell room the plates are bent in over the shell?
A. Over the shells; yes, sir, and right over here [indicating], that is where I found some tanks broken up. About here, I should judge about the end of the ship's bottom, that is the part that is blown out. You can walk in on it.

By the COURT:

Q. In speaking of being able to walk on the top of the plate——
A. The plate seemed to be flat, like that [indicating], and I could walk on it.
Q. Was there nothing above that?
A. No, sir.
Q. How deep was that under water?
A. I judge between 4 and 5 fathoms—about 5 fathoms, I think.
Q. Pretty well down toward the bottom?
A. Yes, sir.
Q. That would be from frame 36 to frame 41?
A. I walked on them, and then they began to take their proper shape again. As you feel the bottom up, you can feel the shape of it. I crawled over in the mud, and that is where I found the plate bent up—the bottom plate, the bottom of the ship, bent up. As I walked in a place higher up I found them bent out.
Q. But under the bottom, about in the vicinity of the 6-inch spare magazine, they were bent up?
A. This place must be abaft here [indicating].
Q. That is between frames 30 and 32?
A. About here there is a space that is nothing.
Q. What I am trying to get at is where you found the bottom of the ship bent in?
A. That is where I found it, right about here [indicating].
Q. Between frames 30 and 32?
A. Yes, sir; right abaft where this armor plate is.
Q. How far out from the middle line of the ship?
A. I couldn't say exactly how far from the middle line of the ship on account of I could not get underneath the mud far enough to tell the middle line on that part.
Q. Was it a hole blown into the ship, apparently?

A. In most places the plate is cracked off, spread in ragged edges, and in three or four places the plates are bent in like a curve. Then as far as you go up the ship's bottom from there up, she is bent out that way [indicating].

Q. I will draw a little sketch here to indicate what I mean. That is the ship's side [indicating]. Do you mean that is bent in so here and out so here?

A. This plate I am talking about on the bottom is complete, like that [indicating]. There are no holes through the bottom at all. It is just the edge where, seemingly, it has been blown apart, and here the plates are bent in, curved in a little, and up here they are bent out on that side like that [indicating]. They seemed to be about that curve. That is about the curve of the bottom itself, right there.

Q. Is there not a hole blown through?

A. No, sir; it is no hole. It is a ragged edge which is bent out. From here aft the bottom is whole [indicating].

Q. What do you mean by bent in? Is it simply a depression or a hole?

A. It is no hole. It is a cave. The plate is warped like, like some external force drove it in like that [indicating].

Q. You did not find a hole?

A. No, sir; no hole, not in that part. From here aft the bottom is complete as far as you can see for the mud. Where I struck those 10-inch shells there are plates bent in like that right over them. You go down like in a little hole and find plates over you like that [indicating]. You can stand right underneath that plate. It is bent from the outboard in, over the starboard, and the shells are down below. I tried to dig down underneath the shells; but if there was anything underneath in the bottom I could not find it. I couldn't get below them. If you go away over to starboard like that [indicating], you strike mud again. There is nothing there. Then you go over where this plate is. You can climb over that until it is bent over like that [indicating], and you go down into some 6-inch shell. That is seemingly outside of this outboard plate, which is bent over like that. Going from that place over there [indicating], there are some pieces of wreckage. Then there is a lot of wreckage blown over to starboard. Then underneath of that I put my hands way underneath. I couldn't get my body in there. I pulled out two 6-pound cartridges.

Q. What was the condition of the tanks?

A. The majority of the tanks—I found a few pieces blown up entirely—that is, small pieces left of the tanks; but the majority of the tanks I seen down there were split in the center—that is, the seam of the tank was split, just melted away like.

Q. Can you imagine a 10-inch charge bursting inside of a tank? Would they look like that?

A. If a 10-inch charge burst inside of a tank, there would be nothing left of the tank. It would be blown into small pieces.

Q. Did you bring up any tanks?

A. Yes, sir.

Q. What did you bring up?

A. Six-inch and 10-inch tanks.

Q. Describe fully the condition of those tanks.

A. The 6-inch tanks I brought up were corrugated, the outside of the tanks, and the seam was split. The tank, seemingly, was not hurt, merely the seam being split, and the whole tank was corrugated.

Q. Crushed in?

A. No; corrugated, in waves like; the whole tank itself on the outside.

Q. Was it empty?
A. It was empty; yes, sir.
Q. Were both cylinder heads on?
A. No, sir; the top was out of one of them. In fact, I didn't fetch up the whole tank. One of the tanks I fetched up the lid was on it and the bottom was out of it. It was corrugated and split up. Then I fetched up a 10-inch tank that was merely the sheeting of it. The lid was gone and the bottom was gone, and the tank was all bent in as though it struck some place and was doubled out of shape. In the fire-room, or where the fire-room had been, where I found those grate bars, I found a couple of tanks.
Q. Were they full or empty?
A. Empty.
Q. Apparently blown to pieces by a charge inside?
A. No, sir; not blown to pieces. They were ripped, the same as the rest of them, in the seam.
Q. You have given considerable testimony according to your best knowledge and belief, as you have sworn. Do you think that all you have stated is quite correct, or do you imagine considerable of this? You know you are not supposed to be as good a judge under water as you are above water. Above water I would not question your testimony at all; but do you feel positive of what you have stated here, and are you satisfied that it is perfectly correct?
A. Yes, sir. I am perfectly sure it is all correct, the way I found the deck.
Q. Are you a good diver?
A. I have had a couple of years' experience of it, sir.
Q. Do you feel comfortable under the water?
A. Yes, sir.
Q. Do you know what you are feeling when you feel anything?
A. Yes, sir.
Q. Did you have your gloves on?
A. No, sir; bare hands.
Q. You do not feel ill under water?
A. No, sir.
Q. You fully believe that what you have testified to is quite correct?
A. Yes, sir.
Q. Were you able to see at all?
A. Yes, sir; I could see, and when I was not quite sure of what I did see I used to wait until the mud cleared away, so I could see perfectly clear.
Q. Were you using any electric lights in diving?
A. Yes, sir; but the electric light was not much use to me. It merely showed a red glare, and I came to the conclusion that I was better without the light.

By the COURT:

Q. You could make out forms better?
A. Yes, sir; better without a light.

By Lieutenant-Commander WAINWRIGHT:

Q. In describing where you saw the plate blown in from the outside, was there any part of the outside of the ship above that plate? You say it did not make a hole. I want to know whether that was the upper plate, or whether there were other plates above it?
A. On the outside of this armor plate were a couple of frames of the ship sticking up, bent inboard on the outside of the plate.
Q. The armor plate I am speaking of now?

A. On the outboard port side of the armor plate.
Q. What I particularly wanted to know was this. Captain Chadwick asked you whether it was a hole or whether it was bent in, and you said it was no hole.
A. No hole.
Q. Was there anything above it; was it a plate bent in, or was it just an indentation in the plate?
A. It was a plate bent in.
Q. Were there any plates above that?
A. Yes, sir; I could feel above it something that felt like a coal bunker, above it and abaft. Where this place was bent in I found a lot of cement.
Q. We will say this was the plate bent in [indicating].
A. Yes, sir.
Q. Was that plate attached to any other plate, or was it the last plate you could get hold of?
A. It was not attached to anything.
Q. It was bent in?
A. Yes, sir; and above it there seemed to be some cement inside. I could reach away in, and then from there up was something like a coal bunker. I couldn't say whether it was a coal bunker or what it was.
Q. Did you make any effort to reach the region of the 6-inch magazine forward?
A. Yes, sir; but I couldn't get there on account of mud. To get there I will have to go on the starboard side where this 6-inch magazine was originally. Down among that wreckage is where I want to go down. Abaft that wreckage, sticking up out of the water, there is nothing but mud right beneath that.
Q. You find wreckage above where you think the 6-inch magazine was?
A. Yes, sir; it must be right where that big pile of wreckage is, over there.

By the COURT:

Q. Speaking of this plate that is doubled back over the 10-inch magazine, is that, do you think, a bulkhead, or is it the outside of the ship?
A. Over the 10-inch magazine?
Q. Yes, or the 6-inch. Which was it you referred to?
A. The 10-inch shell room. If it had been outside of the ship, I should have judged there must be green paint on it, but I couldn't find any green paint on that part of the plate. It seems to be a plate inside of the double bottom.
Q. It might be a vertical bulkhead, might it not?
A. It might have been a bulkhead or an inside part of a double bottom. It turned inward over to starboard.
Q. To have a clear understanding of where that plate was bent in, was it separated from any plate above, or was the ship's side continuous?
A. Where this plate in the 10-inch shell room was bent in?
Q. This plate you speak of. You walked forward on what had been the ship's side, bent outward? Then you came to a place where the ship's side was bent in?
A. That is on the bottom. To get into where these 10-inch shells are, I get clear of that entirely. That is above me, and I get into those 10-inch shells, and there seems to be a plate. Outside of this plate is mud, nothing but the bottom, and right over here is this plate bent in, like that. By that I mean that the ship seems to be broken off for-

ward, and a little way from the midship line the plating is bent in. Higher up, in the same section, it is bent out—that is, on the cross-section of the ship. The last plate I refer to is the one that is thrown over to starboard, over the shell, but not the bottom plate.

Q. That is, it is bent in parallel to the keel of the ship?

A. It is bent in, not exactly parallel with the ship. It is more on an angle over to starboard. Take this as the line of the ship, it is thrown over like that—thrown over to starboard.

Q. Here is the keel of the ship [illustrating with a piece of paper]; here is the magazine. Is that bent in over it like that? [Placing the piece of paper parallel to the keel of the ship on the magazine plan.]

A No, sir; there is a piece sticking down at the bottom and bent in, and it comes up to a point like that [indicating]. That is the way it is bent in. There was a vertical fore and aft plate, the lower part stuck in the mud, and the top part bent over to starboard on top of the shell in the 10-inch shell room.

Q. You say outside of that is nothing but the mud bottom?

A. Nothing but mud; and between this plate here and this part that is blown away, where the bottom stops, there is no more bottom there. There is a plate. It seems to lay over a part of the plate. It lays over where this plate is bent in, and it is rolled up from port to starboard.

Q. Is that a part of the ship's skin?

A. I can't tell what part of the ship that is, sir; it is very thin plate, whatever it is.

Q. Do you think the ship is cut right in two there?

A. It is cut in two from out here to pretty near the midship line, but I couldn't get underneath it. I found that part is down in the mud, but from here in here it is blown right in two. That is about the bend of it, like that, and here it is blown out, like that, and here it is bent in.

(Witness points to the region of the afterpart of the 6-inch reserve magazine.)

By the COURT:

Q. Do you know how many salient angles there are in a 6 and a 10 inch charge as made up? You know, when you build up a 10-inch charge, it is made of a number of grains. How many salient angles are there; how many edges when it is piled up there?

A. I don't know how many in a 10-inch charge. Every part of the powder comes out and forms an angle in itself. I don't know just how many grains of powder there are on the outside of it. I don't know exactly the amount.

The PRESIDENT. The question that occurred to me was whether these corrugations on the outside of the powder tank are produced by a pressure on the outside, which makes the circular section of the tank press in to take the hexagonal form of the powder charge itself, or whether it is due, in the first place, to the first ignition of the powder, acting outward and making the tank take the hexagonal form of the powder charge. It does not look very probable that it is due to a pressure from the inside, but that it is due to a pressure from the outside, in which the hexagonal pile of powder forms the base on which the pressure forces the tanks to take the same shape.

The judge advocate requested that the testimony given by the witness be not read to him by the stenographer, but that he be directed to report to-morrow morning at 10 o'clock, when he will be furnished with so much of the record as contains his testimony and asked to withdraw for the consideration of the same, upon the completion of which he will be again called before the court, and be given an opportunity to amend his testimony as recorded, or pronounce it correct.

The request was granted, and the witness was instructed accordingly; whereupon he withdrew, after being cautioned by the president not to discuss matters pertaining to the inquiry.

The court then (at 4.15 o'clock p. m.) adjourned until to-morrow, the 25th instant, at 10 o'clock a. m.

FIFTH DAY.

U. S. L. H. TENDER MANGROVE,
Harbor of Havana, Cuba—10 a. m., Friday, February 25, 1898.

The court met pursuant to adjournment of yesterday, the fourth day of the inquiry.

Present: All the members of the court, the judge-advocate, the stenographer, and Captain Sigsbee.

The record of the proceedings of yesterday was read and approved.

Gunner's Mate THOMAS SMITH, U. S. Navy, appeared as a witness before the court, and was sworn by the president.

Examined by the JUDGE-ADVOCATE:

Q. State your full name, rate, and to what ship you are attached.
A. My name is Thomas Smith; gunner's mate, second class, serving on board the U. S. S. *Iowa*, lying at Key West, Fla.
Q. You have been engaged in diving here recently?
A. Yes, sir.
Q. How many times have you been down?
A. I have been down altogether four times.
Q. In the wreck of the *Maine?*
A. Yes, sir.
Q. About how long a time in all?
A. Eight hours.
Q. Are you a good diver?
A. Yes, sir; I am a fair one. I have been down lots of times.
Q. Do you get sick under water?
A. No, sir; I do not.
Q. Do you feel perfectly well?
A. Yes, sir.
Q. Strong?
A. Yes, sir.
Q. Can you see well?
A. I can see well, when the water is anyway clear, but this water is not clear. We can't see any more than about a foot or eighteen inches out from you.
Q. I want you to give certain testimony, and in giving it I want you to be sure that what you testify to is perfectly correct, and not make any guess. You will please state to the court exactly what you found under water as far as the construction of the *Maine* is concerned, and any other important discoveries, or any discoveries that you may have made.
A. First, when I was lowered over the side I landed into a 10-inch shell room—the flooring of it. I knew it was the 10-inch shell room, as

the 10-inch shells were lying there in good order. Some of them were lying with their noses up, others down. There was also pieces of the wood used as linings in the magazines lying around them. In this 10-inch shell room the fore-and-aft bulkhead is blown from port to starboard, over toward the 10-inch magazine. I crawled up and over this and down behind it. I found a 10-inch powder tank. It was sort of bent, but it was not burst. I didn't see it after it came up. It was full of powder, and the bag and everything was in it, I guess. That was lying in the mud, well underneath this sheet of a bulkhead that was thrown over. Then I came up out of the water and I went down again in the afternoon. I came down from the port crane. I followed the ship right down until I struck plates that were blown from port to starboard, inboard. I followed that right down until I struck the 6-inch shells. The shells there had their slings on them—what is used for sending them up out of the shell room. They were lying with the noses of them pointing up and to starboard. The forward part of the 6-inch reserve magazine, it seems to me, was gone altogether—completely blown away. The ragged edges of the shell-room steel are turned up.

By the COURT:

Q. The ragged edges whereabouts in the shell room? Do you mean in the bottom of the shell room?

A. Right at the bottom of it: yes, sir. As you leave that you walk right over into the mud. There is nothing left there at all.

Q. Going still forward?

A. Still farther forward. I came back on the wreckage, and walked over to my right, and I came across a lot of 6 pounder shells, and also the 6-pounder cases. Some of the cases were not broken away from the shells. They were sent up on the deck of the lighter that we were using.

Q. In your description, include the number of these things.

A. I sent up two shells and one cartridge case. I also found lying around there lots of accumulators, used for accumulating the air for the torpedoes.

Q. You can read these plans, can you not?

A. Yes, sir.

Q. There is the 10-inch magazine [indicating on plan]?

A. I have something else I want to say before that. Lying right across this 10-inch shell room there is an armor plate. The end of it that is sticking up is thinner than the part that is down in the mud. The reason I take this for an armor plate is that the plate has been torn right from the ship's side and turned completely over, so that the thin sheet of steel where the bolts pass through to bolt the oak backing and the armor plate of the ship's side is right over, pointing to port. The thick part of this plate is down in the mud, and the thin part of it is sticking up.

Q. Just where is that plate?

A. Right across this part of the 10-inch shell room [pointing to the middle of the 10-inch shell room], pointing from port to starboard.

Q. It runs from aft forward?

A. Just in that angle, like that, across it [indicating]. I felt the bolts that go through this oak backing and the thin sheet that screws into the armor plate. I felt those. Then around here [indicating] there were lots of those 6-inch powder tanks. In most of them the seams are split. They are lying all over in the 10-inch shell room and the magazine—all around it.

Q. Have they all been sent up?

A. No, sir; they have not. There was a number of them sent up, though, and the excelsior—long strips of stuff, which was put in the bottom to help fill the tanks, is in them yet. There is a number of these tanks down there, that are in pieces as big as your hand, all torn to pieces. This 6-inch forward magazine, I don't think we have been in it. It is away forward. This one here we have been all through and all around, and that one [indicating].

By the JUDGE-ADVOCATE:

Q. Describe what you found the other times you went down?

A. The third time I was lowered down I was landed right about in the same place as the first, and I took the same direction toward the 10-inch magazine, to the starboard side of the ship. I can not make much headway there because the plates and everything seemed to be blown right down that way. I had to climb up and get in under them. That is where the 10-inch powder tank came out of. I traveled well forward there as far as I could where this fixed ammunition was, and I found any number of them still there. There are 6-pounder shells and cartridge cases. Yesterday when I went down—this was the fourth time—I went down where this crane was. I followed the skin of the ship right under. The skin of the ship looks in good condition right there until you walk out to where this 6-inch shell room starts. The plates are bent that way, from out inboard. They are all ragged edges. You can get in there. You can crawl up and go into a place and find the double bottom. I can feel the pieces of cement and things where you crawl over these ragged plates. That is about all I can explain now, I think.

Q. The first time you went down you struck a 10-inch tank, and you described it. Did you find any more 10-inch tanks at that time?

A. I found lots of 10-inch tanks; yes, sir.

Q. None of them had been blown open by a charge exploded inside of them, according to your opinion?

A. The seams in the majority of them are just split fore and aft. It seems as if the solder had been melted away from it, and it burst right in and flatted out. In that one part I was in you would find the lids of them.

Q. You say you never reached, according to your opinion, the forward 6-inch magazine and shell room?

A. No, sir.

Q. Suppose I were to tell you there are no 6-inch shell in that reserve magazine. How would you account for the 6-inch shell you found there?

A. They had been blown there from the forward one.

Q. Blown aft?

A. Yes, sir.

Q. You also said there were certain plates blown inboard. Show on the plan and describe fully where those plates are that you say were blown inboard.

A. Do you want me to take the bottom ones?

Q. Yes; the ones you said were blown inboard. I do not mean the bulkhead that was blown across the 10-inch shell room that you crawled over to get at the magazine. I mean the plates that you said were blown inboard. Describe exactly where they were.

A. They are about in the middle of the 6-inch reserve magazine and the 10-inch shell room, from about frame 26 forward. This plate runs right across. Those other plates are blown up. They are coiled right up in that shape [indicating], from out inward. One of them particularly that I noticed is coiled right over, just the same as if you took a piece of paper like that [indicating].

Q. Do you think that was the bulkhead or the inboard lining of the double bottom?
A. No, sir; I do not.
Q. What do you think it is?
A. It is the ship's bottom.
Q. The outside skin of the ship?
A. Yes, sir.
Q. You place that about the middle of the 6-inch shell room?
A. The middle of the 6-inch shell room.
Q. The reserve shell room?
A. Yes, sir; and from there it comes in a circle, like that [indicating], and there is nothing of the outside of the ship there at all. I do not know what is forward here, because I have not been there. There is nothing of the ship's skin there at all [indicating].
Q. Nothing forward of the reserve shell room?
A. No, sir; as far as I went. About half of that reserve magazine is there, but it is blown that way [indicating to starboard]. There is just the position the shells are sticking [indicating]. They are standing right on their bases, the points sticking up and pointing toward starboard. I counted six of them standing right close together. About three out of that six had the slings on them, the hemp slings used for sending them out of the magazine. In that part of it, there is nothing of the ship's bottom at all [pointing to the forward part of the 6-inch reserve magazine and the 10-inch shell room on the plan].
Q. Give a little more full description of the side and skin of the ship abaft that reserve magazine.

The COURT. May I suggest one thing? He mentioned that [indicating] as the crane. The crane stands about there [pointing to the middle of the side].

A. I started down from the crane.
Q. When you walked forward to the magazine, the skin of the ship was in good condition, you say?
A. In good condition as you go down, in that shape [indicating].
Q. And the first sudden break is abreast of the reserve magazine?
A. Yes, sir.
Q. You think abaft that, as far as the crane where you started your work, it is complete up to the waterways?
A. I think it is all right from there aft, sir.
Q. From where aft?
A. From the break in the 6-inch shell room to the crane.
Q. Here is the crane right here [indicating]. You went down at the crane, did you not?
A. Yes.

By the COURT:

Q. What do you mean, Smith, when you say you walked down? It would seem as though there was an inclined plane there?
A. There is an incline from there down; yes, sir. It is all old wreckage. There is so much of it right in there that I couldn't tell really what it was. We will come across a ventilator or a piece of air compressor or something else right aft there, where the boiler originally was. You can't make any head or tail of anything until you come to this place here [indicating]. My work is confined right around these magazines all the time.

By the JUDGE ADVOCATE:

Q. Have you been down on the starboard side?
A. No, sir.
Q. Anywhere on the starboard side?
A. No, sir; I have been a little over the center line of the ship.
Q. Coming from port?
A. Yes, sir.
Q. But you have not gone down on the starboard side?
A. No, sir.
Q. Do you know whether the bulkhead outboard of the 10-inch magazine is still standing?
A. I can't tell, because I haven't been over there.
Q. You did not reach that far?
A. No, sir.
Q. Will you describe fully the different articles you brought up?
A. The first thing I brought up was a 10-inch powder tank, full. The next thing I sent up was a 6-pounder shell that had been broken away from its case. I sent up a 6-pounder charge complete. I sent up one case that was broken away and one 6-inch powder tank that had been split open. That is all I sent up.
Q. What was inside that last 6-inch powder tank?
A. Excelsior packing.
Q. Was it full or was it empty?
A. Empty.
Q. Were both cylinder heads on?
A. Yes, sir; just the seam was split. That is all.
Q. Was the bag inside that had contained the powder?
A. No, sir.
Q. Then it might have been an empty tank stowed down there?
A. It might have been an empty tank.
Q. You can not account for the powder getting out and the bag getting out with both cylinder heads on, can you?
A. If they had been burst open, the powder would have melted as soon as it got wet and probably have floated out of it.
Q. Was the split in the side big enough to let the bag come out?
A. The whole length of the case; yes, sir.

By Captain SIGSBEE:

Q. Is there any great difficulty in getting over to the starboard side below in the magazine?
A. There is; yes, sir; because everything is blown from port to starboard.
Q. You think, then, it is not possible to get into the 10-inch magazine?
A. Yes, sir; I can get in there. Any one of us can get in there; by very hard work, though.
Q. Nobody has been in there yet?
A. No, sir; not right into it. They have been on the edge of it, but they have not been properly into it.
Q. Would it be very dangerous to go in there?
A. It is a pretty dangerous place; yes, sir, on account of you have to go up some frames and crawl down, and you are right underneath them.
Q. Could you tell anything about the location of the barbette, or turret, while you were down?
A. I didn't run across it at all, sir. I seen no part of it.
Q. Did you come to the conclusion that it was missing from its regular place on the forward side starboard, abreast of where you were?

A. Yes; it was missing from its proper place.
Q. Was it on the port side?
A. It was on the starboard side, forward. It was right plumb over the magazine. I didn't come across anything that would lead me to believe that I was around the turret at all.

By the COURT:
Q. Smith, you described that forward portion of the 6-inch reserve magazine as being entirely gone. The outside of the ship has entirely disappeared?
A. Yes, sir.
Q. There is a hole through the bottom of the ship at that point?
A. The side and everything is gone right away from it.
Q. Then, there must be a hole through the ship?
A. Yes, sir.
Q. How high up does that extend—that hole? Here is the side of the ship, you know, and you go down underneath. This is entirely gone, a certain portion of it [indicating]?
A. Entirely gone; yes, sir.
Q. How high up on the side does it extend, or is that all gone, clear to the water?
A. Yes, sir; you can take me and lower me right from the diving launch down into the mud, and I can walk.
Q. That might be, too, and if you were inside of the ship, there might be continuous metal outside of you?
A. No, sir.
Q. Suppose this were the magazine [indicating].
A. Yes, sir.
Q. You say that portion is all gone?
A. That portion is all gone; yes, sir.
Q. Why do you say this portion is all gone [indicating]?
A. That is the upper part.
Q. That is the upper part, I know, but when you are lowered down, you go right down into the mud?
A. I can walk off in this direction [indicating to port] and I come across nothing. I walk in here [indicating to starboard] and I come across the wreckage.
Q. That is, you say you can go right out there into the mud [indicating]?
A. Yes, sir; and there is nothing there at all until you walk aft.
Q. That is, the whole side has disappeared there?
A. The whole side has disappeared. It is completely gone right up to there [indicating frame 26]. Then you can walk over. I don't know about this side [indicating].
Q. Do you mean all that part of the ship is gone [indicating everything over the 6-inch reserve magazine and 10-inch shell room]?
A. That part of the ship is gone, and everything up here is gone. Taking this for the port side of the ship, it seems that the midship bulkhead and everything on here is off in that direction [pointing to starboard].
Q. You have not been far enough to see what there is beyond? You do not know whether this hole extends clear forward or not?
A. No, sir; I don't know where that part goes. As far as I can give any good explanation, this was up to the fixed ammunition magazine [indicating]. Around in this part here [pointing to the 10-inch maga-

zine] we have not been much. Here is that armor plate [indicating on plan]. If you wish me to give a better explanation than I did before, probably I can do it now. This is the part [indicating the midship section] that is sticking up out of the mud [pointing to the lower part]. That has been torn off the ship altogether, and turned right over, and it is at that angle across the 10-inch room [showing an angle of 45 degrees to the keel].

Q. The greatest force of the explosion seems to have been forward here [indicating]?

A. Yes, sir; in the forward part of the 10-inch shell room, and the 6-inch spare magazine.

Q. Is forward of that?

A. It takes in part of the 6-inch shell room and part of the 10-inch shell room, too. Where these plates are ripped up, and all forward of that, is completely blown out.

By the JUDGE-ADVOCATE:

Q. Suppose the part that you say is blown away is a hole with a portion of the ship's side still over it. Could you walk athwartships out of the ship or into the ship without catching your tubes and life lines?

A. No, sir; I could not.

Q. Then if there were a part of the ship still standing above that hole——

A. I could feel my life lines hauling over it. Besides, I have a guide line right from the diving lines down, and made fast into the shell room—into the after part of it.

Q. Referring to that armor plate, you say it is thin edge up?

A. Thin edge up; yes, sir.

Q. It is at an angle of 45 degrees across the keel?

A. Yes, sir.

Q. The face which used to be outboard. Is that toward the starboard quarter of the ship or the port bow?

A. You take that [indicating] for an angle of 45°. It is pointing to the starboard quarter of the ship.

Q. And the place that has the nuts and bolts on it is facing which way?

A. To the port bow.

Q. I want to ask you one more question in regard to the port side of the ship, from the derrick forward to the part which was exploded most severely. What is the condition of the ship's side from the derrick forward to the reserve magazine?

A. The condition of the side seems to be pretty good.

Q. Give it a little more plainly than that. Is it complete up to the waterways, or is it gradually torn away down to this hole?

A. It is gradually torn away down to that; yes, sir.

Q. Commencing abreast of the derrick, it is gradually torn down until it reaches this hole of the large explosion?

A. Yes, sir.

Q. Is that it?

A. Yes, sir.

By Captain SIGSBEE:

Q. Did you see any indications in the direction of the metal below or otherwise to indicate that the 10-inch magazine had exploded?

A. No, sir; I can't see anything that indicates that the 10-inch magazine has exploded so far, because the plates all point to starboard.

Q. Did you notice any tendency of plates away from this 10-inch

magazine over toward the port side—of the plates bent from the magazine to port?
A. No, sir.
Q. They were all in the other direction?
A. They were all in the other direction—to starboard.

The testimony of the witness was then read over to him by the stenographer, and by him pronounced correct.

The witness then withdrew, after being cautioned by the president not to converse about matters pertaining to the inquiry.

Seaman MARTIN REDEN, U. S. Navy, appeared as a witness before the court, and was sworn by the president.

Examined by the JUDGE-ADVOCATE:
Q. Please state your full name, rate, and to what ship you are attached.
A. Martin Reden; seaman; attached to the *Maine*.
Q. Have you been diving into the wreck of the *Maine* since her explosion?
A. Yes, sir.
Q. How many times have you been down forward?
A. Twice.
Q. Twice forward?
A. Yes, sir.
Q. What was your profession before you entered the Navy?
A. Diving, sir.
Q. You are a professional diver?
A. Yes, sir.
Q. For how many years?
A. Seven or eight years; eight years, I think, sir.
Q. Have you done much wrecking diving?
A. Yes, sir.
Q. Where?
A. Key West, Oldtown, Mexico, Colon, and on the Mosquito Coast.
Q. Were you in good health when you went down to the wreck of the *Maine?*
A. Yes, sir.
Q. Do you think you can give testimony correctly as to what you saw and felt down there?
A. Yes, sir.
Q. How long were you down each time forward?
A. The first time, I think, I was down about three hours, sir.
Q. Tell the court all you saw down there during that time which can give them information as to the condition of the *Maine*, and any discoveries you made, and describe anything you may have brought up during that dive.
A. The first time I went down, I went down about where the dynamo room is. There is nothing left whatever, only some plates and beams. I can not tell if there has been a dynamo there, or anything else. Everything is gone entirely. I felt away down in the mud as far as I could go from outside. I walked from outside the ship into the ship, and I could feel nothing else there. I only came across a plate or a beam or a shell. That is all, sir. I went from aft the superstructure, and went right down, and the mud goes aft I couldn't say how far. It is very dark there. I struck one bottom plate away down in the mud, and the plate is bent in this way, and up that way [indicating].
Q. It is bent in and up?

A. It is bent in this way, right underneath the bulge of the plate. I went into the mud down to the plate, and the rivet is bent out. The plate is bent in this way.

By the COURT:

Q. You say it is bent "in this way." Which way do you mean; bent to starboard, or to port?

A. Bent right out. That is the ship's side [indicating]. The plate is bent this way, and the rivet comes out that way, and so the plate lies.

Q. Inboard or outboard?

A. That is outboard, sir. The plate goes this way [indicating]. The lower part of the plate is bent in, and the upper part is thrown out.

By the JUDGE-ADVOCATE:

Q. The middle of the plate is bent in, and the upper part, where it is fastened to another plate, is thrown outboard?

A. Yes, sir.

By the COURT:

Q. Let him tell where that is. Is that near the keel?

A. I can't tell how far it is from the keel, sir, because I can't see nothing. I can only feel, and put my face close up and see these plates. I don't know what part of the ship it is. I can't even see the paint, if it is green paint, or red paint, or white paint. As I walk along forward from aft on the port side, there is nothing left. When I get about 20 feet from that break, there is nothing left of the ship whatever, out for 30 feet I should think. Everything is gone underneath there. You can walk from the bottom right into the ship, only you go down in mud about 2 feet. There are lots of shells. Then when I get past them shells, I come to the armor plate. It is thrown into the ship. The armor lies about like that [indicating].

Q. Describe it. When you say "like that" we can not put it on paper.

A. It lies at an angle.

Q. At an angle with the keel?

A. Yes, sir; I should think at that place about midship; right inside, you know, there is nothing the matter with the plate whatever. I could find only two of them armor bolts or screws on the plate below. That is the only bolt you can find. The rest of them is so far down in the mud you can't find them. I should think that plate is about 7 or 8 inches thick. I didn't measure them, sir. Then forward of that plate I find nothing else but iron heaped up all over. I can't make nothing out of it, sir. They are bursted in and bursted out in all kinds of directions. There was lots of rope here [indicating], and one thing and another. I believe that came out of the holds way down below. There is no deck in there, and nothing whatever, only plates all torn up.

Q. In what part of the ship should you say that bent plate was?

A. I should think that plate is about 10 feet from the break of the superstructure.

Q. Forward or aft?

A. Forward.

Q. Then it was about abreast of the forward turret?

A. Somewhere around the forward turret; yes, sir.

Q. Only on the port side?

A. Only on the port side; yes, sir.

Q. This armor plate, you say, was thrown in at an angle to the keel. Is the edge sticking up?

A. The edge is sticking up.

Q. Is the thick edge or the thin edge sticking up?

A. The thick edge.
Q. How do you know?
A. If there is a top place, it must be smaller on top and thicker underneath, about as broad as that [indicating]. I could feel right down.
Q. How many inches should you say it was on top—the top edge?
A. Seven or eight.
Q. You do not know whether it was thicker at the bottom part or not?
A. No, sir.
Q. You only felt the top part?
A. Yes, sir.
Q. If it was at an angle to the keel, one side must have been facing one of the quarters of the ship?
A. Yes, sir.
Q. One was facing forward and the other was facing aft?
A. Yes, sir.
Q. Which was facing aft, the original outboard portion or the original inboard portion?
A. The inboard portion is facing out, sir.
Q. The inboard portion which has the nuts on it is facing forward?
A. Facing out and forward; yes, sir.
Q. And the smooth side, which used to be against the water, is facing how?
A. Inside, aft and starboard.
Q. Did you bring anything up this time when you went down diving?
A. Only about three tanks of powder—powder tanks.
Q. Describe what they were, and what condition they were in.
A. They was all torn up, mashed together in that way [indicating]. Another one was burst right out, torn right in pieces.
Q. Were they 10 or 6 inch tanks?
A. Ten-inch.
Q. You used to work at the 10-inch guns, I believe?
A. Yes, sir.
Q. Your second descent—describe that, where you went down and what you did.
A. I mixed it about all up, the second descent and the first one.
Q. You have described both descents, have you?
A. Yes, sir; both of them.
Q. Did you approach the starboard side of the ship—the forward turret?
A. No, sir.
Q. How far toward the starboard side of the ship did you go when you were down?
A. I must have been, I should judge, away over—right where the turret ought to be.
Q. You do not think there was any ship's side left there?
A. No, sir.
Q. But you are not certain you went beyond?
A. No, sir.
Q. Did you find anything of the turret at all?
A. Nothing at all—nothing whatever.
Q. Your explorations were more on the port side than on the starboard side, though?
A. Yes, sir.
Q. Did you go into what you thought to be the 10-inch magazine?
A. I felt holes there. I couldn't say whether it was the magazine or not.

Q. It was full of holes there?
A. Yes, sir; I don't know what it was. I found a heap of shells there, and I found them all over there—them shells.
Q. You found more shells than powder?
A. Yes, sir.
Q. You probably got as far as the 10-inch shell room, but not to starboard of it. The forward 10-inch magazine is to starboard of the shell room?
A. Yes, sir.
Q. And you went in from the port side?
A. Yes, sir.
Q. So, probably, you did not go farther than the shell room. Do you think that is so?
A. No; I walked farther than that. I passed them shell.
Q. Did you strike the tanks?
A. No, sir.
Q. Where did you find the tanks you brought up?
A. I found them tanks not very far from them 10-inch shells.
Q. On top of them?
A. No, sir; on one side.
Q. Which side?
A. On the starboard side of them.
Q. That must have been the magazine?
A. You can't tell nothing. Everything is only a piece of iron. There is nothing left at all.
Q. Do you think there is anything of the forward part of the ship left, forward of this 10-inch shell room?
A. There is some plates left there, all bent out. You can't make out what it is. I was away up amongst those.
Q. How far forward do you think you got in you travels?
A. I went as far as I could. I couldn't say exactly.
Q. Did you reach this fixed-ammunition room?
A. No, sir.
Q. You did not strike any 6-pounders or 1-pounders?
A. No, sir.
Q. Did you find any paymasters' stores of any kind?
A. Yes, sir; I found them all over the ship—canned stuff.
Q. What condition were the cans in?
A. I picked up a few cans that were all right. Some was busted.
Q. What was the character of the break of the vegetable cans?
A. They were torn up. Some of them was crushed together and some of them torn out—all kinds of shapes.
Q. Split open along the seams?
A. Some was split and some was crushed together.

By Captain SIGSBEE:

Q. Was the metal of the ship, in a general way, bent from port to starboard or from starboard to port, below the water?
A. The plates of the ship, you mean?
Q. Yes.
A. The plates was bent in from port to starboard.
Q. Inboard, you mean?
A. Inboard; yes, sir.
Q. From port to starboard?
A. Yes, sir.
Q. Was there anything in the condition of the metal below to indicate that the 10-inch magazine had exploded?

A. Why, no.

Q. That is, did you see any tendency of the metal from starboard to port to indicate that the 10-inch magazine had exploded?

A. I don't understand you.

Q. Was the bending of the metal below—the direction in which the metal was bent—such as to indicate that the starboard magazine had exploded? That is to say, did you see the metal bent from starboard to port?

A. Yes, sir.

Q. Let me ask that question over again. I assume that if the starboard magazine had exploded, it would have shown a certain amount of the metal bent from starboard over to port. Did you see metal bent that way in general—anything to indicate it?

A. There was metal all around there. I couldn't say, sir.

By the COURT:

Q. Then you did not notice any general tendency of the metal. For instance, we will assume that it is fastened at the bottom of the ship, unless you go into the space where the bottom is entirely gone; but outside of that, where the ship is less completely destroyed, there must be bulkheads that stand up around there?

A. There are some.

Q. Suppose it is fore and aft. Is it bent that way, or is it bent that way [indicating]?

A. They are bent in all directions. Them pieces that are left inside the ship are bent in all shapes, sir.

By the JUDGE-ADVOCATE:

Q. Where were you at the time of the explosion of the *Maine?*

A. In the after turret, sir.

Q. Were you asleep?

A. Yes, sir.

Q. What was the first thing you knew?

A. The first thing I knew, I didn't see nothing else but flames, and everything come in the turret, and the roar of the water.

Q. You got out?

A. Yes, sir; I got out.

Q. How?

A. I am not certain whether I come through the hatch or the ventilator; I don't know.

By Captain SIGSBEE:

Q. Were you well acquainted with the compartments of the *Maine* forward?

A. Yes, sir.

By the JUDGE-ADVOCATE:

Q. Did you say you are well acquainted with them?

A. Yes; I know the compartments.

Q. When you went down did you recognize anything that you can describe?

A. I couldn't recognize nothing, sir. I know the compartments well, and if I had seen anything I could have recognized them; but there was nothing left to recognize, sir.

The testimony of the witness was then read over to him by the stenographer and by him pronounced correct.

The witness then withdrew, after being cautioned by the president not to converse about matters pertaining to the inquiry.

Gunner's Mate W. H. F. SCHLUTER, U. S. Navy, appeared as a witness before the court and was sworn by the president.

Examined by the JUDGE-ADVOCATE:

Q. State your full name, rate, and the ship to which you are attached.

A. W. H. F. Schluter, gunner's mate, second class, serving aboard the U. S. S. *New York*, lying off Key West, Fla.

Q. Have you been engaged in diving in Havana Harbor since the explosion of the *Maine?*

A. Yes, sir; I was down once for one hour.

Q. What part of the ship did you go down in?

A. I was lowered down from the side a little forward of the turret, which was broke off. I was let down about 6 feet or 8 feet, I can't exactly say which. I landed on some ragged edges, bent inboard from the port side over to the starboard side. I crawled then a little ways, and I dropped down about 3 or 4 feet farther, and I landed on something solid. It was something like little lumps laying along. Then I crawled along and landed on some coal. The coal was in good condition, for I picked it up and looked at it. Then I crawled along over ——

Q. Which way were you going?

A. Forward, on the port side. Then I ran against something that was going up. It looked like a partition. I crawled up on the top of that, and it was one of them beams going down that was broke off. I crawled around that, and it was kind of bulged under like, inboard. Then I stood there a little while, and I come back again and went on the inside of this plate. I went down a little ways, and I couldn't touch no bottom, so I crawled back again. That is as far as I went.

Q. You really recognized nothing?

A. No, sir.

Q. You brought up nothing?

A. I went after one of them haversacks. I found that right near the coal.

Q. Were you feeling well when you went down under the water?

A. Yes, sir; I felt well. I am sure it was coal, because I picked it up and looked at it.

Q. Were you yourself feeling well?

A. Yes, sir.

Q. Were you all right?

A. Yes, sir.

Q. Why did you not go down again?

A. It was dinner time, and after that we were told to come over to the court.

Q. You had just commenced?

A. Yes, sir.

Q. On what day did you go down—yesterday?

A. It was yesterday morning; yes, sir. Most of the diving I have done in Havana has been aft except this one time I have just described.

The testimony of the witness was then read over to him by the stenographer, and by him pronounced correct.

The witness then withdrew, after being cautioned by the president not to converse about matters pertaining to the inquiry.

Gunner's Mate CARL RUNDQUIST, U. S. Navy, appeared as a witness before the court and was sworn by the president.

Examined by the JUDGE-ADVOCATE:

Q. Please state your full name, rate, and to what ship you are attached.

A. My name is Carl Rundquist; gunner's mate, first class; on board U. S. S. *New York*.

Q. Have you been diving in the harbor of Havana since the *Maine* exploded?

A. Yes, sir.

Q. Have you been down forward?

A. I have been down forward.

Q. How often?

A. I have been down once, sir.

Q. How long did you remain down?

A. I should judge a little over two hours.

Q. Have you been down aft?

A. No, sir.

Q. Are you a good diver?

A. I have been down before, sir.

Q. Can you see well under water?

A. I could see not very well, but when I put my face close to an object I had a pretty good view of it.

Q. Did you feel well whilst you were under water?

A. Yes, sir; I never felt bad.

Q. Please describe to the court just what you saw as to what was left of the *Maine*, and any objects that you recognized; their condition, or anything you may have brought up. Give us the whole history of your descent.

A. When I left the lighter I got, as far as I could judge, down in the after part of the 10-inch magazine, because when I came down I came down among plates, etc. I walked 2 or 3 feet more, and I came across a lot of empty 10-inch powder tanks. Some of the seams were open, and others looked like they had been in a pressure from both ends. I sent one of them up, and there was lots of them down there.

Q. Just tell us how many.

A. I couldn't say how many, because I had to feel for it, but there were dozens of them—pieces of them blown in all directions. I left then, and went aft from where I was standing. I should judge that would be aft. I came across lots of cans that looked like it was preserved stuff. It looked to be the paymaster's stores or something, and close to there I found a piece of armor plate. On one side of it was the backing, and that plate looked to be turned over, because the end I got hold of was between 6 and 7 inches in thickness. I measured with my fingers. I put the end of my thumb on one edge and my middle finger on the other. It looked to be thicker downward. I went down as far as I could, down in the mud, and the edge of it was down in the mud. I couldn't find out the exact thickness there. From there I went outside. I went to the left. That would be to the port side of the ship, and I followed the bottom there for about 8 or 10 feet. I know I was on the bottom of the ship, because I could see the green paint on it, and as far as I could judge——

Q. Was this green paint inside the ship or outside the ship?

A. This was on the outside of the ship, because I put my face close to it, and it looked to be the bottom of the ship, because that must have been below the armor plates, where the armor belts go, because it was only the exact thickness of the skin of the ship—the thickness of a plate. One side was pretty rough. It must have been inside the double bottom or something. It was a rough paint, and the outside was slippery and green. In some places it was all ragged. The pieces were all torn ragged and it looked to be inward. That is about all I saw down there, sir.

Q. Where were you lowered down; on the starboard side of the ship?
A. No, sir; I was lowered down about midships, a little to the port side. We had a lighter lying right across the ship.

Q. You think you landed in the 10-inch magazine?
A. I landed close to it, because there was lots of empty powder tanks.

Q. Of all those tanks that were there, were any of them in good condition?
A. None that I came across. They were all bent over. I came across two or three of them that the seams were opened.

Q. Were any of them full?
A. No, sir; none of them I came across.

Q. Do you think they had been exploded by a charge inside?
A. It didn't look that way, sir, from where I was. It looked like there had been a pressure from the outside that opened them up.

Q. What was the condition of the cans of provisions you found?
A. They were in good condition.

Q. Describe a little more plainly this hole that you found. You say the ragged edges were pointing inboard. How large were these ragged edges; how long?
A. Of the plates?

Q. Yes.
A. This plate I found. It looked to be the whole plate or the biggest part of a plate, and it looked like it had been torn off from another plate, because there was only one side of it I found was raggy, and I found a plate standing in that direction [indicating].

Q. Describe it.
A. It was pointing to port, aft, and the raggy end, I found, was the upper end. I landed on it, and I slipped down from it once and crawled up on it again.

Q. Was that a plate still made fast to the ship's bottom?
A. No, sir; that was a plate that was loose. It looked to be turned completely over.

Q. That is the armor plate?
A. The armor plate.

Q. I am not speaking of the armor plate. You said when you went further along you found a place where the ship's side had a hole in it, you saw the green paint; and you said the edges were ragged and bent in. I want you to describe the edges a little better.
A. That looked to be the bottom of the ship, or a piece solid, fastened to the plate.

Q. Was it a round hole, or was it completely turned up to the water's edge?
A. Completely turned up to the water's edge.

Q. There was nothing above this place?
A. Nothing above it whatever. It looked to be no plates there, or anything there.

Q. The ragged edges were directly bent inboard?

A. Bent inboard.
Q. You are sure they were not bent out?
A. Yes, sir; I am sure.
Q. And the green paint you saw was on the part bent inboard?
A. The green paint was on the part bent inboard, that was coming on top like.
Q. About this piece of armor plate you speak of, the part that had the bolts on it. Which way was that facing in regard to the ship?
A. That was facing outboard.
Q. Which way—forward or aft?
A. Facing aft.
Q. Explain fully how this piece of armor plate was lying, and the direction of the keel, and how the original outboard side was facing, and also how the side with nuts was facing?
A. That plate was fast in the mud so I couldn't get hold of the lower edge of it. The top edge, I should say, was about 7 inches in thickness, and that side of the plate where the bolts and backing was on, was facing to port.

By the COURT:

Q. Did it stand that way, or did it stand that way [indicating]?
A. It stood the way it is on that drawing, sir, so far as I could make it out down there.
Q. How does that plate face now?
A. The part of the plate that is supposed to be inboard is facing outboard.
Q. That is, it was turned clean over?
A. Turned clean over, sir.
Q. I would like to ask, for my own information, whether this armor plate was inside of the ship?
A. It was on the inside of the ship; yes, sir. It was about half way from the midship, and out to the portside of the ship, half way inboard.
Q. Yet you say that it was not resting on anything but the mud?
A. It was resting on the mud. There was a big piece of the ship there that was entirely gone. The bottom of the ship was all blown up. There was nothing there.
Q. You speak of starting from some point near these copper tanks or powder tanks and walking toward the port side, and you say you were walking on the bottom; that you knew it to be the bottom because it was painted green?
A. I didn't mean to say that I walked on the ship's bottom. I was walking in the mud, or rather crawling in the mud, because in some places I had to haul myself along. I was going alongside the ship's bottom, on the piece that was left of the ship's bottom. I know it was the ship's bottom because I could see the paint was green and slippery.
Q. Was this piece detached from the ship?
A. That looked to be just on the edges of the ship.
Q. You said you walked some distance, you thought about 10 feet?
A. About 10 feet.
Q. You could not have been walking on the bottom of the ship?
A. No, sir; not on the bottom of the ship. On the bottom of the harbor, in the mud.
Q. You said you were walking on the bottom of the ship, and you knew it to be so because it was painted green?
A. I mean to say that I was walking on the outside of the ship, close to the ship's bottom.

Q. You were walking in the hole where the ship's bottom ought to have been?
A. No, sir; on the outside of the ship, sir.
Q. How did you come to go outside of the ship?
A. There was lots of wreckage out there. I slipped on from one piece to another, and I happened to get on it more by accident than anything else, because I slipped on, and I landed on the mud.
Q. How do you know you were outside the ship when you landed in the mud?
A. I couldn't see anything around me. I was crawling around for a couple of feet on each side, and couldn't see anything. It must have been on the outside, or else it was an empty space, where there was nothing, or else the ship must be completely blown away.
Q. That is the ship's section there [indicating]. You understand that?
A. Yes, sir; I understand that.
Q. Were you out here, or were you here [pointing to outboard and then inboard], or where were you?
A. I judge I was somewhere around here [pointing to the longitudinal shown on the midship section], by the curve of the ship.
Q. I thought you said that was all blown away there?
A. This was on the forward part of it; but I took a walk aft 8 or 10 feet, somewhere around there—I couldn't say exactly how far—after I left this hole, and found this plate; and going from one piece of the wreckage to another I came down in the mud, and I was rolling along in the mud when I happened to strike my hand up against something. I felt, and I felt this green slippery piece of steel or something. I put my face close to the plate and I could see it was this green paint. It must have been the outside of the ship. I followed that along, I could not say how far—some 8 or 10 feet—and I come to this raggy edge of it, and there at the edge it was standing in this direction, like [indicating].
Q. Describe the direction. "This direction" does not describe it on paper.
A. It looked to be inboard, bent over—more rolled up than anything else, on the edge of it.
Q. Was that all around the edge?
A. It was all around the edge. It was all torn.
Q. I understand it was torn if there was a hole there, but you must be very careful when you say that that edge of it was turned inboard.
A. It looked to me it was laying inboard.
Q. How much of it did you examine?
A. I examined parts of the edges of it. This piece I followed along in the bottom, that looked to be a good solid piece of the ship. That must have been close to the hole where the explosion took place, because that seemed to be a good solid piece.
Q. How did you think this hole was made in the bottom of the ship?
A. My opinion is, I believe that she was blown up from the outside and in, because there was no explosion from the inside could make a hole like that, from the way them plates stood around in different directions.
Q. Do you think there was no explosion from the inside that could make that hole?
A. There may have been an explosion from the inside afterwards, but in the first place there was an explosion from the outside.
Q. Why do you think so?
A. Because I would never have found them plates in the way I did.

This piece of armor plate and the edges of that hole, I would never have found it that way.

Q. What strikes me is this—that you did not examine enough of that edge to form an opinion.

A. I didn't examine all of it, no; but I examined some parts of it, and that part that I examined looked like it had been bent inboard.

The testimony of the witness was then read over to him by the stenographer, and by him pronounced correct.

The witness then withdrew, after being cautioned by the president not to converse about matters pertaining to the inquiry.

The JUDGE-ADVOCATE. I notify the court that Ensign Powelson has a little additional testimony to give this afternoon, and that besides him Gunner Morgan and Gunner's Mate Olsen have to read over and correct their testimony. I have no other evidence to offer at present.

The court then (at 12.50 o'clock p. m.) took a recess until 2 o'clock.

The court assembled at the expiration of the recess.

Present: All the members of the court, the judge-advocate, the stenographer, and Captain Sigsbee.

Gunner MORGAN here appeared before the court and was handed so much of the record as contained his testimony. He was directed to withdraw, read it over, return to the court and state whether it is correct as recorded.

The JUDGE-ADVOCATE. If the court please, I ask permission to introduce Mr. Henry Drain, clerk at the United States consulate in Havana, and have him sworn, to act as interpreter.

Mr. HENRY DRAIN, by permission of the court, was duly sworn by the judge-advocate, in accordance with the United States Navy regulations, and took his seat as interpreter of the court.

A witness then appeared before the court, whose name and address are suppressed by agreement with the witness that his identity should not be revealed, and was sworn by the president, through the interpreter.

Examined by JUDGE-ADVOCATE (through the interpreter):

Q. I have heard that on Tuesday morning you overheard a certain conversation in a ferryboat which referred to the possible sinking of the *Maine*. Will you please state to the court all you can in regard to that matter?

The INTERPRETER. At about half-past 7 on the morning of the 15th, he was crossing from Havana to Reglas. He was sitting on a front seat in the bow of the vessel—the ferryboat. There were, about 4 feet distant, three officers, two of the army and one of the navy, of Spain, and besides a citizen, a stout man, about fifty years of age. They were conversing about the *Maine*. He says one of the army officers said that in the circulio militario, the military club here on the Prado, "That is nearly arranged." The citizen inquired: "Will not making explosions in the bay run great risk to the city of Havana?" The citizen inquired that from the Spanish officer who had made the first remark. He says that the officer replied "no;" that it was arranged so that it would simply explode, open the vessel, and she would sink immediately. Then the other man, with an exclamation apparently of joy, said: "I will take plenty of beer on that occasion." At that moment a cartman came forward and one of the men touched the other and stopped the conversation, and then he could not hear any more. He said they kept on speaking, but he did not hear any more.

Q. What was the first remark made by the army officer?

The INTERPRETER. That he had heard in the circulo militario that the plans were all arranged, and they were going to blow her up anyhow; that it was a shame to Spain that she should be here in the bay. The lieutenant said: "Then if you blow her up, there would be another one come," and the superior officer said: "They would take care not to send another."

Q. Did the second army officer make any other remark?

The INTERPRETER. He says yes; they were all speaking, but they were speaking in a low voice; he could not catch all they said. He was standing up, close to the wall, so that they would not notice he was listening to them.

Q. Could you distinguish what the navy officer said?

The INTERPRETER. No; he could not.

Q. Are you personally acquainted with any one of these four persons?

The INTERPRETER. He says that he does not know any of them. He could not recognize any of the three officers, but that very probably he could recognize the citizen.

Q. How often do you cross in the ferry from Havana to Reglas?

The INTERPRETER. He says in those days he crossed twice, in the morning and in the afternoon, but now he only crosses in the afternoon, there and back again; that he went at half past 7 in the morning, and would return at 10 to breakfast; that he would go at 4 or 5 o'clock in the afternoon back to Reglas again; and that about 9 or half past 9 or 10 o'clock in the evening he would return to Havana.

Q. Did you ever meet any of these four men before on the ferryboat?

The INTERPRETER. He can not say, because he had never noticed them. He went every day, and he did not notice them.

Q. What was the character of the uniform of the army officers?

The INTERPRETER. One was a lieutenant, and the other one had stars down below the stripes. He had two stripes, which would indicate that he was from a major upward. He also had a belt—that would indicate that he is of the general's staff.

Q. What was the color of the uniform?

The INTERPRETER. All of that little stripe that they wear here.

Q. Blue linen?

The INTERPRETER. Yes; blue linen. The marine officer was dressed in dark blue, but he did not notice the insignias that he had on at all.

Q. Which one of the army officers made the remark you spoke about—the staff officer or the lieutenant?

The INTERPRETER. The staff officer. He spoke with the citizen.

Q. What was that you said about a diamond?

The INTERPRETER. The citizen had on a big diamond ring.

Q. Please describe the citizen.

The INTERPRETER. He was a large, stout man, about 50 years of age. He had a mustache only, somewhat gray. He used one of these black derby hats, and dark clothes.

Q. Can you describe the staff officer a little more fully, his age and appearance?

The INTERPRETER. Somewhere around about the same age, about 50 years of age. He did not notice very well, but he thinks he used chin whiskers.

Q. And the lieutenant?

The INTERPRETER. He says he must be about 40 or 42 years of age, and used a mustache.

Q. And the naval officer?

The INTERPRETER. He was over 40.

Q. Did they wear swords?

The INTERPRETER. None of them used swords.

Q. Would you be able to recognize these persons again?

The INTERPRETER. He sticks to the same thing, that the officers he could not recognize, because he did not pay much attention, that the thing went out of his head afterwards; but he thinks he would recognize the citizen. He says there are a great many officers crossing continually.

Q. Are you quite positive of the conversation you have repeated?

The INTERPRETER. Yes, sir.

Q. What object did you have in informing the consul-general of this conversation?

The INTERPRETER. The substance of what he says is that he was talking with a friend of his in the Café San Nicholas after this occurrence, and he told him all the conversation he had heard. The friend told him: "Why don't you go and say something about this to the consulate?" He says he was afraid to say anything about it, that he would get himself into trouble. The friend said: "I will go and inquire from some of these newspapers—the Journal or the World—and see if there is any danger in it." The friend went and inquired, and said there would be no danger whatever, and he then determined to tell the consul.

Q. Did you go to the consul at all?

The INTERPRETER. No, sir.

Q. What was the name of the friend you spoke to?

The INTERPRETER. He says he will find out the name; that he is one of these friends whom you know without knowing who they are. He will find out the name. He sees him every day.

Q. Is he a Spaniard?

The INTERPRETER. He is a Cuban.

Q. Are you a married man?

The INTERPRETER. No, sir; single.

Q. Have you any family here?

The INTERPRETER. He says he and his father are here, and he has been living eighteen years with a woman, but he is not married to her.

Q. How many people were on board the ferryboat at the time of this conversation? State about how many; whether it was crowded or not crowded is the main issue.

The INTERPRETER. Very few, and nearly all were in the after part It was somewhat cool, and there were very few people.

There being no further questions to ask this witness, his testimony was read over to him by the stenographer through the interpreter, and by him pronounced correct.

The witness then withdrew, after being cautioned by the president, through the interpreter, not to converse about matters pertaining to the inquiry, and after saying that it was not to his interest to converse with anybody about it.

Gunner's Mate OLSEN here appeared before the court.

The JUDGE-ADVOCATE. Olsen, I now hand you so much of the record of the court as contains the testimony given by you. Please withdraw, read it over, and then return to the court and state whether it is correct as recorded, or whether you desire to make any corrections.

The witness then withdrew.

Gunner MORGAN here appeared before the court.

The JUDGE-ADVOCATE. Gunner Morgan, have you read over the testimony given by you before this court on yesterday?

Gunner MORGAN. Yes, sir.

The JUDGE-ADVOCATE. Is it correct as recorded in the smooth record?

Gunner MORGAN. It is.

The witness then withdrew, after being cautioned by the president not to converse about matters pertaining to the inquiry.

Ensign POWLESON, U. S. Navy, a witness heretofore examined, was recalled to the witness stand, and, after being cautioned by the president that the oath previously taken by him was still binding, testified as follows:

Examined by the JUDGE-ADVOCATE:

Q. Have you any further information to give to the court in regard to the wreck of the *Maine?*

A. Yes, sir.

Q. Please state what you have.

A. May I refer to some drawings that I have brought with me?

Q. Certainly.

A. These are the blue prints of the drainage system of the *Maine*, taken from the wreck. I have succeeded in identifying the part of the protective deck of which I submitted a sketch yesterday or the day before. This is a plan of the protective deck of the *Maine*. The frame spaces aft of frame 18 are 4 feet; forward of frame 18 they are 3 feet 6 inches; forward of frame 12 they are 3 feet. This is drawn to the scale of 1 inch equals 1 foot. These frame spaces in between frames 18 and 12 are 3½ feet; those aft of frame 18, as I said, are 4 feet. In the sketch which I have submitted the distance between beams I have made 3 feet 7 inches, which was the measurement that I took from the wreck. That was probably an error of an inch. That, then, places this part of the protective deck somewhere between frame 18 and frame 12. At frame 16 is a water-tight bulkhead and at frame 18 is a water-tight bulkhead. The surface of this plate submitted shows no evidence of bulkhead angle iron on the upper surface. This, then, eliminates the space between frames 18 and 16. Therefore the plate is somewhere between 16 and 13.

As you will see, the outward plate of the protective deck is cut off a little on one point. The width of the plates of the protective deck is 4 feet. The width of the ship at frame 13 is 12 feet 9 nine inches. Then, if the edge of the protective-deck plating at the midship line were exactly at the midship line, this would take three full plates with 9 inches left over. Between the upper plating of the two plates of the protective deck and the side is an angle iron, running along the side with 4-inch flange. That would leave, then, a space of about 5 inches to be filled in by a wedge-shaped piece. It is not probable that the edge of the upper plating of the protective deck is exactly at the midship line. It is probable that it is to one side or the other, to allow for the lapping of the upper plating on the lower plating. This frame 13 corresponds more closely with the drawing measurements taken from the wreck than would frame 14. Since these two frames are confined to frames 15, 14, and 13, that narrows the deck down to the parts between 15 and 12 along the port side compartment A36. This plate, which I have shown in the sketch I submitted yesterday, shows the rivets for the cofferdam bulkhead. My conclusion is that the sketch which I have shown comes from compartment A36, between frames 15 and 12.

Q. What is there in the ship above compartment A36 between frames 12 and 15?

A. A36 is the cellulose compartment, and just inside of that is A34. This is part of A34. This plate is taken from both A36 and A34.

Q. Then that would be forward of the forward 6-inch magazine?

A. Yes, sir. I have also succeeded in identifying a part of the bottom plating, which is now about 4 feet above water, 12 feet abaft the piece of protective deck which I have just referred to.

Q. That is over the magazine, is it?

A. No, sir; I will explain where that plate comes from and my reasons for believing so. This plate shows the split in the reverse, and the frame angle irons, where the floor plating first begins at the ship's side. It also shows a water-tight longitudinal with the cement along the bottom and a part of the inner bottom plating. The distance between the frame that is highest out of water and the frame next below it is 3 feet 6 inches. The distance between this frame and the one next below that is 4 feet. There is only one place in the ship at which such frame spacing occurs. That is at bulkhead 18, the space between 18 and 19 being 4 feet and between 18 and 17 being 3 feet 6 inches. Between frames 18 and 17 I found a sluice valve about 3 inches square. This sluice valve is on the under side of the water-tight longitudinal. The longitudinal at this point was about $17\frac{1}{2}$ inches in depth. From the drawings of the inner bottom of the *Maine*, I locate this sluice valve at the second longitudinal, near the water-tight bulkhead at frame 18. This drawing which I have does not show a sluice valve at that point, nor does it show that the second longitudinal is water-tight.

There has evidently been some change since these plans, and the second longitudinal has been made water-tight, and a sluice valve has been put in the after part of it next to the bulkhead at frame 18, to drain from compartment A41. Frame 17 shows about 5 feet above the water-tight longitudinal to which I have referred at the point where the frame and reverse angle irons divide and the floor plates are first inserted. That can be seen better on the sectional plan at frame 18. This is the sectional plan at frame 18. Here is the second longitudinal at which I fixed the sluice valve to which I have referred. The height of the second longitudinal at this point is 18 inches, which corresponds very closely with the measurement taken from the wreck. In this piece of bottom plating, to which the longitudinal was attached, I found an opening in the ship's side, being the Kingston valve or a similar valve. The inner bottom drawings show such a valve to exist in that compartment for the purpose of flushing the main drains and secondary drains at this point. The plates of the inner bottom are plainly visible for a distance of 8 feet from the longitudinal to which I have referred and about two or three feet under water. Forward of frame 17 the outside plating has been again split, forming a V, with the outboard wing of higher plating than the starboard or inboard wing.

The angle of the V is about horizontal, and the ridge stands nearly fore and aft. The plating just abaft this V seems to have been broken across and pushed up to form a V, of which frame 17 is the apex. This shows that the bottom plating, about 11 feet from the keel, has been raised to a point about 4 feet out of water now. This bottom to which I referred is almost directly under the forward port edge of the forward 6-inch magazine.

S. Doc. 207——7

Q. The forward edge of it comes to frame 18?
A. The forward edge of it stops at frame 18.

By the JUDGE-ADVOCATE:

Q. Where is that sluice valve situated—also under the forward part of the 6-inch magazine?
A. Yes, sir; at frame 18.
Q. That forward 6-inch magazine is between what frames?
A. Between frames 18 and 21. There are several other sluice valves in the longitudinals of the double bottoms, but with the exception of sluice valve No. 4, are in frame spaces of 4 feet. All other sluice valves in the longitudinals, according to the drawings, are in frame spaces of 4 feet, showing that this sluice valve is forward of frame 18. The only other water-tight bulkhead forward of frame 18 is at frame 12, and in the space forward of frame 12 there are no water-tight longitudinals.
Q. Then the appearance of that V-shape that you saw, and the appearance of the plate, now makes you feel convinced that the bottom of the ship was thrown up?
A. Yes, sir.
Q. And not out?
A. Not out.
Q. This is under the forward part of the forward 6-inch magazine?
A. Yes, sir.
Q. And you have seen no other bottom plating as yet to confirm this?
A. This bottom plating is very large in extent. It extends down under the water on both sides from the angle of the V as far as I could touch with an oar or boat hook. I took one of the divers over this afternoon and explained to him what I wanted him to do. I wanted him to go down and follow the frames along as far as possible, and follow the longitudinals and keep track of them, so that he could tell me at what point the bottom plate ended, and the condition of the break at that point.
Q. Who was the diver?
A. The diver's name is Olsen.
Q. Can you state the amount of ship's bottom that is now visible and between what frames?
A. I can see now frames 16, 17, 18, 19. I can see water-tight longitudinal No. 2, port. I can feel with the boat hook longitudinal No. 1. I can see plating running down under the water for about 15 feet aft of frame 17 and 20 feet forward of frame 17.

By the COURT:

Q. All on the port side?
A. Yes, sir.
Q. How far from the center line of the ship do you place the upper plate of the bottom plates now showing above the water, which is bent into this V form?
A. The upper plate is between 11 and 15 feet from the center line of the ship.
Q. You mean that is the highest point?
A. The highest point; the upper plate.
Q. Taking the section, at what depth would that be?
A. Six and a quarter feet, sir, above the plane of the keel.
Q. How much has that been raised; that is, according to the draft of the ship before the explosion?
A. The forecastle superstructure would be about at the water now—

about where the water line is now—so that it would have been lifted about 38 or 39 feet from its original position when the ship was floating.

Q. Was there any paint on the outside of that bottom plating?

A. The outside of the bottom plating is covered with greenish paint. Inside, between frames 17 and 18, it is cemented for a distance of 18 inches above the longitudinal. It is calk paint beyond that. Abaft frame 18 it is cemented as far as the plate extends to the points broken off, about 4 feet from the longitudinal. I also found between frames 18 and 19 a piece of piping, with two right-angle turns, such as is represented on the drawing of the inner bottom at compartment A10. Compartment A4 contained piping of this description. This piping showed the caps at right angles, the same as shown here, and I found this piece of piping lying in an angle of one of the frames and the longitudinal.

Q. Mr. Powelson, you have not come across any portion except that protective deck of either of the decks above that point, have you?

A. Yes, sir; there is a part of the berth deck which was thrown some 20 feet forward of the part of the protective deck of which I have made a sketch; but as to just where that was on the berth deck I am unable to determine. It has the planking and red shellac of the main deck.

Q. Is there any of the main deck visible?

A. No, sir; none of the main deck is visible forward.

Q. None of the main deck is visible forward of the end of the midship superstructure?

A. No, sir.

Q. Forward of frame 30?

A. No, sir.

Q. Starting from the point at which this bottom has been lifted, frame 11, and running aft to the points where the divers have testified that the bottom plating is cut through to the after side of that opening, how many frames are there? What is the distance?

A. The frame which I said formed the apex of this V?

Q. Yes.

A. I do not know, of course, what they testified to. I only know what they tell me. The diver to-day told me that he had found a hole just starboard of that plate I was speaking of, down below—a hole through the ship's side; and that is what I sent him down to investigate still further. He bent a line on some plating around this hole. I think myself this plating on the port side was torn from that on the starboard. The diver told me this morning that he had found the ammunition from the 6-pounder magazine pushed over to the starboard side.

Q. Was that Olsen?

A. Yes, sir.

The judge-advocate requested that the testimony be not read over to the witness by the stenographer, but that he be directed to report to-morrow morning at 10 o'clock, when he will be furnished with so much of the record as contains his testimony, and asked to withdraw for the consideration of the same, upon the completion of which he will be again called before the court and be given an opportunity to amend his testimony as recorded, or pronounce it correct.

The request was granted, and the witness was instructed accordingly; whereupon he withdrew, after being cautioned by the president not to discuss matters pertaining to the trial.

Gunner's Mate OLSEN appeared before the court.

The JUDGE-ADVOCATE. Olsen, do you wish to make any corrections in your testimony?

Gunner's Mate OLSEN. I wish to make the following corrections:

On page 140, line 14, after the word "right" strike out "over in that direction [indicating]" and insert "over to starboard."

On page 141, line 5, after the words, "paper inboard," strike out "from stem to stern." In line 7, after "one plate complete," strike out "the top of the plate standing up." In line 17, after "hexagonal," strike out "ends" and insert "nuts." In line 27, after the words "10-inch," strike out "leaves" and insert "covers," so as to read "10-inch covers." In line 28, after the word "in," at the beginning of the line, strike out "by" and insert "over," so as to read "in over the 10-inch shell room."

On page 148, line 19, after the words "the way I found the," strike out "deck" and insert "wreck."

The JUDGE-ADVOCATE. Is your testimony, as now amended, correct?

Gunner's Mate OLSEN. Yes, sir.

The court then (at 4.40 o'clock p. m.) adjourned until to-morrow, the 26th instant, at 10 o'clock a. m.

SIXTH DAY.

U. S. L. H. TENDER MANGROVE,
Harbor of Havana, 10 a. m. Saturday, February 26, 1898.

The court met pursuant to the adjournment of yesterday, the 25th instant.

Present: All the members of the court, the judge-advocate, and the stenographer.

Captain Sigsbee had not yet appeared.

The record of the proceedings of yesterday, the fifth day of the inquiry, was read and approved.

The court then took a recess, ready to assemble at any moment when any additional evidence might be ready to be presented to the court.

The court (at 12 o'clock noon) took a recess until 1.30 o'clock p. m.

The court reassembled at the expiration of the recess.

Present: All the members of the court, the judge-advocate, the stenographer, and Captain Sigsbee.

Mr. HENRY DRAIN, who acted as interpreter before the court yesterday, appeared as a witness before the court, and was duly sworn by the president.

Examined by the JUDGE-ADVOCATE:

Q. Please give your name, residence, and profession.

A. Henry Drain, 91 San Lazero street, Havana; clerk in the United States consulate at Havana.

Q. Do you know of an anonymous letter received by the consul-general in regard to the explosion of the *Maine*?

A. I do.

Q. Can you produce it?

A. I can. [Witness produces letter.]

Q. What is the date?

A. February 18, 1898.

Q. Is there any signature to it?
A. No signature. It is signed "An admirer."
Q. Have you read the letter?
A. I have.
Q. Is it the document of an educated man?
A. I would say a man of common education, as far as I can judge.
Q. In what language is it written?
A. In Spanish.
(The letter was shown to the court.)
Q. Have you made a correct translation of this letter?
A. To the best of my ability, I have.
Q. Please produce the translation.
(The translation of the letter referred to was handed to the judge-advocate, and by him read aloud.)
The JUDGE-ADVOCATE. If the court please, I ask permission to append this letter to the record.
(The request was granted, and said letter is appended hereto, marked F.)
Q. Has anything been done to ascertain the truth of the statements contained in this letter?
A. I myself tried to discover the whereabouts of this Pepe Taco, and the one to whom I spoke said that the name was a mistake; that the Pepe Taco mentioned had died a few days before the explosion of the *Maine*, and that the letter referred to a Pepe Barquin; that he also had died suddenly about two or three days after the explosion of the *Maine*.
Q. Who was your informant?
A. Mr. Charles Carbonell.
Q. How do you suppose he knows so much about this?
A. In the first place, he is an American citizen, and interested in anything that pertains to the matter. I think he brought to General Lee's attention the clipping from La Lucha, and this letter. He told me that his boatman gave him the information of the death of this man. His boatman lives in Reglas.
Q. Did you ask General Lee to look into this matter?
A. I did, and he did not know just what to do, saying he has no secret-service money; but he told me to consult with Mr. Carbonell, who would probably know more about it than anybody else.
Q. Do you consider Mr. Carbonell a perfectly reliable man?
A. I do, from having known him several years.
Q. Could it not be ascertained whether this dead man's family have really moved from a poorhouse into a good one?
A. I think it could.
Q. Will you kindly have it tried?
A. I will try. I was consulting with him yesterday afternoon. He said he would send his boatman to see about it. I think it would be better to send some reliable person.
Q. I suppose you informed Consul-General Lee that the court would be glad to have the matter of the letter investigated?
A. I did.
The witness here stated that in the evidence given by witness of previous day the latter spoke of a man whom he had consulted in regard to giving the evidence which he gave before the court. The witness now states that man's name to be Aurelio Pla.

By the JUDGE-ADVOCATE:
Q. Do you know anything of this Aurelio Pla?

A. I never heard of him, sir.
Q. Who told you it was Aurelio Pla?
A. The witness himself came up to the consulate this morning.

The testimony of the witness was then read over to him by the stenographer, and by him pronounced correct. The witness then withdrew, after being cautioned by the president not to converse about matters pertaining to the inquiry.

The JUDGE-ADVOCATE. I ask that Captain Sigsbee take the stand.

Capt. CHARLES D. SIGSBEE, U. S. Navy, heretofore examined as a witness, resumed the stand, and was cautioned by the president that the oath previously taken by him was still binding.

Examined by the JUDGE-ADVOCATE:

Q. I have a letter here, Captain Sigsbee, which was sent to me by the chief constructor of the Navy, which purports to be a copy of a letter sent by you, dated June 30, 1897, at Hampton Roads, to the commandant of the navy-yard and station at Norfolk. I will read this letter to you.

(The judge-advocate then read aloud the letter above referred to.)

Q. As far as you can remember, you think this is a correct copy of your letter?
A. I think so.

The JUDGE-ADVOCATE. I ask permission of the court to append this letter to the record.

Permission was granted, and the letter above referred to is hereto appended, marked "G."

By the JUDGE-ADVOCATE:

Q. What changes do you know of having been been made in the storage rooms of the *Maine* and the shell rooms of the *Maine*, as stated in this letter, from June 30, 1897, up to the time of her explosion?
A. I could not give it in figures. I think there has been considerable change in the 6-inch reserve magazine forward, because we have done a good deal of saluting. I had so many figures to remember that I could not tell exactly. I want to see first how many shell there were. (After examination.) I think there were several more shell stowed in the forward 10-inch loading room and forward 10-inch passing room. A great deal of the small-arm ammunition shown in the forward fixed-ammunition room had been discharged, sent on shore, on the acquisition of the new navy rifle. We had just gotten in, before leaving Key West, a new supply of the new ammunition. I have forgotten whether it was our complete supply. It came at a time when I was exceedingly busy, looking forward to coming to Havana.

(Lieutenant-Commander Wainwright here entered the court.)

The WITNESS. I know we had 6,000 rounds before we got the last supply. Mr. Holman could state the exact amount of that. Although we had had target firing after this letter was written, we had practically filled up again on going to Norfolk the last time; so that I take it, except perhaps in regard to stuff stowed in the 6-inch reserve magazine forward and in the fixed ammunition room forward, at the time of the explosion the state of things was practically as shown in that letter.

Q. Do you know where the additional charges for the new rifle were stowed when they were received on board; in the forward or in the after fixed ammunition room?
A. My impression is that they were stowed forward.
Q. You spoke of the changes in the 6-inch reserve magazine, and

then you spoke of saluting. The changes you refer to apply to saluting powder?

A. Chiefly; but I have also understood that there was very little left in that magazine. It was probably put in other places—in the regular 6-inch.

Q. Do you remember when the last changes were made in your magazines, taking powder out of the reserve and stowing them in the regular magazines?

A. No; I do not remember. It was probably referred to me at the time. It undoubtedly was, but I can not now recall. I suppose three months ago I visited all the magazines and shell rooms, personally, and inspected them, going over every one and examining them in detail, but I have not the happy faculty of remembering details and figures.

Q. In a part of your letter here, you speak of the after torpedo head and fixed-ammunition room. Are those one compartment?

A. No.

Q. The torpedo heads are stowed in a different compartment from the fixed ammunition?

A. Yes, sir.

Q. Forward of it?

A. Yes; it is forward of it.

Q. When you wrote this letter you gave a statement of all the ammunition that was in the different compartments, and there is no statement of high explosives or gun cotton, or detonators, or any other material which the regulations prohibit from being in magazines and shell rooms. None of that material is mentioned in this letter. In that respect the letter is correct?

A. The letter is correct.

Q. Was that also the state of affairs in regard to such material on the day of the explosion?

A. It was.

Q. You are quite certain that no torpedo warhead was fitted to a torpedo on board the *Maine* the day of the explosion?

A. I am certain I gave no order to fit them, and it was well known to the executive officer that I did not intend to fit them.

Q. Did you enter the harbor of Havana with a torpedo warhead fixed?

A. No.

By the COURT:

Q. Did you, at any time subsequent to your entry of the harbor, have the warheads on any of the torpedoes?

A. The warheads have not been disturbed in any respect since I have had command of the ship.

The testimony of the witness was then read over to him by the stenographer, and by him pronounced correct.

The witness then left the witness stand and resumed his seat in the court room.

Lieut. Commander RICHARD WAINWRIGHT, U. S. Navy, a witness heretofore examined, resumed the witness stand, and was cautioned by the president that the oath previously taken by him was still binding.

Examined by the JUDGE-ADVOCATE:

Q. I believe, Mr. Wainwright, that you were on board the *Maine* all the time during her last stay in Havana?

A. Yes, sir.

Q. Were you on board the whole day on the evening of which the explosion occurred?

A. Yes, sir.

Q. Are you certain that no warheads were fitted to the torpedoes of the *Maine* on that day?

A. I am positive of it. It could not have been done without my seeing it. I knew what work was going on on the torpedoes, always. I took a special interest in them and consulted frequently with the officer in charge of the division. The Captain has ordered us not to put the warheads on. I mentioned the subject of the warheads to the commanding officer at least twice, and both times he told me not to do so.

Q. Had the warheads ever been fitted to the torpedoes at any time while you were executive officer of the *Maine?*

A. They had not.

Q. Do you remember when there was any large transfer of ammunition from one magazine into another on board the *Maine?*

A. None during my stay on board, to my knowledge.

Q. Then you do not believe that any large amount of 6-inch charges had been taken out of the reserve 6-inch magazine and sent to the others?

A. I should say not, during the two months and over I was on board.

Q. As you were on board the *Maine* during her last stay in Havana, and were frequently on deck, did it ever occur to you that the ship was almost always swinging in any certain direction?

A. A large portion of the time the wind was to the eastward, and we always swung to the wind, generally a little to the southward of east, as I remember now, though I am not positive about the points of the compass. We generally pointed to the eastern shore.

Q. Do you consider that the way she swung at the time she blew up was an unusual way for her to swing?

A. I never remember her swinging in that direction—remaining in that direction—for any length of time. She probably swung past that direction several times, but not to remain in that direction for any length of time.

Q. Are you able to testify whether she was heading in that direction for any length of time previous to the explosion?

A. Not in the absolute direction she is now; but after the usual morning drill, I directed the officer of the deck to get up the gallery target and rifle. They placed that always on the starboard turret, forward. Therefore we would have to fire in the direction of the keel. The officer of the deck, after some little time had elapsed, said that we were swinging in the general direction of the *Alfonso* and the other Spanish vessel. He asked me if it was safe to fire, and I told him not to fire. I thought it was safe, but I considered it better not to fire in the direction of those ships. We held that general direction, which was quite as much toward the shore as we were afterwards, but more to the westward than usual, but not as much as she was when she went down. As far as I can remember, she was heading in the general direction in which she went down when the *City of Washington* came in, and remained about in that direction up to the time of the explosion.

Q. Could you tell us how the *City of Washington* was lying at the time of the explosion, in regard to the *Maine?*

A. She was on the port quarter of the *Maine*, at a distance of about 400 feet, I should say. I thought she was too close to swing properly, only I knew that almost every vessel followed the direction of the wind, and there was very little danger of fouling.

Q. Was she heading in the same direction as the *Maine?*
A. The same general direction—yes, sir.

There being no further question to ask, the testimony of the witness was read over to him by the stenographer, and by him pronounced correct.

The witness then left the witness stand and resumed his seat in the court room.

Ensign POWELSON here entered the court.

The JUDGE-ADVOCATE. Mr. Powelson, is the testimony given by you yesterday, as recorded, correct?

Ensign POWELSON. It is, with the exception of the corrections which I have made.

The JUDGE-ADVOCATE. Please give them to the stenographer.

Ensign POWELSON. On page 201, in the ninth line from the bottom, "one inch" should read "a quarter inch."

On page 203, in the thirteenth line from the bottom, insert "plating" after "bottom."

On page 204, in line 10, scratch out the word "at." In the fourth line from the bottom insert "are" between "and" and "about." The last line should read "wing of after plating and the starboard wing of forward plating. The V occurs at about frame 15."

On page 205, in the eleventh line from the bottom, after "but" omit everything down to the sentence commencing in the next line with "All other sluice valves."

On page 207, in the ninth line from the bottom, change "calk" to "cork."

On page 208, in the ninth line, change "main" to "berth." In the twelfth line from the bottom "eleven" should read "seventeen."

The JUDGE-ADVOCATE. Is your testimony as now amended correct?
Ensign POWELSON. Yes, sir.

Ensign POWELSON, U. S. Navy, resumed the witness stand, and was cautioned by the president that the oath previously taken by him was still binding.

Examined by the JUDGE-ADVOCATE:

Q. Since you gave your testimony yesterday, have you received a book of specifications of the *Maine?*
A. I have; yes, sir.

Q. Have you done anything toward verifying your testimony by that book in regard to the thickness of the plates that you referred to in your testimony?
A. I do not think I mentioned the thickness of any plates in my testimony.

Q. But by reading the book and seeing the thickness of the plates you can tell whether you are sure in your surmises.
A. I have looked over the drawings again with reference to what I said in my last testimony. The only plates to which I could refer for thickness would be those of the protective deck. Those that I measured were 1 inch in thickness.

By the COURT:

Q. Double plating?
A. Double plating, each 1 inch in thickness. (After examination of book.) Forty pounds per square foot. That is, 1-inch plating.

Q. You spoke of a plate which had green paint on it. Did you verify the thickness of that with what you testified to by the specifications?

A. No, sir; I did not.

The JUDGE-ADVOCATE. I would like to say to the court that Mr. Powelson has some additional testimony to give. All this forenoon he has worked in unison with the diver, and the diver has made explanations to him which it would be impossible, so it is thought by Mr. Wainwright, who is in charge of that work, to give to the court intelligibly by the diver. I would request that the diver, Olsen, be admitted to the court room while Mr. Powelson gives his testimony, in order to correct him in anything he might not state correctly, and in that way we will get the testimony of the two men who worked together at the same time.

Permission was granted, and Gunner's Mate Olsen entered the court and was warned by the president that the oath previously taken by him was still binding.

By the JUDGE-ADVOCATE:

Q. Olsen, Mr. Powelson is going to give testimony in regard to your work and his work this morning. You reported to him, and he has put the work together, and is going to testify. If he says anything at all which is not exactly according to your recollection, you must at once state it and correct him.

A. All right, sir.

The examination of Ensign POWELSON was then resumed.

Examined by the JUDGE-ADVOCATE:

Q. Mr. Powelson, we are now ready for your additional testimony.

A. On February 26, to-day, at 10 a. m., Diver Olsen reported to me on coming up from below that he had followed the forward and after wings of the V-shape made by the bottom plating at frame 17. He said on the forward wing of the V the plates ran down on a very steep slant, and then turned under and out under the starboard side. That just above where the plates turned to go under the starboard side he found two dents, as if the plating had been bulged in between the frames from outside in.

By the COURT:

Q. How big were those?

A. He reported to me in this way: He held up his hands at a distance which I measured with a ruler. He said they were about $2\frac{1}{2}$ feet long and bulged in about 6 inches, if I remember correctly. He then went down again, and came to the surface at 11 o'clock. I asked him what he saw, and he said: "I think I have found the flat keel." I asked him what reasons he had for thinking this. Then he made me a sketch in the notebook which I have in my hand. This sketch is approximately the shape of the section at about frame 10 or 11.

(The sketch referred to by the witness was shown to the court.)

On this sketch he has correctly arranged the garboard strake, showing that his idea of the construction was correct. He reported that the keel was sloping downward about 45 degrees and to port, with the after part of the keep uppermost. I then asked him to describe to me the method in which he managed to reach the keel, as the V formed by the bottom plating at frame 17 spread out at the water line. He told me that after going down some distance under the water, these two wings of the bottom plating again converged, so that he was able to put his feet against one wing and his back against the other and support himself. There was nothing to stand on below. He said he put his back against the after wing and his feet against the forward wing and worked himself from port to starboard. He drew a sketch to illustrate to me the manner in which he did it.

(The sketch referred to by the witness was shown to the court.)

The WITNESS. He felt along the forward wing with his right hand, wedging himself between the forward and after wings. With his right hand he felt an angle in the plate. He ran his hand along it, and found on the other side of the angle a flat piece of plate. He ran his hand along a little farther, and found another angle. He ran his arm around the angle, and up, until he found the edge of the plate, which he described by a measurement I took between his hands as he held them up, as being about 10 inches. He said the flat plate was about 16 inches in width between the two angles to which I have referred. I took this measurement with a ruler, Olsen holding up his hands. Then he told me that he reached around to feel still farther, and in doing so lost his balance and fell down. I asked him if he struck bottom. He said that he did not; that he brought up on the life line. He then signaled to the attendant on the scow to pull him up. He told me that the plate next to the point which he had just felt when he fell over—as I took it, the starboard edge of the outer flat keel plate—was lapped under the keel plate, which is the construction with the garboard strake. I then asked him if he had explored any of the after wing of the V. He told me that he had. He told me that he had found a semicircular hole about two feet in diameter, with rivet holes all around it.

I asked him about how far on this plating that semicircular hole was from the top of the V made by the bottom plating. He told me it was about 20 feet. I asked him whether the edge of the plate at which he found this semicircular hole was the natural edge, with rivet holes, or whether it presented a jagged appearance. He told me that the plate at this point presented a jagged appearance, as if it had been torn. He also told me that a crack had extended from the bottom edge of the semicircular hole to a distance of about 8 inches, and that the plates about this hole were bent away from the green side of the plating. He told me that he followed the after wing still farther, and at a point about 25 feet from the angle of the V he found a plate about 2 feet 6 inches in width, from a measurement I took from his hands as he indicated the width, and that this plate was at right angles to the inside plating and at right angles to the edge of the plating. He told me that this plate had a round hole cut in it. I then asked him to be particular about the direction in which he found the keel. I drew a sketch, indicating a direction upward and a direction to port and a direction to starboard, and I asked him to draw upon this sketch a direction of the keel looking from aft forward. He did so, and this is the sketch.

(The sketch above referred to by the witness was shown to the court.)

The WITNESS. The line sloped about 65 degrees below the horizontal down and to port. I then made another sketch indicating forward, aft, starboard, and port, and I asked him to draw the position of the keel upon this sketch, looking down upon it. This is the sketch that he drew me.

(The sketch above referred to by the witness was shown to the court.)

The WITNESS: That shows a line from port to starboard, the port end about 80 degrees in azimuth from a head. He told me that the highest point of this keel was the starboard part. The point where he found the keel, he told me, was about 20 feet under water. I asked him why he did not follow the keel up farther, and he told me that the platings between which he was wedged opened out so that he had nothing to support him. I asked him if he could see any more of the keel above, and he said he could see the keel for 5 feet. I asked him if the keel ended there, and he said no, it continued still farther. He then told me that the general direction of the keel was parallel to the upper edge of the forward wing of the V-shaped plating at frame 17. This is what it should be, by a deduction from the appearance of the plating above. When I got on board the *Fern* I showed Olsen a plan of the ship, having sections at frame 6 and at frame 16. I pointed to the frame at 16, and I asked him if the angle he felt was as great as that at frame 16 on the plan. He told me that the angle was not. I am now referring to the angle made by the flat plate of the keel and the plating on the port side.

I then pointed to frame 6, and I asked him if the angle he saw was as sharp as that at frame 6. He told me that it was not. This, then, would make the point at which it found the keel, according to his statement, somewhere between frame 16 and frame 6. Now, frame 17 is at the water's edge, and as he went down on the forward wing of the V-plating, he went forward, as the ship was in its original position. He says he went down 20 feet. This would put him, as the frame spacing here is 3 feet 6 inches, about six frame spaces, or he was at that time at about frame 10, which checks up very well with his statement as to the angles at frame 16 and frame 6. On the plan of the inner-bottom drainage system, I find there is an opening in the ship's side for sea suction along the edge of the plating where Olsen said he found it, and at a distance of 21 feet from the angle of the V. Olsen told me that he found it at 20 feet, which agrees very closely.

By the COURT:

Q. That is, in which direction?
A. Along the edge of the plating.

By the JUDGE-ADVOCATE:

Q. Are you now through with what Olsen told you?
A. Yes, sir; I am through with what Olsen told me.

The JUDGE-ADVOCATE. I ask that Olsen be directed to withdraw, and to stand by for recall.

Gunner's Mate Olsen then withdrew, after being directed to stand by for recall, and cautioned not to converse about matters pertaining to the inquiry.

The witness Powelson then produced the drainage plans, and testified as follows:

At frame 18, the second longitudinal, is where I found the sluice valve. Olsen testified that at about 20 feet from the sluice valve he found an opening in the ship's side. The sea suction in compartment A-10 follows the direction taken by Olsen, and is situated about 21 feet from the sluice valve, which checks up very well. I found some boarding forward of frame 17. This boarding was originally horizontal, and next the ship's side, under the pieces of the protective deck to which I have already referred, and of which I have made a sketch. These boards are now in an almost vertical position, and the plating is now away from the after end of these boards in a plane almost at right angles to them. If you consider the section of the ship between frames 18 and 13, and consider that the part of the bottom plating between frame 18 and frame 15 is bent out at a right angle, and then that the whole section is turned forward through 90°, you will picture the position in which the plates are now found. This plating could either have been shoved out from the after side or it could have been pushed in from the forward side. The only indication as to how this was done is the wooden boarding. If the after part of the plating had been pushed out from the inside, the boarding would have broken at the V which the plates make. If the forward part of the plating had been pushed in, the boards would have been pulled away from the after plating, as is the case with the plates now. In other words, the side of the ship between frames 13 and 18 has two V's. Frame 17 has been pushed in, forming a V from a point 4 feet above the second longitudinal downward. The plating has been pushed in at about frame 15, from a point 4 feet above the second longitudinal forward.

By the COURT:

Q. All you have told us relates to the part of the ship between frames 18 and 24?

A. Yes, sir; and from frames 13 to 24. I sent the diver down, and he found where that piece of protective deck is fast to the outside plating. He found that, and when it got down there by the protective deck a lot of cellulose came up, showing he was walking in the cellulose compartment.

Q. That piece of plating is fastened to the starboard side of the ship, is it?

A. The port side. You can see it, sir.

Q. There is no hole in the outside plating at that point?

A. It is torn. I do not know where the rest of it is.

Q. Was he able to follow the after side of the V until he came to the end of that?

A. The forward side of the V took him right up toward the waterways of the spar deck, where that V is turned. It starts down and is broken off. All that you can see going along horizontally is fastened to the deck. He followed the forward wing, and went around down in under the ship, and the keel is fast to the forward wing.

By the JUDGE-ADVOCATE:

Q. From your knowledge of the *Maine* and the drawings of the *Maine*, how do you look upon the information that diver Olsen gave you?

A. I think it is extremely accurate.

The JUDGE-ADVOCATE. Shall I ask the witness what deduction he derives from all this?

The COURT. Yes; you can.

By the JUDGE-ADVOCATE:

Q. What do you deduce from this information received from the diver this forenoon, together with such information as you had before?

A. I think that an explosion occurred on the port side somewhere about frame 18, center of impact.

Q. Would you put 18 as the center of impact? Because it seems to me that has to be taken in connection with other injuries.

A. Frame 18 was the water-tight bulkhead, and consequently was stronger than frame 16. The ship yielded at 17, and also yielded at 15. It is pretty hard to say where it came. Frame 15 was blown in.

Q. You see everything at frame 26 is gone?

A. Yes, sir; there is nothing there. I should say, then, between frames 16 and 18 was the center of impact, and that this was under the ship, a little on the port side.

Q. How far from the keel?

A. Frame 17 is broken off at the third longitudinal, approximately, so that I should say the distance from the keel would be 15 feet in a horizontal line.

By the JUDGE-ADVOCATE:

Q. How high up would that be, up the ship's side from the keel?
A. That point of the ship's side is about 10 feet above the plane of the keel.

Q. Ten vertical feet?
A. Yes, sir.

Q. How do you account for the immense damage done abreast of the reserve magazine, where there is nothing left, whereas between frames 16 and 18 you have found damaged plates?
A. My idea is that after the ship was raised up at frame 18, the magazines, one or all of them, after that were exploded, for some powder tanks that I have seen I think were exploded, while others I have seen were not exploded. I saw a coffee can that was brought up this morning which was about as badly battered as most of the powder cases that came up. It looked in very much the same condition.

Q. When you say some of the powder tanks had, in your opinion, exploded, and some had not, do you refer to 6-inch tanks only or to 10-inch tanks also?
A. I refer to both, as I have seen a 6-inch tank that was very little ripped open, and I saw one this morning that had been first opened and flattened out, with evidences of burnt powder upon it. I saw one 10-inch tank that was scarcely battered at all, and only the head of it gone. I also saw 10-inch tanks with the packing, which looked like excelsior, unburnt; so that, in my opinion, some but not all of the 10-inch and 6-inch charges were exploded.

Q. Do you know how many tanks were brought up this morning?
A. The divers started getting tanks so late in the forenoon that they did not get many. I think probably four or five.

Q. And of these how many were exploded and how many were not?
A. I did not see all of them. The only one I remember distinctly was the one to which I have referred, which was exploded and burst out, so that the case formed almost a plane surface.

Q. You say one had the head gone. Did you see that one?
A. I saw the 10-inch tank with the head gone. That was not brought up this morning. It had preserved its proximate shape, and did not look much more damaged than if it had been dropped or rolled down the staircase.

Q. Had the head of the cylinder been torn off?
A. The head of the cylinder was a removable head. The fastenings were still there.

Q. Who could give testimony about the tanks brought up to-day?
A. Ensign Brumby or Gunner Morgan.

By the COURT:

Q. I suppose you saw the 10 inch full tank that was recovered some days ago, did you?
A. No, sir; I did not see that tank, but I was told by the officer of the deck of the *Fern* that such tank had been recovered, and was now in the magazine of the *Fern*.

Q. Do you suppose you could make a perspective sketch of the different parts of the ship as you understand them to exist at present?
A. No, sir; I tried, but I have no talent at all for perspective drawing. I tried to do it.

Q. We would not expect a finished drawing, but I think you understand it better than anybody else.

A. I could try to do it, sir.

Q. I do not mean immediately, but putting together the sketches which you have obtained from time to time, so that if the board should return at some future day you might be able to give us a drawing which would show the present condition of the bottom of the ship?

A. I think I can get someone who does perspective drawing, tell him just what I want, and have him make it. I could tell whether it is correct or not when I see it, although I can not make it myself.

Q. I would like to ask whether you do not think that this same means carried away the body of the ship just forward of frame 26, that is, the forward part of the reserve 6-inch magazine, and produced the distortion that we have been discussing?

A. That question, sir, is rather a difficult one, because it brings in so much conjecture. If anything definite were known about the amount of powder that was under the ship——

Q. Or what shape it was in?

A. Or what shape it was in, you might draw some conclusion.

Q. Is it not likely that if there is a large hole in the ship abaft the point we have been discussing, say frame 18, and also if there were a large hole driven up through the ship at frame 26, is it not likely that that same force would be the force that lifted and distorted the ship at frame 18, 25 or 30 feet away?

A. I think a very heavy explosion farther aft than frame 18—as the ship was much weaker forward of frame 24 than aft—such an explosion of the forward body could have been produced by a force farther aft.

Q. It is only a question of the area of the effect of the explosion. It is not likely there were two outside forces.

The PRESIDENT. No; but suppose it were a mine, and if it were circular or spherical and placed in a certain position, say 10 or 15 feet from the keel, then the center of effort and the destruction produced would be around the center, and it would be circular; but if it were a cylinder and, instead of being parallel to the keel, it inclined from, say, frame 26, where it approached the keel, outward—not parallel to the keel, but crosswise across the bottom of the ship—then the destruction would be greatest at the after end.

A. That is such a difficult question that I think I would rather not answer.

By the COURT:

Q. Then I think I would not say definitely that it was at that particular place.

The PRESIDENT. Yes; he is basing his opinion now on what he has seen. When you come to take in the big hole, as we imagine it to be, that may have been produced by still another mine.

Q. It was only with reference to the question of fixing it definitely that I asked the question.

A. On the bottom forward, where that frame was thrown up, it would seem to me the force was communicated some distance through the water, because this thing was lifted up instead of being battered in. It was a force that was cushioned in some way, because the diver tells me there was a bulge in plates between the two frames, and such a force as that would be a cushion pressure. So, the plates not having been broken in, or anything of that kind, this explosion may have occurred aft, and the frames forward of the transverse armor being weaker than they are aft, the ship might have been lifted up there by this cushion pressure from farther aft.

Q. You have never been down in a diving suit, have you?

A. No, sir; I never have. It struck me, as I was looking at it, that the mine there could not have been very close to those plates that were lifted up, because, as I say, the plates are not so much damaged as bent in the form of a V and raised up a vertical distance. It seemed to me that mine was somewhat removed, and the pressure came through the water, which produced that cushioned sort of pressure.

The testimony of the witness was then read over to him by the stenographer, and by him pronounced correct.

The witness then desired to add the following testimony:

I desire to amend my answer as to the center of impact of the explosion. Not being in possession of information as to the condition of the bottom plating aft of frame 18, I based my answer entirely upon what I had seen above water. If the bottom plating aft of frame 18 is in a broken condition from outside in, I should say that an explosion at this point could very easily have produced, by lifting that part of the ship, the corrugated appearance which the forward body at frames 18 and 15 now presents.

The additional testimony was then read over by the stenographer to the witness, and by him pronounced correct.

The witness then withdrew, after being cautioned by the president not to converse about matters relating to the inquiry.

Gunner's Mate OLSEN was then called before the court and warned by the president that the oath previously taken by him was still binding.

Examined by the JUDGE-ADVOCATE:

Q. You have heard the statements made by Mr. Powelson before this court in your presence. Are they correct in every way?

A. Yes; they are correct.

Q. All the statements that he told the court you had made to him—are they quoted correctly?

A. Yes, sir.

The testimony of the witness was then read over to him by the stenographer, and by him pronounced correct.

The witness then withdrew, after being cautioned by the president not to converse about matters relating to the inquiry.

The court then (at 5.15 o'clock p. m.) adjourned to meet at Key West, Fla., Monday, February 28, at 10 o'clock a. m.

SEVENTH DAY.

U. S. COURT-HOUSE, KEY WEST, FLA.,
Monday, February 28, 1898—10 a. m.

The court met pursuant to adjournment of Saturday, which adjournment took place on board the *Mangrove*, in the harbor of Havana. The court reconvened in the United States court-house at Key West, Fla.

Present: All the members of the court, the judge-advocate, and the stenographer.

Captain Sigsbee, who remained in Havana, informed the judge-advocate that he would waive the right to be present during the sessions of the court, provided the judge-advocate would inform him in case he considered Captain Sigsbee's presence necessary for his interests.

No other officer desired to be present at the meeting except Lieutenant-Commander Wainwright, who is also in Havana, and who desired to be present only when the testimony of the divers is being taken.

The record of the proceedings of Saturday, the sixth day of the inquiry, was read and approved.

Lieut. JOHN J. BLANDIN, U. S. Navy, appeared as a witness before the court, and was sworn by the president.

Examined by the JUDGE-ADVOCATE:

Q. Please state your name, rank, and to what ship you are attached at present.
A. Lieut. John J. Blandin, U. S. Navy, attached to the U. S. S. *Maine*.
Q. How long were you attached to the *Maine* before her destruction?
A. Since the 20th of June, 1897.
Q. What duty did you perform during that time?
A. Watch and division officer.
Q. What division did you have?
A. The fourth division.
Q. Is that the after division of the ship?
A. That was the after division of the ship.
Q. While in the harbor of Havana were you doing the duty of an officer of the deck?
A. I was.
Q. Do you know of any special orders that were issued by the commanding officer while in Havana in order to guard the ship more securely than at any other place?
A. The quarter watch was on watch all night. Small-arm ammunition was placed in the belts of the marines and of the quarter watch in the gun divisions, one hundred rounds. The boxes of 1-pounder and 6-pounder ammunition were stored in the cabin pantry (which is not used for anything else), the armory, and the pilot house. Sentries were posted on the forecastle and on the poop, with cartridges in their belts, but with orders not to load their pieces unless ordered by an officer. Orders were given to see that strict watch was kept, which was done. I think those were the principal precautions taken.
Q. During the time you stood watch in the harbor of Havana, did you ever know of any hostile demonstration afloat, in the way of boats approaching the ship that had to be warned off?
A. None whatever.
Q. On the night of the explosion were all the orders that you have just named faithfully carried out?
A. They were, sir.
Q. What was your duty on that night?
A. I had the watch from 8 until 12.
Q. P. m.?
A. P. m.
Q. What time did you relieve the deck?
A. At 8 o'clock. I relieved Lieutenant Blow.
Q. Had the 8 p. m. reports been made when you took the deck?
A. They were being made when I was relieving.
Q. Did you hear them made?
A. I did not.
Q. Mr. Blow received those reports?
A. The first lieutenant received them, sir.
Q. The reports of lights and fires. Who received those?

A. Those reports were received by Naval Cadet Cluverius, as I remember, just as I was relieving.

Q. What was Naval Cadet Cluverius doing there?

A. He was the midshipman who had two deck watches under Mr. Blow.

Q. Mr. Blow was there?

A. Mr. Blow was there, sir.

Q. When you took the deck, was everything reported perfectly secure to you, and the ordinary state of affairs?

A. Everything was perfectly normal. The usual reports were made.

Q. After 8 p. m. did you attend to your duties faithfully as an officer of the deck?

A. I did.

Q. Please state to the court fully your experience of the explosion, giving all the noises you heard, all the shocks you felt, and everything you can tell the court in regard to the matter.

A. After the third quarter watch at 9 o'clock was piped down, I was on the starboard side of the deck walking up and down. I looked over the side and then went over to the port side and took a look. I don't remember seeing any boats at all in sight. I thought at the time the harbor was very free from boats. I thought it was about 3 bells, and I walked over to the port side of the deck just abaft the after turret. Mr. Hood came up shortly afterwards and was talking to me when the explosion occurred. I am under the impression that there were two explosions, though I could not be sure of it. Mr. Hood started aft to get on the poop to lower the boats, I suppose, and I followed him. Something struck me on the head. My cap was in my hand. My head was slightly cut and I was partially knocked over, but not stunned. I climbed on the poop and went on the starboard side and found Captain Sigsbee there. I reported to him. He ordered the boats lowered at once to pick up any of the wounded. The officers very rapidly got on the poop, and there were one or two men there, but very few.

The barge and gig were lowered, and just then I heard a man crying out down on the quarter deck. I went to the ladder, and I saw Mr. Hood trying to pull a ventilator off the man's legs. He was lying in the wreckage; jammed there. The water then was not deep. I went down and helped Mr. Hood pull this ventilator off and carried the man on the poop, with the help of Private Loftus, I think it was. It was a private man. Then the captain told Mr. Wainwright to see if anything could be done to put out the fire. Mr. Wainwright went forward to the middle superstructure, and shortly afterwards came back and reported to the captain that it was hopeless to try to do anything. Then in a very few moments the captain decided that it was hopeless, and gave the order to abandon ship. Boats came from the *Alfonso Doce,* and two boats from the *City of Washington,* and those, with our boats, picked up the wounded and sent most of them, by the captain's order, to the *Alfonso.* There were thirty-four sent there. We abandoned ship, the captain getting in his gig after everybody had left, and went to the *City of Washington.*

Q. When you first felt the explosion did you notice any list of the ship?

A. None whatever.

Q. Was there a very severe shock where you were standing?

A. No; it was a shock, but I should not call it a very severe shock?

Q. I suppose you at once looked forward?

A. I at once looked over the port side, as I thought the explosion occurred on the port side, forward. That was my impression.
Q. Did you see any water thrown up?
A. Not a particle.
Q. Tell us what you did see go up in the air?
A. I didn't see anything go up in the air, but I saw all kinds of stuff falling down—wreckage.
Q. You saw no upshoot of flame?
A. Mr. Hood saw the flame. It was on the starboard side, and he looked to starboard.
Q. You saw none?
A. I saw a flare. I didn't see the actual flame.
Q. You spoke of ammunition being stowed forward for ready use. Will you please state where that was stowed?
A. In the pilot house.
Q. How high up is the pilot house? It is some distance above the superstructure deck, is it not?
A. It is about 10 feet, I should say, above the superstructure deck.
Q. There was no ammunition forward below that?
A. None below that; no, sir. This was only secondary battery ammunition that was in the pilot house.
Q. How was the ship swinging at the time of that explosion?
A. She was riding to the ebb current.
Q. The ship is now lying pointing almost toward the admiralty house or Machina. I suppose that is the way she was when she exploded?
A. I don't remember her heading, but the *Alfonso* was on our starboard quarter, the little gunboat was almost astern, and the *City of Washington* was on our port quarter.
Q. Would you be able to tell the court whether she was riding in an unusual direction for that harbor?
A. It didn't strike me so from the general appearance. I took no notice of her heading. She swung around the buoy for three weeks, about. She had probably been on every heading.
Q. Did she seem to be pretty steady on that heading that night?
A. Yes, sir.
Q. She was heading steadily in that direction?
A. She seemed to be. I had no cause to suspect any change.
Q. You know that ships swing a great deal in the harbor of Havana. Could you not tell us whether, from the time you took the deck until the time of the explosion, the *Maine* seemed to be heading almost steadily in one direction?
A. So far as I know, she was, from the bearings of other ships.

By the COURT:

Q. Were you so situated that you could see the point at which the explosion took place?
A. No, sir; I was abaft the after turret and could see on the port side well aft, but the turret bulges a little and would cut off the sight of the side of the ship forward of the gangway. I do not know where the explosion took place, but my impression is it was on the port side forward.
Q. You were not so situated that you could have seen the burst of flame or the effect of the first explosion—whether it was thrown up?
A. I could have seen the burst of flame where I was if I had looked in that direction. I looked over the port side. I saw the glare as it

went up, but I didn't see this burst of flame that others have described. That was more amidships.

Q. You did not notice any ascent of a column of water as the result of the explosion?

A. None at all, and none fell, to my knowledge. None fell on me, and I saw none fall around me.

Q. How soon after the explosion do you think the forward part of the ship was under water?

A. The forward part, almost within a minute. I should estimate that, at the most, two minutes after the explosion the quarter deck was knee deep in water. She was on bottom in, I think, less than three minutes, all over.

Q. You say you heard two explosions?

A. That is my impression, sir; though I could not be positive. I think there were two.

Q. Similar explosions?

A. So far as I can judge, sir. When the first explosion took place the ship quivered. The shock, as I said, was not so great where I was, and my impression is there was a second one, but the difference in similarity I could not describe.

Q. As I understand, Mr. Blandin, you only saw the fragments coming down?

A. Yes, sir.

Q. You did not see anything go up?

A. No, sir.

Q. So that whatever was thrown upward was not under your observation?

A. No, sir; I really saw very little coming down, but I heard them and felt them.

Q. Was there any perceptible upheaval of the ship that you noticed?

A. Not that I noticed; no, sir.

By the JUDGE-ADVOCATE:

Q. Were you riding head to the wind?

A. There was practically no wind. It was, if anything, a very light air.

The judge-advocate requested that the testimony given by the witness be not read to him by the stenographer, but that he be directed to report to-morrow morning at 10 o'clock, when he will be furnished with so much of the record as contains his testimony, and asked to withdraw for the consideration of the same, upon the completion of which he will be again called before the court, and be given an opportunity to amend his testimony as recorded, or pronounce it correct. The request was granted, and the witness was instructed accordingly; whereupon he withdrew, after being cautioned by the president not to discuss matters pertaining to the inquiry.

Lieut. JOHN HOOD, U. S. Navy, appeared as a witness before the court, and was sworn by the president:

Examined by the JUDGE-ADVOCATE:

Q. Please state your full name, rank, and to what ship you are attached.

A. John Hood, lieutenant, U. S. Navy, attached to the late U. S. S. *Maine*.

Q. Since when have you been attached to the *Maine?*

A. Since November 5, 1897.
Q. What was your duty during that time?
A. My duty was as watch officer.
Q. Senior watch officer?
A. Senior watch officer.
Q. In charge of the powder division?
A. Yes, sir; in charge of the powder division and the torpedo division.
Q. Since you have been senior watch officer in charge of the powder division have you been down in the magazines and shell rooms?
A. I have been through all of them.
Q. Do you know of any matter being stowed in the shell rooms or magazines which was prohibited by ordnance instructions and regulations from being stowed there?
A. I do not. I inspected all the magazines after I joined the ship, and saw them all properly stowed. I saw nothing there except the proper and authorized articles.
Q. You consider that on the night of the explosion there was existing the same state of affairs—no violation of the ordnance regulations in regard to the stowage of explosives?
A. I do. I did not inspect it then, but I am absolutely sure that there was nothing done beyond the ordinary work down there.
Q. Who was acting in the gunner's place at the time of the explosion, and who had been for some time previously?
A. Chief Gunner's Mate Brofelt.
Q. What is the record and character of that man?
A. His record and character are both excellent. He is a very excellent man, a thoroughly reliable man, and a very intelligent man.
Q. Whenever the magazines or shell rooms are open for drill or otherwise are the keys always returned to the captain and the magazines and shell rooms reported locked?
A. The keys are always returned. The magazine is reported closed. The report is made to the officer of the deck, and by him to the captain. The keys are never gotten out except by a report, first, to the officer of the deck, as to what they are wanted for. That report has to be turned in to the captain, and the captain sends them out.
Q. Do you remember whether on the day of the explosion, February 15, the magazines or shell rooms had been opened for any purpose?
A. They were not opened that day for drill; but it is the routine of the ship to open them to take the temperature. That I had nothing to do with personally. I know that is the routine of the ship.
Q. The temperature can be taken from the small plate holes, can it not?
A. Yes.
Q. And it is done that way?
A. It can be taken through the small holes. I never examined that personally at all. All the magazines were opened the day before at drill, and I passed up and down through all the magazines of the ship.
Q. That was Monday gunnery drill there?
A. Gunnery drill day.
Q. Did you ever pay any attention to the temperature of magazines and shell rooms?
A. No; that was not my special business. I noticed the temperature of the magazines myself when I was in them, but that was all.
Q. Which were the hottest magazines?

A. The hottest magazines were what we called amidship magazines; the midship 10-inch and 6-inch.

Q. Which is the midship, the forward or the after 10-inch?

A. The after 10-inch, down between the engine room and fire room, and they were much warmer than any of the forward magazines. The forward magazines were comparatively cool.

Q. During drill, were all regulations properly carried out in regard to men going down to magazines and shell rooms?

A. I think I am sure they were. They were, so far as I know.

Q. You had no drills since Monday forenoon, the day before?

A. I had no drill after Monday forenoon, the day before.

Q. Do you know where the rockets were stowed?

A. They were stowed on deck, aft somewhere. I never paid any attention to that, because I had nothing to do with that.

Q. I suppose a few were in the pilot house?

A. A few were always up in the pilot house for use. That is all I ever looked at.

Q. While you were officer of the deck, in the harbor of Havana, were there any special regulations made by your commanding officer, and any special orders given in regard to keeping an extra lookout; and, if so, were they faithfully carried out?

A. They were, while I was on watch. Of course, I did not see it all the time.

Q. That is what I mean. Did you ever notice any hostile demonstration afloat in the way of boats approaching the ship that had to be warned off?

A. No; I never saw any demonstration of any kind afloat. The only passing crafts were ordinary passing boats, and they were all hailed as they went along.

Q. Where were the torpedo war heads stowed?

A. They were stowed in the storeroom for them, down underneath the forward end of the wardroom.

Q. When had they been handled last before the explosion?

A. About the 26th or 27th of December, if I recollect right. They were taken up just at the end of December and weighed, and restowed again, and they had not been touched since.

Q. No torpedo war heads were fitted at the time of the explosion?

A. No, sir; no torpedo war heads were out of the torpedo storeroom.

Q. Do you remember the kind of ammunition and, as near as you can tell us, the amount that was stowed in the reserve 6-inch magazine?

A. The reserve 6-inch magazine struck me as being practically empty when I went through it. I didn't take any account of the stock, but there was very little ammunition of any kind in it, and the gunner who went through the magazine with me told me that he had the saluting charges and a few extra shell stowed in there, I think. I am not sure about that, but it was a very small quantity of ammunition of any kind that was stowed in that reserve magazine.

Q. On June 30, 1897, it was reported that there was quite an amount of 6-inch charges there. Do you know whether there were any there at the time of the explosion?

A. I do not know. I did not take any account of the stock there.

Q. Are there any wooden linings to the magazines of the *Maine*?

A. There were gratings on the floors, but I don't recollect how the sides of the magazines were fitted.

Q. During your inspections, did you notice whether there were any electric wires which might endanger the magazines?

A. I never saw any wires there except the light wires which were in the light box. They were not in the magazines.

Q. Did you notice any steam pipes which might endanger the magazines?

A. No, sir; I don't think there were any steam pipes in the magazines at all.

Q. I believe, in answer to a previous question, you stated that while you were officer of the deck all ordnance regulations were faithfully carried out. I believe you were on deck at the time of the explosion. For how long previous to that moment were you on deck?

A. I came on deck about half past 9. It may have been a little before that; and the explosion occurred about 9.40. It might have been a little longer. I was on deck probably about fifteen minutes.

Q. Could you state whether proper vigilance was exercised or not in respect to these orders?

A. The men were on watch on deck and all the sentries were posted.

Q. The officers were at their stations?

A. No other officer was on deck except the officer of the deck and myself. The officer of the deck was on deck at his station, but there was no other officer on deck that I saw.

Q. Did you notice which way the ship was riding?

A. I did.

Q. From your experience while at Havana, did you think she was riding in an unusual way or in a way in which she had frequently been riding?

A. She was riding in a direction that I never remember having seen her ride in before.

Q. Was she heading steadily in that direction, so far as you could judge?

A. Just at that time she was pretty still.

Q. Will you please state to the court your experience of the explosion in full—what you felt, what you heard, and what you saw.

A. I was sitting on the port side of the deck with my feet on the rail, and I both heard and felt—felt more than I heard—a big explosion, that sounded and felt like an under-water explosion. I was under the impression that it came from forward, starboard, at the time. I instantly turned my head, and the instant I turned my head there was a second explosion. I saw the whole starboard side of the deck and everything above it as far aft as the after end of the superstructure spring up in the air with all kinds of objects in it—a regular crater-like performance, with flames and everything else coming up. I immediately sprang myself behind the edge of the superstructure, as there were a number of objects flying in my direction, for shelter. I ran very quickly aft, as fast as I could, along the after end of the superstructure, and climbed up on a kind of step. I went under the barge, and by the time I went up on the superstructure this explosion had passed. The objects had stopped flying around. Then I saw on the starboard side there was an immense mass of foaming water and wreckage and groaning men out there. It was scattered around in a circle, I should say about a hundred yards in diameter, off on the starboard side. I immediately proceeded to lower the gig, with the help of another man. After I got that in the water several officers jumped in it and one or two men. In the meantime somebody else was lowering the other boat on the port side. I heard some groans forward, and ran forward on the quarter deck down the poop ladder, and I immediately brought up on an immense pile of wreckage. I saw one man there, who had been thrown from somewhere, pinned down by a ventilator.

The COURT. May I interrupt Mr. Hood a moment. He said several officers jumped into the gig. He does not say for what purpose or what they did. That might leave a bad impression unless he states what the object was.

A. They jumped into the gig, commanded to pick up these wounded men whom we heard out in the water. The orders had been given by the captain and the executive officer to lower the boats as soon as they came on deck. I spoke of lowering the gig, because I was on the deck before they got up there, and began to lower it anyway, to pick up these men. As I was saying a minute ago, I found this one man lying there on the quarter deck in this wreckage, pinned down by a ventilator. With Mr. Blandin's help, we got him up just in time before the water rose over him. The captain and the executive officer ordered the magazines to be closed. We all saw at once that it would be no use flooding the magazines. We saw that the magazines were flooding themselves. Then the captain said he wanted the fire put out that was starting up in the wreckage. I made my way forward through the wreck and débris, up to the middle superstructure, to see if anything could be done toward putting out this fire. When I got there I found nothing could be done because the whole thing was gone.

When I climbed up on this wreck on the superstructure I saw similar piles of wreckage on the port side which I had not seen before, and I saw some men struggling in that, in the water; but there were half a dozen boats there, I suppose, picking them up and hauling them out; and after pulling down some burning swings and things that were starting to burn aft, to stop any fire from catching aft, I came aft again out of the wreckage. There was no living thing up there at that time. Shortly after that we all left the ship. There were two distinct explosions—big ones—and they were followed by a number of smaller explosions, which I took at once to be what they were, I suppose—explosions of separate charges of the blown-up magazine. The instant this first explosion occurred, I knew the ship was gone completely, and the second explosion only assisted her to go a little quicker. She began to go down instantly. The interval between the two was so short that I only had time to turn my head and see the second. She sank on the forward end—went down like a shot. In the short time that I took to run the length of that short superstructure aft the deck canted down, showing that her bow had gone at once.

At the same time the ship heeled over considerably to port, I should say about 10 degrees, the highest amount, and then the stern began to sink very rapidly, too; so rapidly that by the time I got that gig lowered, with the assistance of another man or two, the upper quarter deck was under water, and the stern was sinking so quickly that when I began to pick this man up, whom I spoke of on the quarter deck, the deck was still out of water. Before I got this ventilator off him—it didn't take very long, as Mr. Blandin assisted to move that to get him up—the water was up over my knees, and just catching this fellow's head. The stern was sinking that quickly. The bow had gone down, as I say, instantly. I do not suppose you want my impressions.

By the JUDGE-ADVOCATE:

Q. No; I will ask you some questions. Which was the larger explosion; which gave you the greater shock, the first or the second?

A. The first was more of a feel. I mean, you felt the first explosion rather more than you saw it. I felt the whole ship just go up and tremble and vibrate all over. The first explosion was a duller sound, to me. The second was a kind of an open explosion, you might say, which was the one that I saw, which came right up at once. The other one had come up, too, but I had not been able to see it.

Q. Was there any lifting of the ship at the time of the first explosion?

A. The ship began to list immediately. The explosions followed each other very quickly. I just had time to turn my head, and the ship began to list to port immediately. There was no appreciable interval of time between these two explosions.

Q. What I mean is, Did the ship give a sudden list to either starboard or port at the first explosion, as if something had struck her on either side? I don't mean a gradual sinking, as she did afterwards.

A. I didn't notice any special list at the first shot, but she began to list immediately.

Q. As I understand from your description, the first explosion was more as if something had run into her, and trembled the whole ship?

A. No; not as if something had run into her at all; as though something had exploded under her.

Q. It affected the whole ship more than the second explosion, which has a bursting of the forward part?

A. Yes, sir.

Q. On which side did you think the explosion was, at the moment?

A. My instantaneous impression was that it was on the starboard side; but that was an impression. It was the starboard side that I saw blow up myself. I couldn't see the port side. I was sitting behind the after turret, and the awning was spread, coming down, and I couldn't see that at all. I felt the explosion was forward, and rather to starboard. I naturally supposed it must have been to starboard, because it was to starboard that I looked.

Q. And could see?

A. And could see.

Q. The turret obstructed the view of the port gangway, did it not?

A. It entirely obstructed the view of the port gangway. I could not see anything at all to port. The turret was there, and the awning was spread, coming down through the top of the turret, so that I could see neither above nor ahead.

Q. The quarter-deck awning was spread, was it?

A. Yes; and my only line of sight forward was in a diagonal starboard line, between the after superstructure and the turret gun, looking out toward the starboard gangway.

Q. Was any water thrown up at the time of either explosion?

A. I didn't see any water thrown up.

Q. Did you feel any?

A. I didn't feel any.

Q. Were there any upshoots of flame in either explosion?

A. The first explosion, I do not know what there was, because I did not see it; but in the second explosion, there was an upshoot of flame, and deck and everything else in sight, along the starboard side. I saw the whole starboard side of the deck, as far as I could see it, nearly as far aft as the after end of the middle superstructure—I saw the whole thing go up in the air, and the part of the superstructure there along with it.

Q. Did you notice any explosions in the air?

A. No.

By the COURT:

Q. You connect that movement of the lifting of the deck of the middle superstructure distinctly with the second explosion, do you?

A. The deck, not the superstructure at all. During this first explosion there was nothing in the way of the starboard gangway of that vast mass of wreckage that is lying there now. My first sight through the starboard side was a perfectly clear sight, and there was nothing lying there, or there was no wreckage there, of that immense pile of wreckage that is piled on the starboard and after side of the ship after the whole thing was over. There was nothing there at that time. There was a clear view through, right past that superstructure, and I just happened to get a look in time to see all that go up itself. When I climbed up after the thing was over, and we got the boats out, and I climbed up in this mass of wreckage at night, I found an immense mass of wreckage piled up where I had seen this thing go up. In the darkness of the night I took that mass of wreckage to be the starboard side of the ship, that had just blown up and tilted up. That was my impression during that night, that this big mass of wreckage was the end of those beams that I discovered the next morning. That night I thought they might be the end of the beams themselves thrown up in the air. When that second explosion took place there was nothing in the line of my sight forward. It was perfectly clear.

By the JUDGE-ADVOCATE:

Q. Where were you at the time of the first explosion? What was exactly your position?

A. I was sitting, I should say, just between—I can point it out exactly on the plan.

Q. We would rather have you tell where you were, because your pointing can not go in the record.

A. I was sitting almost opposite the door. I should say, almost under the forward davit of the whaleboat.

Q. On the port side?

A. On the port side.

By the COURT:

Q. Fix it exactly by the number of the frame?

A. I don't know what the number of the frame is. I was sitting right there, almost opposite this door [indicating].

Q. The door that leads into the admiral's cabin?

A. The door that leads into the admiral's cabin, yes, sir.

Q. The frames are numbered here.

A. (After examination of the plan.) I was sitting about on frame 66, close to the port rail.

By the JUDGE-ADVOCATE:

Q. I understand you to say you jumped right up and ran over to starboard?

A. First, before I jumped out of my chair, I turned. I was sitting in the chair with my feet on the rail. Before I jumped, I turned to the right to look forward, and I had a view just between the turret and the aftersuperstructure, across the deck, over to the starboard gangway. I did not start to run until after the second explosion, when I saw the whole deck and everything above there, and below, too, I suppose, rise up in the air. I saw various missiles of all kinds flying around loose, and some of them were flying toward me. One of them whisked off my cap as it came by. It didn't touch my head, but I felt the wind of it as it went by, and I quickly jumped against the port side of the aftersuperstructure, to be under shelter from these flying missiles.

Q. Your position did not give you a full view of the starboard gangway?

A. No.

Q. The wreck shows now that the forward part of the superstructure was thrown forward of the afterpart?
A. Yes, sir.
Q. Do you think it might have been possible that it was thrown up at the first explosion but not landed in time for you to see the wreckage?
A. That is exactly what I think. It was not there when I saw this second explosion. Just immediately after I got up on the superstructure, the thing was there. My belief is that the whole forward part of the superstructure that is lying there on the starboard gangway now was in the air at the time I saw the second explosion.
Q. You think the first explosion threw up the middle superstructure?
A. I do. The explosion that I saw myself was on the starboard side, and that would have raised and thrown anything in the other direction—thrown it off.
Q. You saw the second explosion on the starboard side?
A. Yes, sir.
Q. But could it not have been on both sides and you not able to see it?
A. It could have been, except that when I examined the wreck the next morning the afterpart of the port side of the middle superstructure was apparently intact. It is intact there yet, almost, and the starboard side aft is all gone. As I say, I saw this deck go up almost as far aft as the after end of the superstructure.
Q. Then it is your belief that the deck was raised at the first explosion?
A. It is my belief that the forward deck—that main deck forward—was raised at the first explosion.
Q. And the second explosion might have been on the port side as well as the starboard, but you would only see the starboard? Is that correct?
A. No; I think the second explosion was more to starboard. The flames and the crater that I saw were to starboard.
Q. None on the port side?
A. I could not see the port side. I do not know what was on the port.
Q. That is what I am trying to say. You could not testify as to the port side?
A. I could not see the port side at all. Of course, I only have my impressions of it after I climbed up on the wreckage and saw what was left—saw what the thing was; but I could not see anything to port. I did see the starboard side go up, and when I saw that starboard side go up my first sight of it was clear. There was nothing piled up there, and it was perfectly clear. Shortly after the explosion, the next time I saw it, there was a great mass of wreckage piled up there, which I saw afterwards was the forward end of the main deck and the middle superstructure. That was not there when this second explosion that I saw took place.
Q. You could not be positive, then, which explosion threw up the forward part of the superstructure, but you are positive that it was not there when you got a view?
A. I am positive it was not there when I saw it, and that the explosion that I saw on the starboard side would have thrown things away from there.

By the COURT:

Q. How do you account, Mr. Hood, for the fact that the missiles which you saw, some of which were coming your way, followed the second explosion?

A. They were things that had blown up from below in this explosion—parts of the deck and parts of the superstructure, the starboard side of the superstructure, and whatever was in the way there. The thing opened out just like a big crater. It is only a matter of judgment, of course, as to just how far aft that came; but my line of sight did not take so very far forward of the line of the after end of the superstructure from where I was sitting.

Q. It is only a question of separating the impression, or estimating the interval between the first and the second explosion, and whether the first one could have produced a result which you did not see at the time of the second explosion. That is, the wreckage which had been produced by the first explosion only landed in its place after the second explosion?

A. After the second explosion.

Q. Or whether the result of the second explosion was what you subsequently saw and recognized as being the result of either the first explosion or of both explosions, or of only the second explosion. That is, you can not separate the result of the two explosions?

A. No; I could not separate them fully, of course, but I know that my line of sight was perfectly clear when I saw this thing open up.

Q. Until the second explosion occurred?

A. Yes; they followed so closely on each other that of course it is a mere matter of impression as to how close they were together.

Q. Yes; I am aware of that.

A. I turned my head, and before I got my head around I heard the second one, and I just got around in time to see.

Q. You saw that your view at that time was unobstructed.

A. Was unobstructed. Of course it was an instantaneous action on my part—as near as a human action can be to look—around.

Q. Why do you think the second explosion occurred on the starboard side?

A. Because I saw the starboard side of the deck go up in the air, and everything about there going up. As soon as I got on top of the after superstructure, I saw this mass of wreckage, and foam, and things skimming in a semicircle around on the starboard side.

Q. Could you see the port side from the superstructure after you got up there?

A. No; the wreckage and other things were in the way from where I was. I did not see that until a minute or two after that, when I climbed forward on the wreck of the middle superstructure. Then I saw the port side, too. That was the first I had seen of the port side.

Q. Will you tell us what your impression was the following day, or when you had a distinct impression of the wreck, as to the point at which the explosion had taken place.

A. In the morning I went around the wreck when it was not absolutely full daylight. Mr. Wainwright and myself got in a boat and pulled around it, and my impression that morning in this darkness was that——

Q. But you were there how long afterwards?

A. I was not near the wreck at all after that. I watched it through glasses as I was coming out on the steamer, but the steamer did not pass very near the wreck. I was in doubt as to just what that mass of wreckage that is turned up there was at that time. I knew those were beams, and that was a part of the superstructure, but whether that was the main deck in the after end of the superstructure, turned up in the air, or whether it was the port end of the forward part of the superstructure that was turned up in the air I could not exactly make out. I could not place exactly what that protuberance was that stuck out there on the starboard side.

Q. You know now, do you?

A. I know what it is; yes. I have studied the thing out since, and I know it is the base of the conning tower. I thought that is what it looked like, but I could not see that morning how it could get there. I could not place it. I thought it might have been the starboard side of the deck, aft, blown up in the air, with the starboard ends of the beam sticking up. At the distance I saw it from the steamer I took it that it might have been one of the drying rooms—I think they call them—around the smokestack, or something of that kind; but I saw that the whole ship was gone from the cranes forward.

Q. Bearing in mind the second impression, or the impressions you got the following day of the condition of the wreck, does that accord with the impression made upon you at the time the explosion occurred?

A. Yes, sir; my impression has never changed at all, except in that I was not sure at the first instant just where the explosion took place, whether it was more to starboard or more to port.

Q. Your impression was at first——

A. My impression at first was that it was a little starboard.

Q. That it was on the starboard side, and now, after knowing the position of the wreck, you are still of the same impression, are you?

A. No; I am of the impression that the explosion was on the port side.

Q. Yes; but the second one?

A. The second explosion, I am under the impression, was on the starboard side. It may have been, of course, that the main explosion at first threw a lot of these things out to starboard, but I could not see that.

Q. I would like to ask a question about the agitation of the water. What did you notice about the agitation of the water?

A. I just noticed a semicircular space of water opposite the starboard side. It was just a mass of foam and wreckage. There were quite a lot of groaning men in it. It extended out, I thought at the time, about 75 yards.

Q. Was there any wave?

A. There was no big wave; no. There would not be any wave.

Q. How close to the port side of the magazine was any of the powder stowed—I mean the 6-inch reserve magazine?

A. The 6-inch reserve magazine was well in. Just the exact distance I do not know; but it was well in from the side of the ship. It was on the port side of amidships.

Q. I mean from the coal-bunker bulkhead, which is the outboard bulkhead of the magazine?

A. I do not remember.

Q. You did not notice any smoke or flame rising above the deck until the second explosion occurred?

A. I did not; but I could not see anything on the port side at all.

Q. You did not notice?

A. I did not notice, because I could not see anything, except on the starboard side.

Q. I mean above the deck. I do not refer to either side. You did not notice any smoke or flame rising above the decks until the second explosion occurred?

A. No; I could not see.

By the Judge-Advocate:

Q. When did you see the steam launch last, or did you see her at all?

A. I didn't notice her that night at all.

The judge-advocate requested that the testimony given by the witness be not read to him by the stenographer, but that he be directed to report to-morrow morning at 10 o'clock, when he will be furnished with so much of the record as contains his testimony and asked to withdraw for the consideration of the same, upon the completion of which he will be again called before the court and be given an oportunity to amend his testimony as recorded, or pronounce it correct. The request was granted, and the witness was instructed accordingly; whereupon he withdrew, after being cautioned by the president not to discuss matters pertaining to the trial.

Lieut. GEORGE P. BLOW, U. S. Navy, appeared as a witness before the court and was sworn by the president:

Examined by the JUDGE-ADVOCATE:

Q. Please state your name, rank, and to what ship you are attached.

A. George P. Blow, lieutenant, United States Navy, attached to the U. S. battle ship *Maine*.

Q. How long have you been in the *Maine?*

A. I have been in the *Maine* since September, 1895, I think it was.

Q. As what?

A. As lieutenant and watch officer.

Q. What division have you?

A. I had the fourth division first, and later the third division, in charge of the after turret.

Q. When did you last have gunnery drill in the *Maine?*

A. On Monday.

Q. The day previous to the explosion?

A. Yes, sir.

Q. Was all powder that was sent up sent below and properly stowed away?

A. No powder was sent up, sir.

Q. While you were watch officer of the Maine did you ever notice any hostile demonstrations afloat, in the way of boats attempting to approach the vessel at night that had to be warned off?

A. No, sir; nothing hostile. I have noticed a number of shore boats which were warned off by the sentries; but nothing of a hostile nature.

Q. Do you know the direction in which the *Maine* was heading at the time of the explosion?

A. I know the direction, approximately.

Q. Was that an unusual heading, from your experience during your stay in that harbor, for that ship?

A. Rather unusual; yes, sir. As a rule, we swung so that the *Alfonso*, which was lying at the buoy inside of us, was either on our port quarter or starboard quarter. That was the customary heading.

Q. Were you officer of the deck from 4 to 8 p. m. the night of this explosion?

A. I was the officer of the day—officer on day's duty.

Q. Were you on duty when the reports at 8 p. m. were made?

A. Yes, sir.

Q. Who made them?
A. Do you mean the regular reports to the executive officer?
Q. Yes.
A. The usual reports were made at the mast by the warrant officers, and by petty officers in charge of their departments.
Q. What reports were made to the officer of the deck in your presence or hearing?
A. The reports were made that the captain, the executive officer, and other officers were on board.
Q. I refer to the master at arms' reports about lights and fires.
A. The usual report was made and repeated by Mr. Cluverius, before the deck was delivered over to the orderly, that the lights and fires were secure and everything was secure.
Q. You were officer of the day of the *Maine* on February 15 up to 8 p. m., and you consider that everything was secure below on the ship at 8 p. m.?
A. To the best of my knowledge, everything was secure as usual.
Q. Did you, as an officer who had been on the ship for a long while, have perfect confidence in the reports of these men that everything below was secure?
A. Yes, sir.
Q. Where were you at the time of the explosion?
A. I was in my room, writing.
Q. Where is your room situated?
A. My room is the after room on the starboard side, in the wardroom proper, just forward of the bulkhead separating it from the after compartment.
Q. Do you remember the number of that bulkhead?
A. No, sir. (After looking at the plan.) It was just abaft of frame No. 76 on the starboard side.
Q. Will you state to the court what you experienced during that explosion? We wish to know what you felt, what you heard, or what you saw.
A. I was writing at the time, and heard forward, and apparently at some distance—that is to say, well up in the bow, as far as I could judge from the sound—an explosion.
Instantly the lights went out. I rushed out of my room to see the cause of it, and before I could get more than probably 6 feet from my room a second and much more violent explosion followed. This explosion I would describe as being a continuous explosion, lasting for some seconds, and accompanied by the falling of lights, electric fittings, furniture, and by a crashing and rending of metal, and immediately by a sharp heel of the ship to port; the sound of rushing water from forward, and the cries and screams of men from about amidships. My first impression was that we had been fired on, and I remember feeling surprised that it should have been by such a heavy gun. When the second explosion occurred, followed by the listing of the ship, I recognized the fact that the ship was sinking, and had been blown up.
My impulse had been at first to go to my quarters, but at the second explosion I abandoned all thought of this, and realized that it was a question of whether I could reach the deck or not before the ship sank. A sharp heel of the ship, as I rushed forward feeling my way along the starboard bulkhead, caused me to lose my way amidst the wreckage, and for probably a moment I was confused as to my position. I soon found the bulkhead again, and, feeling my way along, reached a small china jar on top of the starboard steam heater, and recognizing

this by feeling, found the starboard door leading forward. This door was closed and jammed. It could not be opened. I then felt my way across the deck to the port door. The list of the ship, which had probably closed the starboard door, had kept the port door open, and I had no difficulty in finding it. Stepping through the door, I reached the ladder, and ran into someone in the dark.

By the COURT:

Q. What ladder was that? The one just outside the bulkhead?

A. Yes, sir; just outside the bulkhead, leading up to the wardroom proper.

By the JUDGE-ADVOCATE:

Q. It leads into the cabin passage?

A. Yes, sir. We both fell, owing to the inclination of the deck, but, helping each other up again, we immediately crawled up the ladder, which was then nearly vertical. I am under the impression that this ladder fell immediately afterwards, as I heard a crash behind us. The water was then rushing in on the berth deck, though it was not quite up to the ladder, as she was heeled to port. Reaching the main deck, I felt my way through the starboard door in the after superstructure out on deck, and was surprised to find that everything was pitch dark, as dark as it had been below.

By the COURT:

Q. That starboard door opens right out on the starboard deck?

A. It opens right out on the starboard deck; yes, sir.

Q. After passing through that you found it dark?

A. I found it perfectly dark there. I was surprised at the time to find it so dark. This was probably due to the fact that the quarter-deck awning had been dragged down by the fall of the third cutter. As I passed through the door I ran against someone hanging from the poop-deck rail, who asked me to give him a push up on deck. This I did, and believing that there must be some good cause for his having taken that way of reaching safety, I quickly followed. At this time the main deck was still above water. On reaching the poop deck I glanced forward and found the whole forward part of the ship a mass of confused wreckage, and apparently submerged up to and above the main deck. There were about a dozen men only to be seen on the poop deck. Among these I recognized the captain and the executive officer, Lieutenant-Commander Wainright, who were giving orders to get out the boats for the purpose of saving the lives of the men in the water.

On the starboard side the beam and forward there were cries for help. Realizing at a glance that my boat, the third cutter, and that all the boats, in fact, forward, were gone, I turned aft to help to get out the only boats remaining. I found the gig manned and about to be lowered. I lowered the forward fall, and was surprised to find that the boat only went down about 6 or 8 feet. Thinking the stopper might have passed, or the blocks jammed, I asked the man in the bow if everything was all right. He replied yes. I asked him why the boat would not go down. He informed me that the boat was afloat. By that time the water had nearly reached the top of the superstructure deck. I then went forward again, and noticed that the wreckage had broken into flames, and I heard someone, I think the executive officer, say to the captain. "There is the wreck of the fire ship which they have sent down on us," pointing to the wreckage forward, which was now illuminated from the burning cellulose.

I then went to the port side to assist in lowering the barge. I found that she had already been lowered and was afloat. Before that, however, I would like to insert something. I am a little too fast. Before going forward again one of the midshipmen—I think it was Mr. Cluverius—came and asked me if he could be of any service. I told him to jump in the gig and take charge and save what life he could on the starboard side, which I believe he did. After this I went to the port side to assist in lowering the barge and I found that she was already in the water and afloat. There were already, I think, four men in her, however, to man her. So I went back again and called several who were standing on the poop and put them in the boat, and afterwards got in myself. I took charge of the boat, ordering the man at the helm to steer around on the starboard side, where most of the cries for help had been heard. After shoving off I found Lieutenant Jungen was in the boat, and he being my senior I turned the boat over to him and requested that he put me back. He said it was impossible, which was perfectly right. He pulled completely around the ship, and only succeeded in picking up one man on the starboard side, as we became involved in the wreckage and débris which was floating from a beam around the bow. The barge being very long, and only half manned, was very difficult to maneuver. We were continually backing and pulling out.

In that way we did not get around as quickly as we might have done. By this time the wreckage was all in flames, and I called Mr. Jungen's attention to the fact that I thought I saw men on the forecastle, as I supposed it to be, and asked him to pull in there and see if he could not get them off. We headed in for the wreckage, but ran into other wreckage, which we found out there to be the submerged portion of the forecastle and forward superstructure. We backed out and again pulled in toward the flames. We then found that it was the after part of the middle superstructure, abreast of the port crane. There were several boats there, which had already taken off all the men, so we pulled around on the port quarter, and again reported to the captain that the boat was there ready to take off anybody else. In the meanwhile, the captain had ordered the ship to be abandoned. Mr. Wainwright asked us if we were all right. We told him yes, and asked the captain if he would not get in the barge. He replied, "No; I want my own boat," and then ordered all of our boats to go on board of the Ward Line steamer the *City of Washington*. He then put his orderly and everyone else into the gig and got into the gig himself. We obeyed orders and went aboard the *City of Washington*. Do you wish me to go any further?

By the JUDGE-ADVOCATE:

Q. No. Will you please describe your sensation of the first shock a little more fully?

A. The first shock was not a very severe one, although it was sufficient to put all of the lights out. It impressed me as sounding, as nearly as I can recollect, like a 10-inch gun fired close aboard. My recollection is that I was surprised that they should fire on us with such large guns so close aboard.

Q. I suppose you had heard no report in connection with this—what would you have supposed? What was the shock like?

A. It was a dull concussion; not like the shock of a rapid-firing gun

S. Doc. 207——9

or a 6 inch gun. It was longer and deeper in tone, and also with more of a shake.

Q. Did this first explosion, or whatever it was, list the ship any?
A. I think not.
Q. By the time you had reached the deck in the method you have described, had the second explosion finished completely?
A. Yes, sir.
Q. Then by the time you reached the deck there was no more upshoot of flame or debris or anything?
A. Only a few cinders and sparks.

By the COURT:

Q. When you got up on the poop deck, did you notice whether the men who had been thrown into the water were all on one side of the ship or not?
A. My impression was that those in the water were all on the starboard side; but I was on the starboard side myself, and it is possible that there may have been men on the port side whom I did not hear. That was my impression, and I ordered the boat to pull to the starboard side to pick up the men rather than the port side.
Q. How did you reach the starboard side?
A. We pulled around the stern, sir. The stern was cleared of wreckage and debris. We had no difficulty around the stern.
Q. Yet the ship, you say, was listed sharply to port at this time?
A. To port at this time. She had straightened up more, which led me to believe that she was on bottom.
Q. But she was listed?
A. Yes, sir; she was still listed; not so much, I think, as when she was sinking.
Q. From where you were could you tell from the shock, etc., about where the explosion occurred?
A. Only that the explosion seemed to me to come from well forward.
Q. Could you tell from which side it came from?
A. No, sir. I had an impression, but I do not think it is strong enough. My impression was at the time—that is to say, my impression now is—that it came from port, if there is any distinction; but I do not think it was strong enough at the time to notice—simply that it was an explosion from forward.

The judge-advocate requested that the testimony given by the witness be not read to him by the stenographer, but that he be directed to report to-morrow morning at 10 o'clock, when he will be furnished with so much of the record as contains his testimony and asked to withdraw for the consideration of the same, upon the completion of which he will be again called before the court and be given an opportunity to amend his testimony as recorded, or pronounce it correct. The request was granted, and the witness was instructed accordingly; whereupon he withdrew, after being cautioned by the president not to discuss matters pertaining to the inquiry.

Lieut. CARL W. JUNGEN, U. S. Navy, appeared as a witness before the court, and was duly sworn by the president:

Examined by the JUDGE-ADVOCATE:

Q. Please state your name, rank, and to what ship you are attached.
A. Carl W. Jungen, lieutenant, United States Navy, attached to the U. S. S. Maine.

Q. How long have you been aboard the *Maine?*
A. Nearly two years and a half, sir.
Q. Ever since her commission?
A. Ever since her commission. I went into commission with her.
Q. What have been your duties since that time?
A. Watch and division officer, sir.
Q. What division did you have at the time of her destruction?
A. I had command of the second division, the forward turret.
Q. How long had you had that division?
A. About a year and a half, sir.
Q. When did you last have gunnery drill on board the *Maine?*
A. On the Thursday previous to the accident. I don't remember the date—general quarters.
Q. Did you not have gunnery drill the day before, on Monday?
A. Yes, sir; we did.
Q. After that drill, was all powder that was gotten up properly sent below and stowed away?
A. We didn't get up any powder at all at that drill.
Q. Then there was no powder outside the magazines, as far as you know, subsequent to the last time it was gotten up?
A. No, sir.
Q. It was all properly stowed in the magazine?
A. All properly stowed away. That is, I have not charge of the stowing away, but there was none gotten up.
Q. Was there anything kept in the loading or passing rooms which should not be there?
A. No, sir; nothing that should not be there, although there was an extra supply of 10-inch shell ready for immediate use, which had been gotten up on the night that we started over for Havana from Tortugas.
Q. Who was the gunner's mate of your division?
A. Rieger. I don't remember his first name.
Q. He was a reliable man?
A. Yes, sir; he was.
Q. Do you know a seaman by the name of Neilson, who used to be on the steam launch of the *Maine?*
A. I do, sir.
Q. What duties was he performing just lately before the explosion?
A. I don't know, sir, that he was performing any special duties other than those of seaman in the forecastle, where he belonged.
Q. What was the man's record and character?
A. Excellent, sir.
Q. Was he a very reliable man?
A. I should say he was.
Q. At the time of the explosion he was in Lieutenant Jenkins's division, was he not?
A. Yes, in the first division.
Q. And the regular captain of the hold, was he in the ship?
A. No, sir; the regular captain of the hold was sent to the marine hospital some days before we left Key West, on or about the 20th of January.
Q. I have reason to believe, and I shall prove before the court that this seaman, Neilson, was acting captain of the hold at the time of the explosion. I therefore ask you his character. It was thoroughly reliable?
A. I consider him so, sir.
Q. While officer of the deck of the *Maine,* in the harbor of Havana,

did you ever notice any hostile demonstration afloat, in the way of boats attempting to approach the ship, that had to be warned off?

A. No, sir; I never did.

Q. From your knowledge of the swinging of the ship, do you think that at the time of her explosion she was swinging in an unusual direction?

A. I could not tell that positively without referring to the log book, but I think not.

Q. Were you below at the time of the explosion?

A. I was, sir.

Q. Where?

A. I was sitting in the mess room, the after part, at the small table. Assuming that the ship was heading north, I was sitting at the southwest corner of that table, talking to Mr. Jenkins and Mr. Holman. Mr. Holman was sitting at nearly the opposite corner, and Mr. Jenkins, I think, was standing at the time.

Q. Will you please describe to the court your experiences of this explosion, all you saw, heard, and felt up to the time that the whole thing was over?

A. I had just arisen from my seat. I had finished smoking a cigar which I had in a cigar holder. I had flicked the cigar out of it, and a piece of the wrapper was adhering to the inside, which I pulled out. As I pulled that out the explosion occurred. I remember that distinctly. It was not an explosion. It was a dull, deafening roar, followed immediately by a tremendous crash, and it seemed as though the whole ship was falling to pieces. Mr. Holman jumped up and remarked, "We have been torpedoed," which was the general impression we all had. He added: "Follow me."

There was a sufficient interval between the time it took me to get from that end of the table to the door opposite in the mess room before the lights were extinguished, so that I saw what appeared to me a thick dust or ashes or brown smoke. It may have been the dust that was shaken up from the ship. I detected no odor, nor did I experience any discomfort from it in passing through it. This lasted long enough—that is, the interval of time was sufficiently long—for me to reach the door and see that. I believed at the time that Mr. Jenkins and Mr. Holman were—I know Mr. Holman was and I believe Mr. Jenkins was—right ahead of me. Total darkness followed, and I saw no one then. I stretched out my hands. I knew where I was, but I was afraid of missing my way. So I stretched out my hands to catch hold of the engine-room hatch, which was right there. I followed along that with my other hand and reached the ladder. I got up the ladder and into the passageway of the after superstructure. I thought I saw the captain's orderly there, though I am not sure it was he. I ran out through that passageway and turned to the left, with the intention of going forward. As I was coming up the ladder I heard three—I think it was three—distinct explosions. One of them was more powerful than the other two. The other two were of a character that at the moment impressed me as being the fire of a 6 or 8 inch gun, and the thought flashed through my mind that we were being fired on, after being torpedoed, by the Spanish cruiser that was lying within 200 yards of us at her usual buoy, where she had been ever since we had been in there.

Q. The *Alfonso Doce?*

A. Yes, sir. As I turned to the left, I encountered a mass of wreckage and débris which had fallen on top of the awning. The awnings had been spread, so that I could not get forward. I intended at the time to go to my station at general quarters. Then I made an effort to get to the ladder, and I could not—the ladder that leads up the poop. Finding that I could not get on the poop that way, I turned around and caught hold of the iron water-tight door on that superstructure—the door that I had passed through—and tried to raise myself on it. I failed the first time, and then, by a superhuman effort, I swung myself up. I got my foot up on the waterway, and then I let go one hand and grabbed where I knew there ought to be a rail. It was a chain that had been replaced by a rail. I caught hold of that and swung myself up. The captain and the executive officer were on deck at the time. They had gotten there in the meanwhile, and I heard the captain give some order about flooding the magazines.

Mr. Wainwright made the remark, "There is no use flooding the magazines; the ship is sinking." I, myself, then realized that the ship was settling. Then the captain gave the order to lower the boats. There were very few people on the poop that I could see. I groped my way aft, over the skylights and the wreckage that was there, to the barge. I found Mr. Morris at the forward boat. I recognized him and Mr. Catlin at the after boat. I directed Mr. Catlin to get into the boat and see that the plug was in it. I could not see then. There was a dark shadow, I suppose, which was cast on the water by the light forward, and I could not see how high the water was up on the ship's side. He said at first he could not find the plug. I told him to throw the grating overboard and see if he could not get at it. Finally he got it, and I reported that the boat was ready for lowering. Without waiting for further orders I lowered the boat. I lowered it about 8 feet, I suppose, when I sung out to Mr. Catlin to let me know when the boat was in the water. He said she was in the water then. Then the sentry on the poop, who had loaded his rifle when the explosion took place—he had orders in a sudden emergency to load his rifle, which he did—got in the boat.

There were two men—I don't remember who they were; I think one of them was a mess attendant and a man by the name of Rush—who I directed to get in the boat. Then I got in the boat myself to go around and help pick up the men who were in the water. There was a great deal of hallooing and screaming for help. As I was about to shove off, only having four people in the boat, Mr. Morris got in. The paymaster and the chaplain, and Mr. Blow, and another man appeared at the rail, and I told them to get in. It was the barge—a large boat. They got in and they all took oars, and I took the boat and pulled around. I had to pull around clear of all the wreckage that had fallen in the water, which was very thick, like the driftwood you see sometimes in the Mississippi River. You could not pull through it. You had to pull around it. We pulled around on the starboard side. I saw no one aft, but I picked up a man opposite the forward turret. Then I went around the bows of the ship, or what has since transpired were the bows, but which we took at the time to be the wreck of a fireship, because I heard someone remark while I was on the poop that there was a fire ship down on us. I worked my way aft on the starboard side again to the quarter, and the ship by that time was, as near as I could make out, sunk until the upper superstructure was flush with the water.

There were several boats standing by to take the captain and executive officer, who were the last people to leave, as I remember. I offered the captain my boat and he said he wanted to go in his own. Other officers offered their boats. When I got around on the starboad side, I found several boats there, two Spanish boats, and two boats which I took to be merchant boats, and some smaller boats from shore. Besides our two boats, I believe, and the second whaleboat, which had been lowered, they all had survivors, people they had picked up. When I got around to the quarter again, the captain gave the order, before he got in his boat, for all the boats to go alongside the Ward Line steamer. I shoved off then with the people I had in the boat and went alongside. I put this man on board, and just then it began to rain quite hard. It rained harder a little later, for about ten or fifteen minutes, I should say. Then I got all the officers and the wounded man out. I directed them to go ahead, as the other boats were coming alongside. Then I went down into the cabin, and my first thought was to see if Doctor Henneberger was there. I found him attending the wounded. Mr. Blow went down to assist him. That is all that I can think of.

Q. In the first part of your evidence you spoke of an interval several times. What interval do you refer to?

A. It seemed to me an appreciable interval between the roar and the crash and the extinguishment of the lights, which was, as I say, sufficiently long to enable me to travel from that end of the table to the door, which was probably 8 feet, but the way I went around the table it was probably a longer distance.

Q. Did you not testify to two shocks, two explosions?

A. I testified to the original roar and crash, and then, as I remember, three distinct explosions, one of them being more violent than the rest of them. The other two that I speak of reminded me of the firing of a 6 or 8 inch gun.

Q. Will you describe a little more distinctly the three different explosions; how they took place and the interval between them?

A. I can not give you a proper conception of the time.

Q. You have not stated yet whether the big explosion was the first or the second or the third, and you have not stated definitely at which time the lights went out. Which explosion came first; the small one?

A. The first explosion, as I said, was a dull, deafening roar, followed immediately by a crash. By the time I got to the door, I should say, the lights all went out. Then there was another explosion, which was more violent than any explosion I had heard, that I could not liken to anything except possibly the explosion of a magazine.

Q. When did the lights go out in reference to this second explosion?

A. About simultaneously.

Q. Then you think the dynamo may have been destroyed at the second explosion.

A. Yes, sir.

Q. And not by the first?

A. Not by the first.

Q. Was there any perceptible list or lifting of the ship at the first explosion?

A. I did not notice that.

Q. Did you locate in your own mind this first explosion?

A. Yes, sir; I located it on the starboard side, as I supposed.

Q. Forward or aft?

A. Starboard forward, and as I supposed about under the forward turret.

Q. That was your impression?

A. That was my impression.

Q. And the second one; where did you locate that?

A. Forward; but I could not tell whether it was a magazine or whether it was a second explosion similar to the first.

Q. By the time you reached the deck the explosions had finished?
A. The explosion had finished; yes, sir.
Q. As to the boats in the water; were there more on one side than on the other, and which side?
A. I couldn't tell you that, sir; because when I went around to the stern of the ship I only saw one man in the water on the starboard side.
Q. You went around on the port side from starboard?
A. I went around; yes, sir.
Q. Why did you not go right out to port?
A. Because I thought the explosion was on the starboard side.
Q. You heard the hallooing more on the starboard side?
A. I didn't hear any hallooing at first. My attention was called to it. The men were yelling, and it appeared to me to come from the other side of the ship.

By the COURT:
Q. When did you first notice the list of the ship?
A. I didn't notice that until I caught hold of the door to go up on the superstructure. Then I noticed that the ship listed.
Q. After you had been up through——
A. Up over the ladder and through this passageway to turn to go forward.
Q. Which ladder did you go up from the berth deck to the main deck?
A. The ladder that is usually designated as the wardroom ladder.
Q. Which one is that?
A. That goes up from forward of the water-tight bulkhead separating the wardroom proper from the after torpedo room.
Q. That is not quite the answer I want. Was it the starboard ladder? Did it land you on the starboard side of the main deck or the port side?
A. It landed me on the starboard side of the main deck.
Q. So you did not notice that that ladder was unusually steep?
A. No, sir; I did not.
Q. You did not notice whether it was or not?
A. No, sir.
Q. Are there two ladders there?
A. There are two ladders there, alongside of each other. It is really all one ladder. There is a crossbar from the hatch to the grating.
Q. The ladders lead the same way?
A. Yes, sir; the ladders lead from port to starboard.
Q. To make it perfectly clear, between these two heavy explosions you had time after the first explosion to turn around and go about 10 feet?
A. Yes, sir; so it appeared to me.
Q. The other explosions to which you refer were smaller ones?
A. Smaller; yes, sir.
Q. And occurred some time after?
A. They occurred while I was going up the ladder and before I got to the superstructure door.
Q. But the fact that there were at first two explosions made a distinct impression upon your mind?
A. Yes, sir.
Q. Which would you designate as the more severe explosion, the first one or the second one?
A. The first one; because the crash and everything came with that,

and the second one sounded as though it were an explosion without being attended with the same effects. Where I was at the time, as I found out afterwards, toward that part of the ship the smokestacks had fallen—and I suppose they made as much crash as anything—one on one side and one on the other.

By the JUDGE-ADVOCATE:

Q. I want to ask you about two more men in the ship, as you have been in her since her commission. Sailmaker's Mate Roos—is he on board ship a reliable man?

A. In his duties he is a very reliable man. He was sometimes given to insobriety when he went on liberty, but I never noticed anything on board ship.

Q. I believe he was one of the two men who made the 8 p. m. reports to the executive officer?

A. Yes, sir.

Q. How do you consider Master-at-Arms White as to reliability?

A. He seemed to be a very reliable man—very attentive to his duties.

The judge advocate requested that the testimony given by the witness be not read to him by the stenographer, but that he be directed to report to-morrow morning at 10 o'clock, when he will be furnished with so much of the record as contains his testimony and asked to withdraw for the consideration of the same, upon the completion of which he will be again called before the court and be given an opportunity to amend his testimony as recorded or pronounce it correct. The request was granted, and the witness was instructed accordingly; whereupon he withdrew, after being cautioned by the president not to discuss matters pertaining to the inquiry.

Naval Cadet AMON BRONSON, Jr., U. S. Navy, appeared as a witness before the court, and was sworn by the president.

Examined by the JUDGE-ADVOCATE:

Q. State your name, rank, and to what ship you are attached?

A. Amon Bronson, jr., naval cadet, attached to the U. S. S. *Maine*.

Q. How long have you been attached to the *Maine*?

A. Since May 17, 1897.

Q. What duties have you performed during that time?

A. I have performed boat duty, deck duty—that is, supervision as the commissioned officer of the deck—and mate of the deck.

Q. Mate of the upper deck?

A. Mate of the upper deck and mate of the main deck.

Q. What division were you in last?

A. The second division, all the time I was on the ship.

Q. That is the forward turret division?

A. The forward turret division.

Q. At all times when gunnery occurred in that division, has powder always been sent below properly after the exercise?

A. Yes, sir.

Q. Where were you at the time of the explosion of the *Maine*?

A. I was lying in my bunk in my room.

Q. Which room is that?

A. The forward room of the steerage.

Q. Please describe what you heard and felt and saw.

A. My first impression was that a salute was being fired. That was before the crash came. That is the impression which I have now. That was the first thought that entered my mind. Then my bunk was lifted beneath me, and the ship listed over to port. The lights were out, and I heard the water rushing outside in the passageway. I could hear the cries of the men in the marines' compartment. For a very small amount of time I listened to these cries.

Q. When you thought there was a salute being fired, did you feel a shock of the ship?
A. Yes, sir; that was just merely the first idea that flashed through my mind. I felt a tremendous shock.
Q. How long after that shock did you feel the explosion?
A. I can not state, sir.
Q. Was there a distinct interval?
A. I am not prepared to state, sir.
Q. Was there a list of the ship at the first explosion?
A. Almost simultaneously with the explosion.
Q. There was a list?
A. Yes, sir.
Q. Which way?
A. To port.
Q. The ship settled to port?
A. Yes, sir.
Q. But she never was lifted up?
A. I was lying in my bunk, and I felt the bunk lifted beneath me.
Q. That was at the first shock?
A. The first shock; yes, sir.
Q. Everything was over by the time you reached the deck in the way of explosions and small shots?
A. I heard no small shots until about half an hour afterwards, when I heard the small-arm ammunition going off. I heard no small shot. The explosion did not sound loud in the steerage at all.

By the COURT:
Q. You are only conscious of one shock?
The JUDGE-ADVOCATE. He says he is not prepared to say. He says there was a shock and an explosion, but he is not prepared to state there was a distinct interval.

By the JUDGE-ADVOCATE:
Q. Were you asleep at the time?
A. No, sir; I was reading.
Q. In your bunk?
A. In my bunk.
Q. Upper bunk?
A. Lower bunk.

By the COURT:
Q. You say you do not remember; you did not say that either, but you say you did not separate the explosion into two parts?
A. No, sir; I simply know that the first idea that flashed across my mind was——
Q. We do not care about that. You are convinced yourself that that was not correct; that there was no salute being fired?
A. Yes, sir.
Q. You are convinced that that is not so?
A. Yes, sir.
Q. And you were convinced immediately of that, were you not?
A. Yes, sir.

Q. When you felt the bunk being lifted?
A. Yes, sir.
Q. And from what followed, you knew that it was not a salute?
A. Yes, sir.
Q. Do you or do you not remember that there were two parts to that?
A. I do not remember.

The judge-advocate requested that the testimony given by the witness be not read to him by the stenographer, but that he be directed to report to-morrow morning at 10 o'clock, when he will be furnished with so much of the record as contains his testimony and asked to withdraw for the consideration of the same, upon the completion of which he will be again called before the court and be given an opportunity to amend his testimony as recorded, or pronounce it correct. The request was granted, and the witness was instructed accordingly; whereupon he withdrew, after being cautioned by the president not to discuss matters pertaining to the inquiry.

Naval Cadet D. F. BOYD, Jr., U. S. Navy, appeared as a witness before the court, and was sworn by the president.

Examined by the JUDGE-ADVOCATE:

Q. Please state your name, rank, and to what ship you are attached.
A. David F. Boyd, jr.; naval cadet, U. S. Navy; attached to and serving on board the U. S. S. *Maine*.
Q. How long have you been attached to the *Maine*?
A. Since the 19th of June, 1897.
Q. What duties have you performed in that time?
A. The duties of junior officer of division, junior watch officer, and mate of the deck.
Q. What deck have you been mate of?
A. Mate of the berth deck and mate of the superstructure deck.
Q. How long were you mate of the berth deck?
A. From the latter part of August until the 1st of January.
Q. Who relieved you then?
A. Naval Cadet W. T. Cluverius.
Q. What are your duties as mate of the berth deck?
A. To see that all compartments are not open, except those authorized to be open, and to see that those compartments are water-tight.
Q. Which compartments are authorized to be kept open by the rules of the ship?
A. The clothing issuing room, the dynamo room, the forward and after 10-inch handling room, and the passage between the steerage and wardroom.
Q. What do you mean by keeping the forward 10-inch handling room open?
A. It necessarily must be kept open, because there is a track running in to the base of the turret. The compartment can not be water-tight.
Q. That compartment is open below deck?
A. Yes, sir.
Q. It does not open on the berth deck at all?
A. No, sir.
Q. But the after 10-inch handling room does open on the berth deck?
A. Yes, sir.
Q. On account of there being more heat there?
A. Yes, sir; it is over the evaporating room.

Q. Everything else is locked up at night, and reported so at 8 o'clock?
A. Yes, sir.
Q. Who are the men who make these reports?
A. The captain of the hold, the equipment yeoman, and the sailmaker's mate.
Q. Are they reliable men on board ship?
A. So far as I know; yes, sir.
Q. Did you yourself see these compartments closed at night, as a rule?
A. Yes, sir.
Q. Did you always find the duty properly executed by the men doing it?
A. I did.
Q. The regular captain of the hold, I believe, was sick at the time of the explosion. Do you know anything about the acting captain of the hold?
A. I do not.
Q. What division were you in last?
A. The third division.
Q. That is the after-turret division?
A. Yes, sir.
Q. Where were you at the time of the explosion?
A. I was in the steerage messroom—the junior officers' messroom.
Q. Please state what you saw, heard, and felt.
A. I was sitting in the steerage reading at the time. The lights went out. A crashing booming was heard. I was struck in the back of the head with a splinter, and remember no more of the explosion.
Q. Were you made senseless?
A. Yes, sir; so far as I know. I have an indistinct memory at the time.
Q. You rushed up on deck, you say, and were struck in the head there?
A. No, sir; I was in the steerage.
Q. Do you remember how many shocks you felt?
A. It was one continuous shock.
Q. One continuous shock was all you felt?
A. All I felt.
Q. You do not know how you got on deck?
A. Yes, sir; I remember perfectly.
Q. Did you feel any list of the ship or any lift of the ship?
A. Yes, sir.
Q. Describe it a little more fully, please.
A. When I collected my wits I grasped Assistant Engineer Merritt by the hand and told him to go up on deck. I pulled him out in the passage in the after torpedo room. We groped along the bulkhead until we came to the turn going over to the port side. At this moment the ship sank down amidships and heeled over on the port side. The rush of water swept us apart. I grasped the steam pipe overhead—the small steam-heater pipe—and worked my way down toward the steerage ladder, but it was gone. I worked my way over to the port side—on this steam-heater pipe—hoping to escape through some hole on the port side. The water was rushing through the air ports, so that I was not able to hang onto this small pipe. I grasped the torpedoes that were triced up under the deck beam, and, twining both arms and legs around it, I worked my way inboard toward the hatch, feeling the deck most of the time to find the hatch. The water at this time

was almost over my head; almost up to the deck. Some burning cellulose flared up on deck, and I saw the hatch and made for it. I escaped through a mass of débris, on the hatch part of which was the second cutter.

Q. Again referring to the shocks, what kind of a shock did you first feel?
A. As well as I can describe, the shock was more that of a large freight train being coupled up together.
Q. That was the first shock?
A. That was the first shock.
Q. The other was continuous, so far as you can remember, you say?
A. Yes, sir.
Q. A continual roar?
A. Yes, sir; and splinters and glass falling in the steerage.
Q. Was there any list to the ship?
A. Not until we got in the passage.
Q. Then she listed which way?
A. She listed to port.
Q. Was there any lifting of the ship?
A. She sank amidships.
Q. Was there any lifting of the ship?
A. No, sir; none that I remember.

By the COURT:

Q. You speak of being knocked senseless by a splinter. What kind of a splinter?
A. I think it must have been wooden.
Q. Where did the wood come from? The thing in my mind is, if you were knocked senseless with a splinter, how could you state that it was by a splinter?
A. I was struck on the back of the head. That is all I know.
Q. By something?
A. By something. There was a wooden bulkhead at the forward bulkhead of the steerage. I suppose it was wood from that.
Q. Did you, as mate of the deck, have anything to do with the care of the decks below the berth deck?
A. I did.
Q. How far down did your duties extend?
A. My duties extended to every compartment below the berth deck except the engine room and fire room and the engineer's storeroom.
Q. How did you get from the platform deck down to the hold or level of the magazines?
A. How could you get from the berth deck down to the hold?
Q. Yes; from the platform deck?
A. The fore hold?
Q. Yes; the fore hold.
A. There is a hatch in forward compartment A101. You go down two flights of ladders. The first is in the passage between the rooms. The second goes down to the fore hold itself. A101 is a berth-deck compartment.
Q. How did you get down to the magazines?
A. From the 10-inch magazine hatch in the loading room for the 10-inch turret.

The judge-advocate requested that the testimony given by the witness be not read to him by the stenographer, but that he be directed to report to-morrow morning at 10 o'clock, when he will be furnished with so much of the record as contains his testimony and asked to withdraw for the consideration of the same, upon the completion of which he will be again called before the court and be given an opportunity to amend his testimony as recorded, or pronounce it correct. The request was granted, and the witness was instructed accordingly. Whereupon he withdrew, after being cautioned by the president not to discuss matters pertaining to the inquiry.

The court then (at 1 o'clock p. m.) took a recess until 2 o'clock p. m.

The court reassembled at the expiration of the recess.
Present: All the members of the court, the judge-advocate, and the stenographer.

Lieut. GEORGE F. W. HOLMAN, U. S. Navy, a witness heretofore examined, was recalled as a witness before the court, and after being cautioned by the president of the court that the oath previously taken by him was still binding, testified as follows:

Examined by the JUDGE-ADVOCATE:

Q. Mr. Holman, on June 30, 1897, the commanding officer of the *Maine*, Captain Sigsbee, made out a report, giving the amount of ammunition in each magazine and shell room. I hold a copy of that report in my hand. Will you look at it and tell us whether it is a report made out from data furnished by you? (Exhibit G shown to the witness.)

A. I have no doubt it is. I can not recognize it from anything except the official letter transmitting it.

Q. You did assist your commanding officer in making up such a report?

A. I did; yes.

Q. Can you state what material changes have been made in the stowage since that report was made?

A. No material changes.

Q. Then you think it is a practically correct report at the time of the explosion?

A. I do.

Q. Will you please state where rockets and blue lights and such things were stowed on board the *Maine*?

A. In the chart house or the pilot house, upon the bridge.

Q. All of them?

A. All of them, I think. I do not know of any having been moved from there. They were stowed there originally, and I know of no move having been made.

By the COURT:

Q. Were you asked in your testimony before how many explosions you heard?

A. I heard and felt two, one a small one, a grumble I may call it, and then, after a very short interval, probably a fraction of a second, came the heavy, loud, booming explosion.

There being no further questions to ask this witness, his testimony was read over to him by the stenographer and by him pronounced correct.

The witness then withdrew, after being cautioned by the president not to converse about matters pertaining to the inquiry.

Lieut. A. W. CATLIN, U. S. Marine Corps, appeared as a witness before the court and was duly sworn by the president.

Examined by the JUDGE-ADVOCATE:

Q. Please state your name, rank, and to what ship you are attached.
A. A. W. Catlin, first lieutenant U. S. Marine Corps, attached to the U. S. S. *Maine*.
Q. How long have you been attached to the *Maine?*
A. Since the 1st of August.
Q. In charge of the marine guard of that ship?
A. In charge of the marine guard; yes, sir.
Q. August of last year?
A. August of last year, 1897; yes, sir.
Q. What special orders were given the marine guard of your ship during her last stay in Havana Harbor in the way of special precautions?
A. When we first went into the harbor, there were two extra sentinels put on, one on the forecastle and one on the poop, armed with rifles. They had special orders to challenge all boats which approached the ship near enough for a challenge, and in case any boat came toward the ship, evidently coming to the ship, to report immediately to the corporal of the guard, by the sentinel, and to the officer of the deck. These sentinels were on from 7 o'clock at night until daylight.
Q. Where was the corporal of the guard stationed?
A. The corporal of the guard was stationed in the starboard gangway.
Q. Was there an extra man in the port gangway?
A. There was a patrol in the port gangway.
Q. What do you mean by a patrol?
A. He went by the name of patrol, because his beat went up in the forward superstructure, as well as in the port gangway.
Q. He was a picked man?
A. Yes, sir.
Q. Acting as corporal?
A. He was an acting corporal; yes, sir.
Q. Doing a corporal's duties?
A. Yes, sir.
Q. What duties did the corporal of the guard and the patrol have, in the way of inspecting the ship at night?
A. The corporal's guard went below every half hour to inspect the ship lights, etc., and the patrol took his place in the starboard gangway while he was gone.
Q. All this was faithfully carried out to the best of your knowledge?
A. It was. I visited the sentries every night, once before and once after midnight, while we were in Havana Harbor, and always found them vigilant and attending to their duties properly.
Q. Where were you at the time of the explosion?
A. On the port side, in the wardroom. I was in room No. 8, which is the fourth room from forward.
Q. Just state to the court what you felt, heard, and saw of the actual explosion or explosions that may have occurred.
A. I was sitting in my room reading, when I heard—I do not know how to explain it—a dull sound, a loud concussion, and the shaking of the ship. What impressed me most was the falling of things around the deck—I suppose electric-light fixtures, etc. I immediately rushed up on deck. The lights went out immediately. I rushed up on deck, and as I came on deck I saw the whole heavens full of sparks. There

was no flame then, only sparks up above. Lieut. Commander Wainwright had just called away the boats. I went to where the barge was hanging. Do you wish me to go on from there?
Q. No; I only want the actual explosion.
A. That is all I know, sir.
Q. How many shocks did you feel?
A. I only felt one, sir.
Q. The lights went out at that shock?
A. Yes, sir; immediately.
Q. And it was all over by the time you reached the deck?
A. Yes, sir.
Q. Was there any listing of the ship?
A. The ship listed to port.
Q. Immediately?
A. I don't know, sir. She was listed by the time I got on deck.
Q. Did she seem to be lifted at the time of the shock?
A. I didn't notice it, sir.

The judge-advocate requested that the testimony given by the witness be not read to him by the stenographer, but that he be directed to report to-morrow morning at 10 o'clock, when he will be furnished with so much of the record as contains his testimony and asked to withdraw for the consideration of the same, upon the completion of which he will be again called before the court and be given an opportunity to amend his testimony as recorded, or pronounce it correct. The request was granted, and the witness was instructed accordingly; whereupon he withdrew, after being cautioned by the president not to discuss matters pertaining to the inquiry.

Gunner JOSEPH HILL, U. S. Navy, appeared as a witness before the court, and was duly sworn by the president.

Examined by the JUDGE-ADVOCATE:
Q. Please state your name, rank, and to what ship you are attached.
A. Joseph Hill, gunner, United States Navy, attached to the U. S. S. *Maine*.
Q. How long have you been attached to the *Maine*?
A. About twenty-nine months.
Q. Ever since her commission?
A. Yes, sir.
Q. When were you relieved from duty as gunner last?
A. It was on or about the 18th of January, 1898.
Q. Will you look at this report of Captain Sigsbee, this being a copy of it, and state whether that seems to be practically correct in regard to the stowage of ammunition on board the *Maine* [Exhibit G shown to the witness].
A. This is about it. Do you mean at the time of the accident?
Q. I mean whether that is a correct report on June 30?
A. Yes, sir; that is about right.
Q. State to the court what material changes have been made since June 30, 1897, of any kind, in the stowage of ammunition.
A. I believe we have had small-arm target practice once. I think most of the small-arm ammunition was used up on board, but, as I understand, some time after I was put under suspension, they received about 70,000 rounds of 6-minimeter ball cartridges; also about 7,000 rounds of blank cartridges, 6-minimeter, and as near as I can understand there was some of that stored in the forward fixed-ammunition

room and some in the after fixed-ammunition room, and perhaps some was stowed in the armory. I am not sure about it.
Q. Where was the armory situated?
A. It was a little abaft of the midship line.
Q. On the main deck?
A. On the upper deck; yes, sir.
Q. Will you look specially at the amount of ammunition in the 6-inch reserve magazine, and tell us whether that was practically the amount there at the time of the explosion?
A. I see there is a lot of saluting powder here. Of course at the time I was put under suspension I believe it was somewhere about that, but since that I could not state what changes have been made there.
Q. Do you think the 6-inch charges were put there at that time?
A. Yes, sir.
Q. How were those 6-inch charges stowed? Were they stowed against the bulkheads or clear of the bulkheads, or how?
A. They were stowed on wooden racks that were made fast to the metal bulkheads.
Q. Did the powder tanks abut against the bulkheads?
A. Yes, sir.
Q. Did they abut against the bulkhead which divided the coal bunker from the 6-inch reserve magazine?
A. Yes, sir; the after tier did. The forward tier did not, because they were still forward.
Q. They were against the bulkhead?
A. Yes, sir.
Q. They abutted against the outboard bulkhead, I understand you to say?
A. In the reserve magazine?
Q. Yes.
A. No, sir; in the after one.
Q. You do not know which bunker that was against?
A. No, sir.
Q. But they did not abut against the fore and aft bulkhead on the outboard of the magazine?
A. The side of the tank was laying up there, I understand, but the end of the tank was aft. The tanks were stored fore and aft.
Q. You think they touched that outboard bulkhead which divides the magazine from the coal bunker?
A. Yes, sir.
Q. I will show you the plan. This bulkhead [pointing to a fore-and-aft bulkhead] divides the magazine from coal bunker A16. Did powder touch that bulkhead in its stowage?
A. Yes, sir; it did aft here.
Q. It did in the after part of the magazine.
A. Yes, sir; and it did in the forward part, too, because there was a lot of spare saluting powder stowed there.
Q. And that was close against the bulkhead?
A. Yes, sir; as near as I can remember the date of my suspension.
Q. Did you take the temperature of the magazines and shell rooms, as prescribed by regulations, regularly?
A. Yes, sir; I always made a practice of seeing the gunners take it.
Q. It was regularly taken, was it?
A. Once a day.
Q. Was there anything stowed in the magazines and shell rooms in

the way of high explosives or anything of that kind which should not have been stowed there according to ordnance instructions?
    A. No, sir; I don't know of anything, to the date of my suspension.
    Q. Were magazines and shell rooms always carefully locked after they had been opened?
    A. Yes, sir.
    Q. And the keys turned in?
    A. Yes, sir.
    Q. There was always a regular care taken in the delivery of the keys and the locking of the shell room and magazines?
    A. Yes, sir.
    Q. Are the magazines lined with wood?
    A. No, sir; not as I remember. The plates are bare, of course, and the only woodwork I remember there is the stowage racks, holding powder, tanks, and shells. They are made fast to the metal bulkhead.
    Q. Is there any electric wiring that leads into the magazine that would be dangerous?
    A. No, sir; the wires seemed to be well insulated. Of course they led into the light box, but, as I remember, they came down through the deck, and then went at an angle into the light box itself. As I remember it, the wires went through a metal casing.
    Q. You considered the wiring perfectly secure?
    A. Yes, sir; of course it may have been woodwork painted over white, but I never examined it very closely. It looked very much to me as if it was metal.
    Q. You never had any trouble with the light boxes in the way of grounding—with the lights in the light boxes?
    A. Yes, sir; the dynamo tenders found considerable trouble in keeping the magazine lights in order. They always gave as an excuse that the system was grounded down around the boxes.
    Q. But the wiring laid directly from the upper deck into the boxes, in two metal cases?
    A. Yes, sir; but as I remember it, I think it went down through the deck in some places, and then went at an angle into the light box itself.
    Q. Where were you at the time of the explosion?
    A. I was in Havana.
    Q. On shore?
    A. Yes, sir.

    By the COURT:
    Q. How were the 6-inch powder tanks stowed with reference to the keel of the ship in the reserve magazines?
    A. They are stowed in line with the keel, I should judge about 5 or 10 feet away from the keel, to port.
    Q. How were they stowed? What kept them in place?
    A. Some wooden racks which secured the metal bulkheads in the magazine, and the powder was stowed right on the racks.
    Q. Tell us how these racks were made.
    A. The magazine itself seemed to be divided. The after half of it was divided into two compartments, fore and aft like, and there were strong wooden uprights, secured in place to the deck above and to the inner bottom of the ship, and from this ran athwartships some other battens, a sufficient distance apart so as to have the bottom tank rest on one and the lid or upper part of the tank on the other.
    Q. They were stowed on the side, were they not?
    A. Yes, sir; the tanks were stowed on the side.

Q. Were these battens on which the tanks rested straight?
A. Yes, sir; they were horizontal.
Q. They were not cut out to receive the tank?
A. No, sir.
Q. Were these upright supports between the horizontal battens placed on both sides, at the ends of these horizontal battens?
A. Yes, sir; as near as I can remember.
Q. Then one was against the bulkhead and the other was inside the magazine?
A. Yes, sir.
Q. Please explain how the powder tanks could have rested against the bulkheads.
A. The racks were secured with crosspieces, horizontal and athwartships. When the tank was shoved in place, it was shoved right aft, directly against the metal bulkheads.
Q. Where were these upright strips?
A. The upright strips were fore and aft in the magazine, making two bends like that [indicating].
Q. Fore and aft?
A. Two compartments, like.
(The witness here drew a sketch and explained what he meant by reference to the sketch.)

The judge-advocate requested that the testimony given by the witness be not read to him by the stenographer, but that he be directed to report to-morrow morning at 10 o'clock, when he will be furnished with so much of the record as contains his testimony, and asked to withdraw for the consideration of the same, upon the completion of which he will be again called before the court and be given an opportunity to amend his testimony as recorded, or pronounce it correct. The request was granted, and the witness was instructed accordingly; whereupon he withdrew, after being cautioned by the president not to discuss matters pertaining to the inquiry.

Boatswain FRANCIS E. LARKIN, U. S. Navy, appeared as a witness before the court and was duly sworn by the president:

Examined by the JUDGE-ADVOCATE:

Q. Please state your name, rank, and to what ship you are attached.
A. Francis E. Larkin, boatswain, U. S. Navy, attached to the U. S. S. Maine.
Q. How long have you been attached to the Maine?
A. From September, at the time of going in commission, until the present time.
Q. Were you on board the Maine the night of her explosion?
A. I was.
Q. Did you make the usual 8 p. m. reports to the executive officer?
A. Yes, sir; I did.
Q. Was everything secure in your department when you so reported?
A. Yes, sir.
Q. Where were you at the time of the explosion?
A. Sitting abaft the after turret.
Q. On the main deck?
A. On the main deck.
Q. Please describe what you saw, felt, and heard.
A. I remember hearing an explosion. I do not remember the violence of it. I was struck on the head about the same time and dazed. I

attempted to rise and fell again. Then I remember crawling over the wing awning on the port side of the cabin up on the poop deck.

Q. How did you get there?

A. I climbed over a small wing awning on the poop deck. I helped to lower the gig, letting down a 6-inch gun port in the rear, and breasting the gig off as she lowered. I then jumped in and took an oar.

Q. You do not remember distinctly the explosions, then?

A. No, sir.

Q. You do not know whether there was one or whether there was two, three, or four explosions?

A. No, sir.

Q. You do not remember any movement of the ship when the explosion first occurred?

A. Just a rendering and swaying all around me. It may have been from my dazed condition, or it may have been from the ship.

By the COURT:

Q. You went out in the boat to pick up the people in the water?

A. Yes, sir; we were pretty close to the wreck all the time. We picked up two or three men and handed them in other boats alongside.

Q. Where were these men?

A. There was one man picked out of a mass of wreckage there. I don't know what it was. I think Thompson was the man's name. I remember him being landed in the gig and given to another boat.

Q. On which side of the ship did you pick the man up?

A. On the starboard side.

Q. Were you at any time on the port side?

A. No, sir.

Q. Were there any men in the water on that side?

A. I didn't see any.

Q. You did not see any men on the port side?

A. On the starboard side. I didn't see anything at all on the port side.

Q. I asked you if you saw any men on the port side, and you said you did not.

A. No, sir.

Q. The gig lowered on the starboard side?

A. Yes, sir.

The judge-advocate requested that the testimony given by the witness be not read to him by the stenographer, but that he be directed to report to-morrow morning at 10 o'clock, when he will be furnished with so much of the record as contains his testimony and asked to withdraw for the consideration of the same, upon the completion of which he will be again called before the court and be given an opportunity to amend his testimony as recorded or pronounce it correct. The request was granted, and the witness was instructed accordingly; whereupon he withdrew, after being cautioned by the president not to discuss matters pertaining to the inquiry.

Carpenter GEORGE HELM, U. S. Navy, appeared as a witness before the court, and was duly sworn by the president.

Examined by the JUDGE-ADVOCATE:

Q. State your name, rank, and to what ship you are attached.

A. George Helm; carpenter, U. S. Navy; attached to U. S. S. *Maine*.

Q. How long have you been attached to the *Maine?*

A. Since the 17th of September, 1895.
Q. That is, since her commission?
A. I was ordered to her two weeks before then.
Q. And you became acquainted with the *Maine*, then, some time before she went into commission?
A. About two weeks.
Q. Since you have been attached to the *Maine* you have done a great deal of work below the berth deck in regard to keeping the compartments clean and in proper order, and all that?
A. Yes, sir.
Q. You are well acquainted with the *Maine?*
A. Yes, sir; thoroughly.
Q. Do you know anything about the construction of the magazines of the *Maine?*
A. I have an idea.
Q. Could you tell how the powder is stored in the reserve 6-inch magazines?
A. No, sir.
Q. You do not know how the racks are constructed?
A. No, sir.
Q. What is the thickness of the bulkhead between the reserve magazine and the 10-inch shell room?
A. A quarter of an inch, 10 pounds plating.
Q. And the same between the 10-inch shell room and the 10-inch magazine?
A. The same.
Q. Where is the water-tight bulkhead abaft the reserve magazine; immediately next to it?
A. I don't quite understand that.
Q. What water-tight bulkhead is there abaft the reserve magazine? Does it abut against it or not?
A. That is a continuous bulkhead.
Q. There is a water-tight bulkhead immediately abaft it?
A. Yes, sir.
Q. What is the thickness of that bulkhead?
A. Quarter inch 10 pound plating.
Q. Is there one immediately forward of the reserve magazine?
A. Yes; that is a water-tight bulkhead.
Q. Is there one between the forward 6-inch magazine and the fixed ammunition room?
A. Yes; that is water-tight.
Q. Is there one immediately forward of the forward 6-inch magazine?
A. That is water-tight.
Q. Were all bulkheads and everything in good condition on board the *Maine* just previous to her explosion?
A. First-class condition.
Q. What water-tight doors were in good condition?
A. They were all in good condition.
Q. Had the regular inspections been made all the time the ship was in commission?
A. Yes, sir.
Q. Did you make the 8 p. m. reports on the night of her explosion to the executive officer?
A. I did, sir.
Q. Was everything secure, as you reported it?
A. Everything was secure.
Q. Where were you at the time of the explosion?

A. I was in my bunk.
Q. Where is your bunk located?
A. Compartment C100.
Q. The forward end of that compartment?
A. The forward end, right alongside of the armor of the barbette or turret.
Q. It is on the berth deck?
A. On the port side.
Q. Well outboard?
A. Well outboard, near the skin of the ship.
Q. Just forward of the torpedoes?
A. Just forward of the torpedoes.
Q. Please state what you felt, heard, and saw during the time of the explosions.
A. I only heard one report.
Q. What did it feel like?
A. It just felt about like a 6-inch or a 10-inch gun going off, as near as I can remember.
Q. That is all you heard?
A. That is all I heard.
Q. Were you injured in any way?
A. None that I know of; no, sir.
Q. You got on deck without any trouble?
A. I got on deck with considerable trouble; that is, onto the main deck.
Q. Did the ship seem to shake or shiver any during this report?
A. None that I can remember.
Q. Did she list any?
A. She listed to starboard. That is about all I can say.
Q. Were you wide awake when the thing first happened?
A. No, sir.
Q. Were you asleep?
A. Yes, sir.

By the COURT:

Q. Are you so intimately acquainted with the construction of the *Maine* that you could recognize portions of the wreck—that is, I mean of the hull—take a part of the hull detached from where it belongs entirely?
A. I don't know about that.
Q. Longitudinals and so on?
A. I guess they would be pretty hard to recognize, unless there is something there to go by, such as main drains or sluice valves, or something like that, that you could locate.
Q. Could you tell anything of the longitudinals? Are they not different in width or in depth?
A. Very little. I don't suppose there is more than 3 or 4 inches difference.
Q. How many longitudinals were there?
A. There were three, first, second, and third, and the bottom of the lower wing passage formed the fourth, and the upper wing passage formed the fifth.
Q. How high did the highest longitudinal come?
A. The third longitudinal is water-tight. The fifth is formed by the upper wing passage.
Q. Are not these longitudinals sufficient in depth to be able to recognize them from their depth?

A. Forward you could; yes. I guess you could recognize them forward as they taper so low there.
Q. What was the thickness of the protective deck of that ship?
A. Two inches. That is, two 1-inch plates riveted together.
Q. What was the thickness of her side armor?
A. Her side armor was 11 inch.
Q. All over?
A. No; it tapered down to 7 inches.
Q. Did it taper fore and aft?
A. It tapered aft.
Q. What was the thickness of the wood backing?
A. That I don't know.
Q. What were the sizes of the armor bolts?
A. The wooden backing was 8 inches.
Q. As far as you remember, how big were the bolts?
A. The bolts for screwing the armor were between $3\frac{3}{4}$ and 4 inches in diameter.

By the JUDGE-ADVOCATE:

Q. You said the armor belt was 11 inches. Are you certain of that? Was it not 12?
A. All I have to go by is the plan. [After examination of the plan.] They are 12 inches on top; yes, sir.
Q. What do you mean by saying the armor belt tapered aft?
A. She tapered aft abaft the engine room.
Q. You mean it sloped down aft?
A. It sloped; yes, sir.
Q. It did not taper and get thinner as it went aft, did it?
A. Oh, no.

By the COURT:

Q. That is what I understood you to mean.
A. That they get thinner?
Q. Yes.
A. No; it slopes.

By the JUDGE-ADVOCATE:

Q. How far down did the double bottoms extend?
A. The double bottoms extended from frame 12 forward to frame 73 forward.
Q. How far did the bilge keel extend forward?
A. The bilge keel started in, I think, at frame 28.
Q. Do you know how far they were from the keel?
A. No, I do not.

The judge advocate requested that the testimony given by the witness be not read to him by the stenographer, but that he be directed to report to-morrow morning at 10 o'clock, when he will be furnished with so much of the record as contains his testimony and asked to withdraw for the consideration of the same, upon the completion of which he will be again called before the court and be given an opportunity to amend his testimony as recorded, or pronounce it correct. The request was granted and the witness was instructed accordingly; whereupon he withdrew, after being cautioned by the president not to discuss matters pertaining to the inquiry.

The court then, at 3.10 o'clock p. m., adjourned until 10 o'clock to-morrow morning, Tuesday, March 1, 1898.

EIGHTH DAY.

U. S. COURT-HOUSE, KEY WEST, FLA.,
Tuesday, March 1, 1898—10 a. m.

The court met pursuant to adjournment of yesterday.

Present: All the members of the court, the judge-advocate, and the stenographer.

The record of the proceedings of yesterday, the seventh day of the trial, was read and approved.

Lieutenant BLANDIN, U. S. Navy, was called before the court and handed so much of the record of yesterday as contained his testimony, whereupon he withdrew.

Lieutenant HOOD was called before the court and handed so much of the record of yesterday as contained his testimony, whereupon he withdrew.

Lieutenant BLOW was called before the court and handed so much of the record of yesterday as contained his testimony, whereupon he withdrew.

Lieutenant JUNGEN was called before the court and handed so much of the record of yesterday as contained his testimony, whereupon he withdrew.

Naval Cadet BRONSON was called before the court and handed so much of the record of yesterday as contained his testimony, whereupon he withdrew.

Lieutenant CATLIN was called before the court and handed so much of the record of yesterday as contained his testimony, whereupon he withdrew.

Gunner HILL was called before the court and handed so much of the record of yesterday as contained his testimony, whereupon he withdrew.

Boatswain LARKIN was called before the court and handed so much of the record of yesterday as contained his testimony, whereupon he withdrew.

Carpenter HELM was called before the court and handed so much of the record of yesterday as contained his testimony, whereupon he withdrew.

P. A. Eng. FREDERICK C. BOWERS, U. S. Navy, appeared as a witness before the court, and was duly sworn by the president.

Examined by the JUDGE-ADVOCATE:

Q. Please state your full name, rank, and to what ship you are attached.

A. Frederick C. Bowers; passed assistant engineer, U. S. Navy; attached to the U. S. S. *Maine*.

Q. How long have you been attached to the *Maine*; since her commission?

A. Since her commission.

Q. Are you the senior assistant engineer to the chief?

A. Yes, sir.

Q. And you have been all the time since the ship has been in commission?

A. I have.

Q. Please state to the court what precautions have been taken on board the *Maine* during her commission against spontaneous combustion of coal?

A. The order has been to inspect the bunkers every day, and log it. In the case of every bunker that had an escape door, we have always opened those doors to examine the bunkers; and generally the coal that has been in the ship the longest has been used the first, as near as possible.

Q. As far as you know, these orders have been carried out, have they?

A. Whenever I was on duty they were.

Q. When were you on duty last on board the *Maine?*

A. The 14th day of February.

Q. The day before the explosion?

A. Yes, sir.

Q. You came off that morning at what time?

A. At 8 o'clock.

Q. Can you give the history of bunker A16, which is the port bunker forward abreast of the 6-inch reserve magazine? Give the history of the coal inside.

A. That bunker was stored in either Newport News, Va., or at Norfolk. It contained soft coal; Pocahontas, I think. If it came from Norfolk, I inspected it. It was full of soft coal, about 40 tons.

Q. Were not the bunkers immediately abaft of it, B4 and B6, empty?

A. Yes, sir.

Q. The after bulkhead of A16 was easily accessible?

A. Yes, sir.

Q. What other sides were accessible to ascertain the temperature in case it should have been over hot?

A. You could feel it from the wing passage, and there was an escape door on platform deck A. There was a sign there, "Keep that door closed." That was on account of the opening into the passing room, the loading room.

Q. The 10-inch loading room?

A. Yes, sir; I have a sketch here that I made of the bunker showing the capacity.

Q. We only care for A16.

By the COURT:

Q. Just show me on the plan here where that bunker was accessible. Was it on that deck [indicating]?

A. No, sir; it was the deck above that—on the dynamo deck. That escape door came out here to go into the wing passage. There was an escape door in this corner, away forward—the inboard forward corner.

Q. That was not on the same deck as the magazines?

A. No, sir.

Q. The magazine was below that?

A. Below that; yes, sir. It was just the reverse of the other side. The other tank had an escape door below on the hydraulic room, platform B deck, at the after end. I mean the bunker on the other side, No. A15. That escape door was aft, and was on the platform deck below.

Q. There were two platform decks?

A. Yes; one for the dynamos, and the other for the hydraulic plant.

Q. On this deck [indicating] there was no way of reaching that bunker on the inside, was there?

A. On the outside.

Q. On the outside, but next to the 6-inch magazine?

A. No, sir.

Q. There was no way of reaching that?
A. We generally stored that bunker full, and did not use that escape door for the man to come out. We let him come out of the chute. We always wanted to keep that bunker full.

By the JUDGE-ADVOCATE:

Q. You say you inspected that coal when it was put into bunker A16?
A. If the coal came from Norfolk, I did. I was sent over there to inspect it.
Q. Did you consider it safe and reliable coal, from your inspection?
A. Yes, sir.
Q What is your opinion as to the heat generated in a bunker which has become lighted by spontaneous combustion in the bottom? Would it affect the upper part of the bottom materially and heat the bulkheads?
A. We could notice it very materially, I should think.
Q. In the upper part of the bunker?
A. Yes, sir.
Q. Was bunker A15 being used at the time?
A. When I went off watch we were using what we used from No. 4 bunker. We numbered them all.
Q. It is the forward starboard bunker, is it not?
A. Yes; when I went off watch we were using the after bunker in the forward fire room—the wing bunker—at 8 o'clock.
Q. Please point it out on the plan.
A. We were using coal out of this bunker, B10.
Q. Had you not been using coal out of A15?
A. Previously; yes, sir. When we were using coal out of B10, we had possibly about fifteen tons in this bunker.
Q. That is all?
A. Yes, sir.
Q. How much would it hold?
A. Twenty-five tons, when full.
Q. Do you know of any steam pipes in the *Maine* that were in dangerous proximity to the magazines and shell rooms?
A. No, sir.
Q. What was the condition of the after boilers—the two that were used for auxiliary purposes?
A. The fires were practically banked on the six furnaces of the two boilers. In what respect do you mean?
Q. The condition of the boilers.
A. The boilers were in good condition—in very good condition.
Q. You do not consider there was any danger of their having too much pressure on for safety when you were working them for auxiliary purposes on the evening of the explosion?
A. No, sir; the safety valves blow at about 130 pounds, and we usually carried 80 to 100 for auxiliary purposes.
Q. Where were you at the time of the explosion?
A. I was ashore.

By the COURT:

Q. In reference to taking the temperature of the bunkers, you say there was an order to examine them daily where they were accessible?
A. Yes, sir.
Q. In what did the examination consist?
A. Opening the escape doors where they had them, and feeling around the sides of the bunkers.

Q. Did you have the usual thermostats in the bunkers?
A. Yes, sir; but they didn't work very well. Sometimes they rang when there was no coal in the bunker.
Q. I believe you never had a fire from spontaneous combustion in that ship, did you?
A. No, sir. We thought we did once, but it was a leaky steampipe— a leaky exhaust pipe from the ice machine.

By the JUDGE-ADVOCATE:
Q. It gave the alarm?
A. It gave the alarm, and they moved the coal.

The Judge-Advocate requested that the testimony given by the witness be not read to him by the stenographer, but that he be directed to report to-morrow morning at 10 o'clock, when he will be furnished with so much of the record as contains his testimony and asked to withdraw for the consideration of the same, upon the completion of which he will be again called before the court and be given an opportunity to amend his testimony as recorded, or pronounce it correct. The request was granted, and the witness was instructed accordingly; whereupon he withdrew, after being cautioned by the president not to discuss matters pertaining to the trial.

Lieutenant JUNGEN was called before the court and handed so much of the record of yesterday as contained his testimony, whereupon he withdrew.

Asst. Eng. JOHN R. MORRIS, U. S. Navy, appeared as a witness before the court, and was duly sworn by the president.

Examined by the JUDGE-ADVOCATE:
Q. State your full name, rank, and to what ship you are at present attached.
A. John R. Morris, assistant engineer, U. S. Navy; attached to the U. S. S. *Maine*.
Q. How long have you been attached to the *Maine*?
A. Fourteen months and fifteen days.
Q. What has been your duty?
A. Serving as assistant engineer.
Q. Do you know of the orders of the ship in regard to taking temperatures of coal bunkers when you were on duty?
A. The bunkers were to be inspected every day, to see how they were heated. They were taken every day.
Q. Have you always carried out that order when on duty?
A. Yes, sir.
Q. When were you on duty last in the *Maine*?
A. February 15.
Q. You were on duty the day of the explosion?
A. Yes, sir.
Q. When did you inspect the bunkers on that day?
A. It was some time during the forenoon; I think between 10 and 11 o'clock.
Q. Can you remember distinctly making a careful inspection of bunker A16, the port forward bunker?
A. I remember of opening the escape doors, and there was no heat perceptible, more than just the temperature of the hydraulic room, which is next to the bunker.

Q. You made a careful inspection of that bunker on that day?
A. Yes, sir.
Q. In the forenoon?
A. In the forenoon; yes, sir.
Q. About what time?
A. About 10.30.
Q. Had you any occasion to go in coal bunkers B4 and B6, which were being painted? They are just abaft A16.
A. Yes, sir; I had had those bunker doors closed that night—the bunkers we had been painting.
Q. Which night?
A. The night of the explosion. The inspection was at 7.45.
Q. P. m.?
A. Yes, sir.
Q. Did you go into B4 and B6 at 7.45 p. m.?
A. Yes, sir; I went into B6.
Q. If there had been any combustion going on in A16 would you have noticed it when you went in B6?
A. Yes, sir; I looked into A15.
Q. I am speaking of A16, the port bunker. Which bunker did you go into at 7.45?
A. It was A15 that closed the door to B4.
Q. You did not go into B4?
A. I looked inside; yes, sir. There was nothing unusual there. I simply had the door closed down, as it was night inspection. I did not enter B6.
Q. What work had been going on in B4 and B6 that day?
A. None at all, sir. We had completed painting in those bunkers.
Q. Before you came on duty?
A. Yes, sir.
Q. Where were you at the time of the explosion?
A. I was sitting on the quarter deck—on the port side of the quarter deck, just abaft the after turret.
Q. Will you please state to the court what you felt, heard, and saw of the explosion?
A. I was thrown from a chair, and what I remember of the explosion seemed to me continuous for an appreciable length of time. I was then partially overcome by escaping gases from the smokestack from live boilers, and I was not conscious of anything further so that I could recall anything until I had gained the poop deck.
Q. What was the first sensation you had—the first shock you felt?
A. I saw fire and felt the ship going from under me. I can hardly describe my sensation.
Q. Were you asleep at the time in your chair?
A. No, sir; I was talking.
Q. Your view forward was obstructed by the turret, was it not?
A. Yes, sir.
Q. You could not describe any sensation you had or what you really heard or felt?
A. No, sir, I can not. I don't even remember the noise.

By the COURT:

Q. How were you thrown from your chair?
A. I was thrown aft, sir. At least I thought I was. I think I remember falling over that way. I was sitting talking to one of the other officers.

Q. Were you sitting abaft Mr. Hood?
A. Mr. Hood was on the other side of the deck. I was sitting abaft Mr. Larkin.
Q. On which side?
A. On the port side.
Q. You were on the port side?
A. I was on the port side, yes, sir; right out to the rail.
Q. That was Mr. Hood's side.
A. I don't remember where he was.
Q. You were thrown from your chair by the motion of the deck of the ship on which you sat?
A. Yes, sir; that is my recollection.
Q. You can not say what that motion was?
A. No, sir; I can not.

The judge-advocate requested that the testimony given by the witness be not read to him by the stenographer, but that he be directed to report to-morrow morning at 10 o'clock, when he will be furnished with so much of the record as contains his testimony and asked to withdraw for the consideration of the same, upon the completion of which he will be again called before the court and be given an opportunity to amend his testimony as recorded or pronounce it correct. The request was granted, and the witness was instructed accordingly; whereupon he withdrew, after being cautioned by the president not to discuss matters pertaining to the inquiry.

Naval Cadet POPE WASHINGTON, U. S. Navy, appeared as a witness before the court and was duly sworn by the president.

Examined by the JUDGE-ADVOCATE:

Q. State your name, rank, and to what ship you are attached.
A. Pope Washington; naval cadet; U. S. Navy.
Q. You are in the engineer department?
A. I am an engineer cadet; yes, sir.
Q. Attached to the U. S. S. *Maine?*
A. Yes, sir.
Q. How long have you been attached to the *Maine?*
A. Since the 17th of May, 1897.
Q. Where were you on the night of the destruction of the *Maine?*
A. I was in Havana.
Q. You were not on board?
A. No, sir.

There being no further questions to ask this witness, his testimony was read over to him by the stenographer and by him pronounced correct.

The witness then withdrew, after being cautioned by the president not to converse about matters pertaining to the inquiry.

Naval Cadet ARTHUR CRENSHAW, U. S. Navy, appeared as a witness before the court and was duly sworn by the president.

Examined by the JUDGE-ADVOCATE:

Q. State your name, rank, and to what ship you are attached.
A. Arthur Crenshaw; naval cadet, engineer division; attached to the U. S. S. *Maine.*
Q. Where were you on the night of the destruction of the *Maine?*
A. I was in my room, sir.

DESTRUCTION OF THE U. S. BATTLE SHIP MAINE.

Q. Which was your room?
A. The forward room of the junior officers' quarters.
Q. Was there anyone else in you room?
A. Mr. Bronson.
Q. Please state to the court what you felt, heard, and saw of the destruction of the *Maine?*
A. I don't remember of hearing anything. The lights went out, and I felt a shock, but I don't remember of hearing any noise of any kind.
Q. Were you asleep at the time?
A. No, sir.
Q. How many shocks did you feel?
A. I can't say that I felt but one, sir.
Q. Was it a lurch of the ship or a shaking of the ship, or what?
A. It seemed to be a lurch of the ship.
Q. You are quite sure you were not asleep and that this woke you up?
A. I am quite sure I was not asleep sir.
Q. That is all you know about it?
A. Yes, sir.

By the COURT:

Q. You say you were in your room?
A. Yes, sir.
Q. Your room was which one?
A. The forward room of the junior officers' quarters.
Q. Was there anybody else in that room with you?
A. Yes, sir.
Q. Who was it?
A. Mr. Bronson.
Q. Were you in your berth?
A. No, sir; I was sitting down at my desk.
Q. You heard no noise?
A. No, sir; not that I can remember. It was simply a shock and the lights were extinguished.
Q. When the lights went out what did you do?
A. I rushed out of my room, sir, into the junior officers' mess room and then out of the forward door of the junior officers' mess room, and, it seemed to me, through the door that leads into the compartment just forward of that. There was a rushing noise of some kind. I couldn't tell just exactly what it was, so I made my way aft.
Q. You went aft through the passage?
A. Yes, sir.
Q. Then what did you do?
A. I ran for the steerage ladder.
Q. Just abaft the turret?
A. Yes, sir; it leads up just abaft the turret. There was no ladder there, though.
Q. There was no ladder there?
A. No, sir; not that I could feel. I couldn't see anything. I could feel no ladder there.
Q. Then what did you do?
A. Then I felt for the engine hatch bulkhead, that leads up in that compartment and felt my way along that to the wardroom ladder.
Q. You went up the wardroom ladder?
A. Yes, sir.
Q. Do you know what the other officer, your roommate, did?
A. No, sir; I do not. I supposed he was right behind me, though, sir. I couldn't say.

Q. Was he in the room at the time you were?
A. Yes, sir.
Q. Did the water reach the compartment where you were before you left it?
A. No, sir.

The judge-advocate requested that the testimony given by the witness be not read to him by the stenographer, but that he be directed to report to-morrow morning at 10 o'clock, when he will be furnished with so much of the record as contains his testimony and asked to withdraw for the consideration of the same, upon the completion of which he will be again called before the court and be given an opportunity to amend his testimony as recorded or pronounce it correct. The request was granted, and the witness was instructed accordingly; whereupon he withdrew, after being cautioned by the president not to discuss matters pertaining to the inquiry.

Lieutenant BLANDIN here entered the court.
The JUDGE-ADVOCATE. Do you wish to make some corrections in your testimony?
Lieutenant BLANDIN. Yes, sir.
The JUDGE-ADVOCATE. Please state them to the stenographer.
Lieutenant BLANDIN. On page 242, in next to the last line, it should read "dog watches" instead of "deck watches."
On page 243, the last paragraph should read: "After the third quarter watch was set at 9 o'clock at pipe down."
On page 244, in the eighth line, it should be "knee deep" instead of "not deep."
In the tenth line, on the same page, it should read, after the word "poop," "it was Private Loftus, I think,"
On page 246, in the tenth line, insert "had" before "swung."
On page 247, in the seventh paragraph, it should read "almost immediate" instead of "almost within a minute."
The JUDGE-ADVOCATE. Is your testimony as amended correct?
Lieutenant BLANDIN. Yes, sir.

The witness then withdrew, after being cautioned by the president not to converse about matters pertaining to the inquiry.

Naval Cadet BRONSON entered.
The JUDGE-ADVOCATE. You have read over your testimony?
Naval Cadet BRONSON. Yes, sir.
The JUDGE-ADVOCATE. Is it correct?
Naval Cadet BRONSON. With the exception of two small mistakes.
The JUDGE-ADVOCATE. Please state what the mistakes are that you wish to correct.
Naval Cadet BRONSON. In the third answer, on page 294, it should read: "I have performed boat duty, deck duty under the supervision of the commissioned officer of the deck."
On page 295, the third answer—the third sentence of that answer—should be removed—"That is the impression which I have now." I have not any such impression as that now.
The JUDGE-ADVOCATE. What is the third sentence which you wish removed?
Naval Cadet BRONSON. "That is the impression which I have now."
The JUDGE-ADVOCATE. You want that stricken out?
Naval Cadet BRONSON. Yes, sir.
The JUDGE-ADVOCATE. Is your testimony as amended correct?

Naval-Cadet BRONSON. Yes, sir.

The witness then withdrew, after being cautioned by the president not to converse on matters pertaining to the inquiry.

Lieutenant CATLIN entered.

The JUDGE-ADVOCATE. You have read over your testimony?
Lieutenant CATLIN. Yes, sir.
The JUDGE-ADVOCATE. Is it correct?
Lieutenant CATLIN. Except in one instance.
The JUDGE-ADVOCATE. Please read to the stenographer the corrections you wish to make.
Lieutenant CATLIN. In answer to question 5, on page 306, I wish to change the language as follows:

When we first went into the harbor, there were two extra sentinels put on—one on the forecastle and one on the poop—armed with rifles. They had special orders to challenge all boats which approached the ship near enough for a challenge, and in case any boat came toward the ship—evidently coming to the ship—to report immediately to the corporal of the guard, who would report to the officer of the deck.

On page 307, line 12, it should read, "The corporal of the guard," instead of "The corporal's guard."
At the bottom of the page it should be "a heavy concussion," instead of "a loud concussion."
The JUDGE-ADVOCATE. Is your testimony as amended now correct?
Lieutenant CATLIN. Yes, sir.

The witness then withdrew, after being cautioned by the president not to converse on matters pertaining to the inquiry.

Boatswain LARKIN entered.
The JUDGE-ADVOCATE. You have read over your testimony?
Boatswain LARKIN. Yes, sir.
The JUDGE-ADVOCATE. Is it correct, as recorded?
Boatswain LARKIN. With two changes.
The JUDGE-ADVOCATE. State what corrections you wish to make.
Boatswain LARKIN. I wish the answer to the question "How did you get there?" meaning the poop deck, on page 318, to appear as follows: "I climbed over a small wing awning on the main deck leading to the poop deck, on the port side of the cabin."
The JUDGE-ADVOCATE. You wish to change the first sentence in that answer, do you, to what you have just said?
Boatswain LARKIN. "I climbed over a small wing awning on the poop deck" should be "I climbed over a small wing awning on the main deck leading to the poop deck, on the port side of the cabin."
The JUDGE-ADVOCATE. That is the way you want it to read—that first sentence?
Boatswain LARKIN. Yes, sir.
On page 319, in answer to the question "You did not see any men on the port side?" I wish to say, "I didn't see anything at all on the port side."
The JUDGE-ADVOCATE. That is the way you wish your answer to read?
Boatswain LARKIN. Yes, sir.
The JUDGE-ADVOCATE. Is your testimony, as amended, correct?
Boatswain LARKIN. Yes, sir.

The witness then withdrew, after being cautioned by the president not to converse on matters pertaining to the inquiry.

Private EDWARD MCKAY, U. S. Marine Corps, appeared as a witness before the court, and was duly sworn by the president.

Examined by the JUDGE-ADVOCATE:

Q. State your full name, rank, and to what ship you are attached?
A. Edward McKay, private, U. S. Marine Corps, attached to U. S. battle ship *Maine*.
Q. Were you on board the *Maine* at the time of her destruction?
A. Yes, sir.
Q. State exactly where you were at the first intimation there was of any trouble.
A. I was right on the poop.
Q. On which side?
A. I was on the starboard side.
Q. Aft or forward?
A. Aft.
Q. What were you doing there?
A. I was on watch, sir.
Q. Tell the court what you felt, heard, and saw, in regard to the destruction of the *Maine*.
A. I walked over to the starboard side and was looking over the side to see if there was any boats around the ship, and there didn't seem to be a ripple on the water at all. There wasn't a boat in sight; I didn't have to challenge a boat that night above all nights. I was looking over the starboard side, and all at once there was a flash of fire hit me right in the face and knocked me about half way across the deck, and during the flash the explosion came—just immediately afterwards. After the flash hit me in the face, then the explosion was, and the wood and iron commenced to fall around and lit on the awning all around me; and shortly after the officers came up. I thought I was the only one left on the ship when the explosion came, and the officers came up and we lowered the two boats and jumped into the boats to pick up the men floating around.
Q. Were the poop awnings spread?
A. Yes, sir.
Q. What was the first thing you felt?
A. The first thing I felt was a shock.
Q. Of the ship?
A. Yes, sir.
Q. How did it feel?
A. It felt as if it was rising up.
Q. Did you feel more than one of these shocks?
A. Only one, sir.
Q. Did you hear any noise?
A. I didn't hear a bit of noise, only the explosion.
Q. One explosion?
A. One explosion.
Q. Did the explosion come before this first shock or afterwards?
A. It came after the shock.
Q. Did you feel any water thrown up into the air?
A. No, sir.
Q. Did you see any shoot of flame up into the air?
A. No, sir; I did not.
Q. The awning obstructed your view, did it?
A. Yes; the forward part of the ship. All I saw was the flash hit me in the face; the flash of fire, and then the explosion.

By the COURT:

Q. What do you mean by a flash in your face?
A. The same as if anything would strike you in the face. It seemed like a flash of fire.
Q. You do not mean that it was right in your face?
A. No, sir; but it seemed as if it was striking you in the face—the flash was, and then the explosion followed afterwards.
Q. Where was the fire?
A. It seemed to be coming from about the middle part of the ship.
Q. It was a long way from where you were?
A. Yes, sir; it was.
Q. How far forward could you see?
A. I could see to the superstructure, about amidships, sir.
Q. Why could you not see farther than that?
A. The awnings stopped my view, sir.
Q. You were sensitive of a vivid flash of flame or light, as I understand it?
A. Yes, sir.
Q. Did you have the sensation of the shock to the ship before that, or at the same instant?
A. They came both very near the same instant, but there was a small shock before the flame came up.
Q. The ship seemed to rise, did it?
A. Yes, sir; it seemed as if something lifted her up and tipped her right over on the port side.
Q. Then was there an explosion besides that?
A. The explosion was just after the light was, when the fire seemed to strike me in the face. The fire came right instantly afterwards. Then the ship blew up and keeled over onto the port side.
Q. But the first shock, the lifting of the deck under your feet, was the first thing you felt?
A. Yes, sir; there was only one shock that I felt.
Q. Do you mean to say you did not feel the explosion?
A. Oh, yes, sir.
Q. Was that the shock?
A. The shock and the explosion was at the same time.
Q. Where did the flash come in with reference to the lifting of the deck and the explosion?
A. It seemed to come from about——
Q. I did not ask where it came from. You were standing on your feet when the shock came?
A. Yes, sir.
Q. When you heard the explosion?
A. Yes, sir.
Q. Were they together, instantly?
A. They were instantly together. You could not notice the difference between. It was just like that [indicating].
Q. Was the flash between them?
A. Yes, sir.

The judge-advocate requested that the testimony given by the witness be not read to him by the stenographer, but that he be directed to report to-morrow morning at 10 o'clock, when he will be furnished with so much of the record as contains his testimony and asked to withdraw for the consideration of the same, upon the completion of which he will be again called before the court and be given an opportunity to amend his testimony as recorded, or pronounce it correct. The request was granted and the witness was instructed accordingly; whereupon he withdrew, after being cautioned by the president not to discuss matters pertaining to the inquiry.

Apprentice AMBROSE HAM, U. S. Navy, appeared as a witness before the court, and was duly sworn by the president.

Examined by the JUDGE-ADVOCATE:

Q. Give your full name, rate, and to what ship you are attached.
A. Ambrose Ham, apprentice, first class, U. S. Navy.
Q. What ship?
A. U. S. S. *Maine.*
Q. Were you on board the *Maine* at the time of her destruction?
A. Yes, sir.
Q. At the first intimation of any trouble, tell us exactly where you were.
A. I was on the starboard side of the poop, near the forward 6 pounder.
Q. Near the forward break of the poop?
A. Yes, sir.
Q. What were you doing there?
A. I was standing there. I had just been talking to Waters. I don't know his first name. He was a lamplighter.
Q. What were you doing there; were you on duty?
A. Yes, sir; I was on duty.
Q. What duty?
A. Signal duty.
Q. Tell the court exactly what you felt, heard, and saw of the destruction of the Maine.
A. I was standing facing forward, and I was about to turn around when I saw a flash of light—a flame, which seemed to envelop the whole ship—followed by a report. I was struck in the face by a flying piece of iron. Then there was a perfect hail of flying iron fell all about me. Then the second report. I saw the things flying from forward. I didn't know exactly where the explosion was. After that the officers came up on the poop, and I assisted in lowering the gig.
Q. You speak of two explosions?
A. Yes, sir; it sounded like a roar, the second one.
Q. What did the first one sound like?
A. It was a sharp report.
Q. How far were they apart?
A. There was only an interval of a couple of seconds.
Q. Did you feel the ship shake at either explosion?
A. The ship seemed to lift right out of the water.
Q. At which explosion?
A. At the second explosion.
Q. Did you feel any trembling or shaking or lifting of the ship at the first explosion?
A. No, sir.
Q. When did you see the flame you speak of?
A. The first thing.
Q. Before you heard either explosion?
A. Yes, sir.
Q. You say there was a decided, distinct interval between the two explosions?

A. Yes, sir.
Q. One was like a shot and the other like a roar?
A. Yes, sir.
Q. The second one being the roar?
A. Yes, sir.
Q. Could you see any large upshoot of flame forward?
A. Yes, sir; there is where I saw it first.
Q. Before either one?
A. Yes, sir.
Q. But at the second explosion did you see any large upshoot of flame?
A. No, sir. At the second explosion I was hit in the face, and I had to cover my face like that [indicating] to avoid some flying pieces of iron. So I couldn't see no more after that.
Q. Was there any trembling of the ship at the first shot?
A. No, sir.

By the COURT:

Q. Were you looking forward at the time?
A. I was about to turn around when I saw the flash.

The judge-advocate requested that the testimony given by the witness be not read to him by the stenographer, but that he be directed to report to-morrow morning at 10 o'clock, when he will be furnished with so much of the record as contains his testimony and asked to withdraw for the consideration of the same, upon the completion of which he will be again called before the court and be given an opportunity to amend his testimony as recorded or pronounce it correct. The request was granted and the witness was instructed accordingly; whereupon he withdrew after being cautioned by the president not to discuss matters pertaining to the inquiry.

Lieutenant HOOD here appeared before the court.
The JUDGE-ADVOCATE. Lieutenant Hood, have you read over your testimony?
Lieutenant HOOD. I have.
The JUDGE-ADVOCATE. Do you find it correct?
Lieutenant HOOD. I find it correct with the exception of a few slight changes.
The JUDGE-ADVOCATE. Will you please read them to the stenographer?
Lieutenant HOOD. On page 249, in the first answer, leave out "late."
On page 251, in the second answer, leave out "I" and substitute "ammunition was."
On page 256, in the first line, leave out "went up on" and substitute "reached." On the same page, in the ninth line, insert "had" at the beginning of the line.
On page 260, in the third line, substitute "to" for "through." In the second answer on the same page, leave out the word "gun." In the third line from the bottom on page 261, put a period after "air" and leave out the word "but."
The JUDGE-ADVOCATE. Is your testimony as amended correct?
Lieutenant HOOD. It is correct.
The witness then withdrew, after being cautioned by the president not to converse about matters pertaining to the inquiry.

Lieutenant BLOW here entered the court.
The JUDGE-ADVOCATE. Lieutenant Blow, have you read over your testimony?

Lieutenant BLOW. Yes, sir.

The JUDGE-ADVOCATE. Is it correct as recorded?

Lieutenant BLOW. It is practically correct, with one exception. On page 272, I wish to say: "I can recall two occasions when the ship was heading in the same direction, approximately."

Lieutenant BLOW, U. S. Navy, a witness heretofore examined, resumed the witness stand, and, after being cautioned by the president that the oath previously taken by him was still binding, testified as follows:

Examined by the JUDGE-ADVOCATE:

Q. I wish to ask you, Mr. Blow, the comparative amount of wreckage on the port and starboard sides, as you pulled around the ship.

A. The wreckage on the starboard side was much greater. It began, I should say, about on the starboard beam, and extended completely around w..at was the bow of the ship. There was wreckage on the port bow, but a small amount, as I remember it. I should think the wreckage on the starboard side extended as much as half a ship's length from the side.

The testimony of the witness was then read over to him by the stenographer, and by him pronounced correct. The witness then withdrew, after being cautioned not to converse about matters pertaining to the inquiry.

Naval Cadet BOYD here entered the court.

The JUDGE-ADVOCATE. Mr. Boyd, have you read over your testimony?

Naval Cadet BOYD. I have.

The JUDGE-ADVOCATE. Is it correct as recorded?

Naval Cadet BOYD. It is not.

The JUDGE-ADVOCATE. Do you wish to make some corrections?

Naval Cadet BOYD. Yes, sir.

The JUDGE-ADVOCATE. Please state them to the stenographer.

Naval Cadet BOYD. On page 298 the question is understood to mean "What are your duties as mate of the berth deck after sunset?" My answer should read: "To see that all compartments are water-tight except those authorized to be open." One unnecessary sentence should be struck out.

On page 302, "Was there any listing of the ship?" should be: "Was there any lifting of the ship," the word "lifting" being emphatic.

On page 303, in the answer reading "There is a hatch in the forward compartment," strike out the word "forward." On the same page, in the sentence reading "There is a passage between the rooms," the word "sail" should be inserted before the word "room." On the same page the question "How did you get down to the magazines?" is understood as "How did you get down to the 10-inch magazine?"

The JUDGE-ADVOCATE. As amended, your testimony is correct?

Naval Cadet BOYD. It is correct.

The witness then withdrew after being cautioned by the president not to discuss matters pertaining to the inquiry.

Apprentice C. J. DRESSLER, U. S. Navy, appeared as a witness before the court, and was duly sworn by the president.

Examined by the JUDGE-ADVOCATE:

Q. State your full name, rate, and to what ship you are attached.

A. G. J. Dressler; apprentice, first-class, U. S. Navy; attached to the U. S. S. *Maine*.

Q. Were you on board the *Maine* at the time of her destruction?
A. Yes, sir.
Q. State to the court exactly where you were at the first intimation there was of any trouble.
A. I was up in the midship superstructure, on the port side, right abreast the crane locker.
Q. What were you doing there?
A. I had been writing a letter at the time.
Q. You were writing at the time it started?
A. Yes, sir.
Q. Tell the court exactly what you heard, felt, and saw.
A. I didn't feel anything, nor I didn't see anything; but I must have lost my senses at the time, because when I came to again I had been sitting on the hammock netting on the same side. I didn't feel no shock, nor I didn't see anything at all. I guess something must have struck me and knocked me senseless; but as soon as I came to, two or three minutes afterwards, I had been sitting on a hammock netting.
Q. I understood you to tell me yesterday that you felt the shocks. Did I misunderstand you?
A. I believe you misunderstood me.
Q. The first thing you knew was when you recovered from being knocked senseless?
A. Yes, sir.

By the COURT:

Q. What did you see?
A. While I was sitting on the hammock netting I saw the boats. Mr. Bronson was in the whaleboat. He pulled around the ship and tried to save those that he could. There was two or three Spanish boats came alongside, and all those that they could rescue they took off, I suppose. I didn't see anything further, because I went in one of the Spanish boats and went aboard of the Spanish man-of-war myself.
Q. You were sitting on the hammock rail of the superstructure deck, were you?
A. Yes, sir.
Q. Whereabouts? Which side?
A. On the port side.
Q. On the port side of the ship?
A. Yes, sir.
Q. What was just in front of you that was not there usually?
A. The boats were there—the two Spanish boats—right there on the port side.
Q. I am not speaking about that. I am speaking about the wreck now.
A. The smokestacks. They went right over the superstructure. They laid right slantingly across the after part of the superstructure, and the crane was doubled right up. It hadn't been knocked down though.
Q. That was on which side?
A. On the port side. The water was just even with the awning on that side. The awning was flapping up and down in the water.
Q. What awning was that?
A. That was the main-deck awning.
Q. You were sitting above that?
A. Yes, sir; I was over on top of the hammock netting.
Q. How far was this from the place you were sitting before the explosion?

A. I don't suppose more than two or three steps. I was sitting right down on deck, under a light.

The judge-advocate requested that the testimony given by the witness be not read to him by the stenographer, but that he be directed to report to-morrow morning at 10 o'clock, when he will be furnished with so much of the record as contains his testimony and asked to withdraw for the consideration of the same, upon the completion of which he will be again called before the court and be given an opportunity to amend his testimony as recorded or pronounce it correct. The request was granted and the witness was instructed accordingly; whereupon he withdrew after being cautioned by the president not to discuss matters pertaining to the inquiry.

Carpenter HELM here appeared before the court.

The JUDGE-ADVOCATE. Mr. Helm, is your testimony, as recorded, correct?

Carpenter HELM. It is except for the following corrections:

On page 322 my answer should read, "One water-tight door frame of paymaster's issuing room was not in good condition, and was recommenced to be repaired at the navy-yard, as it could not be repaired by the ship's force."

By the JUDGE-ADVOCATE:

Q. You wish to add that to the answer you have given?
A. Yes, sir.
Q. Where was this issuing room?
A. It was forward, over the 6-inch magazine, two decks above.

On page 323 I would like to change "she listed to starboard" to "she listed to port." I would like to have the word "none" changed, on that same page, to "not" in answer to the question "Were you injured in any way?"

On page 324, in the fourth answer, I wish to strike out "as they taper so low there." and in the same answer strike out the word "guess" and insert "think."

On page 325, in the third answer, change "three and three-quarters" to "four and three-quarters."

Q. As amended, is your testimony correct?
A. It is.

The witness then withdrew after being cautioned by the president not to converse about matters pertaining to the inquiry.

Sergeant MICHAEL MEHAN, U. S. Marine Corps, appeared as a witness before the court, and was duly sworn by the president.

Examined by the JUDGE-ADVOCATE:

Q. State your full name, rank, and to what ship you are attached.
A. Michael Mehan: sergeant U. S. Marine Corps; serving on board the U. S. S. *Maine.*
Q. Were you on board the *Maine* at the time of her destruction?
A. Yes, sir.
Q. What were you doing? Were you on duty?
A. On duty, sir.
Q. As what?
A. As sergeant of the guard, sir.
Q. Where were you at the first sign of any trouble?
A. On the starboard gangway.

Q. On what part of the gangway?
A. It was about midways in the gangway, between the forward turret and the after part of the gangway.
Q. About abreast of the crane?
A. About abreast of the crane; yes, sir.
Q. On the main deck?
A. On the main deck.
Q. You were standing up?
A. Standing up.
Q. Looking which way?
A. I was looking outboard, sir.
Q. State exactly what you felt, heard, and saw.
A. I was in the gangway when I first heard this explosion. The next thing I knew about it I was fired overboard in the water—lifted clean off the gangway and fired in the water. The next thing I was picked up by a boat.
Q. You heard only one explosion?
A. Only one explosion.
Q. Did you feel any shock before that explosion?
A. The explosion and the shock, I thought, was both together.
Q. How far from the ship were you thrown?
A. When I came up from the surface of the water I was about 15 or 20 feet out from the gangway on the starboard side of the ship.
Q. Were you knocked senseless?
A. No.
Q. Simply lifted up and out?
A. Lifted up and thrown out in the water.
Q. How high did you go?
A. I don't think I went very high in the air. I was simply thrown out in the water. When I left the ship I must have swam out, because when I came up I was about 15 or 20 feet from the side of the ship. That is about all I know about it. Afterwards I was picked up by a boat.

By the COURT:
Q. You were thrown off where?
A. I was thrown off the starboard gangway out in the water.
Q. Could you describe the kind of motion of the deck?
A. I could not, sir; I thought the deck came right up and fired me out.

The judge-advocate requested that the testimony given by the witness be not read to him by the stenographer, but that he be directed to report to-morrow morning at 10 o'clock, when he will be furnished with so much of the record as contains his testimony, and asked to withdraw for the consideration of the same, upon the completion of which he will be again called before the court and be given an opportunity to amend his testimony as recorded or pronounce it correct. The request was granted, and the witness was instructed accordingly; whereupon he withdrew, after being cautioned by the president not to discuss matters pertaining to the inquiry.

Corporal FRANK G. THOMPSON, U. S. Marine Corps, appeared as a witness before the court, and was duly sworn by the president.

Examined by the JUDGE-ADVOCATE:
Q. State your full name, rate, and to what ship you are attached.
A. Frank G. Thompson; corporal, U. S. Marine Corps; attached to and serving on board of the U. S. S. *Maine*.

Q. Were you on board the *Maine* at the time of her destruction?
A. I was, sir.
Q. Where were you at the first intimation of any trouble?
A. Lying in my hammock.
Q. Where was your hammock?
A. On the port gangway.
Q. Describe where on the port gangway and how it was slung.
A. It was slung from the first stanchion forward of the gangway—from the stanchion to the port.
Q. Right across the main deck, then?
A. Right across the main deck.
Q. In the afterpart of the gangway?
A. In the afterpart of the gangway.
Q. About how far forward of the turret?
A. About 25 feet—20 feet.
Q. Which way was your head?
A. Inboard, sir.
Q. Were you wide awake?
A. I was wide awake. I was looking aft, with the blanket just over my head. I was lying there just making myself comfortable. It seems as though I had made myself comfortable to have a night's rest. It was my night off, and I had just turned in. I hadn't turned in more than fifteen minutes—ten minutes, I don't believe, at the latest.
Q. Tell the court exactly what you felt, heard, and saw of the destruction of the *Maine*.
A. The first I realized, lying in my hammock, I was deliberately thrown in the air through the port awning on the port side. I went as high as the superstructure, because I could see the superstructure. I landed on my side, here where I have the scar. I laid on the deck stunned for about two or three seconds, it would seem. Just then the ship seemed to give a lurch, and she gradually commenced to sink. As she commenced to sink I realized where my position was and I regained my feet. I grasped the ridgerope, and hung onto the ridgerope until the water had come up almost to my neck. Just then naval cadet Mr. Bronson came along in the boat and threw me a line. He told me I would either have to sink or swim for my life. I let go, and I went down once and came up. I grasped the rope and they pulled me to the boat.
Q. That was the ridgerope that was going along the port gangway?
A. The port gangway, where the awning was made fast.
Q. The awning was in the port gangway?
A. In the port gangway.
Q. You think you were thrown through that awning?
A. I was thrown deliberately through it, because I remember coming down through it to where I was lying there.
Q. I suppose the awning itself was thrown up?
A. It must have been, because I remember there was a rent in the awning where I came through.
Q. Did you go up in the air at the very first shock you felt?
A. That was the first thing I realized.
Q. What did you hear at that time?
A. I didn't hear anything.
Q. Did you see anything?
A. I couldn't see anything on account of the darkness and smoke, and I smelt steam.
Q. Were you stunned?

A. I was stunned; yes, sir. I was stunned for two or three seconds before I realized where I was. I thought at first that war had taken place and the Spaniards had opened on us. I heard groaning and men crying for help.

By the COURT:

Q. This was outside the superstructure? You were on the main deck?

A. On the main deck; yes, sir; port side.

Q. That, of course, was not your billet?

A. No, sir; my billet was below in the marine quarters, but being so close down below, there was two or three of the boys slept on the port gangway.

Q. Were you forward or abaft of the crane?

A. I was abaft the crane. I had been reading up to 9 o'clock that night. Sergeant Brown, the mail orderly, wanted me to give him the book I had after I was through with it. I read until very nearly 10 minutes past 9. Then I took the book down below to the master-at-arms compartment. Sergeant Brown was lying down there, where he always slept, and I gave him the book and went up to the head. From the head I came down to the port gangway, and had just turned in in my hammock.

The judge-advocate requested that the testimony given by the witness be not read to him by the stenographer, but that he be directed to report to-morrow morning at 10 o'clock, when he will be furnished with so much of the record as contains his testimony, and asked to withdraw for the consideration of the same, upon the completion of which he will be again called before the court and be given an opportunity to amend his testimony as recorded, or pronounce it correct. The request was granted, and the witness was instructed accordingly; whereupon he withdrew, after being cautioned by the president not to discuss matters pertaining to the inquiry.

Lieutenant JUNGEN here entered the court.

The JUDGE-ADVOCATE. Mr. Jungen, you have read over your testimony?

A. I have, sir.

Q. Is it correct as recorded?

A. I desire to make some corrections, as follows:

Page 283, line 14, for the word "watch" substitute the word "hold."

Page 284, line 16, for the word "an" substitute the word "a," and between "a" and the word "explosion" insert the words "well defined," so that the whole sentence will read "It was not a well-defined explosion."

Same page, line 25, erase the word "or" after the word "ashes," and in place thereof insert "mingled with," so as to read "ashes mingled with brown smoke."

Same page, last line, for the word "try" insert "see."

Page 285, line 4, for the word "then" substitute the words "after that."

Same page, line 21, erase the word "there" and substitute the words "the harbor."

Page 286, line 19, after the first word "boat" insert the word "fall."

Same page, same line, after the second word "boat" insert the word "fall."

Page 287, line 2, for the word "got" substitute the word "was."

Same page, line 12, put the following word "having" before the word "only."

Same page, line 13, erase the last two words "and myself."

Same page, line 17, between the words "took" and "the" insert the words "charge of," and in the same line, after the word "around," add the words "the stern of the ship."

Same page, line 23, after the word "turret" insert the words "On the starboard side."

Same page, line 28, for the word "starboard" substitute the word "port" and erase the word "again."

Same page, line 29, erase the word "then" after the word "ship."

Page 290, line 20, for the word "boat" substitute the word "men."

Same page, line 26, after the word "around" add the words "that way."

The JUDGE-ADVOCATE. Is your testimony as amended correct?

A. It is.

Lieut. C. W. JUNGEN, recalled to the witness stand and warned by the president that the oath previously taken by him was still binding.

Examined by the JUDGE-ADVOCATE:

Q. Please state the comparative amount of wreckage on the port and starboard sides when you were pulling around the ship in the barge.

A. It appeared to me most of it was on the starboard side.

Q. Was not nearly all of it on the starboard side?

A. The only noticeable wreckage on the port side that I could see at all was the smoke pipe. I would like to add that my impression at first was, when I saw the wreckage, that the explosion was on the starboard side, because I saw something that looked to me like the starboard forward turret having been thrown up to port. That turned out afterwards to be the superstructure, as I learned; also that what I took to be the port crane was standing.

There being no further questions to ask this witness, his testimony was read over to him by the stenographer and by him pronounced correct.

The witness then withdrew, after being cautioned by the president not to converse about matters pertaining to the inquiry.

Master at Arms JOHN B. LOAD, U. S. Navy, appeared as a witness before the court, and was duly sworn by the president.

Examined by the JUDGE-ADVOCATE:

Q. State your full name, rate, and to what ship you are attached.

A. John B. Load, master at arms, third class, U. S. Navy, attached to the U. S. S. *Maine*.

Q. Were you on duty as master at arms the night of the destruction of the *Maine*?

A. No, sir; I was not. The second-class master at arms was on duty.

Q. Where were you at the first intimation of any trouble?

A. I had just left the second-class master at arms, and he was telling me if I wanted the keys during the night, or in case they should be wanted, where to get them. I left him to go to my hammock, which was slung underneath the middle superstructure, right outside the armory door.

Q. Where were you at the moment you felt the first trouble?

A. I was just taking off my shirt, and was going to turn in. From where I was standing I could look out the after door.
Q. That is right by the armory?
A. Right by the armory, sir; on the starboard side.
Q. On the after part of the superstructure?
A. Yes, sir.
Q. Your hammock was inside the superstructure, forward of the armory?
A. Forward of the armory.
Q. And nearly abreast of the door?
A. Nearly abreast of the door.
Q. You were about abreast of the refrigerator?
A. I was close to where that steerage ice box stood; yes, sir.
Q. You were standing up at the time?
A. I was standing up at the time. I had just put my shirt on the hammock.
Q. Please state to the court exactly what you felt, heard, and saw.
A. You could see a red flame outside the ship. It seemed as if it was a small boat had struck the ship at first. She seemed to tremble, and then the whole deck where I was standing seemed to open, and there was a flash of flame came up, and whether I went up in the air, or whether I went down, I couldn't say at first. Then I found myself down below, and the water rushing in on me. I could hear a second explosion, and it seemed to lift the weight off of what was on me where I was lying down, and I managed to crawl out of there. I found myself on the port side of the upper superstructure. That place all seemed to be cleared. At that time the port awning was burning, and people was lying on it. Schwartz was one. He called me by name and asked me to give him some help to get off of there. The only thing I could find was a piece of wire rope. I helped him and two or three others, but I don't know their names. Privates Lutz, Marine, and Galpin were up there. Then I called out for assistance, for a boat, the Ward Line boat. At that time Mr. Bronson was coming along in the whaleboat, and he called out "Courage." He says: "Help is coming."
Then I asked him for his painter, and I made it fast to one of the cradles that was remaining there, and I helped these others to get into the boat. I was going to get in myself, but Lutz called out "Give me some help here; there is two men dying." We managed to get them and throw them over. We had no way of putting them down. One was Ericson and the other was Smith. Smith fell in the water too far from the boat to receive assistance, and Mr. Bronson jumped out of the boat and swam to him. It was only a short distance, but the water appeared to be boiling up around there at the time. Then I got up from there and was intending to make the boat myself. I walked around the hammock netting a little, and I slipped and fell overboard. I got onto a chest, and I was picked up by a Spanish shore boat. We went all around the ship in the boat and picked up Rau, seaman, and Mike Malone, fireman, but Mike fell out of the boat afterwards; he was so badly hurt we couldn't hold him in. Then I was transferred to another Spanish boat, and we were taken ashore.
Q. You say at the first shock you were knocked down somewhere?
A. Yes, sir.
Q. Below?
A. Yes, sir.
Q. Where did you find yourself?
A. I thought I was on the berth deck.

Q. But you were not on the berth deck, were you?
A. I think not, sir.
Q. The next thing you found yourself on top of the middle superstructure?
A. Yes, sir.
Q. How did you get up there?
A. I can remember coming out of the after hatch, sir.
Q. You got on top?
A. On top, sir. I can remember all that was with me at the time down there. There was Williams, the armorer; he was sleeping on deck close to me; and Kane was standing with his arms on the ice chest. McGinnis, the marine, was sleeping on the port side.
Q. They were all saved?
A. They were all saved, sir, but the man that was sleeping in his hammock above, next to me, was lost.
Q. Who was that?
A. That was Calfield.
The JUDGE-ADVOCATE. These men, I want to say to the court, were mostly asleep. I have questioned most of the men he has mentioned, and they were asleep at the time.

By the COURT:
Q. You mentioned two explosions?
A. Two explosions, sir.

By the JUDGE-ADVOCATE:
Q. How far apart were the two explosions?
A. About a minute, as near as I can judge; that is, from the time the deck opened up until I heard the second explosion.
Q. By a minute you mean a very small period of time?
A. Very small.
Q. Very quick?
A. Very quick.

By the COURT:
Q. You do not mean a minute, then?
A. No, sir; it would hardly be a minute; but it happened a little after three bells, as near as I can judge, and I was ashore before four bells struck.
Q. Describe the two explosions.
A. One seemed to be a deafening report.
Q. Which one?
A. The one when the deck opened. Then, when I was down below, I imagined it was a boiler went up, on account of the water down there. It was hot, but the flame that I saw—the deck seemed to open. It was the same as if some one had taken a revolver and fired it close to your face, and you almost suffocated. It felt as if cotton was in our mouths when we were down below. We were choking down there, and we were drinking water as it was coming up on us, to try to get a little relief.
Q. Do you mean to say that you tried to get a drink of water during this time?
A. I was drinking the water as it was coming up on me, sir. As we were sinking, we were drinking water to get relief. This man Kane and myself were together nearly the whole time.
Q. Did you speak with each other?
A. Oh, yes, sir; we were speaking. I told him I had given up all hope once, and he told me he had given up all hope.

Q. Were the lights out at this time?
A. The lights were out as soon as the first flash. Everything was in darkness.
Q. Then you recognized these people how?
A. By their voices, sir.
Q. How did the second explosion differ from the first one?
A. It didn't seem to be as loud a report, to me, as the first one was.
Q. It did not seem to be as loud?
A. Not as loud, sir.
Q. The first thing you knew following the first report was that you were thrown down through the deck?
A. It seemed to me as if I fell through the deck instead of going up. The whole deck seemed to open. It sounded then as if a wagon with a lot of old iron had been dumped into a hole. That was the noise it was making, cracking up all the time.

The judge-advocate requested that the testimony given by the witness be not read to him by the stenographer, but that he be directed to report to-morrow morning at 10 o'clock, when he will be furnished with so much of the record as contains his testimony and asked to withdraw for the consideration of the same, upon the completion of which he will be again called before the court and be given an opportunity to amend his testimony as recorded, or pronounce it correct. The request was granted and the witness was instructed accordingly; whereupon he withdrew, after being cautioned by the president not to discuss matters pertaining to the inquiry.

Seaman PETER LARSEN, U. S. Navy, appeared as a witness before the court, and was duly sworn by the president.

Examined by the JUDGE-ADVOCATE:

Q. State your full name, rate, and to what ship you are attached.
A. My name is Peter Larsen; I was born in Norway; seaman; attached to the U. S. S. *Maine*.
Q. Were you on board the *Maine* on the night of her destruction?
A. Yes, sir.
Q. You were standing on the quarter-deck of the *Maine* at that time?
A. Yes, sir.
Q. Doing extra duty?
A. Extra duty; yes, sir.
Q. What part of the quarter-deck were you on?
A. Close to the after turret, sir.

By the COURT:

Q. It was not on the superstructure deck?
A. No, sir; just that little passage going between the after turret and the bulkhead.
Q. On the port side?
A. Yes, sir.
Q. Right near the gangway between the turret and the middle superstructure?
A. The galley door that leads out on the superstructure.
Q. Which way were you facing?
A. Port side, sir.
Q. What were you facing?
A. I just came walking up, like this, and I stopped there.
Q. Tell the court exactly what you felt, heard, and saw.
A. The first thing, when I came off to that side and was walking up

and down, I heard some explosion in the port gangway; something like an explosion. I just turned around, and then the big explosion came, and I got thrown aft on the poop.

Q. What do you mean by the first explosion? What did it sound like?

A. Something like a shot, sir.

Q. What did it feel like?

A. It jarred the ship.

Q. Did you see any flame or anything?

A. Yes, sir; just around the corner came the flame.

Q. Show us on the plan where you were.

A. Right here [pointing between the turret and the galley]. The first noise I heard was around the port gangway, where the ice machine is.

Q. The first what?

A. The first explosion, and the next thing I got thrown up here on the poop deck.

Q. You got thrown up there?

A. Yes, sir.

Q. On top of the deck?

A. Yes, sir.

Q. You did not walk up there at all?

A. No, sir.

Q. You were thrown up there?

A. Yes, sir.

Q. You saw the light around this corner?

A. Just coming around this corner; and the next thing I found myself up there.

Q. Were you hurt?

A. No, sir; just across the back a little, and my arm.

By the JUDGE-ADVOCATE:

Q. What kind of a sensation did the second explosion make in regard to the ship?

A. At the second explosion I got thrown away, and everything around me was flying.

Q. Was there a distinct interval between the two, do you think?

A. There was a very little between each other, because I didn't have time to turn around, because I got thrown out.

Q. They were distinct, in your opinion?

A. Yes, sir; they were distinct.

Q. When did you see the flames—after the first and before the second?

A. No, sir; just with the second.

Q. It was the second shot, then, that threw you up on the poop deck?

A. Yes, sir; the second shot, because at the first I had just turned around. The second took me away from the quarter-deck altogether.

Q. Can you describe any more carefully the first shock?

A. No, sir; it was just a jar, shaking all over.

Q. It did not throw you off your feet?

A. No, sir; it didn't throw me off my feet. It was something like the ship had gone aground. She was shaking.

Q. How long do you think it was after the first shock before the second one?

A. I don't think there was more than about two seconds, or something like that.

Q. A very short time?

A. Yes, sir.

Q. The two were perfectly separate?
A. Yes, sir.

The judge-advocate requested that the testimony given by the witness be not read to him by the stenographer, but that he be directed to report to-morrow morning at 10 o'clock, when he will be furnished with so much of the record as contains his testimony and asked to withdraw for the consideration of the same, upon the completion of which he will be again called before the court and be given an opportunity to amend his testimony as recorded or pronounce it correct. The request was granted, and the witness was instructed accordingly; whereupon he withdrew, after being cautioned by the president not to discuss matters pertaining to the inquiry.

Seaman LOUIS MORINIERE, U. S. Navy, appeared as a witness before the court, and was duly sworn by the president:

Examined by the JUDGE-ADVOCATE:
Q. Give your full name.
A. Louis Moriniere.
Q. What rate?
A. Seaman.
Q. Attached to the *Maine?*
A. Yes, sir.
Q. Were you on board the *Maine* at the time of her destruction?
A. Yes, sir.
Q. You were on the quarter-deck, I believe?
A. Yes, sir.
Q. On the main deck?
A. Yes, sir.
Q. Whereabouts?
A. Between the after superstructure and the main superstructure; abreast the after turret, sir.
Q. About halfway between the two superstructures?
A. Yes, sir; closer to the after superstructure.
Q. Near the barbette?
A. No, sir; near that reel there that the fire hose is on, under the ladder; close to the ladder.
Q. That is not the after superstructure. That is the middle superstructure. You were close to the ladder leading up the middle superstructure. I will show it to you on the plan. Which way were you facing at the time the trouble commenced?
A. Aft, sir.
Q. Tell the court exactly what you felt, what you heard, and what you saw; not what you have been told since—what you remember yourself feeling.
A. I heard a jar, and after this jar the explosion went up through the middle superstructure. I heard a jar first, and almost at the same time of this jar the whole middle superstructure went up in fire, sir. I was thrown up off my feet and sent aft against my will, and I fell on all fours.
Q. You were thrown down?
A. Yes, sir; I looked forward and saw no more smokestacks. The smokestacks were done.
Q. They had gone?
A. Yes, sir; the two smokestacks were gone.
Q. That was after you picked yourself up?

A. Yes, sir; I got hold of an awning stanchion and crawled up over something around there; I don't know what it was. I looked around, and I couldn't see no smokestacks.
Q. What did the first explosion feel like to you?
A. Just a jar, sir.
Q. How long was it between that and the second explosion?
A. It was hardly two seconds.
Q. When did you see flame?
A. The flame was in the port gangway.
Q. When did that first come?
A. Just soon after this second explosion started.
Q. Which knocked you down?
A. It was the second explosion.
Q. How far aft were you thrown?
A. Just about fifteen feet, in my judgment.
Q. You landed on your hands and knees?
A. Yes, sir; I couldn't get on my feet again.
Q. You could not get your feet again?
A. No, sir; I couldn't get on my feet. There was so much vibration in the deck that I couldn't stand up. When I got up in the boat alongside the ship, after the captain left the ship, we saw the berth deck on fire through the ports.
Q. That was after you had left the ship?
A. Yes, sir. She was very deep down in the water then. She was almost level with the ports.

The judge-advocate requested that the testimony given by the witness be not read to him by the stenographer, but that he be directed to report to-morrow morning at 10 o'clock, when he will be furnished with so much of the record as contains his testimony and asked to withdraw for the consideration of the same, upon the completion of which he will be again called before the court and be given an opportunity to amend his testimony as recorded, or pronounce it correct. The request was granted, and the witness was instructed accordingly; whereupon he withdrew, after being cautioned by the president not to discuss matters pertaining to the inquiry.

Boatswain's Mate CHARLES BERGMAN, U. S. Navy, appeared as a witness before the court, and was duly sworn by the president.

Examined by the JUDGE-ADVOCATE:

Q. Give your full name, rate, and to what ship you are attached.
A. Charles Bergman; boatswain's mate; first-class; U. S. S. *Maine*.
Q. Were you on board the *Maine* on the night of her destruction?
A. Yes, sir.
Q. Were you asleep when it happened?
A. I was just between waking and sleeping.
Q. Just going to sleep?
A. Yes, sir.
Q. Were you in your hammock?
A. Yes, sir.
Q. Where was your hammock swung?
A. Forward on the berth deck, in the forward compartment.
Q. Which side?
A. The starboard side.
Q. Near the brig?
A. On the afterpart of the starboard brig.

Q. The hammock swung fore and aft?
A. Yes, sir.
Q. Well outboard?
A. Yes, sir; the first hammock outboard, alongside the mess locker. I swung on top from the hooks, and two others were swinging underneath.
Q. What were the other men's names?
A. Atkin and Fountain.
Q. They were both killed?
A. Yes, sir.
Q. Tell us what you felt and what you experienced. Which way was your head?
A. Aft, sir.
Q. Tell us what you felt—what you experienced.
A. I heard a terrible crash, an explosion I suppose that was. Something fell, and then after that I got thrown somewhere in a hot place. Wherever that was I don't know. I got burned on my legs and arms, and I got my mouth full of ashes and one thing and another. Then the next thing I was in the water—away under the water somewhere, with a lot of wreckage on top of me that was sinking me down. After I got clear of that I started to come up to the surface of the water again, and I got afoul of some other wreckage. I got my head jammed in, and I couldn't get loose, so I let myself go down. Then it carried me down farther. I suppose when it touched the bottom somewhere it sort of opened out a bit, and I got my head out and started for the surface of the water again. I hit a lot of other stuff with my head, and then I got my head above the water. I got picked up by a Spanish boat, one of these shore boats, I think.
Q. When you found yourself in the water first, how far were you from this ship?
A. I must have been underneath the ship, as far as I can make out. At least, I come up on the side.
Q. Near the ship?
A. Yes, sir. I got out through the bottom or the side, as near as I can make out.
Q. You were the only man in that compartment that was saved?
A. Yes, sir; the only man from the whole berth deck except Jerry Shea, I believe.
Q. Where was he?
A. He was in the fireman's compartment, I believe, forward of the marines' compartment.
Q. Where is Shea now?
A. He is in the hospital at Havana, I think. I don't know of no other one. When I come up, she was all settled down in the water. She was all torn to pieces then, and settled down.
Q. Had you swallowed much water?
A. I was full of it. I was pretty near drowned when I came up. When I got in the boat the water was running out of me. I must have been under there for a couple of minutes, as far as I can make out.

By the COURT:

Q. Do you remember more than one shock?
A. That is all, sir; one terrible crash. That is all I know about.
Q. You say you went which way; what became of you?
A. That I couldn't say. I must have got out from the bottom or the side. That is what I think. I don't know which way I got thrown

S. Doc. 207——12

or fired. It was something fearful. There is nothing to compare with it at all.

Q. You were not conscious of having your head above water from the start until you were picked up? You did not know during that time that your head had been above water at all?

A. No, sir; I was under all the time. After I once got my head above water I had it there all the time.

Q. You say your legs and arms were burned?

A. Yes, sir.

Q. Those are the burns on your hands now, are they?

A. Yes, sir; and that leg and arm [indicating his left leg and left arm].

Q. How large spaces were burned?

A. It is burned across this leg here [indicating]. My arm is pretty well healed up now. There was a big, raw burn on my left elbow.

Q. You say at one time you felt you were in a very hot place?

A. Yes, sir.

Q. Do you mean that it was hot air, hot gases?

A. It must have been hot iron or something, I guess, that I fell against. I got a lot of ashes in my mouth and face. I know that.

The judge-advocate requested that the testimony given by the witness be not read to him by the stenographer, but that he be directed to report to-morrow morning at 10 o'clock, when he will be furnished with so much of the record as contains his testimony and asked to withdraw for the consideration of the same, upon the completion of which he will be again called before the court and be given an opportunity to amend his testimony as recorded, or pronounce it correct. The request was granted and the witness was instructed accordingly; whereupon he withdrew, after being cautioned by the president not to discuss matters pertaining to the inquiry.

Gunner HILL here entered the court.

The JUDGE-ADVOCATE. Mr. Hill, have you read over your testimony of yesterday?

A. Yes, sir.

Q. Is it correct as recorded?

A. I wish to make a few changes. On page 315, in the fourth answer, strike out the word "yes" and insert "no."

In the fifth answer, add to the answer "I can remember no upright in the after end of the magazine except those in the center forming the two fore and aft bins."

Q. Is your testimony as amended correct?

A. Yes, sir.

The witness then withdrew, after being cautioned by the president not to converse about matters pertaining to the inquiry.

The court then (at 12.40 p. m.) took a recess until 2 p. m.

The court reassembled at the expiration of the recess.

Present: All the members of the court, the judge-advocate, and the stenographer.

Landsman GEORGE FOX, U. S. Navy, appeared as a witness before the court, and was duly sworn by the president.

Examined by the JUDGE-ADVOCATE:

Q. State your full name, rate, and to what ship you are attached?

A. George Fox, landsman, U. S. Navy, attached to the U. S. S. *Maine*.
Q. Were you on board the *Maine* at the time of her destruction?
A. Yes, sir.
Q. I believe you were a lamplighter?
A. Yes, sir.
Q. Where were you at the time it happened?
A. In the lamp room, sir.
Q. Where is that lamp room situated?
A. On the port side of the superstructure forward.
Q. The middle superstructure?
A. The middle superstructure.
Q. Is it inside the 6-inch gun rest?
A. Yes, sir; right under the port 6-inch gun.
Q. Were you in there in your hammock?
A. No, sir; I had a bunk rigged up in there.
Q. Was the door locked?
A. Yes, sir.
Q. In what way was the door locked?
A. I had a catch and a hook, just a kind of a hook. I don't know how to explain it. It was caught over a port.
Q. Were you asleep when this commenced?
A. I was just dozing off.
Q. Tell us what happened to you.
A. As well as I can remember I was thrown up in the air and I came down feet first. I heard the rattling and the roar around me, but it was pitch dark and I couldn't see nothing. I had to feel around. I heard the men groaning around me. I felt a hole and I crawled through that. Then I seen the wreck burning on top, and that gave me light to see to climb up. I found myself in the middle of the wreck, pretty high up, because I could look down and see the boats all around there. Then I went down to the water's edge and swam out to a boat.
Q. Did the lamp room seem to be upside down?
A. Yes, sir; it seemed to be pretty well demolished, as well as I could make out.
Q. Was it perfectly open on the outside for you to crawl out?
A. No, sir; I had to crawl through a pretty small hole. It scratched me all here [indicating].
Q. Did you feel any particular shock except this upheaving?
A. No, sir; I was dazed for a minute. I was stunned.
Q. You were dazed at the very first shock?
A. Yes, sir; but I realized that we had been blown up some way. There was a strong smell of powder there somewhere that nearly gagged me. It was some kind of explosive that smelled like powder, and also the burning of cotton. I don't know what it was or what made it.

By the COURT:

Q. Of cotton?
A. Yes, sir; it smelled like burning cloth of some kind.
Q. Were your own clothes burned?
A. No, sir; not as I know of. I was stripped, myself. Of course my bedding might have taken fire; I don't know. Anyway, that smoke seemed to come from below somewhere.
Q. Do you mean that you were stripped?
A. Yes, sir; I was naked, myself. I didn't have a stitch on me, it being very warm there.
Q. Did you go to bed that way?

A. Yes, sir; I went to bed that way.
Q. You heard but one explosion?
A. Yes, sir; but one explosion.
Q. When you came down to the water's edge to swim out into the water, which side of the ship were you on?
A. I was on the port side, sir. I am sure of that, sir, because I seen Mr. Boyd on top of the wreck. He called out to all hands to turn to and fight the fire. He said we had settled down. That is the first thing I heard when I came on top of the wreck, and I went down to the water's edge and swam out to one of these boats.
Q. You are sure that was on the port side?
A. Yes, sir; I am certain of that.

The judge-advocate requested that the testimony given by the witness be not read to him by the stenographer, but that he be directed to report to-morrow morning at 10 o'clock, when he will be furnished with so much of the record as contains his testimony, and asked to withdraw for the consideration of the same, upon the completion of which he will be again called before the court and be given an opportunity to amend his testimony as recorded, or pronounce it correct. The request was granted, and the witness was instructed accordingly; whereupon he withdrew, after being cautioned by the president not to discuss matters pertaining to the inquiry.

Landsman MICHAEL LANAHAN, U. S. Navy, appeared as a witness before the court, and was duly sworn by the president.

Examined by the JUDGE-ADVOCATE:

Q. State your full name, your rate, and the ship to which you are attached.
A. My name is Michael Lanahan; landsman; U. S. S. *Maine*.
Q. Were you on board the *Maine* at the time of her destruction?
A. Yes, sir.
Q. Where were you?
A. I was in my hammock, over the starboard 6 inch gun, in the forecastle.
Q. Over the starboard 6-inch forecastle gun?
A. Yes, sir; my foot was over the starboard 6-inch gun, and my head was aft.
Q. Inside the forward superstructure?
A. Yes, sir.
Q. What happened to you? Were you asleep when it started?
A. No, sir; I wasn't asleep. I was just turning into my hammock. I was about to lie down in my hammock when I felt a jar, and that is all I remember.
Q. Where did you find yourself?
A. I found myself about 50 feet from the ship, out in the water.
Q. On which side?
A. On the starboard side.
Q. Were you injured?
A. No, sir; I had a slight cut in my head.
Q. Was anyone else in that superstructure saved?
A. Yes, sir.
Q. Who?
A. Michael Flynn, Durkin, Bloomer, and a young fellow—I forget his name. He is out in the hospital. He was a new fellow that had just come. There was four or five of them came out of that first part.

Q. You do not remember anything at all until you landed in the water?
A. No, sir; I didn't know anything at all about it until I came up in the water.
Q. Some distance from the ship?
A. Yes, sir; about 50 feet out in the water.
Q. To starboard?
A. To starboard; yes, sir.
Q. What did you feel in the way of shocks or explosions?
A. I just felt a jar, and that was all—just a trembling, and that is the last I remember of it.

By the COURT:

Q. You did not hear any noise?
A. No, sir; I did not hear any noise; just a trembling, and everything seemed dumb then. When I came up out of the water, I realized what had happened, and I swam for a buoy.
Q. Swam for what?
A. One of those small buoys that are anchored there.
Q. The door into that superstructure was abaft your head, was it not?
A. Yes, sir; just abaft of the gun.
Q. You do not know whether you went through the deck or through the side?
A. No, sir; I went right straight up and went out. The deck must have been blown up. If it hadn't, I would have been hurt worse than I was. I couldn't make any statement about that. I know I went up through it.
Q. Were you burned at all?
A. No, sir; I wasn't burned. I was just cut in the head; that was all.

The judge-advocate requested that the testimony given by the witness be not read to him by the stenographer, but that he be directed to report to-morrow morning at 10 o'clock, when he will be furnished with so much of the record as contains his testimony and asked to withdraw for the consideration of the same, upon the completion of which he will be again called before the court and be given an opportunity to amend his testimony as recorded, or pronounce it correct. The request was granted and the witness was instructed accordingly; whereupon he withdrew, after being cautioned by the president not to discuss matters pertaining to the inquiry.

Coal Passer THOMAS MELVILLE, U. S. Navy, appeared as a witness before the court, and was duly sworn by the president:

Examined by the JUDGE ADVOCATE:

Q. State your full name, rank, and to what ship you are attached.
A. Thomas Melville, coal passer, U. S. S. *Maine*.
Q. I believe you were on the quarter-deck of the *Maine* at the time of her destruction?
A. Yes, sir.
Q. What part of the deck were you on?
A. Just right between the after turret and the bulkhead of the galley.
Q. In that passageway?
A. Yes, sir.
Q. Which way were you facing?

A. With my back turned to it, sir, and my face toward aft.
Q. Were you standing near Larsen?
A. Yes, sir.
Q. Tell the court exactly what you felt, heard, and saw.
A. I felt something like electrician right under my feet.
Q. You felt what?
A. Something that appeared to me like electrician—a loud report—just about amidships.
Q. An electric shock, I suppose you mean?
A. Yes, sir; and she listed over on the port side. The port was under water. Her starboard side was up. I made my way to the starboard gangway, and then I heard the second report. I had an idea that was the boilers, from the ashes and soot and stuff. I tried to make my way amidships on the starboard gangway, and I got hit with ashes. I had an idea it was the boilers had exploded. That opened up the superstructure and carried everything forward. By that time I made my way aft for the second whaleboat. Before me and a man by the name of McCann could reach her she was under water. I came back again to the starboard gangway, when the captain's gig came along aft with the boatswain in her. He hollered for me and McCann to come to him. We dove overboard and swam for the cutter and manned her to save lives, which we couldn't. Then the captain's writer—I don't know what you call him; I guess it was the writer—hollered for us to come back. We came back and stood there, and the first lieutenant and the captain got in the gig. The captain gave orders to shove off and for all boats to leave her, to look out for the magazines. That was the captain's orders. We went around her a couple of times and looked for lives, but couldn't find any. Then we rowed to the *City of Washington*, at the captain's order, with all the men we had in the boat.
Q. When you felt the first shock, were you knocked off your feet?
A. No, sir.
Q. How long was it before the explosion, which you call a boiler explosion, occurred after the first shock?
A. It appeared to me about a half a minute between the two explosions.
Q. Almost immediately, do you think? Half a minute, you know, is quite a little space.
A. The first explosion raised up part of the superstructure, etc., and twisted it right over my head, and the awning came down over my head. I made under it for the starboard gangway. When I got to the starboard gangway the second explosion occurred.
Q. Did the ship shake as much after the second explosion as after the first?
A. No, sir; I think it shook more at the first.
Q. How was the sound?
A. It appeared to me, when she was hit starboard, it came about amidships, and then turned and everything went forward.
Q. Did you see any flame?
A. Not before the second explosion. The first explosion appeared to be right under the berth deck.
Q. Did the ship seem to lift any at the first explosion?
A. No, sir.
Q. She just trembled?
A. She trembled, and the port side went down just as she was struck.

By the COURT:

Q. You say that this second explosion threw everything forward?

A. It threw everything forward, sir. That is what it appeared to me—that it opened up the superstructure, and the second explosion carried the ironwork out and struck the steam launch, made fast to the guess warp of the starboard side. I seen that myself.

Q. You saw what?

A. I saw when the steam launch went down, from the ironwork of the superstructure, at the second explosion.

Q. What seemed to be the cause of the steam launch going down?

A. The ironwork tipped her over like, and everything went right on to her—smothered her right up. It appeared to me that way. There was a good deal of iron blown out from her. Our two boilers was going forward down below. That is what made me think it was so long, half a minute or so, between the two explosions. There was no boilers going aft. We had two going forward.

Q. You had two boilers going forward?

A. Yes, sir; I knew that myself, and we had four primed ready to steam at the time.

Q. You are wrong. The after boilers were in use?

A. Yes, sir; the two after boilers. I know the steam launch was lying there at the second explosion. I am sure of that.

Q. What was the name of the man who was standing in that passageway between the turret and the galley with you?

A. Pete Larsen.

Q. Where did he go; what did he do?

A. I couldn't tell you, sir. I didn't see him at all.

Q. You did not see him afterwards?

A. No, sir.

Q. Larsen simply went overboard?

A. He disappeared from me, sir. I couldn't say how he disappeared. Of course the shock took all the life out of me for a second—for half a second. When I came to myself, I knew where the starboard gangway was, and I made for it. When I got there I found a fellow by the name of Gartrell praying, and one fellow by the name of Lancaster, he was dead, and another fellow was holding on the gangway. I pulled him out of the water, and saw that he was dead, and I left him there.

Q. You are sure that the ship listed after the first explosion?

A. Oh, yes, sir; the port gangway went under water in two seconds, right after she was hit. She went down so quick that when I got to the starboard gangway it was away up. The gangway was clean out of water.

Q. The second explosion had not occurred at that time?

A. No, sir; not before I reached the starboard side.

Q. Were you standing up at the time of the first shock?

A. Yes, sir; me and this man by the name of McCann and Wilber, coxswain of the steam launch, we tried to make for the second whaleboat. We did make it, and we seen it was under water, and couldn't do anything with it. So we came back to the gangway again, and by that time Wilber fell overboard. He disappeared, and he told us afterwards in the hospital that he fell overboard. The boatswain holloed for me and McCann, and we dove overboard and swam to the captain's gig.

The judge advocate requested that the testimony given by the witness be not read to him by the stenographer, but that he be directed to report to-morrow morning at 10 o'clock, when he will be furnished with so much of the record as contains his testimony, and asked to withdraw for the consideration of the same, upon the completion of which he will be again called before the court and be given an opportunity to amend his testimony as recorded or pronounce it correct. The request was granted, and the witness was instructed accordingly; whereupon he withdrew, after being cautioned by the president not to discuss matters pertaining to the inquiry.

Coxswain BENJAMIN R. WILBER, U. S. Navy, appeared as a witness before the court, and was duly sworn by the president.

Examined by the JUDGE-ADVOCATE:

Q. State your full name, your rate, and the ship to which you are attached.
A. Benjamin R. Wilber; coxswain; U. S. S. *Maine*.
Q. Were you on board the *Maine* at the time of her destruction?
A. Yes, sir; not on the *Maine*. I was in the steam launch alongside the ship.
Q. Where was the steam launch?
A. On the starboard boom, sir.
Q. Did you have steam up?
A. Steam up; yes, sir.
Q. Hanging to what; a guess warp?
A. No, sir; made fast to the Jacob's ladder, and the stern hauled aft to the grab rope, so that she couldn't swing and catch the smokestack.
Q. Who were in the boat with you?
A. There was five of us—Pank, Lowman, Nicholson, and Rau—five men with myself.
Q. Are any of those men alive now?
A. All of them are alive; yes, sir.
Q. Were you awake when it happened?
A. Yes, sir.
Q. What part of the boat were you in?
A. In the stern sheets, sir.
Q. Tell the court what happened.
A. What I know of it; it seemed to me as if something hit me in the face, and I didn't know any more until I came up under the water, some distance from the ship, when I came up close to one of our coaling booms or strong back. I don't know what it was. Pank, one of the men in the boat, was on it. I don't know how long I stayed there, but then I happened to think of the sharks that was in the water around there, and I swam to the ship, to the starboard gangway. I took off my clothes and shoes and jumped overboard again, and swam to the Spanish cutter that was pretty close to the ship then, and they took me on board the Spanish man-of-war that was lying there.
Q. You do not know how you got out of the launch?
A. No, sir; I don't remember one single thing. I don't know what became of the boat either.
Q. Did you see any flame?
A. Just like a flash it hit me in the face. I didn't see any flame.
Q. You were immediately knocked senseless?
A. Yes, sir; I think I was knocked senseless.
Q. How far were you from the ship when you found yourself in the water?
A. I can't exactly say. I should say about 20 yards, or something like that.
Q. Which way from the ship?
A. Right directly out—right broadside off from the ship.

Q. You were some distance from where the launch had been?
A. Yes, sir.

By the COURT:

Q. You heard no explosion; you heard nothing?
A. No, sir; I didn't hear nothing.

By the JUDGE-ADVOCATE:

Q. How were you injured?
A. I was struck on the side of the head here by something.
Q. The right side of your face?
A. Yes, right here.
Q. Around the temple?
A. Yes, sir; and I think it has injured the jawbone. I don't know. I can't open my mouth. I can't hear in the left ear, and I am cut on the right arm below the elbow.

The judge-advocate requested that the testimony given by the witness be not read to him by the stenographer, but that he be directed to report to-morrow morning at 10 o'clock, when he will be furnished with so much of the record as contains his testimony, and asked to withdraw for the consideration of the same, upon the completion of which he will be again called before the court and be given an opportunity to amend his testimony as recorded or pronounce it correct. The request was granted, and the witness was instructed accordingly; whereupon he withdrew, after being cautioned by the president not to discuss matters pertaining to the inquiry.

Fireman JOHN H. PANK, U. S. Navy, appeared as a witness before the court, and was duly sworn by the president.

Examined by the JUDGE-ADVOCATE:

Q. State your full name, rate, and the ship to which you are attached.
A. John Henry Pank; fireman, first-class; U. S. S. *Maine*.
Q. Were you the fireman that ran the first steam launch?
A. Yes, sir.
Q. Were you in that launch at the time of her destruction?
A. Yes, sir.
Q. What part of that boat were you in?
A. I was amidships, near the engine room.
Q. Between the boiler and the stern sheets?
A. Yes, sir.
Q. On which side of the boat?
A. On the port side.
Q. Which way were you looking when this thing happened?
A. I was looking out to starboard.
Q. Away from the ship?
A. Yes, sir.
Q. Tell the court what happened to you?
A. All I can say, sir, is that I heard a big explosion, and I was just about to look around to see where it came from, when something must have struck the steam launch on the port side. It just capsized her right over. It taken us about 25 or 30 feet under the water before we could get out. By the time we got up it was all over. We landed about 30 yards from the ship. That is about all I can say, sir.
Q. You heard an explosion on board the ship?
A. Yes, sir.
Q. One or two?

A. I only heard one, sir.
Q. You felt the boat going over?
A. Yes, sir.
Q. You were not blown out of the boat?
A. No, sir.
Q. You scrambled out as the boat turned over?
A. Yes, sir.
Q. What is the matter with your arm?
A. I lost two of the fingers.
Q. How do you suppose that happened?
A. I don't know, sir; unless it was because we had a pretty good fire in the boilers at the time—we had about 160 pounds of steam—and I can't account for it no other way except that when the boiler struck the water, the boiler was so hot at the time it must have exploded.
Q. You were knocked senseless?
A. No, sir; I wasn't knocked senseless at all. The only place I was hurt was on the hand, and I felt that just as I started to come up.
Q. Did you turn toward the ship when you heard the explosion?
A. Yes, sir.
Q. Did you see any flame shoot up?
A. No, sir; I didn't see anything at all.
Q. I suppose the boat was between you and the ship when she was turning over?
A. Yes, sir.
Q. You are sure the boat keeled over and went down that way?
A. Yes, sir; I am certain of that.

By the COURT:

Q. Were you carried down in the boat?
A. Yes, sir; in the boat.
Q. Did the boat turn over toward the ship or from the ship?
A. From the ship, sir.
Q. You say you think the boat must have been struck by something which keeled her over?
A. Yes, sir; something struck her on the starboard side and just keeled her right over.
Q. Was that any of the flying débris? Was it a piece of metal, or was there anything about it that would enable you to form a conclusion as to what it was struck her?
A. No, sir; I couldn't tell what it was struck her.
Q. You do not know whether it was a wave or the water disturbed by the explosion, or whether it was a piece of the débris?
A. No, sir.

There being no further questions to ask this witness, on account of his crippled condition his testimony was read over to him by the stenographer, and by him pronounced correct.

The witness then withdrew, after being cautioned by the president not to converse about matters pertaining to the inquiry.

Seaman OTTO RAU, U. S. Navy, appeared as a witness before the court and was duly sworn by the president.

Examined by the JUDGE-ADVOCATE:

Q. State your name, rate, and the ship to which you are attached.
A. Otto Rau, seaman, U. S. S. *Maine*.
Q. You were in the steam launch at the time of her destruction?

A. Yes, sir.
Q. Were you awake?
A. Yes, sir.
Q. What part of the boat were you in?
A. I was standing right in front of the boilers.
Q. Forward of the boilers?
A. In front of the boilers; yes, sir. I had scrubbed the tape with my shirt and put it on top of the boiler, and at that minute I felt the pressure. I don't know which way I went out of the launch. I only know that I next felt myself coming up from the water. Three times I struck myself against things, and could not come right on top of the water. After I did come on top of the water, I was a good distance from the ship, close up to Nicholson. He cried for help, and so did I, and we got picked up by a boat.
Q. How far do you suppose you came up from where the wreckage originally was?
A. I don't know exactly how far. It was a good distance.
Q. How many explosions did you hear?
A. I can't remember. I didn't hear none at all.
Q. You do not know anything about it?
A. No, sir. I thought at first it was a boiler from the steam launch that had exploded, and after I came on top of the water I took a look around and seen the ship burning.

The judge-advocate requested that the testimony given by the witness be not read to him by the stenographer, but that he be directed to report to-morrow morning at 10 o'clock, when he will be furnished with so much of the record as contains his testimony and asked to withdraw for the consideration of the same, upon the completion of which he will be again called before the court and be given an opportunity to amend his testimony as recorded, or pronounce it correct. The request was granted, and the witness was instructed accordingly; whereupon he withdrew, after being cautioned by the president not to discuss matters pertaining to the inquiry.

Fireman WILLIAM GARTRELL, U. S. Navy, appeared as a witness before the court, and was duly sworn by the president.

Examined by the JUDGE-ADVOCATE:
Q. State your full name, rate, and to what ship you are attached.
A. William Gartrell, born in Washington. I am a first-class fireman by rate; attached to the U. S. S. *Maine*.
Q. Were you on board the *Maine* at the time of her destruction?
A. Yes, sir.
Q. Where were you?
A. I were right down at the magazine, on top of the magazine, when it happened; at the tiller room, right by the storeroom. I was lying down at the time.
Q. You were lying down in the tiller room?
A. Yes, sir; I had just laid down. It wasn't a second. I had no sooner laid down, than it happened.
Q. You were right in front of the storeroom door?
A. No, sir; that is a torpedo on the edge of the storeroom. It was back of that, where the gunners keep their storeroom.
Q. About abreast of the three wheels?
A. Yes, sir.
Q. On which side?

A. On the port side.
Q. You were on the port side, abreast of the three wheels?
A. On the port side; yes, sir.
Q. You were in the steering room, then?
A. Yes, sir.
Q. In the steam steering engine room?
A. Yes, sir.
Q. Not in the tiller room.
A. You know, there are two magazines.
Q. You were right by the three wheels?
A. Yes, sir; I were lying right in here, sir [indicating]. There is a hatch there.
Q. On the starboard side or the port side?
A. On the port side the hatches are. I was lying right on that hatch. I had a mattress there.
Q. You were in the steam steering room?
A. Yes, sir.
Q. The tiller room is abaft that?
A. Yes, sir.
Q. Tell the court exactly what you felt, and heard, and saw.
A. Just a second before that Rushford, chief machinist, came to me and asked me for the loan of the keys to go in the storeroom. He said he was restless and couldn't sleep. I gave him the keys and told him to put the keys near my shoes, that I was going to sleep there that night. I laid there. I had a book in my hand and was going to read. Just then Charley Quinn, an oiler, that was on watch, came up and said: "We want some oil." I said: "It is funny there is no oil out," and everything like that; but I gave him the key and he got the oil and throwed the key back. Then I walked back and laid down and went to sleep. Frank Gardiner, coal passer, was lying down beside of me. Just as soon as I laid down, I was talking to him and I hadn't spoke three words. He was telling me his time was out in May, and I said mine was out in June, and he made the remark that he was going to wait for me—all like that, just fooling, and just then a flash came. It was a blue flash. It seemed to me like it was right by the lamp in the engine room. I could see as plain as day.
Q. How could you see into the engine room?
A. I could see through the door, sir. It was a kind of a blue flame, and it came all at once. The two of us jumped up, and I went on the port side up the engine-room ladder, and Frank Gardiner, he went up the starboard side—at least he didn't go up, because he hollered to me. He struck the door right there where the partition separates the two doors, and he must have struck his head. He hollered to me; he says: "O Jesus, Billy, I am gone." I didn't stop then, because the water was then up to my knees. I made a break as quick as I could up the ladder, and when I got up the ladder into the steerage room the ladder was gone. Everything was dark. I couldn't see nothing; everything was pitch dark, and I gave up, or I started to give up. There was a colored fellow with me; I didn't know his name until afterwards. His name was Harris. We got hold of each other. I says: "Let's give up; there is no hope." I started in to say a prayer the best I knew how, and I heard a voice. It must have been an officer; it couldn't have been a man's voice, because he says: "There is hope, men." I knew from that that he was an officer. After that I seen a little light. It looked like an awful distance from me, but I made for that light, and when I got there it seemed like I could see the heavens. I got jammed in the ladder. My head was right up against the deck. I seen the

ladder, and I caught hold of Harris, and the two of us hugged each other.

Q. You got hold of who?
A. The ladder was hung crossways on top. There wasn't no ladder that we could walk up. The ladder was up above us, and we got jammed in the ladder, the two of us. I don't know whether I got out first or this colored fellow, but when I did get out I tried to say a prayer. I looked where I was and I saw the heavens and everything, and I tried to say a prayer or something, and I fainted away. I felt someone picking me up and they throwed me overboard.

Q. When you saw this blue flame in the engine room, did you feel any shock to the ship?
A. Yes, sir; she was going like this all the time [indicating].

Q. The ship was?
A. Yes, sir.

Q. How long did that last?
A. It lasted until I got up to the top of the ladder. Then I was in the water.

Q. You only felt one continuous shaking?
A. Yes, sir.

Q. Did you hear any noise, any report?
A. Yes, sir; I heard a terrible report.

Q. How did it sound; like a gun?
A. No, sir; it wasn't a gun. I couldn't hardly tell you how it sounded—like the whole earth had opened up.

By the COURT:

Q. There was but one shock—one continuous shock?
A. I don't know. It seemed like it was just the roaring of the ship, and then the shock came.

Q. You felt the ship tremble before this explosion?
A. Before this explosion; yes, sir.

Q. You were right in the bottom of the ship?
A. Yes, sir.

Q. Did you say you were lying on your hammock?
A. On the mattress, on the after magazine on the port side, right in the engineers' storeroom. As you come out of the door and right down about 8 or 9 feet, I think, there are these magazine hatches. I had my mattress there. Frank Gardiner, coal passer, he was lying this way, just between the wheels, with his mattress.

The judge-advocate requested that the testimony given by the witness be not read to him by the stenographer, but that he be directed to report to-morrow morning at 10 o'clock, when he will be furnished with so much of the record as contains his testimony and asked to withdraw for the consideration of the same, upon the completion of which he will be again called before the court and be given an opportunity to amend his testimony as recorded, or pronounce it correct. The request was granted and the witness was instructed accordingly; whereupon he withdrew, after being cautioned by the president not to discuss matters pertaining to the inquiry.

Seaman EDWARD MATTSON, U. S. Navy, appeared as a witness before the court, and was duly sworn by the president.

Examined by the JUDGE-ADVOCATE:

Q. State your full name, rate, and to what ship you are attached.
A. My name is Edward Mattson; ordinary seaman; attached to the U. S. S. *Maine*.

Q. You were on anchor watch at the time the *Maine* was destroyed?
A. We were standing quarter watches, and I had the messenger watch.
Q. You were wide awake at the time it happened, were you?
A. Yes, sir; I and another fellow was walking up in the starboard gangway.
Q. Will you tell the court exactly where you were when you felt the first shock?
A. I was right abreast of the starboard crane.
Q. In the starboard gangway?
A. Yes, sir.
Q. Facing which way?
A. Facing forward.
Q. Then state exactly what you felt, and heard, and saw.
A. It was just the same as if I seen lots of smoke, and I went right up in the air. I don't know where I went to. After that I didn't remember until I was lying aft on the quarter-deck.
Q. What part of the quarter-deck?
A. I was lying right by the smokestack, and when I come to my senses I slid down on the quarter-deck.
Q. When the ship shook were you knocked off your feet immediately?
A. Yes, sir.
Q. At the very first shock?
A. Yes, sir.
Q. Did you see any fire flying up in the air?
A. No, sir; I didn't see anything else but smoke.
Q. You only felt one shock?
A. Yes, sir.
Q. And that landed you aft on the quarter-deck?
A. Yes, sir.
Q. Are you sure you went up in the air?
A. Yes, sir; I didn't strike the water. I must have gone in the air.

By the COURT:

Q. You say you felt but one shock?
A. One shock; that is all, sir.
Q. You were walking up and down the gangway?
A. Yes, sir.
Q. You were facing downward?
A. Yes, sir.
Q. Then you were thrown backward, were you?
A. Backward on the quarter deck.
Q. How did you fall?
A. I suppose I fell on my shoulder, for I felt kind of sore there [indicating left shoulder].
Q. Did you say you were alongside of the smokestack?
A. Yes, sir; by the smokestack, just where the third cutter was standing.
Q. You said you were by the crane, did you not?
A. Yes; abreast of the starboard crane.

The judge-advocate requested that the testimony given by the witness be not read to him by the stenographer, but that he be directed to report to-morrow morning at 10 o'clock, when he will be furnished with so much of the record as contains his testimony and asked to withdraw for the consideration of the same, upon the completion of which he will be again called before the court and be given an opportunity to amend his testimony as recorded, or pronounce it correct. The request was granted, and the witness was instructed accordingly; whereupon he withdrew, after being cautioned by the president not to discuss matters pertaining to the inquiry.

Mess Attendant JOHN H. TURPIN, U. S. Navy, appeared as a witness before the court, and was duly sworn by the president.

Examined by the JUDGE-ADVOCATE:

Q. State your full name, your rate, and the ship to which you are attached.
A. John Henry Turpin, mess attendant, attached to the U. S. S. Maine.
Q. Where were you when the first indication of any trouble occurred on the night the Maine was destroyed?
A. Down below in the wardroom pantry.
Q. In the wardroom pantry?
A. Yes, sir.
Q. Sitting down or standing up?
A. Sitting down.
Q. Facing which way?
A. Facing the door as you come out of the pantry.
Q. Facing the inboard door?
A. Yes, sir.
Q. The pantry is on the starboard side, is it?
A. Yes, sir.
Q. You were facing inboard?
A. The pantry is situated like this [indicating]. As you come in from the wardroom, you come in so [indicating]. I was facing the door as you come out.
Q. Facing the inboard door?
A. The inboard door.
Q. Not the door leading into the wardroom?
A. No, sir; not the door leading into the wardroom.
Q. The door leading into the passage amidships?
A. The door leading into the passage.
Q. How far were you out into the pantry; how far away from the door?
A. Right by the ice box.
Q. Tell us how far that is—about halfway?
A. About halfway.
Q. Tell the court exactly what you felt and heard and saw.
A. I just felt the ship heave, and it seemed to lift, like that [indicating]. I just felt the ship heave and lift.
Q. Lift which way?
A. She lifted up and kind of listed to port.
Q. What made her do that?
A. It was a jarring explosion—just one solid explosion, and the ship heaved and lifted like that, and then all was dark. I met Mr. Jenkins in the mess room, and by that time the water was up to my waist, and the water was running aft. It was all dark in there, and he hollered to me, and he says, "Which way?" I don't know what he meant by that. I says, "I don't know which way." He hollered again, "Which way?" I says, "I don't know, sir, which way." And he hollered the last time; he says, "Which way?" I says, "I don't know, sir." Then I was groping my way, and the water was up to my breast. Mr. Jenkins started forward, and then the whole compartment lit right up. That whole compartment where the torpedoes were lit right up, and

I seen Mr. Jenkins then throw up both hands and fall, right by the steerage pantry. Then I groped my way aft, and got to the captain's ladder—the ladder coming out of the wardroom—just as you come out of the wardroom to go up in the cabin. When I got there the ladder was carried away, and somehow or other the manrope kept fast upon deck, but the ladder got adrift from it down below in the water.

By that time the water was right up even with my chin. Then I commenced to get scared, and in fooling around it happened that a rope touched my arm, and I commenced to climb overhand and got on deck. When I got outside the passageway in the cabin on the starboard side, I climbed up on some—I don't know what it was I climbed up on. Anyhow, I got up on the poop, and as soon as I got up on the poop Mr. Holman gave the order to me. He says, "Go down below and get some cutlasses." I says, "Aye, aye, sir." I went down in the after gunroom, and the water was coming in at such a rush I had to come up again. So I came up again and got on the after search-light rail, and I dove overboard. When I dove overboard I swam a little ways, and John Herbert, an ordinary seaman, was right up behind me. He grabbed hold of my ankle. I says, "Let go, please; you will drown the two of us." He wouldn't let go. He kept climbing on me; so I hit him. By that time he relinquished his hold, and he was picked up afterwards. So I swam out, and the Spanish boat passed me, and I went under the water again. I was afraid there was some danger, so I went under water again, and when I rose again the barge passed, and I got inside.

By the COURT:

Q. Where were you at the time; right astern of the ship?
A. Right astern of the ship; yes, sir. That is my experience about it.

By the JUDGE-ADVOCATE:

Q. You felt only one shock?
A. I felt only one shock.
Q. Only one lift of the ship?
A. Only one lift of the ship.
Q. She lifted first and then went down to port?
A. Yes, sir.
Q. What kind of noises did you hear?
A. It sounded like distant thunder—just a rumbling.

By the COURT:

Q. Were you asleep?
A. No, sir; I was not asleep. I had just as good sense about me and was as wide awake as I am now.
Q. How do you know you were not asleep?
A. I know I was not asleep because I was standing there talking.
Q. I thought you said you were sitting down?
A. I was sitting down. I was talking to a couple of the boys in there—Harris and Robert White.
Q. What became of them?
A. Harris—how he got on deck, I don't remember.

The judge-advocate requested that the testimony given by the witness be not read to him by the stenographer, but that he be directed to report to-morrow morning at 10 o'clock, when he will be furnished with so much of the record as contains his testimony and asked to withdraw for the consideration of the same, upon the completion of which he will be again called before the court and be given an opportunity to amend his testimony as recorded or pronounce it correct. The request was granted, and the witness was instructed accordingly; whereupon he withdrew, after being cautioned by the president not to discuss matters pertaining to the inquiry.

Seaman MARTIN LARSEN, U. S. Navy, appeared as a witness before the court, and was duly sworn by the president.

Examined by the JUDGE-ADVOCATE:

Q. State your full name, rate, and to what ship you are attached.
A. Martin Larsen, captain of the hold, seaman; attached to the U. S. S. *Maine*.
Q. When did you leave the *Maine*?
A. The 21st of January.
Q. How long had you been captain of the hold?
A. Fifteen months, sir.
Q. What were your duties at night in securing the hold?
A. Closing all the hatches, and seeing that everything was secure and all lights out.
Q. You always saw that securely done before reporting at 8 o'clock?
A. Yes, sir.
Q. Who relieved you when you left the ship?
A. Neilson.
Q. What kind of a man is Neilson?
A. He is a very good man.
Q. A reliable man?
A. Yes, sir.
Q. Did you explain all of your duties to him?
A. Yes, sir; I didn't have time to. I was sick at the time, and they seemed to be in a hurry to get me off the ship.
Q. He is a very good man?
A. Yes, sir.
Q. Looking after everything is always done before reporting?
A. Yes, sir.
Q. Neilson was killed?
A. Yes, sir.
Q. You were not on board at the time of the explosion?
A. No, sir.
Q. Tell the court what places you closed at night before making your 8 p. m. report.
A. In port we closed the hatches leading down from the berth deck— leading down through A33.
Q. And at sea?
A. At sea every hatch was closed.

The judge-advocate requested that the testimony given by the witness be not read to him by the stenographer, but that he be directed to report to-morrow morning at 10 o'clock, when he will be furnished with so much of the record as contains his testimony and asked to withdraw for the consideration of the same, upon the completion of which he will be again called before the court and be given an opportunity to amend his testimony as recorded or pronounce it correct. The request was granted, and the witness was instructed accordingly; whereupon he withdrew, after being cautioned by the president not to discuss matters pertaining to the inquiry.

The court then (at 3.35 p. m.) adjourned until to-morrow morning, March 2, 1898, at 11 o'clock.

NINTH DAY.

United States Court-House,
Key West, Fla., 10 a. m., Wednesday, March 2, 1898.

The court met pursuant to adjournment of yesterday, the first instant.

Present: All the members of the court, the judge-advocate, and the stenographers.

The record of the proceedings of yesterday, the eighth day of the inquiry, was read and approved.

Passed Assistant Engineer BOWERS here appeared before the court.

The JUDGE-ADVOCATE. Mr. Bowers, have you read over the record of your testimony given yesterday?

Mr. BOWERS. Yes, sir.

The JUDGE-ADVOCATE. Is it correct as recorded?

Mr. BOWERS. I should like to make some few corrections.

The JUDGE-ADVOCATE. Please name them.

Mr. BOWERS. On page 330, in the second line from the bottom, I should like to leave out the words "the other tank," and say "the starboard bunker."

On page 332, the fourth line from the top, "When I went off watch we were using what we used, No. 4 bunker," should be, "When I went off watch we were using No. 4 bunker."

The JUDGE-ADVOCATE. You wish to leave out, "what we used"?

Mr. BOWERS. Yes, sir.

The JUDGE-ADVOCATE. Is your testimony as amended correct?

Mr. BOWERS. Yes, sir.

Assistant Engineer MORRIS appeared before the court:

The JUDGE-ADVOCATE. Have you read over the testimony given by you yesterday as recorded?

Mr. MORRIS. Yes, sir.

The JUDGE-ADVOCATE. Is it correct as recorded?

Mr. MORRIS. No, sir; I have one change to make.

The JUDGE-ADVOCATE. State what it is.

Mr. MORRIS. On page 336, in the twelfth line, the answer should be: "I looked into B4." The record from there down to the tenth line from the bottom of the page should be struck out.

The JUDGE-ADVOCATE. I can not strike out the record. I will have to repeat the questions to you as I put them, and you can answer them any way you like. I will repeat them:

"By the JUDGE-ADVOCATE:

"Q. If there had been any combustion going on in A16, would you have noticed it when you went into B6"?

"A. I did not go into B6."

Q. You want to strike out "I did not go into B6"?

A. Yes, sir.

"Q. I am speaking of A16, not A15, the port bunker. Which bunker did you go into at 7.45?"

A. There is a misunderstanding there. I was in B3, B5, and A15.

Q. Which port bunker did you go into at 7.45?

A. I looked into B4.

Q. Your previous answer read: "I looked inside; yes, sir, into B4.

There was nothing unusual there. I simply had the door closed down, as it was night inspection. I did not enter B6." Is that correct?
A. That is correct.
The JUDGE-ADVOCATE. Then your testimony as amended is correct?
Mr. MORRIS. Yes, sir.
The judge-advocate asked and received permission to ask some additional questions of Lieutenant Bowers.

Examined by the JUDGE-ADVOCATE:

Q. You were on watch during the day of February 15?
A. Yes, sir.
Q. What boilers were in use?
A. Boilers G and H.
Q. Those were the two after boilers?
A. The two after boilers.
Q. What was the condition of these boilers?
A. I looked at the fires and noted the water in the glass. There was three-quarters of a column of water. The boilers were in every way in a normal condition.
Q. At what time did you make this inspection last?
A. 7.45.
Q. Was there a careful watch on over these boilers?
A. Yes, sir.
Q. Good men?
A. Yes, sir.
Q. They were all at their stations?
A. Yes, sir.
Q. They all went to their stations at 8 o'clock, the relief watch?
A. Half the relief was down there at the time. The water tender was down there and one of the firemen.
Q. At what time?
A. At 7.45, or when I came out. At about five minutes to 8 I left the compartment.
Q. I am speaking of the first watch that night. You have every reason to believe the watch was carefully set at 8 o'clock, and that they did their duty?
A. Yes, sir.
Q. They were good men in that watch?
A. Yes, sir; the water tender was the most reliable water tender in the ship.

There being no further questions to ask this witness, his testimony was read over to him by the stenographer, and by him pronounced correct.

The witness then retired, after being cautioned by the president not to converse about matters pertaining to the inquiry.

Naval Cadet CRENSHAW here entered the court.

The JUDGE-ADVOCATE. You have read over your testimony of yesterday as recorded?
Mr. CRENSHAW. Yes, sir.
The JUDGE-ADVOCATE. Is it correct?
Mr. CRENSHAW. No, sir; there is one mistake.
The JUDGE-ADVOCATE. Please state what correction you wish to make.

Mr. CRENSHAW. At the end of line 23, page 311, strike out the period, so that it will read: "It seemed to me that through the door that leads into the compartment just forward of that there was a rushing noise of some kind."

The JUDGE-ADVOCATE. Is your testimony as amended correct?

Mr. CRENSHAW. It is.

The witness then retired after being cautioned by the president not to converse about matters pertaining to the inquiry.

Private McKAY, U. S. Marine Corps, here entered the court.

The JUDGE-ADVOCATE. Private McKay, you have had read to you the testimony which you gave yesterday?

Private McKAY. Yes, sir.

The JUDGE-ADVOCATE. Is it correct as recorded?

Private McKAY. Yes, sir.

The witness then retired after being cautioned by the president not to converse about matters pertaining to the inquiry.

Apprentice HAM here entered the court.

The JUDGE-ADVOCATE. Apprentice Ham, you have had read to you the testimony which you gave yesterday?

Apprentice HAM. Yes, sir.

The JUDGE-ADVOCATE. Is it correct as recorded?

Apprentice HAM. Yes, sir.

The witness then retired after being cautioned by the president not to converse about matters pertaining to the inquiry.

Apprentice DRESSLER here entered the court.

The JUDGE-ADVOCATE. Apprentice Dressler, you have had read to you the testimony which you gave yesterday?

Apprentice DRESSLER. Yes, sir.

The JUDGE-ADVOCATE. Is it correct as recorded?

Apprentice DRESSLER. Yes, sir.

The witness then retired, after being cautioned by the president not to converse about matters pertaining to the inquiry.

Sergeant MEHAN here entered the court.

The JUDGE-ADVOCATE. Sergeant Mehan, you have had read to you the testimony which you gave yesterday?

Sergeant MEHAN. Yes, sir.

The JUDGE-ADVOCATE. Is it correct as recorded?

Sergeant MEHAN. Yes, sir.

The witness then retired, after being cautioned by the president not to converse about matters pertaining to the inquiry.

Corporal THOMPSON here entered the court.

The JUDGE-ADVOCATE. Corporal Thompson, you have had read to you the testimony which you gave yesterday?

Corporal THOMPSON. Yes, sir.

The JUDGE-ADVOCATE. Is it correct as recorded?

Corporal THOMPSON. Yes, sir.

The witness then retired, after being cautioned by the president not to converse about matters pertaining to the inquiry.

Master-at-Arms LOAD here entered the court.

The JUDGE-ADVOCATE. Master-at-Arms Load, you have had read to you the testimony which you gave yesterday?
Master-at-Arms LOAD. Yes, sir.
The JUDGE-ADVOCATE. Is it correct as recorded?
Master-at-Arms LOAD. Yes, sir.

The witness then retired, after being cautioned by the president not to converse about matters pertaining to the inquiry.

Seaman PETER LARSEN here entered the court.

The JUDGE-ADVOCATE. Seaman Peter Larsen, you have had read to you the testimony which you gave yesterday.
Seaman PETER LARSEN. Yes, sir.
The JUDGE-ADVOCATE. Is it correct as recorded?
Seaman PETER LARSEN. Yes, sir.

The witness then retired, after being cautioned by the president not to converse about matters pertaining to the inquiry.

Seaman MOLINIERE here entered the court.

The JUDGE-ADVOCATE. Seaman Moliniere, you have had read to you the testimony which you gave yesterday.
Seaman MOLINIERE. Yes, sir.
The JUDGE-ADVOCATE. Is it correct as recorded?
Seaman MOLINIERE. Yes, sir.

The witness then retired, after being cautioned by the president not to converse about matters pertaining to the inquiry.

Boatswain's Mate BERGMAN here entered the court.

The JUDGE-ADVOCATE. Boatswain's Mate Bergman, you have had read to you the testimony which you gave yesterday?
Boatswain's Mate BERGMAN. Yes, sir.
The JUDGE-ADVOCATE. Is it correct as recorded?
Boatswain's Mate BERGMAN. Yes, sir.

The witness then retired, after being cautioned by the president not to converse about matters pertaining to the inquiry.

Landsman FOX here entered the court.

The JUDGE-ADVOCATE. Landsman Fox, you have had read to you the testimony which you gave yesterday?
Landsman FOX. Yes, sir.
The JUDGE-ADVOCATE. Is it correct as recorded?
Landsman FOX. Yes, sir.

The witness then retired, after being cautioned by the president not to converse about matters pertaining to the inquiry.

Landsman LANAHAN here entered the court.

The JUDGE-ADVOCATE. Landsman Lanahan, you have had read to you the testimony which you gave yesterday?
Landsman LANAHAN. Yes, sir.
The JUDGE-ADVOCATE. Is it correct as recorded?
Landsman LANAHAN. Yes, sir.

The witness then retired, after being cautioned by the president not to converse about matters pertaining to the inquiry.

Coal Passer MELVILLE here entered the court.

The JUDGE-ADVOCATE. Coal Passer Melville, you have had read to you the testimony which you gave yesterday?
Coal Passer MELVILLE. Yes, sir.
The JUDGE-ADVOCATE. Is it correct as recorded?
Coal Passer MELVILLE. Yes, sir.

The witness then retired, after being cautioned by the president not to converse about matters pertaining to the inquiry.

Coxswain WILBER here entered the court.

The JUDGE-ADVOCATE. Coxswain Wilber, you have had read to you the testimony which you gave yesterday?
Coxswain WILBER. Yes, sir.
The JUDGE-ADVOCATE. Is it correct as recorded?
Coxswain WILBER. Yes, sir.

The witness then retired, after being cautioned by the president not to converse about matters pertaining to the inquiry.

Seaman RAU here entered the court.

The JUDGE-ADVOCATE. Seaman Rau, you have had read to you the testimony which you gave yesterday?
Seaman RAU. Yes, sir.
The JUDGE-ADVOCATE. Is it correct as recorded?
Seaman RAU. Yes, sir.

The witness then retired, after being cautioned by the president not to converse about matters pertaining to the inquiry.

Fireman GARTRELL here entered the court.

The JUDGE-ADVOCATE. Fireman Gartrell, you have had read to you the testimony which you gave yesterday?
Fireman GARTRELL. Yes, sir.
The JUDGE-ADVOCATE. Is it correct as recorded?
Fireman GARTRELL. Yes, sir.

The witness then retired, after being cautioned by the president not to converse about matters pertaining to the inquiry.

Seaman MATTSON here entered the court.

The JUDGE-ADVOCATE. Seaman Mattson, you have had read to you the testimony which you gave yesterday?
Seaman MATTSON. Yes, sir.
The JUDGE-ADVOCATE. Is it correct as recorded?
Seaman MATTSON. Yes, sir.

The witness then retired, after being cautioned by the president not to converse about matters pertaining to the inquiry.

Mess Attendant TURPIN here entered the court.

The JUDGE-ADVOCATE. Mess Attendant Turpin, you have had read to you the testimony which you gave yesterday?
Mess Attendant TURPIN. Yes, sir.
The JUDGE-ADVOCATE. Is it correct as recorded?
Mess Attendant TURPIN. Yes, sir.

The witness then retired, after being cautioned by the president not to converse about matters pertaining to the inquiry.

DESTRUCTION OF THE U. S. BATTLE SHIP MAINE.

Seaman HARRY S. MCCANN, U. S. Navy, appeared as a witness before the court, and was duly sworn by the president.

Examined by the JUDGE-ADVOCATE:

Q. Please state your full name, your rate, and to what ship you are attached.
A. Harry S. McCann; seaman; serving on board the U. S. S. *Maine.*
Q. Were you on board the *Maine* at the time of her destruction in Havana?
A. Yes, sir.
Q. What part of the ship were you in at the moment it commenced?
A. I was in the after part of the ship, on the quarter deck, right abaft the middle superstructure.
Q. What part of the superstructure were you nearest to?
A. I was nearest to the ladder leading up to the superstructure.
Q. The one that has the rail underneath?
A. Yes, sir; I was within 5 feet of the ladder.
Q. Which way were you facing?
A. Outboard. My head was facing the superstructure. My feet was aft—lying down.
Q. You were lying down?
A. Yes, sir.
Q. Were you asleep?
A. I was neither awake nor asleep. I was in a sort of doze.
Q. Tell the court exactly what you felt, saw, and heard.
A. I felt a jar and I saw a flash of light—a red fire and an explosion. That is all, sir.
Q. What kind of a jar was it you felt?
A. I don't know—like a lifting.
Q. Did the ship tremble?
A. Yes, sir.
Q. How soon did the explosion come in regard to the jar?
A. I should say about an interval of a second or so.
Q. Did that jar the ship—did the explosion jar the ship much?
A. Yes, sir.
Q. What became of you?
A. I remained where I was. I wasn't thrown. I just stayed right there.
Q. Were you knocked senseless?
A. No, sir.
Q. What made you stay there?
A. I waited there until the débris and stuff stopped dropping, and I came from underneath the awning and went to the starboard rail, right there at the starboard gangway; then I jumped overboard and got under the gig.

By the COURT:

Q. Was the first shock that you felt accompanied by any sound; was there any report?
A. No; not the jar. There was no report to the jar, sir. I got in a sitting position; then came the flash and the report.
Q. Then there was but one report, was there?
A. That is all I remember hearing; there might have been more.
Q. That is what we want to know.
A. I couldn't swear there was any more, sir.
Q. That is what we want. You heard only one report, but you felt the jar before the report came?
A. Yes, sir.

There being no further questions to ask this witness, his testimony was read over to him by the stenographer and by him pronounced correct.

The witness then withdrew, after being cautioned by the president not to converse about matters pertaining to the inquiry.

Landsman KANE, U. S. Navy, appeared as a witness before the court, and was duly sworn by the president.

Examined by the JUDGE-ADVOCATE:

Q. Please state your full name, rate, and to what ship you are attached.
A. Joseph H. Kane; landsman; U. S. S. *Maine*.
Q. Were you on board the *Maine* at the time of her destruction in Havana?
A. Yes, sir.
Q. Tell the court exactly where you were at the beginning of the trouble.
A. I was in the after part of the superstructure, on the starboard side.
Q. Which superstructure; the middle superstructure?
A. Yes, sir.
Q. You were right over the armory?
A. Right forward of the armory; as far aft as I could be on that side.
Q. Inside?
A. Yes, sir; on the starboard side.
Q. You were inside the superstructure?
A. Yes, sir; looking out to port, where the ice chest is. I was looking out to port on the starboard side, and I seen a flash, followed by an explosion. I didn't see the fire itself, but I seen the reflection, as from a fire, a light. I was thrown below decks somewhere; I don't know where. I guess it must have been below decks. When I emerged I was on the port side, under the port crane. I came out on the main deck. It must have been below decks, and I came through a manhole.

By the COURT:

Q. You stood looking out of this air port [indicating]?
A. I was standing abaft the 6-inch gun support, and I saw a flash of light in the starboard gangway.
Q. Were you under water during that time?
A. When I first went down I was pinned down. It must have been wood, and the water came and lifted the weight off my body, and I was able to get up. By that time the water was up to my waist.
Q. It is impossible to explain how you got there?
A. Yes, sir; I didn't walk a step. Load was with me all the time.
Q. Did you crawl up?
A. Yes, sir.
Q. You crawled up through this manhole?
A. Yes, sir.
Q. Or bunker plate, whatever it was?
A. It was a natural hole. There was nothing broken in there, because the iron rim on there was perfectly smooth. I think it was a coal chute, or something of that sort.

By the JUDGE-ADVOCATE:

Q. What was the first thing you felt; the very first thing?
A. The first thing I felt was the shock, and I was thrown very quick.

Q. Did you hear a noise with it?
A. Yes; I heard a noise.
Q. What kind of a noise?
A. Like the report of a gun, very close.
Q. What did you hear next?
A. Nothing but a roar right along until I got out.
Q. You mean, when you first heard the noise begin, the roar came immediately; or was there an interval?
A. It sounded like the gun was fired, and you heard the roar for a good while afterwards; for two or three seconds.
Q. Interval?
A. No; following.
Q. The roar lasted two or three seconds?
A. Yes, sir.
Q. Then you found yourself below decks?
A. Yes, sir.
Q. And you crawled out on the port side of the main deck?
A. Yes, sir.

By the COURT.

Q. What is the height between the main and berth decks; could you reach up?
A. It is about 10 feet.
Q. How do you suppose you got hold of that opening to get up?
A. As I say, there was water there, and débris, ditty-boxes, and all such stuff, piled up. Then there was some kind of a tank there—some kind of an iron or copper, or some kind of a metal tank there—that broke. I could see that. That helped me up. I got up on it, and I had a long stick, probably three or four feet long. I stood it upright, and put it straight on the plate, and I hauled myself up. I got my elbows on it, and crawled up through it. The water raised a good deal. It was up to my waist. There was débris of every kind and wreckage lying around there.
Q. What happened to you after that?
A. After that I crawled from the main deck up on to the hammock nettings and into the whaleboat. The painter of the boat was thrown up and made fast. All the men that was there with me got in the boat.
Q. When were you hurt?
A. Where was I hurt?
Q. When or where?
A. The wreckage was falling on me, and I hurt myself trying to lift the wreckage off. Whatever was on me, it must have been wood, because when the water came it lifted off itself.
Q. You broke your arm then, did you?
A. My shoulder. I dislocated it. My breast is hurt, too.

There being no further questions to ask this witness, his testimony was read over to him by the stenographer, and by him pronounced correct.

The witness then withdrew, after being cautioned by the president not to converse about matters pertaining to the inquiry.

Commander JAMES M. FORSYTH, U. S. Navy, appeared before the court as a witness, and was duly sworn by the president.

Examined by the JUDGE-ADVOCATE:

Q. Please state your full name, rank, and to what ship duty you are at present assigned.

A. James M. Forsyth; commander, U. S. Navy; commandant of the Key West Naval Station.

Q. Did you receive any orders recently in regard to examining the coal pile at Key West, which is the property of the Government?

A. I did.

Q. Please state what orders you received.

A. On the 17th of February I received a telegram from the Chief of the Bureau of Equipment to "examine anthracite coal pile thoroughly for infernals. Signed, Bradford."

Q. What steps did you take to carry out this order?

A. I appointed three of the employees as inspectors, and hired a gang of shovelers to turn the coal over with shovels—to shift it with shovels.

Q. Whom did you put in charge of the whole work?

A. Charles Goodwin, machinist.

Q. A reliable man?

A. I consider him a very reliable man.

Q. Has the work been completed?

A. The work was completed in about three days.

Q. How much coal was in the pile, about?

A. About one thousand tons.

Q. When did the *Maine* coal here recently—since her coming down from the north?

A. Twice.

Q. What coal did she receive, and how much each time; the kind of coal, I mean?

A. She received anthracite coal, 280 tons at the first coaling, and I think 270 tons at the second. I have a memorandum of that.

Q. Refer to that paper.

A. This is taken from the log of the station; 280 tons at the first, and 271 tons at the last coaling.

Q. Can you give the dates of the coalings?

A. Yes, sir; the first was December 20 to 22, 1897, and the second January 18 and 19, 1898.

Q. Did she receive the coal from the pile which you have examined?

A. No, sir.

Q. What became of the coal that was in that pile at that time?

A. The coal that she received was mostly Morea coal from the Morea coal mine; anthracite Morea coal.

Q. That has all been given to ships?

A. It has all been given to ships. There may be a few tons of it left outside, on the eastern end, but I am not sure, because the two coals were mixed; but her main body of coal that she received was Morea coal. I would further say that she may have received some red-ash coal that was sent down later from the *Natalie*. There may have been some carloads of the *Natalie* coal; but the main body of her coal was Morea.

Q. How did the coal arrive here that she received?

A. In schooners.

Q. Alongside the wharf?

A. Alongside the wharf.

Q. It was taken up in the regular method to the storehouse?

A. Taken up in the regular method to the storehouse, and handled in the regular way.

Q. How long had that coal been here which the *Maine* received?

A. It was received in January, 1897.

Q. What report did Mr. Goodwin make to you after his inspection?
A. He reported that there had been nothing unusual discovered. I can also say that I visited the work at intervals myself, and also had Paymaster Jewett visit the work at intervals while it was going on, to see that it was carried on so that the inspector could see every shovelful of coal that was moved; and they said that all of it was examined lump by lump.

Q. The coal was taken to the *Maine* in the usual method pursued in the coaling of ships?
A. No, sir; rather unusual. It was coaled by lighter. Ships generally come alongside the wharf and coal, but the *Maine's* draft was excessive. The draft was too great. The captain did not wish to bring her alongside the wharf; so it was put on lighters. So the coal was really handled twice more than it would have been if it had been coaled in the usual way.

There being no further questions to ask this witness, his testimony was read over to him by the stenographer and by him pronounced correct.

The witness then withdrew, after being cautioned by the president not to converse about matters pertaining to the inquiry.

Machinist CHARLES GOODWIN appeared as a witness before the court, and was duly sworn by the president.

Examined by the JUDGE-ADVOCATE:

Q. Please state your full name, your business, at present, and your residence.
A. Charles Goodwin; foreman of the Government machine shop in Key West.
Q. You reside in Key West?
A. I reside in Key West. I reside in the shop.
Q. Did you, about the middle of February, receive an order from the commandant of this station to make an inspection of the coal pile for infernals?
A. I did, sir.
Q. Do you remember when you received the order?
A. I received it on last Saturday, a week ago.
Q. Did you carry out the order?
A. I did.
Q. In what way?
A. I had all the pile of coal turned directly over, so that I could see through every particle. I had two assistants with me, but I was there all the time myself. Not a particle of coal was left unturned over—of the anthracite coal, not the bituminous coal. There was bituminous coal there, too. Of the anthracite coal there was not a particle that was not turned thoroughly over, so that I could see through the whole of it.
Q. Was anything found wrong by anybody during this work?
A. Nothing at all.

By the COURT:

Q. What did you expect to find?
A. I thought I might find some unforeseen bombs or something like that. That is what I expected. I found one piece of coal with a hole drilled through it, but that was nothing more than where they drilled to blast it. I was careful, of course, to see. I could tell pretty near

the difference between the coal and any substance of iron or anything that way.

Q. You could have seen a bomb or a piece of pipe or anything of that sort?

A. Anything that way. I found one old tin can with some white lead in it. That might have dropped from the ship.

There being no further questions to ask this witness, his testimony was read over to him by the stenographer and by him pronounced correct.

The witness then withdrew, after being cautioned by the president not to converse about matters pertaining to the inquiry.

The JUDGE-ADVOCATE. I would like to inform the court that I have no more testimony to offer from any of the survivors of the *Maine* at Key West. All who can give any testimony in the matter, as far as I can learn, have been before the court. There is only left the testimony of the survivors in a body, which the court desires to take.

At the request of the judge-advocate, the court was then cleared for deliberation. The stenographer withdrew.

The doors were then opened and the stenographer entered.

The court then (at 1.15 p. m.) took a recess until 2 p. m., at which time it was decided that the court would proceed to the military station, Key West, at which place the wounded were being cared for and the other men were quartered.

The court reassembled at the expiration of the recess.

Present: All the members, the judge-advocate, and the stenographer.

The court then proceeded in a body to the army barracks at Key West. On reaching there, all the survivors of the *Maine*, officers and men, who were able to attend, were assembled in the presence of the whole court. The president of the court administered the oath to them which is usually administered to witnesses, whereupon the judge-advocate asked the following questions:

The JUDGE-ADVOCATE. Is there present any officer or man who has any complaint to make or any fault to find with any officer or man belonging to the *Maine* on the night of the destruction of that ship, at Havana, February 15, of this year? If so, let such officer or such man step to the front.

No one stepping to the front, each one of you declares under oath that you have no fault to find and no complaint to make of any officer or man belonging to the *Maine* on that night.

Is there any officer or man here present who has any complaint to make against or fault to find with any officer or man belonging to the *Maine* as to the care and guarding of that ship in the harbor of Havana previous to her destruction on February 15, 1898? If any such officer or man has any such complaint to make or fault to find, let him step to the front.

No one stepping to the front, each one of you declares under oath that you have no complaint to make against or fault to find with any officer or man as to the care and guarding of the ship previous to her destruction.

The court then (at 2.35 p. m.) adjourned to meet to-morrow, at — o'clock — m., at its usual place of meeting, the United States court-house, Key West.

TENTH DAY.

U. S. L. H. TENDER MANGROVE,
Harbor of Havana, 10 a. m., Saturday, March 6, 1898.

The court met pursuant to the last adjournment on Wednesday, the 2d instant, at Key West, Fla.

Present: All the members of the court, the judge-advocate, and the stenographer. Captain Sigsbee and Lieut. Commander Wainwright were also present, at their own request.

The record of the proceedings of the last meeting were read and approved.

Ensign POWELSON here appeared before the court and was warned by the president of the court that he was still under the oath he had previously taken.

Examined by the JUDGE-ADVOCATE:

Q. Ensign Powelson, have you any further evidence to offer to this court—evidence that you may have discovered since the court left Havana?
A. Yes, sir.
Q. Is the nature of the evidence such as is derived from your own observation or from the reports made to you from time to time by the divers?
A. It is from reports made to me by the divers.
Q. Did you take notes at the time such reports were made to you by the divers?
A. I did.
Q. You will please give your evidence as far as possible, giving each diver separately; also, in giving your evidence give it in such a manner that the convening authority and the authorities in Washington will be able to understand it without having before them the sketches upon which you may point out different objects in the course of your testimony. Please proceed.
A. I will first take up the reports of Chief Gunner's Mate Olsen, one of the divers. I will first submit to the court a rough sketch showing the forward body of the ship, forward of about frame 28.

The JUDGE-ADVOCATE. I request that this sketch be appended to the record as one of the exhibits.

The request was granted, and the sketch was appended to the record, marked "H."

The WITNESS. This is the report Diver Olsen made to me at 11.40 a. m. March 1, 1898:

He went down the after wing of the after V, marked "A" in sketch submitted, and he counted 9 frames, counting the highest frame No. 1. This highest frame is frame 17. Frames 21 and 22 had floor plates still attached. The other frames had only the angle irons next the skin left. The floor plates on 21 and 22 were bent forward from their original position. He found the first longitudinal at about frame 24. He saw it for about two frame spaces. This first longitudinal was not shown in the sketch, because it is under the inside plating.

By the COURT:

Q. Will you please put in explanations?
A. He saw it for about two frame spaces. The outer skin was broken with the rivet holes at the edge between the first and second longitudinals, at frame 24. This break was at the butt of the plate. Following

the second longitudinal down, he came to the end where it is broken off and very ragged. He followed the plate A in the sketch until it turns underneath the keel about 10 inches. There it ends with ragged edges touching the flat part of the keel. He then came up and went forward of this plate A of which I have spoken, and went on to the plate marked B in the sketch. He went down the plate B and found it extended 10 frame spaces. There, at the end of 10 frame spaces, he found the plating ended with ragged edges about 2 feet from the green outside bottom plating. Plate B is forward in the sketch, and plate A aft. He followed the longitudinal down. The green plating is underneath the plate B. He went down, and it slopes in the same general direction, inclined about 45 degrees.

He could step at the bottom of plating B down onto the green outside plating. He followed the green plating down about 10 feet and got into the mud. The green plating is attached to the flat keel. The keel seems to go forward under the mud. He could feel the keel sloping upward aft and to starboard where he was standing in the mud. On the flat part of the keel he felt for the outside keel plating, but he could not find where it lapped, although he felt in from the keel about 10 feet. He found a plate with rivets along the edge about 10 inches from the angle of the flat part of the keel. He found no raised and sunken plating. It was smooth for about 12 feet up at right angles to the flat part of the keel. He then found something which he sketched for me, and by the way he described it it was like a small bilge keel. This projection that he found was about 12 feet from the mud. He then went out clear of the ship into the mud and found some boxes of canned goods and some loose cans seemingly unhurt. Some of the cans were square, like beef cans; others were cylindrical. He took a 2-foot rule with him and measured the dimensions of the outside keel plate, and he found that the flat part of the outside keel plate was between 14 and 15 inches wide, and also found it extended up the sides from the flat part on each side a distance of 18 inches.

I would like to say that from the studying of the drawings, after Olsen's report, and his distances, I find that he found the keel go into the mud at about frame 7, and above that he found the ram plate which stick out from the side of the ship on each side at the bows.

Olsen went down the next time in the forenoon of March 3. This time I gave him orders to see if he could find the top part of the keel—that is, the highest point of the keel—as he had reported to me it had extended upward and starboard quite a steep slope. He went down on the top part of the plate marked "A" in the sketch, and followed frame 17 until he found the break in the keel. I had ordered him to take a 2-foot rule with him in order to get the exact dimensions of the plates at the point where he might find a break in the keel. He took the following measurements at the break: First he measured the inner keel plate, and found that the total width of the plate was 35 inches. He then measured the outer keel plate and found the total width to be about 15 inches. It is so dark where the divers work that they can not see the numbers on the 2-foot rule, and they have to guess at the distance of anything under a foot by the proportion, so that these measurements may be in error an inch or two.

He found at the first frame forward of the break in the keel a lightening hole in the floor plate. He took the measurement of this hole, and found that the major axis was 20 inches and the minor axis 12 inches. He then found a manhole in the inner skin just forward of the break in the vertical keel on the port side. He took measurements of this manhole, and found the major axis 22 inches and the minor axis 15 inches. He then measured the spacings of the rivets on the angle irons of the vertical keel, and found them to be 3 inches. He found between the outer and inner skins at the point where the break occurs in the vertical keel a four-way pipe. This was on the port side of the vertical keel. One branch was horizontal, and extended starboard to the vertical keel and ended there with a blank flange. Another branch of the pipe extended athwartships to port. Another extended vertically up through the inner bottom, and the fourth extended vertically downward.

The horizontal branches were found to measure 4 inches in diameter. The lower vertical branch measured 3 inches in diameter. The vertical keel was broken at about the point where the pipe with the blank flange pierced it. He measured the height of the vertical keel and found it to be 36 inches. In this compartment he found a water alarm and sent it up on a line. This was just forward of the break in the vertical keel on the port side, about 9 inches at its lowest point from the outer skin. The angle irons along the vertical keel he measured and found to be 3-inch flange, and the angle between the broken parts of the vertical keel he found to be considerably more than a right angle. He found a manhole 14 or 15 inches below the break in the vertical keel on the port side, in the inner skin. He also found one in a similar place on the starboard side of the vertical keel. About 8 or 10 feet farther down the keel, which at this point runs down in a vertical line, he found on the starboard side a manhole. Near this manhole he found a blank flange and three pipe holes in the inner skin. About 10 or 12 feet farther down than this last manhole he found two more manholes, symmetrically placed on each side of the vertical keel, in the inner skin.

These two manholes were in the part of the keel which in the sketch is represented as turning and going nearly horizontal at the point marked C. He found that abaft this point C the inner bottom was of a corrugated form, having large corrugations bent in it. The bottom plating on each side of the keel along in the vicinity of the point C slopes downward from the keel. Near the starboard manhole of the last pair of manholes he described there was a pipe running down through the inner bottom just to port of it. He could not see whether this pipe belonged there or was driven there. The edges of the plate, I would say, were all ragged. He felt down through the starboard manhole and found a piece of pipe with an elbow in it. This elbow and the piece of pipe he referred to as coming down through the double bottom, looked as if they had originally been the same piece. On top of the inner skin, a little abaft these last two manholes to which he referred, he found two 3-inch pipes running across the ship. He could not say whether they were originally there or not. Between these two manholes and the keel and forward of them was a blank flange. These two manholes were in the level part of the keel about 10 feet abaft where the vertical part comes down to the horizontal part. These two manholes in the inner skin were 6 or 7 feet apart. Abaft these manholes there is a great deal of wreckage, and he could not tell anything about what it was.

The COURT. This is Olsen's report all the time, is it?

A. Olsen; yes, sir.

At about frame 22, on the starboard side, he found, 8 or 10 feet from the keel, 30 or 40 6-pounder shells detached from the cases, a lot of brass cases, 6-pounder, seemingly exploded. He found many more projectiles than cases. He found at the same place one 6-inch shell, which he sent up. I examined this shell and found that it was still in its slings, with its wooden nose cap still attached, the wood of which was uninjured and unburned. The slings were unburned and uninjured, except one part which had been cut. Just forward of that place he found a lot of knapsacks, rubber blankets, haversacks, and canteens, some of which he sent up. They were unburned and uninjured. He also found a lot of blacksmith's tools where he found the 6-inch shell. The place for the 10-inch magazine he found covered with wreckage, which seemed to have been from port to starboard.

On the forenoon of March 4 Olsen went down again. He went down until he found the break in the vertical keel; then he slid down the vertical part of the keel until he came to about frame 24, as I determined from all the measurements and data that he and Smith had in the meantime taken in reference to the keel. Then he walked out to starboard. He found a good many 6-inch shell, and some powder tanks, one of which he sent up.

By the COURT:

Q. What size?

A. Six-inch powder tank. I examined this tank, and found it was battered up and opened up along the seam for only about a foot. It had evidently not exploded. Excelsior in good condition was found in it. The bag was also sent up with it. Olsen then found the outboard bulkhead of the 10-inch magazine bent outward and about horizontal. In this bulkhead was a square box, with one hole in it for a deadlight. The box was built in the bulkhead from the coal bunker side. This box was apparently uninjured, except the glass light in it was gone. The rim holding the circular glass disk was not injured. He took the cover off the box and sent up the frail, light box, which holds the incandescent magazine light. When this box reached the top of the water I examined it and found that it was in very good shape. The joinings at the corner of the box had been shaken loose, but the box itself was very slightly bent, and still had two wires about three feet in length attached to it. The small water-tight cover to the light box was also sent up. It was very slightly bent, and its rubber gasket was not burnt and was intact.

On this starboard 10-inch magazine bulkhead, to which the light box was attached and which is now bent down to starboard and nearly horizontal, he found a manhole plate near the light box. This plate he sent up. I examined it and found that it was bent up a little on one end. The rim which holds the hinges, and which is riveted to the inner skin, was broken in two. Half of it was still attached to the manhole plate by one hinge. This rim was bent up on one side and the rubber gasket in the manhole plate was entirely gone. I found the paint burned on the under side.

Olsen felt under the light box on the bulkhead, to which he referred, the rungs of an iron ladder, riveted to the bulkhead. He followed these rungs down until he reached the floor of the magazine. There he found a crack in the inner bottom about 3 feet wide. I questioned him particularly about the edges, and he told me they were ragged and bent neither in nor out. He crawled into this double-bottom compartment and found a 10-inch gas check and two 10-inch gas-check pads, one in perfect condition, the other jammed. Neither of them was burned. He also found a cutlass scabbard in this double-bottom compartment. While in the compartment he saw the floor plates of a frame, and said the floor plates had lightening holes in them. The plate was buckled a little. He then went farther aft to examine the condition of the aft part of the magazine. He found that that was covered with wreckage, going high up into the air, so that he could not climb over it. He found 6-inch shells on top of the 10-inch tanks; also paymaster's stores on top of the tanks. He broke off a piece of magazine grating and tongued-and-grooved woodwork of the 10-inch magazine, which I secured as it came to the surface. This wood was unburned.

This finishes Olsen's testimony up to this morning. He is now diving.

By the JUDGE-ADVOCATE:

Q. Does any other diver testify by the sketch you have submitted?
A. Yes; Smith's work and Olsen's work are corroborative.

The following is the evidence as derived from information given to me by Diver Smith:

On the morning of February 28 I sent Smith down on plate marked A in the sketch.

By the COURT:

Q. On top or inside?
A. On top the plate marked A in the sketch. He followed the second longitudinal down until he got to frame 19. Then he worked himself down toward the direction of the keel, and there he found the first longitudinal which is not shown on the sketch, because it is covered by inside plating. He found the top part of this first longitudinal at frame 19. He found the bottom plating broken, and edges pushed in from the green paint. This was on the outside of the ship. These edges were pushed in about 18 inches from the original surface of the bottom plate. He then felt along the edge of the break about 2 feet, but could not find the plating lower down, which had originally been attached to this edge. On account of the inner and outer plating being jammed together he could not reach further up than frame 18, nor could he reach lower down than frame 20 for the same reason. He then went down inside of the V formed by the bottom plating at frame 17 at a point marked D in the sketch.

The bottom plating at frame 17 diverges for about 15 feet; lower down it converges and comes nearly together about 20 feet down, at that point being only a few inches apart. The after wing of the V marked "A," ends at the point nearest the bottom plating, near the keel. In the afternoon of February 28, I sent Smith down to look for a circular hole which Olsen had said he found in the upper edge of the plate marked "A" on the sketch. I wished to locate this hole exactly in order to determine exactly whether the highest frame in the sketch was frame 17 or not. He counted the frame spaces along the upper edge of the plate marked "A," and found that the semicircular hole with the rivet holes around it to which sea valve had evidently been attached, was between the sixth and seventh frames, counting frame 18 as No. 1. I referred to the drawing afterwards and found that this checked up exactly, calling the highest frame in the sketch No. 17, as has been done. He found between frames 19 and 20, and near the second longitudinal, a dozen 6-pounder shells with the cartridge gone. He was unable to get any more data connected with the break in the outside plating between the first and second longitudinals at frame 19, to which he referred in his morning report. The testimony in regard to the situations of various holes, and details of construction have checked up exactly on the supposition that the highest frame sketched is frame 17, and with previous testimony given before this court.

On the morning of March 2, I sent Smith down to corroborate the evidence which Olsen had given in regard to the break in the vertical keel at frame 18. Smith took with him a 2-foot ruler. He found the thickness of the vertical keel not quite an inch. He found the four-way pipe which Olsen testified as having found, and he found that the smallest inside diameter of the horizontal branch of the pipe was 3 inches. He found that 5 inches was the largest inside diameter of the vertical branch of the pipe—Olsen testified to having found it 4 inches. He measured the distance from the vertical keel to a flange to which the port horizontal branch of the pipe is riveted. This he found to be 21 inches. He found that the diameter of the blank flange at the end of the pipe which pierced the vertical keel from port to starboard was 5 inches. He found the distance from the break in the vertical keel to the next frame forward to be 36 inches. He found the distance between the outer edges of the horizontal flanges of the two angle irons on each side at the bottom of the vertical keel plating to be 7 inches.

He measured the width of the inner keel plate and found it to be 37 inches. He found the outer keel plate lapped 4 inches beyond the inner keel plate. He found the large pipe in the double bottoms alongside the vertical keel at the point where the break occurs and measured it, and found it to be 12 inches in diameter. This pipe had a flange on the end. He measured the length of the pipe, and found it was 5 feet between this flange and where it went through the next plate. At this point he found two manholes in the inner bottom, on opposite sides of the keel, just forward of the piece of pipe to which he referred.

Smith went down again the afternoon of March 2, and went down to the break in the vertical keel, and followed the vertical point down to the point where it bends up again to the horizontal. He found the after part of the keel almost horizontal—part marked "C." When he was at this point the diving machine registered a depth of 35 feet.

Q. That is the horizontal part of the keel?
A. Yes, sir. The machine is not accurate within 5 feet, I find. At this place, near the point C in the sketch, he found a 10-inch shell, a bunch of knapsacks, and a magazine swab. He reported that the swab was not burned and was uninjured.

Smith took certain measurements of the keel at the point where it bends to go horizontally. He finds that there is a bend in the keel, extending forward for about 3 feet from the lowest part of the keel, which is now vertical; it then turns down and around through about 360 degrees and runs aft. He got in the double bottoms at a point a little way abaft where the vertical keel comes down vertically, and he found that the vertical keel itself was buckled out to starboard. He drew me a sketch of it, showing it was buckled to starboard at about the point marked C.

On February 28, in the afternoon, Smith went down to examine the forward part of the keel as far forward to the bow as he could get. He went down at the point D and walked down on the green plating until he got near the keel. He then put his back against the green side of the plate marked A on the sketch and his feet against the green side of the bottom plating under the point marked D. He worked himself along aft. He worked along about 8 feet and found the bottom to take a form of which he made me a sketch. This sketch is a cross section of the keel of the ship at about frame 12, from the measurements he took. He found the flat part of the keel to be 14 inches wide, and found that the outer keel plate lapped up along the bottom plating on each side a distance of 1 foot 8 inches. He took these measurements with a 2-foot rule. He then worked himself forward until he came to the edge of plate A and then went down to the keel on the bottom plating until he got into the mud. At the point where the flat keel goes into the mud he found a hole in the mud. He made out that the bottom of this hole was about 6 inches deep. He then made me a sketch indicating the form of the hole.

By Captain SIGSBEE:

Q. Six inches, you say?

A. No, sir; he found the hole to be about 6 feet deep and about 15 feet in diameter. In the bottom of the hole he found sticking in the mud a sort of metal tank, which was hauled up by a line bent onto it. This tank was a very thin metal, and riveted together by spacing of rivets, which was not water-tight, and evidently came from part of the ventilating system of the ship. This finishes my evidence from information derived from Smith, the diver.

The court then (at 12.15 p. m.) took a recess until 1.30.

The court reassembled at the expiration of the recess.

Present: All the members of the court, the judge advocate, the stenographer, Captain Sigsbee, and Lieutenant-Commander Wainwright.

Ensign POWELSON, who was on the stand before the recess, resumed the stand and proceeded with his testimony as follows:

On the forenoon of March 1 Rundquist, gunner's mate, went down on the port side of the ship abaft the port crane, and he made a report to me as follows: He said he went down a ladder placed about 5 feet abaft the port crane against the port superstructure and leading down to the main deck. Then he went over the side at a point about 12 feet abaft the break in the main deck. He found still attached to the side, underneath the waterways of the main deck, a strip of plating 3 or 4 feet wide. This plating he said was bent inboard. He lowered himself over the side until his feet struck something about the position of the berth deck. He did not notice any armor at that point. He said the deck sloped down to starboard and aft in such a manner that a ball would roll toward the starboard quarter or a little more aft. He found a hole in this deck, which he supposed to be the berth deck.

The hole was about 6 or 7 feet from where his feet first touched on the berth deck. The wood was all broken at the edge of the hole. He just lowered himself down over the edge. He reached out with his arm, but didn't find the other edge of the deck opposite the break. He went down 10 or 12 feet, perhaps a little more, and then his feet struck in the coal. He reported that there were tons of coal down there. He then moved to port and found a fore-and-aft bulkhead. This bulkhead had rivet holes in it from which the rivets had been pulled. He put his fingers in the rivet holes, and hauled himself up about 6 or 7 feet until he reached the top of the bulkhead. I asked him how he judged his distance, and he said he put his hands up three times, and the fourth time he got hold of the upper edge of the bulkhead. The upper edge was ragged, and the break was clean, meaning that the edge was approximately horizontal.

He climbed over this bulkhead, and went outboard. Across the top of this bulkhead he found a plank. This plank was about a foot wide and the end edge was beveled off about 45 degrees. He went down on the other side of the bulkhead—outboard side—and found lots of small compartments about 3 or 4 feet apart. The upper part of the compartment he was in was large and the bottom of it was divided into small compartments. The outboard side of these compartments looked curved like the ship's side in the sketch, which he drew for me. This sketch showed the portion of the ship's side and fore and aft vertical bulkhead. There was a floor plate with lightening hole in it which went up the lower angle between the ship's side and the bulkhead.

The plates with the round lightening holes in them were loose, some of them, from the curved side of the compartment, and were bent in toward the vertical bulkhead. He then walked with the vertical bulkhead on his right side, and walked forward over four or five of these small compartments. He then struck his helmet against something and climbed back over the vertical bulkhead to which he had referred, and got into some 10-inch powder tanks, one of which he sent up on a line. I examined this tank and found that one end of it was still circular in form. This was the end to which the cover was attached. The other end looked as if it had been struck on the side and flattened together at right angles to its length. It was very much battered. I found in a tear in this tank a piece of the tape sewed on the powder bags to support them. Rundquist told me that when he bent a line on the tank, it had a bag in it. This bag probably fell out on the way up. He then went farther forward and got tangled up among a lot of electric wires. This was 5 or 6 feet forward of where he found the 10-inch powder tank. I asked him what the water looked like at this place, for I thought he had walked outside the ship forward into the gap, which is apparently all blown away. He told me that where he was the water looked pretty clear, meaning there was more light there than there had been inside the ship. He then came up, back through the hole in the berth deck.

Rundquist went down again on the afternoon of March 1. I gave him orders to examine the side plating under the waterways on the port side, abaft the port crane, and also to examine the armor belt, and any details of interest he might find at the point where the ship appears to be broken about frame 41. He went down as before on the port side and examined the strip of side plating attached to the waterways, and found that the break in the side plating extended as far aft as the after boat cradle, abaft the port crane. He then lowered himself down over the side until he felt the armor. He had his body outside of the ship, and his arms over the armor plate. He said the plate looked normal. He followed the armor plate along until he came to the end of it. I asked him about how far, and he said it was the length of a plate and a half. I asked him how he could distinguish the ends of the plates, and he said that at the place where the plates abutted together, the outer surfaces were not flush, that the outer aft corner of the forward plate was about 4 inches farther outboard than the upper forward edge of the after plate. He then followed this seam down to the bottom of the armor plate and found the plates were flush at the bottom. He then went up the seam to the upper edge of the armor and worked his way forward until he came to the end of the armor plating.

This armor ended a little forward of the port crane. He then went down to the lower edge of the armor plate and found the edge about a foot in the mud. He said the forward plate looked to be about in its original position. He went out about 12 feet from the ship's side, trying to find any of the plates. He found some old pieces of tin that appeared to belong to air conductors, and a piece of wire which he sent up. This wire was lead covered and had a junction box attached. He found some small pieces of coal and some small pieces of plating about the size of his hand. He found no large plates. He then went back to the ship's side and examined the backing of the armor. That looked to be pushed from out in, because at the place where the plate was gone the wood backing, about 6 or 7 inches thick, was splintered, and all the splinters pointed inboard. He examined the top of the wood backing level with the armor plate. He drew me a sketch of its condition.

The backing was split in a fore and aft vertical plane, and the inboard part of the backing was torn off. The outboard part of the backing was still attached to the plate. The splinters were on the forward edge of the backing and pointed inboard, as he indicated in a sketch. These splinters were about 6 or 7 inches long, and pointed inboard, as he drew them, at an angle of about 45 degrees. He went over all the work two or three times to make sure, and is positive there is no plating attached to the main deck forward of the break in the ship's side, to which he referred, at a point aft of the crane equal to the length of a plate and a half of armor, with the exception of the strip from 3 to 4 feet wide, running along under and parallel to the waterways.

He sent up a splinter from the backing, on which he had measured the thickness of the armor plate, by cutting nicks in it with a diver's knife. I measured these distances with a ruler, and found them to be 12 and 8 inches.

By the COURT:

Q. Twelve at the top and eight at the bottom, I suppose?

A. Yes, sir. He then came up, and to make perfectly sure of what he had reported, I sent him down again to examine the strip of plating under the waterways more closely. He said he found that way aft, a short distance forward of the turret, side plating was bent out. At this point he slipped from the ship's side and fell out into the mud. He worked himself back to the ship, feeling around in the mud, but did not find any plates. The strip of plating at the waterway he found ragged on the edge. He then came up.

Rundquist went down again the forenoon of March 2. This time he went down on the port side, forward of the port crane, where the break in the ship occurs. He reported that he got in among a lot of wreckage which he could not distinguish. He found some empty powder tanks, 6-inch and 10-inch. Some of them were in pretty good condition. He found rags in three; the others he reported were opened up at the seams. He found one 10-inch tank with only the cover gone. He said there were lots more rags lying about, but it was so dark he could not be positive whether they were powder bags. He walked around and got into a place where there was lots of canvas rolled up. He found a plate standing in the mud on a slant, the upper edge pointing inboard. One side of it was white cork paint, the other was slippery and looked green. The cork side was to port.

On the afternoon of March 3 I sent Rundquist down on the starboard side to make an examination there, similar to the one he had made on the port side. He went down first under the supports of the conning tower as they now are. He went directly down into the mud, and then walked in toward the ship's side. The mud was about 2 feet deep. He found the ship's side at that point intact, and followed it forward until he reached the end of his guide line. He made the guide line fast to a piece of coal, put it in the mud, and followed the side along about 10 feet more, until he came to the break in the ship. I was unable to determine his exact position by the bubbles on account of the wreckage of the superstructure and other plates, which deflected the bubbles and made them come up at widely different places in a very short space of time. The edges in the break were all ragged and looked as if they had been broken between two frames.

The edges were bent neither in nor out, but presented a ragged appearance. He then took hold of the break, which was vertical, and pulled himself up 6 or 7 feet. There the break turned and went aft in a horizontal line about 2 feet. The forward corner of the plate—upper part—at the break was bent down and aft. This horizontal top edge was not ragged, but had rivet holes in it. This was level with the bottom of the armor. He then found the armor and crawled vertically up along the forward edge. He found the wood backing projected farther forward than the armor plate, and in it he found two bolts. The ends of the bolts were smooth and appeared not to have been broken off, and had screw threads. There was a washer on the bolt that felt like rubber. He felt forward of the armor for about a foot and a half, and found the wood backing, but could not feel the end of it. He then climbed up until he got to the top of the armor and worked himself aft, hanging on it with his arms over it and his body outside the ship.

He went aft for about 12 feet. Then his hand slipped, and he fell down in the mud. He worked himself forward again to the break in the ship's side, and worked himself up and over the same corner as before. He found that the bottom of the armor was about 12 feet above the mud and at the place where the break occurred. He worked himself back along the top of the armor as before, and at about the same place slipped again. He put his hands over the armor going back and found a foot of armor and 6 or 7 inches of wood, if not more. He did not have a measure with him. There was something beyond the wood, but he did not have time to examine it. When he slipped from the side he went out about 12 feet in the mud. He found pieces of plating, which he took for side plating. One side was slippery and the other rough. It was so dark he could not distinguish colors. The slippery side was down and about horizontal. The plating was a little curved, and the concave side was up. He then looked for the end of his guide line, and, when he found it, went up. He found a great deal of coal in the mud.

I sent Rundquist down again in the afternoon of March 4 to go over the same ground. He went down near the conning-tower supports, as before, and got into the mud and walked into the ship's side. He followed it forward until he came to the break. I was able to distinguish the bubbles more clearly at this time, and concluded that the break in the ship's side was at the same frame as the frame on the port side—about frame 41. He climbed up the vertical break until he came to the corner, which is bent over as he described before. He followed it a couple of feet until he struck the forward edge of the armor plate. He climbed up the forward edge of the armor plate and examined the backing as he went up. The backing extended fully 5 feet farther forward than the armor plate. The splinters on the forward edge of the backing pointed outboard. Then he went up on top of the armor and crawled along about 4 or 5 feet until his helmet struck up against something which looked like athwartship bulkhead, painted white. It extended above the armor, and the upper part was bent forward. It had an angle iron on the outboard edge, after side.

There was a fore and aft vertical plate riveted to this angle iron at right angles to the bulkhead he had just mentioned. He said he was sure this did not belong to the outside plating. He went farther aft for fully two lengths of an armor plate. I asked him how he could tell the ends of the plate, and he told me that the ends of the plate were not flush at the top; the forward plate was about 4 or 5 inches farther out from the ship than the after one, but they were flush at the bottom. He could not go farther aft than two plates' length, because there was a lot of wreckage from above hanging over him, which seemed to be a part of the forward wreckage of the superstructure. He said as he worked aft the armor projected about 6 inches farther out than the side plating above it. He was not able to determine exactly the distance to which the side plating above the armor was blown out, on account of all the wreckage over the main deck on the starboard side.

The armor stuck out this way about 6 inches all the way aft to where he found the wreckage which he has just spoken of. He then went forward again until he got nearly to the break in the ship's side at the armor belt, and then he went over inside the armor and found what he took to be a deck with two plates riveted together. He is sure the total thickness of both plates together was not more than an inch. These plates were painted reddish brown. The plate was a little curved and extended inboard horizontally about 2 feet, and was then broken off, with ragged edges bent down. This plate was flush with the top of the backing. He then went forward to the end of the armor plating, where the break occurs, and made his guide line fast to one of the bolts going through the wood backing. Then he lowered himself down inside the wood backing. He found a number of pieces of board, planking, and coal, and plates. The boards were about 2½ inches in thickness. He could not distinguish the color.

Inside he found a vertical fore and aft bulkhead, about 4 feet from the wood backing. He found athwartship bulkheads about 4 feet apart and states that he could find no holes in them, and thinks he was in a pocket of some kind. He found some pieces of inch piping in this compartment. He hauled himself up again on the line, and then went over the side at the break of the armor belt, and went down in the mud and found the side plating underneath where the armor plates that are missing had been, and found where it had been torn down in a vertical line and bent out nearly horizontally, and the extreme outboard end bent vertically down in the mud. He scraped away the mud as far as he could, but could not find the end of the plating. He found a small pipe attached to these plates, made of composition, three-fourths of an inch in diameter. He sent this pipe up. He felt in the mud and found a great many pieces of broken crockery, and found six mess plates all together. These were about 15 feet from the ship's side; he also found a 10-inch powder tank with rags of powder bag inside. He sent the tank up. I examined the tank and found that it still preserved its cylindrical shape, but the head and bottom were missing. Otherwise the tank was practically uninjured. He sent up the bag. He found this tank about 15 feet from the ship's side. This bag was ragged in appearance, but on being opened up presented a square foot or more of intact surface.

Q. Were there any signs of fire?

A. I could not tell whether it had been burned or not. The supporting tapes were ragged and were blackened. Everything down on the bottom looked as if the insides of the ship had been blown right out to starboard. He found coal wherever he went. He went out about 20 feet, but believes the coal goes out much farther. I then asked him how this condition compared with what he found on the port side opposite the break, and he told me at that point there was no coal—nothing but mud. That concludes my testimony with reference to the diving of Rundquist.

In the afternoon of March 2 I sent Schluter down on the port side forward of the break. I told him to see if he could find any of the armor of the ship. He went down about 30 feet forward of the port crane and landed on what he thought was a deck light. He said there were planks about it running in athwartship direction. This was about 15 feet from where the ship's side would have been. He felt all around among the wreckage, but did not recognize anything until he found the armor plate, to which he attached a line. He measured the plate with a ruler. This plate stood on an angle with the thick armored side forward. He measured this plate and found that the part which he called the thick armored side was 6 inches in width. Behind that he found 9 inches of wood backing, and behind the wood backing he found 3½-inch plate of armor. The bolt-head came out of this 3½-inch armored side. I plumbed this plate with a line which he attached to it, and found it in line with the mainmast and port crane, about 40 feet forward of the crane, inside the line of the ship.

I sent Schluter down on the morning of the 5th and told him to examine the plating on the port side abaft the crane, just under the main deck. He went over the side to fore and aft above the port crane and felt the side plating. The main deck sloped down to starboard. The outside plating was bent sharply from outside in, making an acute angle at the waterway. Then he crawled away aft and felt over the edge, and in places could not find any side plating attached to the end of the waterways. He went as far aft as the turret. He said the plating about 10 feet forward of the turret is broken right out. A little forward of that was another plate, blown up and out.

Q. On the starboard side?

A. On the port side, sir. This had beams fast to it and looked like a deck. Forward of this plate for about 7 or 8 feet is wreckage inside the line of the ship. It looks as if it had been blown outboard to port. He then crawled along the top of the armor, which was all clear as far forward as the crane, and there it is broken clear off.

Q. What is?

A. The armor.

This is corroborative of the testimony of Rundquist. Just at the break of the armor about 8 inches inboard from the armor the wood backing is blown up and inboard.

Q. Which deck is that?

A. I take that to be the berth-deck, as that was the upper edge of the armor. That covered the protective deck. He did not examine the strip of plating under the waterway farther aft than 10 feet from the crane, but all that he felt was blown inboard. That is as much of the diver's statements as I have up to the present time.

By the JUDGE-ADVOCATE:

Q. Mr. Powelson, look at the sketch you have presented the court of the frame plates and broken keel of the ship. When you look at A, is that in the inboard side of the ship?

A. That is the inboard side of the ship, between frames 26 and 17, and is broken off between the first and second logitudinals and between the second and third longitudinals, embracing a space of about two longitudinals between frames.

Q. Now, the right-hand edge of this plate, as you see it—where would that be if the plate was bent back into its original position?

A. It would be the lower part of the plate—the garboard strake.

Q. And the left-hand edge—what would that be?

A. The upper part of the plating.

Q. And the longitudinal which is marked on Plate A—which longitudinal is that?
A. The second longitudinal, from keel, on the port side.

By the COURT:

Q. That would be this one [indicating on sketch]?
A. Yes, sir; the second one.

By the JUDGE-ADVOCATE:

Q. Looking at plate B, on the sketch, the face which you see there, is that in the inboard side of the ship?
A. It is.
Q. What longitudinal is that marked on this plate?
A. This is a part of the third longitudinal.
Q. If this plate was put back into its original position, in which direction would the right edge be?
A. The lower edge.
Q. And the left edge?
A. That would be the upper edge.
Q. And the dark part marked "D," between plates A and B, what is that?
A. Outside of the outer skin of the ship.
Q. That is painted green?
A. It is.
Q. And above plate A there is a place torn in the keel of the ship, where the keel goes downward. About what frame is that?
A. Between frame 17 and 18.
Q. And how far down does this keel go in the vertical position it now has, between what frames?
A. Between frames 22 and 23.

By the COURT:

Q. Where is the 6-inch shell room, the forward 6-inch shell room, on that keel?
A. The forward 6-inch shell room rested on the upper half of the vertical part of the keel, as shown.
Q. And the fixed ammunition room, where was that?
A. Right over the angle of the keel, at frame 22 and 23.
Q. Where would the 10-inch shell room have been?
A. The 10-inch shell room and magazine are on the flat part of the keel, marked "C."

By the JUDGE-ADVOCATE:

Q. How much plating is there attached to the keel, which is up and down on the sketch, do you know?
A. I could not state that definitely. You might ask Smith or Olsen about that.
Q. But the horizontal keel which is marked "C," has the ship's side attached to it for some distance on the starboard side?
A. The inner skin is for some distance on the starboard side, but through a crack in the inner skin, the diver found the outer skin, but as to the full extent, it would be pretty difficult to find out, on account of all the wreckage thrown down around it.

By the JUDGE-ADVOCATE:

Q. Did you locate that four-way pipe?
A. Yes, sir.

Q. Where was that originally, according to your deduction?
A. Between frame 17 and frame 18.
Smith says he measured 21 inches from the midship line to the flange, and that agrees with the drawing.

There being no further questions to ask this witness to-day, he was directed to come before the court at 10 a. m. on Monday next.

The court then (at 3.40 p. m.) adjourned to meet Monday, March 7, 1898, at 10 a. m., on board the U. S. L. H. tender *Mangrove*, harbor of Havana.

SPECIAL SESSION.

The court reassembled at 5 p. m. to take some additional testimony of the captain and first officer of the *City of Washington*, which is to sail to-night.

Present: All the members of the court, the judge-advocate, and the stenographer.

First Officer GEORGE CORNELL, of the *City of Washington*, appeared as a witness before the court, and was duly sworn by the president.

Examined by the JUDGE-ADVOCATE:

Q. Please state your full name and profession.
A. George Cornell, first officer of the steamer *City of Washington*.
Q. To what line of steamers does she belong?
A. The Ward Line.
Q. Were you on board the *City of Washington*, in the harbor of Havana, on the night of the 15th of February, when the *Maine* was blown up?
A. Yes, sir.
Q. What part of the *City of Washington* were you in?
A. I was standing amidships, on the starboard side.
Q. On the upper deck?
A. On the upper deck; yes, sir.
Q. Were you looking right at the *Maine*?
A. Yes, sir.
Q. Will you please state what you heard and what you saw?
A. Yes, sir; I was standing on the gangway, and giving the quartermaster orders to call the men at 5 o'clock in the morning. While I was standing there I heard a rumbling sound, and we saw the *Maine* raise up forward. After that the explosion occurred, and the stuff was flying in the air in all directions. She sank immediately at the forward end, sir.
Q. At the first noise or rumbling did anything fly up, or did she only lift?
A. The ship lifted.
Q. Forward?
A. Forward; yes, sir.
Q. What interval was there between the rumbling noise and the explosion?
A. I think there must have been about sixteen or eighteen seconds—not a full minute.
Q. That is, a long time?
A. Almost immediately; there was not very much of an interval.
Q. What part of the ship did the explosion come out of when you saw it?
A. Amidships.

Q. Was there much flame coming up?
A. There was not much flame.
Q. Did a large piece of cement drop on your deck?
A. Yes, sir.
Q. Can you identify it?
A. Yes, sir.
(A large piece of cement was brought into the court room and showed to witness.)
Q. Is this the piece of cement?
A. Yes, sir; that is the piece of cement. A small piece has been cut off at one end.

By the COURT:

Q. How were you anchored with reference to the *Maine?*
A. We were anchored fast to a buoy.
Q. But what direction was the *Maine* from you?
A. The *Maine* was lying on her starboard side, sir. We were off the port quarter of the *Maine.*
Q. How much did she lift at the first sound you heard?
A. She lifted most nearly all out of water. She raised up considerably, but it was kind of dark, and how high she lifted up I couldn't exactly say. We saw her raising by her lights.
Q. The next thing you saw was the débris?
A. The débris; yes, sir.
Q. Did you see any water thrown up?
A. No, sir; I don't think so. I only seen these large pieces flying in the air close by where I stood looking over the rail. We couldn't get out of the way of the débris, and it fell on the deck and all over us.
Q. You could not tell whether you saw her ram or not when she was lifted up?
A. No, sir; it was too dark to see that.
Q. You say she raised almost out of the water forward?
A. Yes, sir.
Q. You can not say how much she raised?
A. No, sir; I could not.
Q. There was a very decided interval between the first sound you heard and the explosion, was there?
A. Yes, sir.
Q. There was a very decided interval, was there?
A. There was not much. Between fifteen and eighteen seconds. It might have seemed to me longer than it really was. It was immediately after the rumbling noise.
(The president of the court produced a watch and counted the seconds. The witness stopped him at the third second, saying the time was less than that.)

By the JUDGE-ADVOCATE:

Q. The interval between the two was decided?
A. Yes, sir.

By the COURT:

Q. Did you feel anything?
A. Yes; the ship was kind of shaking.
Q. When did you feel that?
A. Right after the rumbling sound.
Q. Before the explosion?
A. At the same time the explosion happened.

There being no further questions to ask the witness his testimony was read aloud to him by the stenographer and by him pronounced correct. Whereupon he withdrew.

Capt. FRANK STEVENS, of the *City of Washington*, appeared as a witness before the court, and was duly sworn by the president:

Examined by the JUDGE-ADVOCATE:

Q. Please state your full name and profession.
A. Frank Stevens, master mariner.
Q. You are captain of the steamer *City of Washington*, Ward Line?
A. Yes, sir.
Q. Were you in the harbor of Havana last month when the *Maine* exploded?
A. I was.
Q. Were you at that time in command of the *City of Washington*?
A. I was.
Q. How far were you anchored from the *Maine* at the time?
A. About 300 feet.
Q. In what direction was your ship from the *Maine*?
A. We were on the *Maine*'s port quarter, nearly astern.
Q. Nearly astern?
A. Nearly astern; yes, sir.
Q. Where were you at the time this happened?
A. I was standing along amidships, abaft the smokestack on the port side, where I could look through between the smokestack and forward end of the midship deck house, toward the *Maine*.
Q. Please tell the court what you heard and what you saw.
A. I heard a dull, muffled explosion, and commotion, like as though it was under the water, followed instantly by a terrific explosion, lighting up the air with a dull red glare, filling the air full of flying missiles which lit all around us. We were struck, I think, in four places.

By the COURT:

Q. By the fragments?
A. Yes, sir; and I could hear it dropping into the water the other side of us. After getting out the starboard forward boat we found there was a hole in it, and got the port one out. I noticed that the water on the port side of us was full of floating wreckage from the *Maine*. I got out three boats, two quarter boats and the port forward boat, and sent them out in charge of officers to save lives.
Q. Did you feel any trembling of your own ship at either of these explosions?
A. The last one I did, but the first one I did not. Everything shook.
Q. Was there a very decided interval between the first noise and the explosion?
A. There was.
Q. Were you looking at the *Maine* at the time of the first noise?
A. I was.
Q. What did the *Maine* appear to do?
A. My first impression was when I heard this noise that it was a gun or a salute, but that changed instantly, and then it flashed across my mind that there was dynamite under the bottom of that ship. That was my impression.
Q. Did you see the *Maine* lift at all?
A. I did not, I being on the opposite side and looking through. I seen the mainmast and part of her outline, but could not see her lift.

There being no further questions to ask this witness, his testimony was read aloud to him by the stenographer, and by him pronounced correct.

The court then (at 5.20 p. m.) adjourned to meet Monday, March 7, 1898, at 10 a. m., on board the U. S. light-house tender *Mangrove*, harbor of Havana.

ELEVENTH DAY.

U. S. L. H. TENDER MANGROVE,
Harbor of Havana, March 7, 1898—11 a. m.

The court met pursuant to the adjournment of Saturday, after having proceeded in a body to the wreck to make a personal inspection.

Present: All the members of the court, the judge-advocate, the stenographer, and Captain Sigsbee.

The record of the proceedings of Saturday was read and approved.

Chief Engineer HOWELL, a former witness, was then recalled, and cautioned by the president of the court that he was still under oath taken.

Examined by the JUDGE-ADVOCATE:

(The piece of cement here brought into the court on Saturday and identified by the first officer, Cornell, was then shown to the witness).

Q. Will you examine this piece of cement and identify it if you can?

A. I saw that piece of cement on the *City of Washington*, and now identify it as the same piece. My opinion is that it was blown from the *Maine*, and came from underneath the berth-deck blower on the port side.

Q. Upon what do you base your opinion?

A. That blower was not placed at right angles to the bulkhead on the forward side, and this piece of cement shows marks of an angle similar to the acute angle, which is the base of the blower.

Q. Is it not a very heavy piece of cement for the base of the blower?

A. I do not know exactly how this cement was, but I believe it was 2½ inches thick, similar to this. I mean to say, I do not know how thick that cement was, but this piece is about 2½ inches thick, and that is a very reasonable thickness to put either. The cement has also indications of oil on both sides of it, and I also know that that cement had oil on the under side, because I have seen oil drop through from that deck down into the bunker underneath. This cement showed oil on both sides while on the *City of Washington*. The marks of rivet heads on this cement and the imprint also of the angle iron and the running in line, similar to the acute angle I have spoken of before, which is also another indication that it came from the bottom of that blower. I should say that the top and bottom sides are parallel.

Q. There is a set of photographs of 12 views on the table here. Can you inform the court how they were obtained?

A. I received orders from the commanding officer to instruct the photographer of the 12 views that were desirable, and was with the photographer when he took about 8 of these views. After that time there were so many boats around the wreck that I could not get the views that were wanted, and the whole set of 12 was then made up from plates which the photographer had already taken.

Q. Would you be able to get photographs—starboard view and port view—of the three projections above the water, of wreckage, which are forward of the superstructure, the three together, and the three separately?

A. Yes, sir.

Q. Will you consult with Captain Sigsbee and receive orders to that effect?

A. Yes, sir.

By Captain SIGSBEE:

Q. You are a photographer yourself, are you not?

A. I have done a good deal of work in photography; yes, sir.

The JUDGE-ADVOCATE. I request that the above photographs be appended to the record and marked Exhibit I.

The request was granted, and the said photographs were appended to the record marked Exhibit I.

There being no further questions to ask this witness, his testimony was read over to him by the stenographer and by him pronounced correct; whereupon, after being cautioned by the president not to discuss matters pertaining to the inquiry, he withdrew.

Ensign W. V. N. POWELSON, U. S. Navy, a former witness, was then recalled, and cautioned by the president of the court that he was still under oath taken.

Examined by the JUDGE-ADVOCATE:

Q. Have you read over the testimony which you gave before this court on Saturday last?

A. Yes, sir.

Q. Is it correct as recorded?

A. Yes, sir; with some exceptions which I have noted.

Q. Will you please give the corrections to the stenographer?

A. On page 453, fifth line from the bottom, insert "to" before "starboard" and "at" before "quite."

Page 456, fourth line, "I would say" should be "He said."

Page 460, twelfth line from the bottom, change "apart" to "from the keel."

Page 463, last line, insert after "the" "mud at the."

Page 465, tenth line from the bottom, "far aft" should be "fore and aft."

Page 469, eleventh line, insert "the" between "turret" and "side."

Page 476, tenth line, change "to fore and aft above" to "a little baft."

Page 477, third line, change "backing" to "planking of the deck."

Same page, thirteenth line, "between the first and second longitudinal" should be "between the keel and first longitudinal."

That is all.

Q. Is the testimony, as now amended, correct?

A. Yes, sir.

Lieut. Commander RICHARD WAINWRIGHT here entered the court.

The JUDGE-ADVOCATE. Mr. Powelson, have you any further testimony to offer of the nature that you gave on Saturday last—that is, testimony derived from what was reported to you by divers?

Mr. POWELSON. Yes, sir; I have the work of Olsen on Saturday morning.

By the JUDGE-ADVOCATE:

Q. Please give it.

A. On Saturday morning last, March 5, I sent Olsen down to the piece of the keel—the vertical keel—which is now vertical, with instructions to make farther explorations in the region of the 10-inch magazine. He went down to where the keel becomes horizontal at frame 23. Then he walked aft about 25 feet, climbed over a lot of wreckage consisting of plates or bulkheads standing upright. The upper ends of these plates were ragged, and he crawled over them and on the other side found what he thought was part of a boiler.

I asked him how he could distinguish the boiler; whether there was any of its original shape or not, and he could not give me any definite details, but said from the general look of the piece of wreckage he would take it for a boiler. He went a little farther aft from this, which he considered a boiler, and walked out to port, clear of the ship, into the mud. He was at this time forward of the break of the ship at frame No. 41. He found nothing in the mud and came back, walking to starboard. About 10 feet in he found some wreckage. He examined this plate and found that it was curved as if it were a part of the side plating. This, he said, was about 10 feet inboard of the side of the ship. It did not lay exactly fore and aft; it pointed toward the starboard bow. It was so dark he could not distinguish the color. He walked up on top of the plating and found all the edges rough. From the top of the plate he found a horizontal plate about 2 or 3 feet wide, and in a corner some cellulose packed in tightly. He said the compartment seemed to be about $2\frac{1}{2}$ or 3 feet wide. Abaft that he found something like a boiler. It was very black, all crushed up, and he could not recognize any definite form. He was not absolutely sure that it was a boiler.

He went forward from this point about 10 feet and found some loose wreckage, and he lifted up a couple of plates and threw them aside. He felt around and found a 6-inch tank. He found it intact. He lifted it and found it was heavy, and sent it up. This afterwards proved to be a full tank. He found a lot of broken tanks split up on the seams, and in one tank, at the cover, which has holes in it, he found a lot of mud which he brought up, and which he said looked like dissolved powder. He said there was any quantity of similar mud in the same place. The mud around the tanks was very dark in color, but the mud outside, forming the bottom of the harbor, is of a gray color. He also found a plate of angle iron and U-bar stiffeners riveted to it, about 1 foot apart.

Q. Is that all of this nature?

A. That is all up to this morning.

Q. What side did he go down when he found what he supposed to be a broken boiler?

A. He found the boiler first in the midship line, and then walked to port.

Q. Where did you locate Olsen, when he found the full 6-inch tank?

A. I was at that time on board the *Mangrove*.

Q. Have you any further testimony to give?

A. No, sir.

By the COURT:

Q. Did Olsen mention the thickness of this wreckage which he supposed to be the boiler?

A. No, sir; he said it was without shape, and he could not distinguish anything about it.

Q. Do you know the thickness of the *Maine's* boilers?
A. I do not.
There being no further questions to ask this witness, he was directed to hold himself in readiness for further evidence and to read over the evidence just now given. Whereupon he withdrew.

Chief Engineer HOWELL, U. S. Navy, a former witness, was then recalled and cautioned by the president of the court that he was under the oath which he had previously taken.

Examined by the JUDGE-ADVOCATE:
Q. What was the thickness of the *Maine's* boilers—the shell?
A. About 1¼ inches.
Q. All over?
A. All the shell.
Q. What is the thickness of the heads?
A. They were approximately the same. Some parts of the heads were different.

There being no further questions to ask this witness, his testimony was read over to him by the stenographer, and by him pronounced correct; whereupon he withdrew, after being cautioned by the president not to discuss matters pertaining to the inquiry.

Gunner's Mate RUNDQUIST, U. S. Navy, a former witness, was recalled and cautioned by the president of the court that he was still under the oath which he had taken.

Examined by the JUDGE-ADVOCATE:
Q. Since you gave your last testimony, have you done any more diving at the wreck of the *Maine?*
A. Yes, sir.
Q. To whom did you report the results of what you had found when you came up out of the water?
A. Ensign Powelson.
Q. Referring to the reports that you made to him—were they strictly correct as if you had been under oath?
A. Yes, sir.
Q. You went down on the forenoon of March 1. Do you remember going down the ladder on the port side?
A. I went down the ladder on the port side of the *Maine.*
Q. Did you find anything made fast to the waterways?
A. I found a piece of the side plating.
Q. You then went on to what you supposed to be the berth deck, did you not?
A. Yes, sir.
Q. Which way did it slope?
A. It inclined aft and to the starboard side.
Q. Did you find a hole in the berth deck?
A. I found a hole; that is, it looked to me to be a hole.
Q. How large?
A. I could not say how large it was.
Q. Was the wood broken at the edges?
A. Yes, sir.
Q. You then went farther down?
A. I went farther down.
Q. What did you find—do you remember?

A. There was a lot of coal, in the first place. I sent a big piece of coal up.
Q. What part of the ship do you think you were in then?
A. I should judge I was in the port side of the ship, and in one of the coal bunkers. There was lots of coal—two or three feet deep.
Q. How far forward or abaft the crane were you?
A. I must have been on the forward part of the crane.
Q. Was this coal outside of the ship or inside of the ship?
A. Inside of the ship.
Q. None of it had been blown out?
A. No, sir; at least, I could not say not.
Q. You found a vertical bulkhead about this time did you not, on your right side, walking forward?
A. Yes, sir.
Q. What did you do?
A. I examined this bulkhead. I believe I went over it.
Q. Did you strike your helmet against something?
A. I struck my helmet against something, and it prevented my going forward in that direction.
Q. What did you find about this time; do you remember?
A. I believe that is the time I found some powder inside a tank.
Q. What kind of a tank?
A. Ten-inch tank.
Q. Did you send the tank up?
A. Yes, sir; I sent up a tank with what looked to me to be powder bags.
Q. Did the bags fall outside the tank when you sent it up?
A. The men that received it said that they fell out.
Q. You then got tangled up in what?
A. I then got tangled up in a line.
Q. What kind of a line?
A. A line that was leading down.
Q. Did you not find a lot of wires—a lot of electric wires?
A. Yes, sir; about fifty of them in a bunch. That was as much as I could take in two hands.
Q. You went down again on the afternoon of the same day?
A. Yes, sir.
Q. As before?
A. In the same place, sir.
Q. How far aft did you find that the break in the side plate extended?
A. I could not say exactly how far aft from above it was, but I followed the armor plate, and it extended for fully two lengths of the armor plate aft.
Q. What do you call the break in the ship—where?
A. Where the ship was blown apart.
Q. What part of the ship was that?
A. That was where the armor plate ended, on the forward part of the ship.
Q. Can you describe about what part of the ship it was, what you call a break?
A. I could not say exactly; but it was where the ship had been blown up.
Q. Do you mean about opposite the forward part of the middle superstructure, as it was?
A. I should say it was forward of that.
Q. Did you crawl with your arms over the armor?

S. Doc. 207——15

A. No, sir; I was outside the armor, and was walking with my hands on top of the armor plate.

Q. You informed Mr. Powelson that you had gone a certain distance and a certain number of plates. How could you tell that?

A. I could tell by that the two plates had been joined together. One plate extended further out than the other.

Q. Which plate was the one that was farther out?

A. The forward one; the one that was closer to the break.

Q. About how much out were they?

A. About 5 or 6 inches.

Q. In your dive on this occasion you found some pieces of tin with wire attached?

A. I found some wires; I sent some of them up. There was a long string, about 15 feet, of heavy wire.

Q. After you sent that wire up, I understand, you examined the back of the armor plate. What condition did you find this backing then?

A. The end was all twisted and torn and ragged edges; and then they all looked and pointed inboard. I also examined the upper part of the backing and found the inside corner of it was gone.

Q. Did you send a splinter of this backing up?

A. Yes, sir.

Q. Did you measure the armor plate by this splinter?

A. I did, sir.

Q. Top and bottom?

A. Top and bottom.

Q. How could you measure the bottom?

A. The lower edge of the armor plate was a foot beneath the mud, and I could stick my hand beneath it.

Q. Then there was no plate of the ship under the armor plate?

A. This was just at the first break of the armor belt, and there was no plate left underneath of it. There was nothing of the ship's side left. This was just at the end of it.

Q. How much of the armor plating had no ship's plate under it?

A. I could not say, because I did not measure.

Q. How much do you think?

A. I felt a couple of feet and there was nothing there left of it. Fore and aft there was side plating standing, but I do not know how far it extended.

Q. You went down again the next forenoon?

A. Yes, sir.

Q. Do you remember where?

A. I believe I went down on the same place on the port side.

Q. Are you sure you did not go down forward of the port crane?

A. I may have gone down forward of it, but it was on the port side.

Q. You found the powder tanks on this occasion?

A. Yes, sir.

Q. Please describe them.

A. They were all pressed in, and I also found some powder bags. I put this powder bag in a pocket of my overalls for fear of losing it. I was trying to send this tank up, but it got afoul of something and so I let it go. I left it down there.

Q. Do you remember in how many you found rags?

A. I found rags in three or four of them.

Q. Did you find any 10-inch tanks with the covers on?

A. Yes, sir.

Q. What were these tanks, what size, 6 or 10 inch? Can you state about how many?
A. I could not say how many, because there were tanks and pieces of tanks all around. I could not say how many there were.
Q. What do you mean by pieces of tanks?
A. Tanks pressed together. They feel very small down there.
Q. Then you mean tanks which do not have their shape as well as others?
A. Yes, sir.
Q. You then got among a lot of canvas?
A. I got among a lot of canvas all rolled up. It must have been a sail locker.
Q. Did you find a plate standing in the mud at this time?
A. Yes, sir.
Q. Please describe it.
A. I found a plate standing on the edge down in the mud. I believe I went over this plate and I got down along the hole, which looked to be an inner passage or double bottom. It may have been an inner passage, and a lot of compartments and sections, like. The compartment had a big, round, circular hole in it.
Q. This one plate which I referred to, did it have cork paint on it, on one side?
A. Cork paint on one side and on the outside it was slippery.
Q. Was the cork paint to the port or starboard?
A. It was to starboard.
Q. Think again.
A. The slippery side was to starboard and the cork paint to port.
Q. You went down again on the afternoon of the 3d of March, on the same day?
A. Yes, sir.
Q. On which side?
A. Starboard side.
Q. Abreast of what?
A. Abreast of the crane and wreckage, a little forward of the wreckage.
Q. Abreast of the conning tower?
A. Abreast of the conning tower, sir.
Q. What did you drop into?
A. I dropped into a lot of wreckage, pieces of the ship.
Q. Did you not drop into the mud first?
A. Yes, I walked toward inboard of the ship, and got in amongst a lot of wreckage.
Q. How did you find the ship's side at this place?
A. I did not find the ship's side at that time, because I got fouled twice and got pulled up, and then I went forward and aft on the starboard side, from the whaleboat, and dropped down into the mud and walked into the ship's side, and followed that until I came to the break.
Q. Which side were you on then?
A. On the starboard side of the ship.
Q. Where did you find the break on the starboard side?
A. A good way forward. I could not say how many feet. I came to the end of the guide line, and made the line fast to the piece of the keel and followed the ship's side until I came to the break.
Q. Will you please describe the break as you found it?
A. This break was vertical, and with ragged edges. I climbed up the edge until I got to where it went off in the corner, where the lower

edge of the ram plate had been made fast to it. This extended 2 or 3 feet in that direction. The corner of this side plate was nearly doubled over, and bent outboard. I got to the ram plate and found lots of backing there, extending out 5 or 6 feet, and the bolts were left in the backing. This backing was all pointed outboard. I went up to the upper edge of the ram plate and followed it aft for some distance. I could not say how many feet. My hand slipped on account of not having a guide line. I went back to the same break and came to the same place, and slipped again. I did not make any more attempts that day, because I had not enough guide line.

Q. Can you locate this break that you have just described on the starboard side?
A. No, sir; I could not locate it here. When I found this break, I gave a signal on the line. The man told Mr. Powelson about it. He said, when I came up, that he could not tell where the break was, because the bubbles came up from underneath the wreckage.
Q. When you slipped down the second time did you slip into the mud?
A. Yes, sir.
Q. How deep?
A. Above my waist.
Q. How far, about, did you go?
A. I fell down close to the ship's side when I struck the mud.
Q. Did you find pieces of plate when you fell down into the mud?
A. Not where I fell; but I went outboard and forward toward the break, and found pieces that did belong to the ship.
Q. Were they curved?
A. They were curved.
Q. Which way was the concave side?
A. I believe it was up.
Q. You then looked for your guide line?
A. I did; in the meantime I got a signal to get up.
Q. Did you get amongst a lot of coal before you came up?
A. Yes, sir; there was a lot outside of the ship—a good way out.
Q. What do you mean by a good way?
A. Ten or twelve feet from the ship's side.
Q. You went down again in the afternoon of that day, March the 4th?
A. Yes.
Q. Near the conning tower, as in the morning?
A. As in the morning.
Q. You landed in the mud; and then what did you do?
A. I was walking in the mud until I struck the ship's side again. I went over and examined the break in the backing better than I did the day before. I went up the same way and followed up the part of the ram plate aft. I first struck against something that pointed up and forward. I was first trying to walk on top of the ram plate, but my helmet struck against this, so I had to walk on the side of it with my hands hanging over the ship's side. I went aft about the length of two plates, I should say, and then I got stuck. I could not go any further aft.
Q. Why?
A. Because there was lots of wreckage extending over the ship's side which prevented me.
Q. Wreckage under the water, or dropping from above?
A. From above, and extending over the ship's side.
Q. Did you find a plate about this time—two plates riveted together?

A. Afterwards I found these two plates.
Q. How were they painted?
A. These two plates? They looked to be a red-colored brown.
Q. Was the plate curved?
A. Yes, sir.
Q. How far in did it extend in the ship's side.
A. It extended a couple of feet.
Q. Was it ragged where it had broken off?
A. It looked as if it had been carried away; as if something heavy had fallen on it.
Q. Was this plate flush with the top of the backing?
A. Yes, sir; I could barely lay the point of my fingers down there.
Q. You also found a number of pieces of board and planking at this time, did you not?
A. Yes, sir; I did.
Q. You sent up a pipe for examination?
A. Yes, sir.
Q. Where did you find it?
A. I found it made fast to the ship's starboard side—to the bottom plate. I broke it loose and sent it up.
Q. What else did you find about here?
A. I examined the ram plate and where the break was, and found the bottom plate of the ship down in the mud standing outboard. I was following up this plate, trying to find the armor plate, but could not get to the end of it. It looked to be rolled over, and was too deep for me to get hold of it.
Q. This was the plate underneath the armor plate?
A. Yes, sir.
Q. Was there any crockery about here?
A. Yes, sir; I found lots of crockery, pieces of washstands, clothes, and a 10-inch powder tank. I sent the tank up, and there were some power bags inside.
Q. You sent the bag up also?
A. I put the bag in my pocket and brought it up when I came.

The judge-advocate requested that the testimony given by the witness be not read to him by the stenographer, but that he be directed to hold himself in readiness to appear before the court, when he will be furnished with so much of the record as contains his testimony and asked to withdraw for the consideration of the same, upon the completion of which he will be again called before the court and be given an opportunity to amend his testimony as recorded or pronounce it correct. The request was granted, and the witness was instructed accordingly; whereupon he withdrew, after being cautioned by the president not to discuss matters pertaining to the trial.

Gunner's Mate SCHLUTER, U. S. Navy, a former witness, was then recalled and cautioned by the president of the court that he was still under oath which he had taken.

Examined by the JUDGE-ADVOCATE:

Q. Since you gave your last testimony before this court have you been engaged in any diving at the wreck of the *Maine?*
A. Yes, sir.
Q. To whom did you report the results of your diving?
A. To Mr. Powelson.
Q. Were your reports as true as if they had been given under oath?
A. Yes, sir.

Q. I believe you were down on the forenoon of Tuesday, March 2.
A. Yes, sir.
Q. Do you remember where you went down?
A. I believe that was the day I was down after some powder tanks.
Q. I refer to the time you went down on the port side forward of the break. You went down on the port side forward of the break, do you remember?
A. Yes, sir.
Q. Were you told to look for any armor?
A. Yes, sir.
Q. What did you find?
A. I was lowered over the side to the bottom of the ladder until I struck the main deck. The main deck sloped over toward the starboard side. Then I crawled right out straight to the port side of the ship and put my hand over the ship's side and felt the plates were bent inboard up to about 5 or 6 feet along the ship's side and the waterways. Then I crept on over some stanchions going aft on the port side and kept on going aft until I struck up against the after turret, and was crawling along when I made out two distinct plates of the ship's side. Both were bent from port side outboard. I was going to crawl out over one when the signal was made for me to come up on account of the wrecking tug which was going to move the smokestack.
Q. Did you not find the armor-plate, to which you attached a line?
A. That was the next time I went down, sir.
Q. Whenever you did find that armor-plate to which you attached a line, what did you do? Did you measure this plate with a rule?
A. That was the one amidship, which stands in a vertical position; vertical angle on its end. It was leaning a little over forward. The lower end was pointed aft.
Q. The thick side was forward or aft?
A. The thick side was in the mud, sir; the heavy side. I believe I found 6 inches on top.
Q. That is what you call the thick armor side?
A. Yes, sir.
Q. What did you find behind this plate?
A. A wood backing, sir.
Q. How many inches was this wood backing?
A. About 9 inches, I think.
Q. Behind that what did you find?
A. Three and a half inch armor plating.
Q. Was there any bolt there?
A. Yes, sir; there was bolts sticking out 2 or 3 inches, and I felt a soft washer, or something. That is all I could feel right up against the armor plate; and going right through the wood and armor.
Q. Was this, apparently, athwartship armor or fore and aft armor?
A. Athwartship armor. I found the ship's side armor since.
Q. You are quite sure of the wood backing and plate backing?
A. Yes, sir.
Q. You went down again on the morning of the 5th, and were told to examine the port side abaft the crane. Do you remember?
A. Yes, sir.
Q. You found the main deck?
A. Yes, sir.
Q. How did it slope?
A. It sloped to starboard, sir.
Q. Was the outside plate bent?

A. Yes, sir; the outside plate was bent inboard, about the length of 5 feet, at a sharp angle with the waterways.

Q. You then crawled aft?

A. Yes, sir; I crawled up the aft turret and found two distinct breaks—that is, the sheathing was bent over to port side, outboard—and I was going to crawl over the first plate when I got the signal to come up.

Q. You crawled aft and felt over the edge, did you not?

A. Yes, sir; I did.

Q. You could not find any side plating attached to the waterways in places?

A. Yes, sir.

Q. You went as far aft as the after turret?

A. Yes, sir.

Q. How many feet forward of the turret is broken right out—the plates?

A. Six or 7 feet forward of the turret.

Q. What side was this on?

A. Port side, sir. It looked as if it had been blown outboard.

Q. You then crawled along on the top of the armor forward?

A. Yes, sir; the last time I was down there.

Q. How far does that clear?

A. As far forward as the crane.

Q. What happened there?

A. The armor appeared to be broken off, and 2 feet abaft it was all clear. The inside armor backing was hanging on at an angle from port up, and over to starboard at the top of the armor belt. The backing was broken off from the armor as far down as I could reach, and sloped inboard.

Q. Explain what you mean by the armor being broken off.

A. By broken off I mean that it looked as if another piece had been blown right away from it. It was gone.

By the COURT:

Q. In your answers you have spoken of plates attached to the waterways being blown in; also some being blown out. What do you mean?

A. I mean that aft it was blown out and forward it was blown in.

Q. How far apart were these places?

A. Ten or 12 feet, sir. It might have been a little less—8 or 9 feet. It is hard to judge under water how far one goes.

The judge-advocate requested that the testimony given by the witness be not read to him by the stenographer, but that he be directed to report to-morrow morning at 10 o'clock, when he will be furnished with so much of the record as contains his testimony and asked to withdraw for the consideration of the same, upon the completion of which he will be again called before the court and given an opportunity to amend his testimony as recorded or pronounce it correct. The request was granted, and the witness instructed accordingly; whereupon he withdrew, after being cautioned by the president not to discuss matters pertaining to the inquiry.

The court then (at 12.45 p. m.) took a recess until 2 o'clock.

The court reassembled at the expiration of the recess.

Present: All the members of the court, the judge-advocate, the stenographer, Captain Sigsbee, and Mr. Wainwright.

232   DESTRUCTION OF THE U. S. BATTLE SHIP MAINE.

Chief Gunner's Mate OLSEN, U. S. Navy, a former witness, was recalled, and cautioned by the president of the court that he was still under oath which he had taken.

Examined by the JUDGE-ADVOCATE:

Q. Have you done any diving on the wreck of the *Maine* since your last testimony before this court?
A. Yes, sir; I have.
Q. To whom did you report the results of your diving?
A. To Mr. Powelson, of the *Fern*.
Q. When you made these reports to him were they as true as if given under oath?
A. Yes, sir.
Q. You went down on the morning of March 1—Tuesday?
A. Yes, sir; I did.
Q. Do you remember where you went down? Was it not at the after V-shaped plate?
A. Yes; I went down at the after V-shaped plate.
Q. Where did you find the first longitudinal?
A. The first longitudinal I found about 20 feet under water, and about 4 feet abaft of the second longitudinal.
Q. Taking frame 17 as the highest frame on this V, where do you think you found the first longitudinal?
A. About frame 23.
Q. For how many frame spaces did you see?
A. About two frame spaces.
Q. What was the condition of the outer skin of the ship between the first and second longitudinals?
A. Between the first and second longitudinal on the outer skin of the ship?
Q. Yes; was it broken?
A. The skin of the ship was cracked off.
Q. Did you follow the second longitudinal down?
A. Yes, sir; I did.
Q. What did you find at the end?
A. I followed it down to about nine frame spaces. I found a plate on which this longitudinal was attached bent underneath the keel on the afterpart of the V.
Q. What is the condition of the longitudinal at the end?
A. Broken off and ragged.
Q. When you went to plate B, what was the color of plate B; plate plate B being the forward one inside the V?
A. Green inside the V—McInniss's paint.
Q. Did you follow the green plate along to the flat keel?
A. Yes, sir; I did.
Q. How does the keel go from there?
A. I followed the green paint along the ship's bottom until I found the flat part of the keel. It extended down and over to port, up and over to starboard, at an angle, I should judge, of about 60 degrees from the bottom of the mud itself.
Q. Which makes the angle of 60 degrees, the one going forward or the one going aft?
A. The angle between the keel and the mud is about 60 degrees.
Q. Did you find the forward part of the ship and the keel sloping downward?
A. Yes, sir.

Q. About how many degrees?
A. It seemed to me that this part of the ship is lying on the starboard side—the starboard side on the mud, the port side up, and the keel to port.
Q. Does not her ram seem lower than her after part?
A. Yes, sir; it does.
Q. What inclination does her keel seem to be to horizontal?
A. Sixty degrees from the bottom.
Q. Abaft both of these V-shaped plates, how does the keel lay?
A. A little farther to starboard and amidships I found the continuation of the keel and broken part. The inside angle irons standing up and the inside and outside keel plates broken off for the space of about 3 feet from the bottom angle irons and vertical keel, and sloping down.
Q. What direction does the keel take then, aft?
A. Almost vertical, going down.
Q. About how long a space do you think it goes vertical?
A. About 20 feet, I should judge.
Q. Then what does it do?
A. It runs aft parallel to the bottom.
Q. What kind of a break is on the bottom; that is, that part that stands vertical and the part that stands horizontal?
A. A regular bending. It bends forward and then it bends aft.
Q. About how far forward does it bend?
A. About 2 feet.
Q. Referring to this part of the keel which stands vertical, how much plate is attached to that part of the keel which stands vertical?
A. The bottom plate of that part of the keel extends 4 or 5 feet on each side of the keel. Some places along these I slipped.
Q. You went down again on the forenoon of March 3, which was Thursday, did you not?
A. Yes, sir; I did.
Q. Did you have orders to find the top part of the keel?
A. Which top part of the keel do you mean?
Q. The inside of the keel.
A. I was told to locate the keel outside, if I possibly could.
Q. How far did you get down this time?
A. I went down over the break and followed the vertical part down to where it bends aft again. Afterwards I located some manholes with high combings around it. I located two right at the break where the keel goes aft on the vertical part, and two farther aft.
Q. Did you find a lightening hole the first frame forward of the break?
A. Yes, sir.
Q. Did you measure this hole?
A. Yes, sir.
Q. Do you remember the measure in both cases?
A. Twelve by 21 inches.
Q. Did you find a manhole in the inner skin just forward of the break?
A. Yes, sir.
Q. Did you measure that?
A. Yes, sir.
Q. Do you remember the measurements?
A. Fifteen by 22 inches.
Q. You found a four-way pipe?
A. Yes, sir.

Q. Where?
A. Alongside the vertical keel forward of the break. The smaller part of the pipe going through the inner skin of the double bottom. This pipe was 3 inches in diameter, inside diameter of the pipe, and then there was a curved pipe going through the vertical keel. This was a 4-inch pipe.

Q. Did you take measurements of the vertical keel at this time?
A. Yes, sir.

Q. How large?
A. Thirty-six inches between the inner and outer skin of the double bottom.

Q. You found several other manholes, did you not?
A. Yes, sir.

Q. They all had high combings?
A. Yes, sir.

Q. How high would you say these combings were?
A. About 3 inches.

Q. Now, along the flat part of the keel, which is abaft the vertical part, did you find the inner bottom corrugated?
A. Yes, sir; I did.

Q. In what way? Describe the appearance of the keel.
A. It was corrugated right over the keel. I am sure it was the inner bottom. The corrugations ran fore and aft. The inside skin of these plates of the keel were bent downward. The vertical keel stands up and the inside skin alongside of it slopes downward on both sides of the keel.

Q. In accounting for the depression of the bottom on both sides of the keel, did you think that the bottom had been knocked down or the keel been shoved up?
A. It may have been from the keel being shoved up, or the inner plate being shoved down; I could not tell which.

By the COURT:

Q. Was there any keel in the bottom at this place?
A. No, sir. That part of the bottom seemed all right. I could not go further on account of the wreckage.

By the JUDGE-ADVOCATE:

Q. At that place, how much bottom was there on each side of the keel, as far as you could tell?
A. I could feel about 6 feet on each side. It might have gone farther, but I could not tell.

Q. Do you know what frame you were at?
A. I must have gone abaft of frame 24.

Q. Did you find some 6-pounder ammunition?
A. Yes, sir.

Q. On which side of the keel?
A. On the starboard side of the keel.

Q. Did you find any 6-inch shell there?
A. Yes, sir; I did.

Q. On which side of the keel?
A. On the starboard side of the keel.

Q. Did you send the shell up?
A. Yes, sir.

Q. On the next forenoon you went down again. From the break in the vertical keel, which way did you go?
A. I went down the vertical keel; followed the flat part of the keel aft and worked my way over to starboard.

Q. What did you find then?
A. I worked my way over to starboard, and continuing in that direction I found a light box.
Q. Before you found this light box did you not get among a lot of 6-inch shell?
A. Yes, sir.
Q. How far were these shell from the keel?
A. It must have been about 10 or 12 feet on the starboard side.
Q. Are you sure they were 6-inch shell?
A. Yes, sir.
Q. Did you find a powder tank the same place?
A. Yes, sir.
Q. Describe the tank; 6-inch or 10-inch?
A. I can not recollect.
Q. Did you send it up?
A. I sent one 6-inch drill tank up.
Q. Did you then work your way over to starboard?
A. Yes, sir.
Q. What did you find?
A. A light box.
Q. Where was that light box made fast?
A. It was made fast in the proper light box in which the lamps go. I lifted up the cover of the light box proper.
Q. Was this light box in the bulkhead?
A. Yes, sir; between the coal bunker and what I think was formerly the 10-inch magazine.
Q. How do you know?
A. The 10-inch magazine light only shows one light in the drawings, which shows that this is the only place where there was only one light.
Q. What was the general direction of the bulkhead that you found this light box in?
A. It was flat and lying down.
Q. Which way was it bent down?
A. It was lying flat parallel with the bottom.
Q. Had it been bent to starboard or to port?
A. Over to starboard.
Q. Did you feel the end of this bulkhead?
A. Yes, sir.
Q. What did you find?
A. I followed the continuation of this bulkhead down about 10 feet, and underneath it I crawled into the double bottom.
Q. Did you find the rungs of an iron ladder there?
A. Yes, sir; underneath the deadlight in the bulkhead.
Q. You then went into the 10-inch magazine as you suppose?
A. Yes.
Q. Did you find 10-inch tanks there?
A. I found some 6-inch shells in the space; some of them had slings on them and wooden nose pieces; they were in good condition. Digging underneath these shells I located some tanks.
Q. What kind of tanks?
A. I should judge them to be 10-inch tanks.
Q. Were they in good condition?
A. I could not tell. I could only feel them on account of the shell being on top of them, but they showed that they were tanks by their shape.
Q. Did you find in your dive any cutlass or scabbard?
A. Yes, sir; I found a scabbard.

Q. Where?
A. I found one on this plate, going from the light box down about 10 feet and in the double bottom, a scabbard and gas check disks in pads, which I sent up.
Q. Did you find any paymaster's stores on top of the tanks you were just speaking about?
A. Yes, sir; I found canned goods, some low-cut paymaster's shoes.
Q. Did you find a piece of wooden grating from the floor of the magazine?
A. Yes, sir; I did. I sent it up.
Q. Had it been burned?
A. I could not tell. Mr. Powelson looked at it after it came up.
Q. You went down again Saturday?
A. Yes, sir.
Q. Where did you go?
A. I went aft, trying to locate the armor plate.
Q. Did you find anything that looked to you like a boiler?
A. Yes, sir; it looked to me like a boiler, but I did not stay down there long enough to get a good look at it. It was very dark.
Q. Was it very much out of shape?
A. Yes, sir.
Q. You then walked over to starboard, I believe, after walking aft, and found a plate.
A. Yes, sir.
Q. Will you please describe this plate that you found?
A. I found a plate with angle iron— V-iron. These irons were about 12 inches apart, forming a regular square in two rows.
Q. What direction was this plate standing in?
A. Up and over to starboard, standing at an angle up and leaning to starboard.
Q. Did you find any cellulose?
A. Yes, sir; I found the cellulose compartment.
Q. Where were you then?
A. I must have been at the midship line of the ship on the port side aft.
Q. What do you mean by midship line of the ship? About the place of the crane?
A. Yes, sir; about somewhere in that line.
Q. Are you sure this was cellulose?
A. Yes, sir. I took it out in my hand and looked at it. It was packed in the compartment.
Q. What was the size of the compartment and the shape of the compartment that the cellulose was in?
A. I could feel the outside and inside skin of this compartment. It must have been 3 or 4 feet wide from the inside to the outside. It might have been larger or smaller—4 feet I judge it to be. It was standing up and pointed, one pointing aft about the port quarter and the other pointing forward to the starboard bow. It was way abaft. I know exactly where 24 frame is; it is 20 or 30 feet abaft frame 24.

By the COURT:

Q. Do you know where the forward end of the belt is—the armor belt?
A. Yes, sir.
Q. What frame is that?
A. About frame 30.

By the Judge-Advocate:

Q. Did you after this lift up a couple of plates and throw them aside?
A. Yes, sir.
Q. Where were they?
A. They were below this portion described—below and forward of the cellulose compartment. I picked up a 6-inch powder tank. This tank was full of powder, the bottom and head of the tank being on the tank.
Q. Did you send this tank up?
A. Yes, sir.
Q. Did you find a lot of other broken tanks about here?
A. Yes, sir; a lot of them split in the seam. On the head of this tank I sent up there was a lot of black mud. We dried it and found it was powder. Where all the broken tanks were I could pick up a lot of this mud. I found that mud in several places around that place, and I think it is all powder. I can tell the difference between these and the mud which is outside the bottom of the ship. This is very black, and the mud on the outside turns a greenish color when you stir it up.
Q. What made you think it was powder, only the color of it?
A. I tried to burn some, and it burned all right.
Q. Who made this experiment?
A. Chief gunner's mate of the *New York*, Fisher.
Q. You were there?
A. Yes, sir.
Q. And you say there is plenty of this black mud around the ship?
A. Yes, sir; especially where the broken tanks are you will find some of that mud all around. It seemed to me that the tanks in this place had been spilled all around.
Q. What did you do this morning in the way of diving?
A. I went down, took a lead line down plumb in line with the ship. I came up again; I made a line fast at the broken part of the keel, and then I went down again, and was towed outside, clear of the ship, and was told to go down and see if I could find any coal. I went aft until I came to the break where the armor ends, and could not find any sign of coal on the port side.
Q. How far away from the ship did you walk when you were looking for coal?
A. I must have walked about 20 feet out—and I walked in a zigzag out and in, 20 feet clear—and back again to where the armor ends.
Q. How far forward did you commence the search?
A. I started forward, about at the ram, a little further out, and as far forward as the ram.
Q. When you put your lead down had you found the ram itself?
A. The end of the ram: that is, the bow of the ship itself, was down in the mud. I should judge the place was about 6 feet from the bow, that part of the keel and the ram being about 6 feet apart, and the flat part of the keel sloping forward at this point. The ram itself I should judge to be about 6 feet.
Q. Did you find the ram plates?
A. Yes, sir.
Q. And you were well forward of the afterend of the ram plates?
A. Yes, sir. I could not feel the afterpart of the ram plate. It extends underneath the side.
Q. What is the condition of the ship's side under the after one of the two V-shaped plates?
A. Going down about half-way down, on the after end of B, and then getting onto the ship's bottom properly, I found two dents extending between two frames and bulged into the ship's bottom itself.

Q. Are these two dents in a horizontal line?
A. They are in a parallel line to the keel.
Q. How deep should you say they were?
A. About 3 or 4 inches deep.
Q. And about what is their diameter?
A. About 4 feet in diameter.
Q. Is there a frame between the two dents?
A. It looks so from the outside.

The judge-advocate requested that the testimony given by the witness be not read to him by the stenographer, but that he be directed to report to-morrow morning at 10 o'clock, when he will be furnished with so much of the record as contains his testimony, and asked to withdraw for the consideration of the same, upon the completion of which he will be again called before the court and be given an opportunity to amend his testimony as recorded or pronounce it correct. The request was granted, and the witness was instructed accordingly; whereupon he withdrew, after being cautioned by the president not to discuss matters pertaining to the inquiry.

Naval Cadet CLUVERIUS, U. S. Navy, a former witness, was recalled and warned by the president that he was still under the oath that he had taken.

Examined by the JUDGE-ADVOCATE:

Q. Were you the mate of the berth deck of the *Maine* at the time of her destruction?
A. I was.
Q. What were your duties as regards the securing of the ship for the night?
A. The duties I had in securing the ship for the night were to instruct the persons in charge of such departments as by the ship regulations were to be closed at sunset that these departments were to be closed, and that the tag keys placed upon the keyboard, which was at the forward part of the engine room hatch in compartment C100, were placed there.
Q. What part of this duty did you do that night?
A. I was on watch from 4 until 8, and did not personally instruct the men in charge of these compartments, but had warned them the night before, and I remember that they had all been turned in the night before, and on the night of February 15 I am almost positive that these men reported to me that their compartments were closed while I was officer of the deck.
Q. Did you look at the keyboard that night?
A. Yes, sir; when I was relieved for my dinner, in passing the keyboard I glanced at it and remember seeing the numbers solid.
Q. Were the regular 8 p. m. reports made to you that night?
A. They were, sir.
Q. Did you consider Seaman Neilson, temporarily in charge of the hold, a reliable man?
A. I did, sir.
Q. Had the magazines or shell rooms or any of them been open during your tour of duty, the dog watches that day?
A. To my knowledge they had not, sir.
Q. Had any of them been reported to you as open when you took the deck?
A. They had not.

There being no further questions to ask this witness, his testimony was read over to him by the stenographer, and by him pronounced correct; whereupon he withdrew, after being cautioned by the president not to discuss matters pertaining to the inquiry.

The court then (at 3.30 p. m.) adjourned until to-morrow Tuesday, March 8, 1898, at 10 o'clock a. m.

TWELFTH DAY.

U. S. L. H. TENDER MANGROVE,
Harbor of Havana, 10 a. m., Tuesday, March 8, 1898.

The court met pursuant to the adjournment of yesterday.
Present: All the members of the court, the judge-advocate, and the stenographer.
The proceedings of yesterday were then read over and approved.

Gunner's Mate T. SMITH, U. S. Navy, a former witness, was then recalled, and cautioned by the president of the court that he was still under the oath he had taken.

Examined by the JUDGE-ADVOCATE:

Q. Have you done any diving at the wreck of the *Maine* since your last testimony was given before this court?
A. Yes, sir.
Q. To whom did you report the results of your searches?
A. Ensign Powelson.
Q. When you made these reports were they as truthful as if you had been under oath?
A. Yes, sir.
Q. Do you remember going down on Monday morning, February 28?
A. Yes, sir.
Q. Where did you go down?
A. I went down along the after wing which forms the V.
Q. Did you find the first longitudinal?
A. The first longitudinal; yes, sir.
Q. Did you find the bottom plate?
A. Yes, sir; I did.
Q. What was its condition?
A. Condition, it was good.
Q. Did you find any bottom plate broken with the edges pushed in?
A. Yes, sir.
Q. Where?
A. The lower edges of the wing, and all around the edges of it was broken and jagged.
Q. Was it pushed in from the green paint?
A. It comes closer to the forward part of where it forms the V as you go down deep, and it has a sort of corrugated shape to it.
Q. You went down again on the afternoon of the same day, did you not?
A. Yes, sir.
Q. You were sent down, I believe, to look for a circular hole. Do you remember?
A. Yes, sir; that is what I was sent down for.

Q. Where did you locate it?
A. Between the sixth and seventh frame, and from the water's edge down.
Q. What was the nature of the hole?
A. It was a circular hole, sir, like one that had been there. There was just half of it there with the rivet holes.

By the COURT:

Q. The rivet holes were in a straight line?
A. No, sir; in a circular line.

By the JUDGE-ADVOCATE:

Q. Did you find a number of 6-pound shell there?
A. Yes, sir.
Q. Were there cartridges on them?
A. Just the shell, sir.
Q. On the morning of March 2, which is Wednesday morning, you went down again, I believe?
A. Yes, sir.
Q. What was your purpose in going down that time; do you remember?
A. I remember it was to find where the break of the vertical keel was.
Q. Did you take anything with you for measurements?
A. A 2-foot rule, sir.
Q. What was the thickness of the vertical keel as you found it?
A. About 5½ inches, sir, on the flange.
Q. You found a four-way pipe, did you not?
A. Yes, sir.
Q. Did you measure the distance from the vertical-keel break to the next frame forward?
A. Yes, sir.
Q. Do you remember what this measurement was?
A. Thirty six inches, sir.
Q. What was the width of the inner keel plate?
A. The inner keel plate was 37 inches.
Q. You went down again in the afternoon of the same day, did you not?
A. Yes, sir.
Q. You looked then for the keel and found the vertical part, did you not?
A. Yes, sir. The horizontal part abaft the part which is now vertical.
Q. Abaft the vertical part?
A. Yes, sir.
Q. What did you find?
A. I found the vertical keel lying in a horizontal position.
Q. Did you find a 10-inch shell there?
A. Yes, sir.
Q. What else?
A. A powder tank.
Q. What else?
A. A bunch of knapsacks. I sent them up from below.
Q. Did you find a swab?
A. Yes, sir; I found a big magazine swab.
Q. Was it burnt?
A. No, sir; it was not.
Q. What kind of a bend has the keel where it goes to the horizontal again?

DESTRUCTION OF THE U. S. BATTLE SHIP MAINE. 241

A. It forms a sort of a V in there with the two angle irons that are bolted to the vertical keel, and also bolted to the skin of the double bottom, which is broken right in the corner where it forms the V.

Q. Do I understand that the keel first bends forward and then goes aft?

A. It first goes forward and then goes aft.

Q. What is the distance, do you think, that it goes forward?

A. Thirty-six inches, sir.

Q. You then went down the keel into the mud?

A. Yes, sir; I went off to the bottom of the plate.

Q. What did you find there in the mud where the flat keel goes into the mud?

A. I do not remember what I found there.

Q. Do you remember finding a hole in the mud?

A. Yes, but in a different place, sir. It is by the bow where I found the hole.

Q. Now tell us exactly where you found that hole.

A. I followed the forward part of the wing that forms the V down until I came to the mud. I took a couple of steps aft and felt the vertical keel again, and followed it down until I came to the mud; then I was standing up straight until I could take my two hands so [witness illustrated by extending his arms horizontally], out that way, and feel the mud all around.

Q. How deep was this hole, do you think?

A. I should judge 7 feet.

Q. How wide was it—the diameter, I mean?

A. About the same, sir.

Q. Was the bottom of the hole hard at this place?

A. The mud was a little harder than the other mud. You would not sink over 18 inches in that mud.

Q. Can you locate this hole?

A. Yes, sir.

Q. By the frames, where was it? Locate it with the two V-shaped plates. Was it forward of the after V-shaped plate?

A. The hole was about under the forward V-shaped plate. The largest part of the hole is on the port side of the ship. The keel can not be felt from the hole, and it seemed to be under the forward part of the forward V-shaped plate.

Q. What did you find in this hole?

A. I found a tin I should judge to be about 20 inches long and 10 inches square. It looked like a can made up in a square, and 20 inches long. There was a place where a big square hole had been with a gasket. I sent it up to Mr. Powelson.

Q. Were you down yesterday afternoon?

A. Yes, sir.

Q. Tell to the court what you found.

A. I was landed on top of the boiler—the forward boiler on the port side. What I found of it seemed to be in good condition. Between that boiler and the forward athwartship bulkhead I found two 10-inch shells and a 6-inch powder tank, and also a large copper pipe, about 4 inches in diameter. That is all I have to say about that for the present.

Q. Where was this bulkhead, in regard to the boiler?

A. It seemed to me to be between that boiler and some other boiler.

Q. Was it forward of the boiler or abaft the boiler?

A. It was abaft the boiler.

Q. Did you send the 10-inch tank up?

S. Doc. 207——16

A. No, sir; I did not.
Q. What was its condition?
A. It was split in the seam, the same as the rest.
Q. Nothing in it?
A. Excelsior.
Q. You have no other report to make of yesterday's diving, have you?
A. No, sir; I was hauled up at that time.
Q. What is fast to the keel which now stands up and down?
A. The vertical keel. On the starboard side there is the inner skin of the double bottom made fast to it, and on the port side part of the way it is torn off.
Q. Torn off altogether?
A. In some places on the port side it is torn off altogether.
Q. What appearance does it make next to the keel; which way does it bulge?
A. From the present position of the keel it bulges aft.
Q. Were the keel horizontal would it bulge up?
A. Yes, sir.

By the COURT:

Q. All this is the inner bottom?
A. Yes, sir.
Q. In that part of the keel in the inner bend where the inner bottom is torn from the keel, can you tell us anything of the condition of the outer bottom?
A. No, sir; I can not. I would have to walk around there and find that out to see what condition it is in.

There being no further questions to ask this witness he was directed to hold himself in readiness to appear before the court whenever he had further testimony to give; whereupon, after being cautioned by the president not to discuss matters pertaining to the inquiry, he withdrew.

The court was then cleared (at 11.40 a. m.) for further discussion.

The doors being opened, the court at 12.30 took a recess until 2 p. m.

The court reassembled at the expiration of the recess.

Present: All the members of the court, the judge-advocate, and the stenographer.

Naval Constructor J. B. HOOVER appeared as a witness before the court and was duly sworn by the president.

Examined by the JUDGE-ADVOCATE:

Q. Please state your name, rank, and station.
A. John B. Hoover, naval constructor, United States Navy.
Q. Were you ordered by the Secretary of the Navy to assist this court of inquiry in their work?
A. I was.
Q. Have you visited the wreck of the *Maine*, and examined such portions as are above water?
A. I have.
Q. Do you recollect the three portions of wreck which are in a fore-and-aft line some distance forward of the middle superstructure?
A. Yes, sir.
Q. Can you identify the after one of these three of this wreckage?
A. I can. It is a portion of the ship from frame 17 showing a portion of the second longitudinal, and main frame 17, and the outside

platings doubled—thrown up and doubled to starboard. Bottom platings thrown up and doubled back.

Q. What is the direction of frame 17 with regard to the fore-and aft line of the ship at she now lies?

A. Frame 17? In relation to the fore-and-aft line of the ship? Well, it is canted. The port frame is come up and gone over to starboard.

Q. How far from the center line of the ship does the doubling in the plate occur?

A. I can not say.

Q. The frame 17 which appears above water, you say, how near was that to the vertical keel when in its normal state?

A. About 5 feet from the middle line of the ship.

Q. Did you measure the distance of frame 17 from some part of the ship which is in its normal position?

A. Yes. I measured the distance from the after funnel, which is at frame 43, and which is about 93 feet 6 inches; that is, to the after object seen.

Q. What would have been that distance had the ship been in its original shape from frame 43 to frame 17?

A. It would be 103 feet and one-half.

Q. Did you examine the next object forward of this one? What is that?

A. That is a portion of the protective deck abreast of the chain locker.

Q. Which side of the protective deck?

A. The port side.

Q. Did you measure that from the same normal part of the ship?

A. I did.

Q. What was the distance?

A. 109 feet 6 inches.

Q. What would that distance have been with the ship in its normal condition?

A. That was opposite the chain lockers. It ought to be just the same, 103 feet 6 inches.

Q. Did you examine the the third piece of wreckage forward of the second?

A. I did.

Q. What did you identify that to be?

A. As a portion of the berth deck, but broken off at frame 19 with the part of the cellulose compartment bulkhead attached to it, and showing one scupper hole, going up from frame 19 and taking in frames 18 and 17.

Q. Which side of the berth deck was this?

A. That was on the port side, and it was twisted right around to starboard looking forward.

Q. What was the distance from the same normal point in the ship?

A. That would be 130 feet.

Q. Then, according to your statement, the lower portion of the ship near the keel, at frame 17, was thrown up and abaft the same portion of the ship at a higher deck.

A. Thrown up and abaft the same portion of the ship at the berth deck and at the protective deck.

Q. The part of the protective deck was thrown up between the lower portion and the berth deck portion, was it not?

A. Yes.

Q. Did you examine the line of keel which these three pieces of wreckage show you and compare it with the line of keel in the after part of the ship?

A. I did in this way only—by sighting through as near as I could see.

Q. Did you find that this line of keel in the wreck is in line with the after keel line of the ship?

A. They are on the port side of the original keel.

Q. How much?

A. In the neighborhood of 4 to 5 feet, but they are canted to starboard.

Q. Were you able to see anything below water at these three pieces of wreckage?

A. Nothing that I could recognize.

By the COURT:

Q. According to your statement, these three pieces of wreckage—the bottom of the ship, the protective deck, and the berth deck—all three of which show above the water at present, and all coming from points which were nearly in the same vertical plane; Now, then, the piece of the berth deck, forward portion of the three, which is now forward of the other two.

A. The protective deck comes next and the bottom comes last. Then the bottom of the ship, as it now stands, has been turned nearly 90 degrees—revolved nearly 90 degrees.

Q. The protective deck has been revolved how much?

A. About the same.

Q. And the berth deck?

A. The berth deck, I think, a little more than the others. It seems to be twisted more.

Q. With these three decks, one above the other, the upper one has gone forward and been turned through an angle of 90 degrees?

A. Yes.

Q. Did all these pieces that show above water belong to the port side on the port side of the keel?

A. Yes, sir.

Q. Except the protective deck? Is that on the port side?

A. The protective deck is on the port side also, but not all of it.

Q. Yes, but what there is on it came from the port side?

A. I did not mean that, exactly.

Q. What position does the forward 6-inch magazine occupy with reference to this portion of the bottom of the ship, the protective deck, and the berth deck which have been displaced as described?

A. The forward part of the 6-inch magazine is just below the three pieces of deck as they originally were. The forward 6-inch magazine begins at frame 18. The wreckage goes from 17 to 19. 18 is a water-tight bulkhead. The magazine goes from 18 to 21. There are two magazines there. In 18 to 21 is the forward magazine.

There being no further questions to ask this witness, he was directed to appear to-morrow, to read his testimony, at 10 a. m.; and after being warned by the president of the court not to converse regarding the inquiry he withdrew.

Carpenter HELM, U. S. Navy, a former witness, was recalled and warned by the president of the court that he was still under oath which he had taken.

Examined by the JUDGE-ADVOCATE:

Q. Since you have given your last testimony before this court have you made an examination of that portion of the wreck of the *Maine* which is above the water?

A. Yes, sir.

Q. Do you remember the three portions of wreckage which appeared in a normal fore-and-aft line some distance forward of the middle superstructure?

A. Yes, sir.

Q. Can you identify the after one of these three pieces of wreckage?

A. Yes, sir; that is a piece of outside plating with second longitudinal, frame 17 and frame 18.

Q. How near the keel is that portion of frame 17 which you see above the water?

A. About 10 feet.

Q. Can you identify the second piece of wreckage—the one forward of this?

A. Yes, sir; that is the protective deck, in wake of the sheet-chain locker, on the port side. The highest point is frame 18, being below frame 17, and frame 16 just under the water.

Q. Are these three frames 18, 17, and 16 in a vertical line?

A. Well, they are at about an angle of nearly about 60 degrees.

Q. Is the upper frame forward or aft?

A. The upper frame is forward.

Q. What do you mean by the upper frame?

A. Eighteen is the highest one.

Q. What is the third and forward piece of wreckage?

A. That is part of the first deck bulkhead which helped to form the cellulose compartment. The highest point is frame 19, 18 next, and 17 is under the water. The pipe hole through that deck belongs to one of the forward scuppers.

Q. What is the general direction of these three frames 19, 18, and 17?

A. I guess they would be pretty near at an angle of 80 degrees from the horizontal.

Q. The top one forward or aft?

A. No. 19 forward.

Q. Which side of the berth deck and what portion of it do you identify this as being?

A. Port side, frame 19.

Q. And the cellulose bulkhead is also from the port side?

A. Yes, sir.

Q. Do these three pieces of wreckage seem to you to be twisted around?

A. From aft to forward they are twisted about 90 degrees and turned completely around.

By the COURT:

Q. What was originally the relative positions of these three pieces of wreckage?

A. Well, they were all parts of decks running fore and aft. They were practically in a vertical position over one another. 19, 18, and 17 are within the vicinity of 16, 17, 18, and 19 frames.

Q. How do you think they got into their present condition?

A. That is beyond me, Captain.

Q. Are they all in the same position with reference to the horizontal that they were originally?

A. No, they are thrown forward of one another. They are right forward of one another. The inner bottom seems to come right up and over. The berth deck extends nearly vertical now, with the upper side of the deck to port. The protective deck stands about 60 degrees to port and slants about 60 degrees to vertical. The upper side faces forward. The top of the protective deck faces also to port and slightly forward.

Q. Taking the superstructure of the ship between frames 18 and 24, which do you regard as affording the greater resistance, the pressure from the interior or the exterior?

A. I think the double bottom.

By the JUDGE-ADVOCATE:

Q. Where were the knapsacks and infantry equipments stowed in the *Maine?*

A. I think they were stowed in the compartment A11.

There being no further questions to ask this witness he was directed to appear to-morrow at 10 a. m. to read over his testimony; whereupon, after being warned by the president of the court not to discuss matters pertaining to the inquiry, he withdrew.

Consul-General FITZHUGH LEE appeared as a witness before the court, and was duly sworn by the president.

Examined by the JUDGE-ADVOCATE:

Q. Please state your full name and your official position.

A. Fitzhugh Lee, United States consul-general at Havana.

Q. When were you first notified of the intended arrival of the battle ship *Maine?*

A. Twenty-fourth of January, 1898. I have the telegram here and will read it:

> It is the purpose of this Government to resume the friendly naval visits at Cuban ports. In that view the *Maine* will call at the port of Havana in a day or two. Please arrange for the friendly interchange of calls with the authorities.
>
> DAY.

Q. How long after the receipt of this telegram did the *Maine* arrive?

A. She arrived the next morning, at about 11 o'clock, I think.

Q. Had you notified the authorities at Havana of her intended arrival?

A. After receiving that telegram I went down to the palace and notified the authorities, and read the telegram to them. That was on the afternoon of the 24th of January. Immediately after having received the telegram above referred to I sent the following reply to the State Department:

> HAVANA, *January 24.*
>
> Advise visit be postponed six or seven days to give last excitement more time to disappear. Will see authorities and let you know. Governor-General away for two weeks. I should know day and hour visit.
>
> LEE.

The following morning I sent the following telegram to the State Department:

> [In cipher.]
>
> HAVANA, *January 25.*
>
> At an interview authorities profess to think United States has ulterior purpose in sending ship. Say it will obstruct autonomy, produce excitement, and most probably a demonstration. Ask that it is not done until they can get instructions from Madrid, and say that if for friendly purposes, as claimed, delay unimportant.
>
> LEE.

And after arrival of the *Maine* I sent the following telegram to the Department:

HAVANA, *January 25*.

Ship quietly arrived, 11 a. m. to-day; no demonstration so far.

LEE.

After sending the telegram of the 24th I received the following reply on the 25th:

Maine has been ordered. Will probably arrive at Havana some time to-morrow, Tuesday. Can not tell hour. Possibly early. Cooperate with the authorities for her friendly visit. Keep us advised by frequent telegrams.

DAY.

There being no further questions to ask the witness, his testimony was read over to him by the stenographer and by him pronounced correct; whereupon he withdrew, after being cautioned by the president not to discuss matters pertaining to the inquiry.

The court then (at 5 p. m.) adjourned to meet to-morrow, Wednesday, March 9, at 10 o'clock a. m.

THIRTEENTH DAY.

U. S. L. H. TENDER MANGROVE,
Harbor of Havana, Wednesday, March 9, 1898—10 a. m.

The court met, pursuant to adjournment of yesterday, the twelfth day of the inquiry.

Present: All the members of the court, the judge-advocate, and the stenographer.

The record of the proceedings of yesterday was read and approved.

Naval Constructor HOOVER appeared before the court.

By the JUDGE-ADVOCATE:

Q. Have you read over the testimony which you gave yesterday before this court?
A. I have.
Q. Is it correct as recorded?
A. It is.

The witness then withdrew, after being cautioned by the president not to discuss matters pertaining to the inquiry.

Carpenter HELM appeared before the court.

By the JUDGE-ADVOCATE:

Q. Have you read over the testimony which you gave before the court yesterday?
A. Yes, sir.
Q. Is it correct as recorded?
A. Yes, sir; it is.

The witness then withdrew, after being cautioned by the president not to discuss matters pertaining to the inquiry.

Ensign W. V. N. POWELSON, U. S. Navy, a former witness, was recalled, and, having been warned by the president that he was still under the oath he had previously taken, testified as follows:

Examined by the JUDGE-ADVOCATE:

Q. Have you read over the testimony which you gave before this court last Monday?

A. Yes, sir.

Q. Is it correct as recorded?

A. With one exception. On page 492, third line from the bottom, next to the last word, change "of" to "with."

Q. Is your testimony as amended now correct?

A. Yes, sir.

Q. Since giving that testimony have you taken an angle which would show the position of the ram with regard to the keel of the ship?

A. Yes, sir.

Q. Will you please state how you did it, and the result?

A. I sent a diver down to make a lead line fast as near to the point on the ram as possible. He could not find the point of the ram, as it was in the mud, and he made his lead line fast to some weights alongside a ram plate at a distance which he estimated from the curve of the keel at that point and the stem of the ship to be about 5 feet abaft the ram point. I sent a man out in a boat to plumb this point on the ram plate. I also sent a diver down to make a line fast to the vertical keel where this broken place occurs at frame 18. I then got in a boat and plumbed this latter point, and took an angle between the plumb line of the armor plate and the center of the after funnel of the *Maine*, which occupied probably its original position.

This angle I measured to be 104°. Standing in the same position I measured an angle between the funnel to which I have referred and the mainmast of the ship. The angle was 2° 10′. I was at that time to port of the line connecting the funnel and the mainmast. I took a measurement with a tape line from the plumb of the ram and the plumb of the break in the vertical keel, at frame 18. I found this to be 42 feet. I measured the distance from the funnel to the plumb of the ram and found it to be 99 feet. I measured the distance from the funnel to the plumb of the vertical keel at frame 18 and found it to be 86 feet.

Q. Did you yesterday afternoon send Diver Olsen down to examine the break in the ship's side?

A. Yes, sir.

Q. Where did he descend?

A. He went down at about frame 41, that being the most forward point of the armor plate which is now attached to the ship.

Q. On which side of the ship?

A. On the port side.

Q. How much water was there at the plumb line to the ram?

A. I think it was about 35 feet.

By the COURT:

Q. Now, did the measurements which you made with reference to the position of the ram enable you to determine how the keel of the ship attached to the ram laid?

A. I have not made any drawings from these measurements.

Q. That is one thing we would like to know—how the keel lies.

A. I will take measurements of everything and let you know.

There being no further questions to ask this witness, he was directed to hold himself in readiness to give further testimony, and after being cautioned by the president not to converse about matters pertaining to the inquiry he withdrew.

Chief Gunner's Mate A. OLSEN, U. S. Navy, a former witness, was recalled, and, having been warned by the president that he was still under the oath he had previously taken, testified as follows:

Examined by the JUDGE-ADVOCATE:

Q. Have you read over the testimony which you gave before this court last Monday?
A. Yes, sir.
Q. Is it correct as recorded?
A. It is correct except in two places.
On page 523, eleventh line, after the words "with the," insert "ram plate on bow of ship."
On page 521, fifth line, it should be "U iron" instead of "V iron."
Q. Is your testimony, as amended, now correct?
A. Yes, sir.
Q. Olsen, will you state to the court what you mean by the ram plate which you can feel?
A. The ram plate—it is fastened on the bow of the ship. It extends out from the ship about 10 or 12 inches—a heavy plate.
Q. Is it convex on the outside?
A. Yes, sir.
Q. Does this plate you speak of extend fore and aft on the whole of the ship?
A. Fore and aft; yes, sir.
Q. Have you been down diving since you gave your last testimony?
A. Yes, sir; I was down yesterday, Monday evening, and yesterday all day.
Q. Please state what you found.
A. I went down Monday night, after I left the court here, to look for a piece of wire, of which I spoke, but I could not find it. Then I went down again yesterday morning, following the outside of the ship fore and aft, looking for this wire, which I could not find. I gave that up entirely and started to overhaul the bottom of the ship at that point. I found where I went down, at frame 31, at the armor plate, that I could feel the bottom of the ship forward for ten frame spaces. At the end of ten frame spaces and at frame 31, I found her to be cut off entirely. That is as far as I could walk in the mud. Then I went back again, and I counted six frame spaces from the armor plate forward. That is about frame 35, and from there forward I found to be blown up and over to starboard, this point of the bottom being much higher than at any other place along the edge of the bottom abaft this point. Then I tried to locate this point, where she was broken up, and I found a manhole, to which I attached a line, which is fast over there now on the scow. You can plumb that point at any time by the line.

At frame 31 I found the bilge keel, and followed the break in amidships as far as I could. I followed it in to about 4 or 5 feet inside of the bilge keel, and could not go farther on account of wreckage. Then I came up and went down in the afternoon forward to locate the bow. I went down the bow of the ship at the ram plate, and I could not walk any farther forward on account of the wreckage, but I walked out clear of the ship to port and forward about 10 feet. Then I walked in again over to starboard, and I got right down to the bow of the ship and followed the flat surface of the bow right forward until I came to a hawse pipe. I felt all around this to see if I could feel the chain, but I could not; but I dug the mud out underneath and found another hawse pipe with chain.

Q. Which bow was that?

A. The port bow. Then I went farther forward, about 5 or 6 feet, and I could feel the top keel of the ship. I found the shape of the keel bent, the iron keel, around the forecastle. Underneath the keel I found scroll work on the bow of the ship and over this hawse pipe, but I found no chain. I found a cover that covers the hawse pipe, with two hinges and a guy made fast on this plate, down in the mud—I think originally made fast on the bow of the ship—and tried to haul it in, but could not get in the slack, so I cut the mousing that hooks where it was hooked into the plate. Then I followed the chain out from the hawse pipe, out to port from the ship, and found the port anchor in the mud. Then I found another chain leading out, I think, from the starboard bow underneath and out. I think that chain runs to a bow, but I did not locate that spot.

Q. When you first descended where the armor is broken off, what frame is that?

A. Frame 41, sir.

Q. What is the appearance of the edge of the ship's bottom, from frame 41 to frame 35?

A. The edge is ragged, going forward between frames 35 and 41, sir.

Q. Are there any ragged points tending in or out?

A. No, sir.

Q. From frame 35 to frame 31, you say, the ragged edge slopes in toward the keel?

A. Yes, sir; in and up.

Q. Then the appearance of things there at frame 35 would indicate that the ship's keel commences to be lifted?

A. Yes, sir; seemingly on account of the plates here being so much higher, and further aft the rest of the ship being in the mud so far.

Q. Then you are able to get underneath the bottom of the ship forward of frame 35?

A. Yes, sir.

Q. How much plating should you say is left on the keel at frame 35?

A. The bottom of the ship is attached to about the fourth longitudinal.

Q. At frame 31 how much plating is attached to the bottom of the ship from the keel out?

A. To about the fourth longitudinal at this point also.

Q. At frame 31 you say the bottom of the ship seems to have disappeared forward of 31?

A. Forward of 31, yes, sir.

Q. Have you endeavored to find the keel itself forward of 31?

A. Yes, sir; but could not get in amidships as far as the keel ought to be, on account of the wreckage.

Q. Where did you again find the keel forward of 31?

A. The only place forward of 31 where I found the bottom of the keel is at frame 18.

Q. What is the condition of the keel between 18 and 22?

A. From 18 aft the keel goes down vertically—that is, the inner skin of the double bottom, not the keel—goes down vertically for a space of about 20 feet, and then goes aft, sloping lower and lower as far aft as you go.

Q. At what frame did you find the bilge keel?
A. At frame 31.
Q. What was the appearance of this bilge keel?
A. It was the wood part of that keel that was ragged and torn.
Q. Could you feel the after break of the keel—the bilge keel?
A. I could feel the break of the bilge keel where she was broken at frame 31; forward of that it was gone.
Q. What was the condition of the bilge keel and the wood on it, as you say; where you did find it?
A. The steel part of the bilge keel was broken off, showing rough edges, and the wooden part, extending forward of it, was ragged and torn in splinters.
Q. At what frame did you find the fourth longitudinal, clear of the bottom plating of the ship?
A. At frame 31.
Q. How far did the longitudinal extend forward clear of the plating?
A. About 2 or 3 feet. I didn't measure it.
Q. What became of it then?
A. It was broken off. It did not extend any farther forward.
Q. In what direction did this few feet of longitudinal run?
A. Seemingly it appeared to be in its normal condition, not bent out of shape.
Q. When you looked for the bow of the ship did you again find it was over on the starboard side?
A. Yes, sir. I could feel over the rail on the bow of the ship and feel the mud. The starboard side must be covered with mud.
Q. She seemed to be lying on the starboard side?
A. Yes, sir.
Q. Which way did the keel go, with the line of the mud—up and out? Did it go aft and parallel to the line of the mud?
A. The keel is up and over to starboard a little aft.
Q. Counting from the stem aft?
A. Where the keel is out of the mud, up over to starboard, a little aft.
Q. Did you take the depth of water over the break of the keel at frame 18?
A. Yes, sir.
Q. How much was it?
A. Six feet of water, sir.
Q. Did you plumb it at the top of the frame, or where?
A. At the point where the keel plates are broken away from the bottom angle irons of the vertical keel.
Q. Did you plumb and take depths of the bend of the keel lower down?
A. Yes, sir.
Q. What depth did you find?
A. It was 25 feet.
Q. Twenty-three feet?
A. I think so.
Q. I would like you to get that exact. What part of the bend did you plumb with your line?
A. I plumbed the point where she starts to go aft—where the vertical keel comes down and goes aft.
Q. Did you plumb the top of the vertical keel?
A. It was the inner skin of the double bottom.

Q. While down diving since you gave your last testimony have you looked for the keel on the port side of the ship?
A. Yes, sir; I have been looking for the coal. I was told Monday to look for the coal, and every time I have been down since I have looked for it, but have not been able to find it.
Q. On the port side of the ship?
A. Yes, sir.
Q. Have you looked as far forward as "B?"
A. Yes, sir.
Q. And as far aft as frame 41?
A. Yes, sir.
Q. Well out from the ship?
A. Yes, sir; as much as 20 feet from the ship.
Q. In toward the ship?
A. Yes, sir; inside, and bottom.
Q. Did you find much wreckage on the port side?
A. No, sir; no wreckage there.

There being no further questions to ask this witness, he was directed to appear to-morrow to read over his testimony, and to hold himself in readiness to give further testimony. Whereupon, having been cautioned by the president not to discuss matters pertaining to the inquiry, he withdrew.

Gunner's Mate T. SMITH appeared before the court.

By the JUDGE-ADVOCATE:

Q. Have you read over your testimony which you gave before this court yesterday?
A. Yes, sir.
Q. Is it correct as it is recorded?
A. Yes, sir; with the exception of one mistake. On the seventh line of page ——, change "five and one-half" to "five-eighths," so as to read "five eighths of an inch."
Q. Is your testimony as now recorded correct?
A. Yes, sir.
Q. Have you been down since you gave your last testimony?
A. No, sir; I have not.

The witness then withdrew, after being cautioned by the president not to discuss matters pertaining to the inquiry.

The court then, at 11.45, took a recess until 2 p. m.

The court reassembled at the expiration of the recess.

Present: All the members, the judge-advocate, and the stenographer.

Gunner's Mate SCHLUTER, a former witness, was then recalled, and, after being warned by the president of the court that he was still under the oath he had taken, testified as follows:

Examined by JUDGE-ADVOCATE:

Q. Have you read over the record of your testimony which you gave before this court last Monday?
A. Yes, sir.
Q. Is it correct as recorded?
A. It is, sir, with the exception of two lines. On page 507, eighth line, the word "plates" should read "breaks." On page 509, second line, the word "plate" should read "break."
Q. As amended, is it now a correct record?

A. Yes, sir.
Q. Have you been down diving since you gave your last testimony?
A. Yes, sir. I was down yesterday.
Q. Please tell to the court what you did and found.
A. I was dressed and lowered down by order of Mr. Powelson to look for boilers, if I could find them. While I was down, crawling down a little ways I found a boiler. I crawled all around it and all over it, and found it to be in good condition. Then, while I was on top of the boiler, I hit my helmet up against a plate overhead, and while crawling up on top of there I found a piece of wire. This wire looked to me not to belong to the ship, so I cut off a piece of it and sent it up on the line. After Mr. Powelson had inspected it, he called me up, and then sent me down again, telling me to saw off a piece of the wire and send it up. I went down again in the afternoon and tried to locate it, and did so after an hour or so. I tied the line to it and pulled in as much slack as I could, then sawed it off. Then I signaled for them to haul it up. They took it on board the *Fern* to Mr. Wainwright, who said it was telophotos wire.
Q. Where was this boiler situated that you found?
A. This boiler was situated about 20 feet forward of the crane, thwart ships.
Q. On which side of the ship?
A. A little over on the port side, sir.
Q. Did you find any other boilers?
A. No, sir.
Q. Did you look for them?
A. Yes, sir.
Q. Where?
A. In the same place and a little to the left of the one I found and abaft of it.

By the COURT:

Q. What prevented you from finding them?
A. A lot of wreckage, sir, over which I had to crawl.
Q. Looking at the plan of the ship, which boiler is it that you think you found?
A. I think it is the forward one. [Here witness pointed out the port forward boiler.]

There being no further questions to ask this witness, his testimony was read over to him and by him pronounced to be correct; after which he withdrew.

Gunner's Mate RUNDQUIST, a former witness, was then recalled, and after having been cautioned by the president of the court that he was still under the oath which he had taken, he testified as follows:

By the JUDGE-ADVOCATE:

Q. Have you read over the record of your testimony given before this court on Monday last?
A. Yes, sir.
Q. Is it correct as recorded?
A. Yes, sir; it is, with the exception of on page 501, end of line 6, strike out "forward of." Same page, line 16, "piece of keel" should read "piece of coal." After that the word "ram-plate" appears several times, and should in each case read "armor-plate."
Q. Is your testimony, as amended, now correct?

A. Yes, sir.
Q. Have you been down diving since you gave that testimony?
A. Yes, sir.
Q. Tell us what you did.
A. I went down on Monday afternoon and examined the boilers. I landed in a place that looked to be something like a big shell or compartment. It may have been a boiler blown in. The top part of it was blown away; the sides were sloping up. I could not say what it was. I examined it, and it looked to be a place measuring inside 10 feet wide, and of the same length. I found a big square hole in the bottom of it, and going through, got out among a lot of coal. I was feeling around for some time and got hold of some pipe. I sent up a piece of pipe and also got some asbestus after I had come up out of the square hole.

Then I went to the other side of this place where I came down and found some wire netting. I put my hand through this netting, and it was all carried away, and found something that looked to be the end of a boiler or what appeared to be the end of a boiler. There were lots of nuts. I think there were eleven of them; but I found I could not count them all. They were six-cornered nuts and measured 4¼ inches across. The top of the boiler looked to be in good condition. I was sitting on top of this boiler and examining it when I got the signal to come up. I was down only a short time. I also found three 10-inch shells inside this place where I landed when I first came down. That was all that day.

Q. What part of the ship was this place in where you first landed?
A. That was on the port side of the ship. I should say it must have been somewhere about there. [Witness pointed out coal bunker B. 4.]
Q. Where was this boiler that you landed on; can you point that out?
A. No, sir; I do not know where I landed.
Q. Where did you go down when you landed on that boiler?
A. From the lighter on the port side.
Q. Then you went down forward of the crane?
A. Forward of the crane; yes, sir.
Q. Have you looked for any coal on the port side of the ship?
A. Yes, sir; I have been looking for coal. I found some coal after going through the square hole. I was not on the bottom of the ship. It must have been some place inside of the ship. It may have been in a coal bunker.
Q. Did you go down again?
A. Not that day. I went down this morning.
Q. State to the court where you went down and what you found.
A. I had orders to go down and look for powder tanks. I went down from the lighter on the starboard side and landed about midships among a lot of wreckage. I was walking around there and got hold of three 10-inch shells lying flat down. I tried to lift them up, but could not on account of the wreckage. I walked away from there and found a 6-inch shell with the straps on. I sent it up. I also found a 10-inch powder tank, which I sent up. I was walking over a lot of plates and wreckage down there and did not find any more powder tanks, but found different parts of the ship. I then got a signal to come up. The second time to day I landed close to a heavy piece of plating. I examined it and found it to be armor belonging to the transverse armor, because it was about the same thickness all over. I should say that it was about 6 inches thick, as well as I could measure it with my fingers. I went over this and lowered myself over the other

side to what looked to be a wing passage, and this plate was standing up. I examined this for some time, when I got the signal to come up.

Q. When you first landed on the 10-inch shell, were these three shells ranged together?
A. Yes, sir; they were lying side by side.
Q. Noses which way?
A. Toward starboard, I should say, from where I was, down below.
Q. Which way did you walk before you found the 6-inch shell?
A. I found the 6-inch shell close to these—only a few feet apart.
Q. What was the condition of the powder tank you sent up?
A. The top and the bottom of it was gone; the rest of it was in good condition; not split or anything in it.
Q. Empty?
A. Empty.
Q. Which way did you walk when you found the armor that you speak of?
A. I walked aft.
Q. Aft?
A. Aft and to starboard.
Q. Which way was this armor plating standing?
A. It was standing on the end, sloping over to port.
Q. Was it fore and aft, or was it athwartships?
A. No, sir; it was neither way. It was standing in an angle facing the starboard bow and port quarter.
Q. How large was this plate?
A. I did not measure the length of it, but I extended my two arms and could not reach the end of it.
Q. What side of the ship was it in?
A. Starboard side, sir.
Q. Are you sure it did not increase in thickness as it went down?
A. Yes, sir; it may have increased, but if it did, it was very little.
Q. How far from the top did you feel?
A. I felt and followed one edge down until I got to the corner, and felt the same thickness.
Q. How deep did you say it was?
A. Six or seven feet.

By the COURT:

Q. What did it rest on?
A. It looked like it had been jammed in amongst some wreckage, and it also rested on the bottom of the ship and the passageway that I got into. I went over the plate and got into the wing passage on the starboard side of the ship. It was very dark, and I could hardly distinguish anything.
Q. Did you see the armor plate that has been reported in previous testimony?
A. Yes, sir; I seen the armor plate on the port side the first time I went down. This is not the same armor, because that plate had some wood backing, but I could not find any wood backing on this one.
Q. Was not that first plate in the neighborhood of the one you just described?
A. No, sir; the first plate was more on the port side. This one was well out toward starboard.
Q. Did you, on that occasion, feel the side of the ship when you examined that plate?
A. Do you mean the first plate or the one I examined to-day?

Q. The one you examined to-day.
A. Yes, sir; I found the inside of the ship; that is, it felt to me like the inside of the ship. I found the slope of the ship and found beams extending out—4 or 5 feet between each beam.
Q. Were there any bolts in this armor plate?
A. No, sir; I could not feel any. I was feeling all over with my hands, but could not feel either bolts or places for them.

There being no further questions to ask this witness, the testimony was read over to him, and by him pronounced correct, and after being cautioned by the president of the court not to converse upon matters pertaining to the court he withdrew.

There being no further testimony ready to give, the court (at 3.45) adjourned to meet to-morrow, Thursday, at 10 in the morning.

FOURTEENTH DAY.

U. S. L. H. TENDER MANGROVE,
Harbor of Havana, Cuba, Thursday, March 10, 1898—10 a. m.

The court met pursuant to the adjournment of yesterday.
Present: All the members, the judge-advocate, and stenographer, Chief Yeoman F. J. Buenzle, U. S. Navy; Messrs. Hulse and Bisselle having been discharged.
The record of proceedings of yesterday was then read over and approved.
The court was then cleared for deliberation.
The doors were opened at 12 o'clock and the court proceeded to the wreck. On the return of the court from the wreck a recess was taken until 2 p. m.
The court reassembled at the expiration of the recess.
Present: All the members, the judge-advocate, and the stenographer.
The court again visited the wreck.
On returning from the wreck, at 3 p. m., there being no further evidence ready, the court adjourned to meet to-morrow at 10 a. m.

FIFTEENTH DAY.

U. S. L. H. TENDER MANGROVE,
Harbor of Havana, Cuba, Friday, March 11, 1898—10 a. m.

The court met pursuant to the adjournment of yesterday.
Present: All the members, the judge-advocate, and the stenographer.
The court was then cleared for consultation.
Two members of the court visited the wreck, and returned with some of the mud taken from the bottom of the harbor where the wreck of the *Maine* is now lying. This mud, after having been dried, was ignited by a match, and burned readily, the smoke having a strong odor of gunpowder.
At 12.15 the court took a recess until 2 p. m.

The court reassembled at the expiration of the recess.

Present: All the members, the judge-advocate, and the stenographer. Captain Sigsbee also entered the court.

Commander G. A. CONVERSE, U. S. Navy, was summoned by the court as an expert witness, and, having been duly sworn by the president of the court, testified as follows:

Questioned by JUDGE-ADVOCATE:

Q. What is your name, rank, and present station?
A. George A. Converse; commander, U. S. Navy; commanding the U. S. S. *Montgomery.*
Q. How long have you been in the naval service?
A. Thirty-six and one-half years, sir.
Q. Have you made a study of the nature and effects of explosives?
A. Yes, sir; considerable.
Q. Please state to the court what duties you have had on shore which brought you in close contact with this subject.
A. About eleven years at the torpedo station: commencing in 1869.
Q. When were you at the torpedo station last?
A. In June, 1897.
Q. Had you then been in charge of torpedo supplies?
A. Yes, sir; for over four years.

Examined by the COURT:

Q. Did you, while at the torpedo station, have many opportunities to witness the explosion of submarine mines?
A. Yes, sir; very frequent opportunities.
Q. What material—what explosives were used?
A. Gunpowder, nitroglycerin, dynamite, and gun cotton.
Q. What quantities of these materials have you seen used for such purposes at any one time?
A. The largest quantity I have ever seen used consisted of a torpedo containing 300 pounds of gunpowder and 200 pounds of dynamite, all in separate cases—100 pounds in each case—securely lashed together. Single charges of gunpowder of 150 pounds; charges of nitroglycerin of about 100 pounds; charges of dynamite of about 100 pounds, and charges of gun cotton of about 120 pounds.

(A plan of the forward magazine and shell room of the *Maine* was then shown to the witness.)

Q. Examine that blue print, Captain Converse, and tell the court if, in your opinion, one or more of those magazines should explode or partially explode in that ship would such an explosion lift the forward body of the ship partly out of the water?
A. I don't think it would lift the ship out of the water.
Q. Will you please give the court your reasons for thinking so?
A. I think that the body of the ship, water borne in all directions, would tend to offer a resistance which would cause a general effect of a large explosion to be exerted upward; and that an explosion tending to lift the ship up would necessarily have to be diffused over a very large surface.
Q. Suppose that a submarine mine explodes adjacent to the side or bottom of a ship thus water borne; what will be the direction of the explosion?
A. It exerts some effect in all directions, but the most violent effect

in the direction of the least resistance, and that depends entirely upon the depth of the explosion below the surface of the water. I believe it to be possible to explode moderate charges of gunpowder against the sides of a strong ship and do very little damage, if the center of the charge is comparatively near the surface of the water; but if the center of the charge is well below the surface of the water, so that it will afford a large amount of water-tamping, then an injury will be done to the ship, while there will be comparatively little disturbance of the water at the surface.

Q. Supposing the charge to be a large one, and placed under the bottom of the ship where the water is only 8 or 10 feet below the bottom of the ship, what will be the direction of the explosion?

A. It would depend very much upon the position of the torpedo with regard to the bottom of the ship; that is to say, whether the torpedo was in close contact with the bottom, or was lying on the ground at some distance below the bottom of the ship, with water intervening. If the torpedo contained a large amount of explosive, and were placed in contact with the bottom of the ship, it is my opinion that it would endanger the ship by blowing a well-defined hole through it. The size of the hole depends, of course, upon the distance of the center of the charge from the skin of the ship. If, however, the charge is on the bottom of the harbor, and a depth of water of several feet intervened between it and the bottom of the ship, I think the tendency would be to lift the ship bodily; in other words, it would cause a large upheaval of water similar in effect to a large wave striking the ship, at a point directly over the mine—would tend to lift the body of the ship at that place exactly as the crest of a wave.

Q. In case of the explosion of a submarine mine under the bottom of a vessel, as you have described it, the effect upon a vessel, either in lifting her bodily, of blowing a hole in the bottom, would depend upon the size of the charge and its proximity to the bottom of the ship, would it not?

A. Yes, sir.

Q. If the charge is sufficiently large, and near enough to the bottom of the ship, both of these phenomena would take place—ship lifted up and the bottom blown in?

A. Yes, sir. A point to be taken into consideration is the nature of the explosives employed. Gunpowder is the more moderate explosive, and tends to produce a greater upheaval of water, as a rule, than do the more violent explosives, which, in proportion to their violence, seem to cut a hole out of the water, lifting in the shape of a fine spray all that directly above the charge. To illustrate this point, and the injury sometimes done by high explosives, I cite the case of the *Aquidaban*, which, according to authentic photographs, had holes blown completely through from one side to the other by charges of gun cotton; whereas I have seen wooden vessels of comparatively good size, in which large quantities of gunpowder have been exploded, without injuring the vessel to any great extent, there being in the latter case simply a large upheaval of water, to which the vessel rose and fell exactly as she would have done in a heavy sea.

Q. What is your experience, Captain, in the case of the explosion of a submarine mine, as to what becomes of the mine; of the case itself?

A. I have rarely seen any considerable pieces of mine, whether they consisted of powder or of more violent explosives which have been found; they are almost invariably ruptured and lost.

Q. That is to say they are not blown up?

A. They are blown up. That is noticeable in the case of spar torpedoes, in which I have exploded gunpowder and gun cotton, in cases made of wood, cast iron, copper, and steel, and perhaps other metals. In all my experience I do not recollect to have seen any considerable pieces of any case after an explosion. Sometimes small fragments of cast iron have been seen, and, on one or two occasions, thrown into a boat, indicating a complete demolition of the case containing the explosive.

Q. In the case of a submarine mine that was exploded under the bottom of the ship, and containing sufficient explosive to completely destroy the ship in that region, would your remarks about the submarine mine case itself apply to the bottom of the ship which is submerged, not referring at all to the interior portion of the ship?

A. In the case of all mines the form of the mine is usually such as to contain only the amount of the explosives used, and hence there must be a rupture of the case for the gases to escape. Were the mine in contact with the ship, or quite close to it, I think the effect on the bottom of the ship would be—depending, of course, upon the size of the mine—to blow to pieces that part of the ship directly over the center of the explosion, and rending and tearing the bottom of the ship from the center in different directions, the amount of damage depending entirely upon the quantity and nature of the explosive employed. In other words, that the violent explosive would cut a hole, blowing that part that was cut out into small fragments, and that the size of the hole would depend entirely upon the size of the charge employed.

Q. Captain, will you please examine the sketches which have been shown you and tell the court whether, in your opinion, the explosion of one or all of these forward magazines, or their partial explosion, would leave the bottom of the ship in the condition which now exists, as represented in these sketches?

(Exhibit H was shown witness.)

A. The sketch might represent two explosions of entirely different natures. That part of the sketch represented here as frame $14\frac{1}{2}$ to frame $18\frac{1}{2}$, aft, in a direction of frame 23, might be produced by the explosion of a comparatively large mine of not violent explosive matter at some distance below the bottom of the ship; whereas the part abaft of frame 23 has all the appearance of the effect produced on iron plates by a high explosive in close proximity to it. There are in all explosions two general effects: First, the upheaval of the water, caused by the direct action of the explosion, followed almost immediately afterwards by the second upheaval of water and mud, being the reaction of the water from the sides and the bottom, which rushes in to fill the crater produced by the first explosion. But the location of this upheaval and the distortion of the keel in the present instance does not appear to have been formed by the secondary effect referred to above. It is too far forward; too remote. It is too far from the place marked "Débris," which must be somewhere about frame 27. If that is 27, then the distance, as marked, from frame 18, will be eleven frame spaces, or 44 feet forward of what would appear to be the crater of the most violent explosion.

Q. Then to what kind of an explosion do you attribute the force that caused this bending of plates and keel on sketch?

A. I am of the opinion that it could be produced by the explosion of a submarine mine containing a large amount of the lower explosives—

gunpowder or similar—not in contact with the ship, but some distance below it, perhaps on the bottom.

Q. Looking at the sketch shown you, especially at that portion of the keel which has frame 18 on top, and the plates—bent plates—forward of it, excluding entirely all portion abaft of it, could this part which you are now told to consider have become so distorted from the effects of an internal explosion alone?

A. I do not think it could. I have never seen anything in my experience which would lead me to believe that it is possible to produce the effect indicated by any explosion within the interior of the ship in that immediate vicinity.

Q. Looking at the sketch shown you, and informing you that the forward 6 inch magazine and the fixed ammunition room were at that part of the keel which is represented as nearly vertical—that is, frame 18 to frame 24—could the conditions as shown forward of frame 24 have been caused by an explosion of those two magazines, or of any magazine abaft of frame 24?

A. I do not think it could.

Q. Do you think, then, necessarily, there must have been an underwater mine to produce these explosions?

A. Indications are that an under-water explosion produce the conditions there.

Examined by the JUDGE-ADVOCATE:

Q. Looking at the plan of the *Maine's* forward 10-inch and 6-inch magazines, would it be possible for them to have exploded, torn out the ship's side on both sides, and leave that part of the ship forward of frame 18 so water borne as to raise the after portion of that part of the ship, drag it aft, and bring the vertical keel into the condition that you see on the sketch?

A. It is difficult for me to realize that that effect could have been produced by an explosion of the kind supposed.

Q. You said in your previous testimony that the distortion of the plates forward of frame 18 could have been caused by an outside mine of moderate explosive power. Could such a mine, if producing that effect, also set fire to the magazine?

A. I am unable to answer that question.

Q. Can you consider it possible, under any circumstances, to have a portion of the 6-inch magazine exploded and not all the powder in that magazine explode? If so, please state under what circumstances this would be possible.

A. I think I am positively certain an explosion might occur without exploding all the powder in separate tanks.

Q. But if the explosion originated on the inside of the magazine, without any water on the inside of it, would it not be almost certain that all the powder in that magazine would explode?

A. I think it would be much more certain.

There being no further questions to ask this witness, he was directed to hold himself in readiness to appear before the court when summoned, and to give further evidence, if desired, whereupon he withdrew.

The court then adjourned (at 5.20) to meet to-morrow at 10 a. m.

SIXTEENTH DAY.

U. S. L. H. TENDER MANGROVE,
HARBOR OF HAVANA, CUBA,
Saturday, March 12, 1898—10 a. m.

The court met pursuant to the adjournment of yesterday.

Present: All the members, the judge-advocate, and the stenographer.

The record of the proceedings of yesterday was read over and approved.

Capt. JOHN HAGGERTY, of the Merritt Wrecking Company, was called as a witness, and, having been duly sworn by the president of the court, testified as follows:

By JUDGE-ADVOCATE:

Q. Please state to the court your full name and your profession.

A. John Haggerty, a submarine diver of the Merritt & Chapman Derrick and Wrecking Company.

Q. Are you one of the officers of that company?

A. Yes, sir; I am one of the Merritt's divers. I am in charge of the diving department.

Q. How long have you been a diver?

A. Thirty-seven years, sir.

Q. Have you recently gone down to the wreck of the *Maine*, and outside of the wreck of the *Maine*?

A. Yes, sir.

Q. About how many hours in all have you been down?

A. I could not state that exactly; about seven days, at three and one-half hours per day.

Q. Which side of the ship did you go down?

A. Inside first, looking for the dead bodies.

Q. And then did you go down on the port side or the starboard side?

A. I went down both the port and starboard sides; also into the staterooms, and got the doctor's watch and chain and his rings, and in the afterroom I got those gold cups and some other things.

Q. Did you make an examination of the ship itself on the outside?

A. Yes, sir; partly.

Q. Please state to the court how you found the *Maine* when you examined her.

A. I found the deck—that is, the protective deck—aft, and it lays aft now, with the upper side against the ship's side and the waterways and juts out on an angle of about 30 degrees from the horizontal—that is, the thick steel deck—2-inch plate. It lies on the port side, with the outer edge right in the mud. That is what we are trying to pull out, so as to get inside to examine her.

Q. About what part of her did you find the deck in this condition; how far aft and how far forward?

A. It is just forward of the turret on the port side. The forward part of the turret on the port side is about 2 or 3 feet abaft of that. I could stand on that deck and reach my hands over to the forward part of the turret.

Q. How far forward does this deck go in this condition?

A. About 35 to 40 feet forward of the break. On the bottom it runs a little farther forward than it does on top.

Q. Did you feel the armor belt underneath this protective deck?
A. Yes, sir.
Q. Is the court to understand that this protective deck has been pulled over to port so as to bring the beams of the deck on top?
A. Yes, sir; the beams are on top.
Q. And you further mean to say that which is now the outer edge was formerly inboard?
A. Yes, sir; that is, when it was on the ship.
Q. And, furthermore, that this edge extends farther out from the ship's side forward than it does aft?
A. It does. If it is anything, it goes down at more of an angle.
Q. How far forward from the after part can you go under this protective deck to feel the armor belt?
A. About 8 feet; I don't think you can get any farther than 8 feet. Probably 6 or 8 feet.
Q. And what is the condition of this armor belt for these 8 feet?
A. I found it all right. Another thing I found forward of this port turret, I think that the iron is broken, and I have not made a good examination. From the main deck down it looks like a split of about 2 feet.
Q. Does it seem to be an up-and-down break?
A. Yes, sir; up and down.
Q. How wide do you think this piece of protective deck which has been folded outboard is?
A. I dare say it is somewhere about 30 feet.
Q. Is it wider forward or wider aft?
A. It looks to me, if anything, to be wider forward, as it runs out and more down into the mud.
Q. Can you tell whether the break of the protective deck on the inside of the ship runs fore and aft?
A. The break runs athwartship, and the deck is folded back from forward and to port, and the edge which was forward and is now aft is cut off sharp.

By the COURT:

Q. Captain, have you been down forward of this protective deck?
A. Not yet, sir.

There being no further questions to ask this witness, the testimony was read over to him and by him pronounced to be correct, whereupon he withdrew.

WILLIAM HENRY DWYER, a submarine diver, was then called as a witness by the court, and, having been duly sworn by the president of the court, he testified as follows:

By the JUDGE-ADVOCATE:

Q. Please state to the court your full name and your profession.
A. William Henry Dwyer; a submarine diver.
Q. Are you one of the regular divers of the Merritt Wrecking Company?
A. Yes, sir.
Q. How long have you been a diver?
A. Since 1876.
Q. Have you been down to the wreck of the *Maine* recently?
A. Yes, sir.

Q. About how many hours have you been under water examining the *Maine?*

A. Six hours every day; for three days I have been down examining her.

Q. Please tell the court in what condition you found the wreck of the *Maine* where you examined her.

A. On the starboard side, about 20 feet aft of the midship torpedo tube, about frame 43, I found the armor belt started from the side. From that point forward to about 8 feet forward of the torpedo tube the top of the armor belt gradually leaned out until 8 feet forward of the torpedo tube it leaned out the whole thickness of the armor and about 2 inches more. That is all abaft the turret. About 4 feet forward of the torpedo tube—that is, at about frame 36—the top side; that is, from the top of the armor up to the main deck, leaned out until it was almost horizontal at the forward edge, where the armor is broken off. About 18 inches forward of the end of the armor the skin of the ship below the armor was cut down. The next plate forward was gone completely—that is, between that and the turret. Then, I should judge, about 18 inches beyond the end of the last plate, the side itself was cut down plumb for three plates deep—that is, the skin of the ship. It was cut down level with the bottom, so that I could walk right in on the inner bottom. Inside, the fore-and-aft bulkhead, between the side of the wing passage and the bunker, was intact up to the berth deck, and stood perpendicular.

The bulkhead between the coal bunker and the boiler room was also plumb up to the forward end of the bunker back of the starboard forward boiler; but the forward thwartship bulkhead of that bunker was blown aft and torn out completely. There is a thwartship bulkhead about in line with the after side of the forward boiler, and that was also intact, but the protective deck was lifted 3 or 4 feet up off of it. I went over that thwartship bulkhead into the next bunker—that was by the after boiler of the forward fire room. I went over there and went back through the next bunker nearly to the thwartship pocket. It is a coal bunker abaft of the after boiler in the forward fire room. At that point the protective deck is down in its place. The inner bulkhead of the wing passage is intact right forward—as far forward as frame 30. I went in over the top of the armor, at frame 35, over the three bulkheads, and got in on boiler A, and then on boiler C, and after tearing off the felting and wiring I could feel the boiler itself. Then I found the same on boiler A. At the bottom of the armor belt, all along, it is flush with the side. It is not started out.

As far as the armor extends, which is at frame 35, the bottom edge of the armor is all right, but the top leans out. By boiler A I mean the starboard forward boiler, and by boiler C I mean the next after boiler on the starboard side. That ended the inspection on the starboard side. On the port side I went down at about frame 35, dropping a weight at the end of boiler B. I crossed the top of boiler B and then back across the back of it, along the back of the boiler to the starting point. From there I went to boiler D, striking it at about the middle, and went to the back end of it. I took off the cover and felting and felt the iron in that. I found the boilers not materially damaged. The felting was all burned off the forward part of boiler B. The protective deck over boilers B and D seems to have been broken off at about the middle of these boilers, and the outboard edge is resting just above these two boilers, somewhat at an angle from the fore-and-aft line, sloping to starboard and upward.

Outboard of this outer edge the protective deck is gone altogether. The starboard side of the protective deck rests in its place at the after end of boiler C, but is raised at the after end of boiler A about 3 feet. At the forward end of boiler A it is raised almost vertical and projects out of the water. Along the forward side of boiler D I crawled in under the protective deck and crossed the face of boiler D. On the face of boiler D I could feel the tubes, the hand hold, and the forward furnace door. The boiler appeared to have rolled about one-eighth of a turn aft. From that boiler I came out again, and, crossing over the protective deck, found an opening in the protective deck and went down through that about the inner frame 36, and from there I crawled diagonally forward to starboard, and found the front end of boiler A, took the felting off and felt the plates myself. Returned to this starting point, frame 36, amidships, and went down again under the protective deck, through the same opening, and found boiler C. The A, B, and C boilers appeared to be in their proper positions.

I forgot to mention that the forward bulkhead of the coal bunker abaft boiler C is buckled aft and horizontally. That is all.

Q. Could you not describe that opening in the protective deck through which you passed, a little better?
A. I think it is a hatch.
Q. Did you ascertain how far aft the protective deck was carried away?
A. No, sir.

There being no further questions to ask this witness his testimony was read over to him and by him pronounced to be correct, and, after having been cautioned by the president of the court not to converse upon matters pertaining to the inquiry, he withdrew.

The court then proceeded to the wreck.

After returning from the wreck, the court reassembled, and took a recess subject to being reassembled upon being called upon.

At the expiration of the recess, 10 a. m., Sunday, March 13, 1898, the court reassembled.

Present: All the members, the judge-advocate, and the stenographer. Lieutenant-Commander Wainwright entered the court.

Ensign POWELSON, a former witness, was called by the court, and after having been warned by the president of the court that he was still under oath which he had taken, he testified as follows:

By JUDGE-ADVOCATE:

Q. Mr. Powelson, have you read over the testimony which you gave before this court the last time?
A. Yes, sir.
Q. Is it correct as recorded?
A. Yes, sir; it is with the exception of, on page 549, fourth line, next to last word, "a" should be "the." I wish to change the testimony in regard to the horizontal angle that the keel forward of the frame 18 makes with the keel abaft of frame 18. It was 104 degrees, and I have since ascertained that it is about 91 degrees. The angle had been recorded wrong in my notebook.
Q. Have you made any further discoveries that you wish to testify to before this court since your last testimony?
A. I have taken some soundings, and have cut in prominent points in the keel by taking angles on fixed points of the ship, but have not yet completed my work.

Q. When do you think that your drawings will be ready?
A. I think by to-night or early to-morrow morning.

By the COURT:

Q. Is this work that the court had directed you previously to do?
A. Yes, sir.

There being no further questions to ask this witness, his amended testimony of previous day and his testimony of to-day was read over to him and by him approved and pronounced correct, whereupon he withdrew.

Chief Gunner's Mate ANDREW OLSEN, a former witness, appeared before the court, and having been warned by the president of the court that he was still under the oath which he had taken, testified as follows:

By the JUDGE-ADVOCATE:

Q. Have you read over the record of your testimony given before this court on Wednesday last?
A. Yes, sir.
Q. Is it correct as recorded?
A. It is, with a few exceptions. On page 552, eighth line, second word, change 31 to 41. On page 553, ninth line, "keel" should be changed to "rail," and the same corrections made twice on the tenth line. Page 553, seventh line from the bottom, change "bow" to "buoy." Page 557, tenth line, "25" to "23."
Q. Is your testimony, as now amended, correct?
A. Yes, sir.
Q. Have you done any diving since you gave your last testimony before this court?
A. Yes, sir.
Q. About how many hours in all?
A. About eight or ten hours since I gave my last testimony.
Q. With what object did you go down?
A. To look for the armor plate which I had previously reported.
Q. Did you find it?
A. No, sir.
Q. Are you still confident, in your own mind, that you had found it before.
A. Yes, sir.
Q. How can you account for its disappearance?
A. The only way I can account for it is that it sunk in the mud at that point. It is three weeks now since I found it. There has not been any diving since two weeks at that place.
Q. Have you made any further discoveries while down during these last hours which make you wish to change any of your testimony previously given before this court?
A. No, sir.
Q. Have you made any additional discoveries that you wish to testify to before this court?
A. Yes, sir. About some loose powder that I have reported before. I scooped some of it up and sent it up to Mr. Powelson. It was sent up in a bag.
Q. Powder and mud mixed?
A. Both, sir.

By the COURT:

Q. Has that fore-and-aft bulkhead, which was bent over the 10-inch shell room, and which was near the plate which you formerly described, disappeared?

A. Yes, sir; I can not locate it.

Q. What plates have you found there lately?

A. Around the vicinity I found a thwartship bulkhead—an armor bulkhead——

Q. In how many parts?

A. One plate. I found something that looked like the bulkhead plate— 6-inch—farther in amidships, but I could only feel it for a space of a few inches underneath some wreckage.

Q. How high did the fore-and-aft bulkhead which leaned over the 10-inch shell room appear to you when you were down there, as you stood in the 10-inch shell room?

A. I went down in a hole and the curved part just touched my helmet.

Q. And that bulkhead you have not lately been able to locate?

A. No, sir.

Q. Does not that plate lead you to believe that you have not been down in the same place where you at first found the outside armor plate?

A. My belief is that I was down in the vicinity.

Q. Does not that make you doubt that you have not been down in the same place?

A. Yes; I might not have been down in the same place. I might be within 5 or 6 inches of that place without seeing the plate. You can not tell where you are down there.

Q. That would be a more reasonable explanation than to suppose that this plate has disappeared in some way?

A. Yes, sir.

Q. In locating the points under Mr. Powelson's direction, have you been again to the stem of the ship?

A. Yes, sir.

Q. And you are confident of its position?

A. Yes, sir.

Q. Have you followed up again the keel from the stem?

A. Yes, sir.

Q. Does the bottom of the ship, then, forward of frame 17, appear to be fairly intact?

A. It seems to be in a pretty good condition.

Q. Did you get around at all so as to feel up on the forecastle deck?

A. Yes, sir; I could feel the scupper inside the rail.

Q. At what angle did the deck seem to lie?

A. At about 45 or 50 degrees from the horizontal.

Q. That is, the whole bow lies over on its starboard side?

A. Yes, sir; I am confident of that, because I can put my hand over the port rail and down into the mud.

Q. How high does the mud go up on the deck? Does it come pretty nearly up to the port rail?

A. Taking a point level between the two hawse pipes of the sheet chain and of the bow chain, the mud is just on a level at that point.

Q. Are you understood to have said that this stem lies nearly parallel with the general direction of the ship?

A. Nearly parallel with the general direction of the ship.

Q. What is the direction of the keel of this part of the ship, forward of frame 17?

A. The keel there is up and over to starboard and aft, at an angle of about 60 degrees with the horizontal.

Q. Did you see anything of a deep depression in the mud forward there?
A. Yes, sir; right at the bow of the ship.
Q. Under the bow, do you mean?
A. Right where the keel goes into the mud I found a big hole in the mud. I could go right down into the hole, and extend my arms and feel the top of the hole. It was about level with my armpits.
Q. How deep was it?
A. About 4 or 5 feet.
Q. Was it solid at the bottom?
A. It was muddy. It was seemingly more solid than any other mud higher up.
Q. How wide was this at the top?
A. It extended out from the ship about 4 or 5 feet, then it seems to extend around the keel—abaft and around the keel. I was down at this point yesterday. The ship is rapidly sinking into it and the hole is closing up.
Q. When were you there?
A. Yesterday.
Q. Is it to be understood that this hole extends under the after part of the remainder of the bow?
A. Underneath the keel, as it goes aft; yes, sir. The bottom of the stem is in the hole, and the hole goes around and to starboard, underneath the keel.
Q. How far, according to your observation, has the powder been mixed with the mud; over how great an area?
A. In several places where I found tanks split up, in the seams I found this mud and powder mixed. I think it is powder and mud. When you stirred it up you can not see a thing. When you go outside of the ship and walk in the mud it shows a kind of greenish light color. That is what made me think it is powder. Mr. Powelson has what I brought up.
Q. Does the quantity of this mixed material down there seem to be large?
A. No; not very large, sir. You can find it in small spots here and there.

There being no further questions to ask this witness, his testimony was read over to him, and by him pronounced to be correct; and, after being warned by the president of the court not to converse upon matters pertaining to the inquiry, he withdrew.

Gunner's Mate THOMAS SMITH, a former witness, was called by the court, and having been warned by the president of the court that he was still under the oath which he had taken, he testified as follows:

By the JUDGE-ADVOCATE:

Q. Have you done any diving in the wreck of the *Maine* since you gave your last testimony before this court?
A. I was down for about one hour.
Q. What was your object in going down?
A. To search for the armor plate.
Q. Did you find it?
A. No, sir.
Q. What, then, did you find?
A. I found the one that has been already reported—the transverse armor.

Q. Are you confident you found this side armor plate before, as you reported?
A. The plate that I found now I am sure is not the one I found first when I came here.

By the COURT:
Q. Smith, how can you account for the fact that you can not find this plate?
A. The only thing is that it may be in the mud.
Q. What was there near the plate—the side armor plate—as you originally found it, by which you might identify it?
A. I remember there was some of the frames of the ship stood up vertically.
Q. Did you find those frames?
A. No, sir; I have not found those frames yet. Right near this transverse armor plate there seems to be an inner bottom rolled up over on top of it. I can not tell whether it is an inner bottom or a bulkhead.
Q. Referring to the hole that you testified to on a previous occasion, as having found near the bow of the ship, will you please describe that hole and its location again.
A. The hole is chiefly abaft the keel on the port side on the bow, and extends a little way forward along the stem as it lies.
Q. How deep do you think that it was?
A. I should judge it to be about 7 feet deep.
Q. How wide across the top?
A. About the same, sir.

There being no further questions to ask this witness, his testimony was read over to him and by him approved; and, after having been cautioned by the president of the court not to converse upon matters pertaining to the inquiry, he withdrew.

Gunner's Mate RUNDQUIST, a former witness, was called by the court, and after having been warned by the president of the court that he was still under the oath which he had taken, he testified as follows:

By the JUDGE-ADVOCATE:
Q. Have you done any diving in the wreck of the *Maine* since you last testified before this court?
A. Yes, sir.
Q. About how many hours in all?
A. I went down about eight hours.
Q. Did you have any special object in going down?
A. I was sent down to look for the side armor plate.
Q. Did you find it?
A. No, sir.
Q. Are you confident that you found it before?
A. Yes, sir.
Q. By what localities could you identify the spot where it was before?
A. Well, I won't say I am unable to identify the place. I was not down long enough that day. I happened to come across it more by accident than anything else. I slipped and fell, and landed close to this plate.
Q. And that is the only time you saw it before?
A. Yes, sir; the only time I saw it before.

Q. Then you are sure it was the side armor plate, with the thinner edge up?
A. Yes, sir.
Q. During this recent diving of eight hours have you made any further discoveries that would change your previous testimony?
A. No, sir; I have not.
Q. Have you made any additional discoveries that you wish to testify before this court?
A. Yes, sir; I found lots of shells down there—6 pounders and 10-inch; I also found some powder tanks. I sent some of them up—about six of them; and I also found another boiler—two boilers in all. I only saw one before. That is all.
Q. Where did you find the shell; in what part of the ship?
A. I found it right amidships, forward of the boiler.
Q. Where did you find the tanks?
A. In the same localities; close to it; not very far from it.
Q. In which direction from the shell?
A. Forward and to port.
Q. How many tanks did you send up?
A. I sent up about five tanks.
Q. Were these boilers that you found forward boilers?
A. They looked to be forward boilers, sir. I also found a piece of transverse armor which I never saw before.

By the COURT:

Q. Are you certain, absolutely certain, that the piece of armor which you first reported was as much as 11 or 12 inches thick at the thickest part?
A. I could not say what thickness it was, because I did not measure it. I measured the top of it with my fingers, and then followed the armor plate with my two hands, and it felt to me that it was getting thicker down below.
Q. You are confident it was thicker at one part than it was at another?
A. Yes, sir; I am certain of it.
Q. How far down in the mud did you follow it?
A. I followed it to about one-half a foot down into the mud. It extended way down, sir. I could not say how far down.

By Lieutenant-Commander WAINWRIGHT:

Q. Did you notice any difference in the condition of the wood backing of the transverse and side armor?
A. Yes, sir; on the side armor the backing looked to be all ragged, but on the back of the transverse armor the backing is all in good condition. I also found on the side armor, where the bolts went through the backing, the backing is broken away, and left the part of the bolt uncovered where the wood is gone.

By the COURT:

Q. Was there anything besides the nut on it?
A. I found some rubber gaskets, and it felt soft when I put my hand on the bolt. Nothing else.

There being no further questions to ask this witness, his testimony was read out to him and by him pronounced to be correct; and, after having been cautioned by the president of the court not to converse upon matters pertaining to the inquiry, he withdrew.

Gunner's Mate SCHLUTER, a former witness, was called by the court, and, after having been warned by the president of the court that he was still under the oath which he had taken, he testified as follows:

By the JUDGE-ADVOCATE:

Q. Have you done any diving on the wreck of the *Maine* since your last testimony before this court?
A. Yes, sir; I have been down forward in the magazine for shells and powder tanks.
Q. Is that all the diving you have done?
A. I have been looking for the armor plate, sir.
Q. Looking for the side armor plate?
A. Yes, sir.
Q. Did you find it?
A. No, sir.
Q. What did you find in the way of tanks?
A. I found some 6-pounders, sir. Some of them had the shell in them; some of them had the shell out, and there was still some dark stuff left that looked like powder. I brought them up. Some 6-pounder empty ones with the side burst out, and the top of a 10-inch tank.
Q. How many 6-inch tanks did you send up?
A. Three or four.
Q. What part of the ship did you find them in?
A. Right around the 10-inch magazine. I also found another boiler on the starboard side, in good condition, as far as I could feel.
Q. Was it a forward boiler?
A. Yes, sir; it looked to me like the second boiler forward on the starboard side.
Q. Did you make any discoveries which would now cause you to change any of your previous testimony?
A. No, sir.
Q. Did you make any other discoveries which you wish to testify before this court?
A. No, sir.

There being no further questions to ask this witness, his testimony was read over to him and by him pronounced to be correct; and after having been cautioned by the president of the court not to converse upon matters pertaining to the inquiry he withdrew.

Lieutenant-Commander WAINWRIGHT, a former witness, was then called by the court, and after having been warned that he was still under the oath which he had taken he testified as follows:

By the JUDGE-ADVOCATE:

Q. Have you kept an account of the powder tanks that have been sent up out of the wreck of the *Maine?*
A. Only in my memory.
Q. Can you state to the court about how many have been sent up of each kind, and also their condition?
A. About thirty-five 6-inch and about ten 10-inch. I have seen one 10-inch tank and two 6-inch tanks that contained powder in bags, and the remainder were either empty and contained parts of excelsior packing or parts of powder bags. All the tanks were more or less injured, a large proportion opening lengthwise along the seam. Nearly all the tanks show signs of having been subjected to outside pressure, as if pressed against the powder inside; and their ends are also crushed in.

I saw two 6-inch tanks that were opened at the seams and were pressed down flat, as if by an exertion of considerable force. Those two have more the appearance of having been exploded, in my mind, than any other, and though not the appearance I would expect powder tanks to exhibit after a charge inside had burst. Others are not sufficiently destroyed to give me the impression of having been exploded, although I have never seen powder tanks after an explosion and can only draw my own ideas. The damage to the tanks seems to have been caused by contact with some hard object, and as the shells were found on top of these tanks accounts for the damage.

Q. How was the *Maine* made fast to her buoy at the time of her destruction?
A. Starboard bow chain.
Q. Do you know whether there was any private ammunition on board the *Maine*—that is, ammunition belonging to individuals and not to the Government?
A. None that came to my knowledge.

There being no further questions to ask this witness, his testimony was read over to him and by him pronounced to be correct, whereupon he took his seat as an interested party.

Naval Constructor HOOVER, U. S. Navy, a former witness, was called by the court, and having been cautioned that he was still under the oath which he had taken, he testified as follows:

By the COURT:

Q. In the examination you made of the portion of the wreck above water, recognized as being about frame 17, what do you make out the thin plate in that vicinity to be?
A. It is the forward part of the forward water tank, on the port side, beneath the platform deck at frame 18.
Q. What is the portion painted white?
A. It is a portion of the bulkhead at frame 18, forming the forward side of the 6-inch magazine.
Q. Is the forward side of the water tank crushed in at all, or is it approximately still a plane surface?
A. Nearly a plane surface. It is distorted a little; but it is torn away from its fastenings to frame 18. The after side of this water-tank bulkhead now faces forward.

There being no further questions to ask this witness, his testimony was read to him and by him pronounced to be correct, and after being cautioned by the president of the court not to converse upon matters pertaining to the inquiry he withdrew.

The court then took a recess at 12.20 p. m., to meet to-morrow at 10 a. m.

SEVENTEENTH DAY.

U. S. L. H. TENDER MANGROVE,
Harbor of Havana, Cuba, Monday, March 14, 1898—10 a. m.

The court met pursuant to adjournment.
Present: All the members, the judge-advocate, and the stenographer.
The record of yesterday's proceedings was read and approved.

272   DESTRUCTION OF THE U. S. BATTLE SHIP MAINE.

Lieut. H. HUTCHINS, U. S. Navy, a witness called by the court, appeared, and, after having been duly sworn by the president of the court, testified as follows:

By the JUDGE-ADVOCATE:

Q. Please give to the court your full name, rank, and present station?
A. Hamilton Hutchins; lieutenant, U. S. Navy, serving as navigator on the U. S. S. *Montgomery*.
Q. Is the *Montgomery* at Havana?
A. She is; at buoy No. 3.
Q. How long has the *Montgomery* been at Havana?
A. Since the morning of the 9th instant.
Q. Have you, since her arrival here, been engaged in taking soundings around the wreck of the *Maine*?
A. I have; assisted by Lieutenant Fields, of the *Montgomery*.
Q. Have you with you a chart of these soundings?
A. I have; in original and blue-print copy.

(The witness presented to the court the two charts in question.)

Q. This chart was made from soundings taken under your supervision?
A. Yes, sir; from soundings taken under my supervision on the 9th and 10th instants.
Q. Is it a correct chart?
A. It is; as nearly as possible under the conditions. The depths are correct, although their positions may not be accurate.

(The chart was presented to the court, with the request that it be appended to the record, marked I.)

Q. Was the depth of the soundings reduced to datum line, or the mean low water?
A. No, sir; the soundings around the after body were all taken in the forenoon, and the soundings around the forward body in the afternoon. The time of high water on these two days I made to be about 9.30 on the morning of the 9th.

There being no further questions to ask this witness, his testimony was read to him and by him pronounced to be correct; and, after having been cautioned by the president of the court not to converse upon matters pertaining to the inquiry, he withdrew.

Chief Engineer HOWELL, U. S. Navy, a former witness, was recalled by the court, and, after having been cautioned by the president of the court that he was still under the oath which he had taken, he testified as follows:

By the JUDGE-ADVOCATE:

Q. During the stay of the *Maine* at Havana the last time, what forward coal bunkers were painted, and at what times were they painted?
A. B 3, B 5, B 4, and B 6 were painted. They were painted between February 1 and about February 10. Somewhere between the 1st and the 10th.
Q. Did the paint you used contain dryer and turpentine?
A. The first paint we used was made of red lead, oil, and turpentine. The turpentine gave out, and after that the paint was without any turpentine or dryers. I don't remember when this change took place.
Q. After having painted the bunkers, were they kept closed in such a manner as to endanger any accumulation of combustible gases?
A. No, sir; these bunkers were opened frequently by the battle doors and schutes which led up to the open air on the main deck. The

chutes were opened, and the battle doors were worked to keep them in good order; also these bunkers have air-ventilating pipes leading to the open air.

There being no further questions to ask this witness, his testimony was read over to him and by him pronounced to be correct; and, after having been cautioned by the president of the court not to converse upon matters pertaining to the inquiry, he withdrew.

The court thereupon took a recess, to reassemble upon being called.

At 2 p. m. the court reassembled at the expiration of the recess.

Present: All the members, the judge-advocate, and the stenographer.

Commander CONVERSE, U. S. Navy, a former witness, was called by the court, and having been cautioned that he was still under the oath which he had taken, he testified as follows:

By the JUDGE-ADVOCATE:

Q. Have you read over the record of the testimony that you gave before this court on Friday last?

A. Yes, sir.

Q. Is it correct as recorded?

A. Yes, sir.

By the COURT:

Q. Having somewhat examined the wreck, and being informed as to the conditions existing in the forward part of the ship, as she now is, are you able to express an opinion as to the initial cause of the damage?

A. I am unable to form any opinion from the observations of the wreck which I have seen above water. Assuming that the sketch of the forward part of the ship, from frame 18 forward, is approximately correct, [witness here looked at Exhibit II], it would appear to me that the result indicated or shown might have been produced by an explosion of a large quantity of explosive material of small power, which, by causing a large upheaval of water, would lift the vessel bodily, and at the same time throw it slightly over to starboard.

The rupture of the vertical keel, and of the skin plating on the port side occurred, and that, as the vessel was still farther lifted, the edges of the skin plating came in contact with the water, and by being lifted still farther, these fragments, marked B and A, were bent forward and downward in the position shown; and that, when the vessel slowly sank again, having her starboard bow water borne, would naturally cause the whole bow to slide off to port. The amount by which the piece of A and B are bent forward corresponds approximately with the amount by which the vessel has been shortened. I can not realize that pieces of the bottom as large as A and B could have been blown forward and downward by any interior explosion, the surfaces being, as they were, supported by water on the outside.

Q. Supposing the initial cause of the disaster had been exterior, by such a mine as you have described, and this explosion had exploded the forward magazines of the *Maine*, what would have been the result to the *Maine*, caused by this second explosion?

A. The explosion of a magazine, entirely or partially flooded, containing powder in tanks, would undoubtedly, on account of the water tamping given the charges, produce marked local effects. Escaping gases, if in sufficient quantity, would tend to blow open and back the sides and deck of the ship. It is thought that an explosion of this kind would be, in its nature, progressive, and that the accumulation of gases would become more and more rapid until all obstacles were removed. Judging also from the effects of explosions which I have witnessed, much of the explosive material in the magazine, if contained in separate cases or tanks, would be dispersed and scattered without exploding.

Q. Frame 18, as shown on the plan of the *Maine*, represents the highest point of the keel at present, and the point at which the keel is broken. Do you think that, in the case of a powder pressure in this compartment of the berth deck, between frames 12 and 18, sufficient to rend asunder the sides of the ship, it would have been possible for any man to have escaped alive?

A. I think it not impossible.

There being no further questions to ask this witness, his testimony was read over to him and by him pronounced to be correct; and, after having been warned by the president of the court not to converse upon matters pertaining to the inquiry, he withdrew.

The court then adjourned at 3.40 p. m. to meet to-morrow at 10 a. m.

EIGHTEENTH DAY.

U. S. L. H. TENDER MANGROVE,
HARBOR OF HAVANA, CUBA,
Tuesday, March 15, 1898—2 p. m.

The court met pursuant to the adjournment of yesterday, but not until 2 p. m., as no testimony was ready during the forenoon.

Present: All the members, the judge-advocate, and the stenographer.

Lieutenant-Commander WAINWRIGHT entered the court.

The record of yesterday's proceedings was read over and approved.

Submarine Diver DWYER, a former witness, was called by the court, and after having been warned by the president of the court that he was still under the oath which he had taken, he testified as follows:

By the JUDGE-ADVOCATE:

Q. Have you done any diving in the wreck of the *Maine* since you gave your last testimony before this court?

A. Yes, sir; about one-half day on Saturday, one-half day on Sunday, all day Monday, and this forenoon.

Q. Please state to the court what you found.

A. I found the bow portion of the ship laying on its starboard broadside, with the stem laying flat on the bottom. The port side of the main deck to the berth deck was torn loose and thrown forward—bent forward—and slightly upward. The break from the main deck started at the forward shutter of the 6-inch gun port. At the same point the main deck was turned up at right angles from its proper position. The break begins aft and extends as far forward as the forward shutter of the 6-inch port. Forward of this the deck is in place, and also the bow. The port 6-inch gun lays across the knightheads; the port 6 pounder is still attached to the deck, and so is the port anchor davit. The 6-pounder is trained aft on its own deck.

(Sketch H was here shown to the witness.

By the COURT:

Q. Do you recognize that, Mr. Dwyer?

A. On the sketch the stem seems to come up out of the mud. In reality the ram is in the mud and the stem lies flat along the mud. For the first eighteen frames from forward the keel of the ship slants upward. The keel is then thrown up from its original position for a distance of about 18 inches; after that it makes a sharp bend up at an angle of 45 degrees, and then it bends down. At this upper point the vertical keel is broken sharp off and bent right down, comes straight down, almost plumb, for a distance of, I should judge, of about 16 feet. The vertical keel is then bent back on itself for a distance of about 2 feet. The flat keel itself, at this lower point, appears to be broken. Then the keel is bent aft and downward for about 20 feet, when the vertical keel appears to end. I could feel the broken end.

By the JUDGE-ADVOCATE:

Q. How much of the vertical keel, as you have described it, had the flat keel still attached to it?

A. That would be difficult to answer. The inner bottom covers the vertical keel almost the whole length of it, so that it is impossible to see whether the flat keel is underneath or not, except that one point, about ten feet forward of the end of the vertical keel, where it is possible to reach down there. At that point, on feeling the vertical keel, it appeared to be crushed—the lower portion up toward the upper portion or reverse.

The inner bottom on the starboard side of the vertical keel appeared to be pressed downward, showing the sharp outline of the vertical keel. It was in that shape from where I found the vertical keel to end for about fifteen feet forward. The port side of the bow appears to be blown outward to within one or two plates of the keel. On the starboard side, abreast of where the keel is bent, there are two bottom plates attached to the keel, and the outer edge of these plates take the same general curvature as the keel does, but with a larger radius.

Q. What is the general direction of the inner bottom which is attached to the keel, and how much of it is attached to different portions of the keel?

A. From frame 18 down to about frame 21 there is none of the inner bottom attached to the vertical keel on the port side, while there is on the starboard side from 3 to 4 feet. Abaft of this the inner bottom is intact, and the end of the vertical keel, except at one point, about 10 feet forward from the after end, where the inner bottom is split from the vertical keel out to port.

Q. How much of the bottom plating is attached to the keel on each side, as far as you could find? What is its general condition?

A. At about frame 16 I counted five plates from the starboard side of the keel down to the mud. They did not seem to be damaged in any way. About 10 feet forward of that point I counted two plates to port of the keel. Farther forward I could not tell how many plates it was. Near the ram I was unable to find the edge of the plates so as to count them, as the plates appeared to be but seams.

Q. Was there any bottom plating attached to the keel on the port side in the vicinity of frame 17?

A. Yes, sir; on the port side of the keel, at frame 17, there was plating attached, but I could not get the general contour of it.

By the COURT:

Q. Mr. Dwyer, did you examine the outside of the ship, from the turret, forward on the starboard side?

A. Yes, sir.

Q. What condition of things did you find there?
A. It was a bewildering mass of bulkhead and iron plates. I could not keep track of it, especially as I had to work from aft forward.
Q. Could you tell us anything about the armor forward of what you testified to the last time?
A. No, sir.
Q. Did you examine the port side abaft?
A. No, sir.
Q. Where the bow of the ship lies on its bilge, as you might say, on its starboard side, is the position of that portion of the ship due to its form, or is it held there by the keel and by the bow, or stem, sticking in the mud?
A. No, sir; I should say it was the form of the ship. I should say, from the position of the keel in relation to the bottom plating, that she is lying a little farther over than on her beam end. In regard to the depression in the mud which you spoke of, I searched for that, and find no hollow such as was described. What I found was that the ram, when the bow fell over on its side, had turned up quite an amount of mud, and on going from the top of that aft I appeared to go down in a hollow; but going from aft forward you find the general bottom, and then the mound raised up to the ram.
Q. You are assuming, then, that the bow went down first?
A. Yes, sir.
Q. And that it struck a blow in the mud and threw this up?
A. Yes, sir; I assume that from the condition of the bottom just forward of the ram.
Q. Just forward of the ram or just abaft?
A. Well, you might say under the ram. There is one point to mention about the main deck. After turning at right angles it takes a general twist over to starboard, so that the point where the hatch is— the forward hatch—the deck was upside down at that point.
Q. What hatch?
A. Forward hatch on the forecastle.
Q. Are you referring to the upper deck or the main deck?
A. Main deck, sir.
Q. Did you find the foremast?
A. No, sir; I did not. I crossed the deck just by the hatch and found a brass plate on the under side of the deck which spoke of "showers."
Q. Did you come across any projectiles or powder tanks when you were in the vicinity of frame 18 or abaft of it?
A. I found a 10-inch shell laying close to the vertical keel on the inner bottom at about frame 21—a percussion 10-inch shell. I found no powder tanks here. Further aft to port I found quite a number of powder tanks, 6-inch, 6 pounder, and 10-inch shell, and also some brass cartridges about the same diameter as the 6-pounders, but they were exploded.

By Lieutenant-Commander WAINWRIGHT:

Q. When you stood in the mud at the point where the keel entered the mud forward, did there appear to be any depression there—a hollow?
A. No, sir; the mud appeared to be, as I stood at the side of the keel, facing toward the ram, on the left, appeared to be turned up higher on one side, and the ram appeared to be going down into the bottom. Following the keel down with my hands toward the point of the ram I found the ram was covered with the mud.

There being no further questions to ask this witness, his testimony was read over to him, and by him pronounced to be correct, and after being cautioned by the president of the court not to converse upon matters pertaining to the court, he withdrew.

The court thereupon took a recess at 3.30

The court reassembled at the expiration of the recess at 4.30 p. m.

Present: All the members, the judge-advocate, and the stenographer.

Lieutenant HUTCHINS, a former witness, was called by the court, and having been cautioned by the president of the court that he was still under the oath which he had taken, he testified as follows:

By the JUDGE-ADVOCATE:

Q. Have you observed and can you tell the court the magnetic direction of the keel of the *Maine*—the after part of the ship?

A. Yes, sir; I examined it by horizontal angles and checked it as near as possible with the compass. It is north 85 degrees west magnetic, looking forward. The ship is lying head north 85 degrees west.

There being no further questions to ask this witness, his testimony was read over to him and by him pronounced to be correct, and after having been cautioned by the president of the court not to converse upon matters pertaining to the inquiry, he withdrew.

Ensign POWELSON, U. S. Navy, a former witness, was recalled by the court, and after having been cautioned by the president of the court that he was still under the oath which he had taken, he testified as follows:

By the JUDGE-ADVOCATE:

Q. Mr. Powelson, have you made the drawings you were directed to make by the court of the wreck of the *Maine?*

A. They are not quite complete; but nearly so.

Q. Will you please explain to the court how you obtained the data for these drawings?

A. I sent divers down to various points on the line of the keel, and then sent a lead line down to the diver; got into a boat; plumbed the point; took soundings and two angles on stations that I had established on the ship and wreckage near the ship. Station A is the mainmast; Station C the port crane; Station D the forward edge of the after smoke-pipe, and Station B is at a piece of wreckage 126 degrees in azimuth from Station A, measured at Station D, and distant $41\frac{1}{2}$ feet from Station D. Station E is the piece of wreckage in azimuth 64 degrees from Station B, measured at Station D, and distant 94 feet from Station D. After establishing several points on the line of the keel, I sent the diver down to get points on the line of the break of the bottom plating on the port side. These points are one, two, three, and four E. These points were angled on, and depths taken as I have described.

Mr. Powelson was then directed to complete the drawing and send it to the court, at Key West, on board the *Iowa*, to-morrow, and attest the correctness over his signature.

There being no further questions to ask this witness his testimony was read over to him, and by him pronounced to be correct, and after having been cautioned by the president of the court not to converse upon matters pertaining to the court, he withdrew.

The court then, at 5.10, adjourned to hold its next meeting on board the battle ship *Iowa*, off Key West, Fla.

NINETEENTH DAY.

U. S. BATTLE SHIP IOWA (1st rate),
Off Key West, Fla., Thursday, March 17, 1898—10 a. m.

The court met pursuant to the last adjournment.
Present: All the members, the judge-advocate, and the stenographer.
The record of last day's proceedings was read over and approved.
The court was then cleared for deliberation.
The doors being opened at 5 p. m., the court adjourned to meet tomorrow at 10 a. m.

TWENTIETH DAY.

U. S. BATTLE SHIP IOWA (1st rate),
Off Key West, Fla., Friday, March 18, 1898—10 a. m.

The court met pursuant to the adjournment of yesterday.
Present: All the members, the judge-advocate, and the stenographer.
The record of yesterday's proceedings was read over and approved.
The judge-advocate informed the court that he had received seven more photographs from Chief Engineer C. P. Howell—the ones that Chief Engineer C. P. Howell had been directed by the court to have taken—and asked permission of the court to place them with Exhibit I.
The request was granted.
The judge-advocate then informed the court that he had received the plan of the wreck of the *Maine* that Ensign Powelson had not finished before the court had left Havana.
The plan was shown to the court, with the request to have it appended to the record, marked L.
The request was granted.
The judge-advocate then informed the court that he had also received the plan of the broken part of the vertical and flat keel of the *Maine* which Gunner's Mate A. Olsen had sent to him, the same not having been quite complete when the court left Havana.
This plan was shown to the court, with the request that it be appended to the record, marked M.
This request was granted.
The judge-advocate also requested to have five views taken by Photographer Hart—which he had requested Photographer Hart to take—and added to Exhibit I.
The request was granted.
The court was then cleared for deliberation.
At 3.50 p. m. the doors were opened, and court adjourned to meet to-morrow at 10 a. m.

TWENTY-FIRST DAY.

U. S. BATTLE SHIP IOWA (1st rate).
Off Key West, Fla., Saturday, March 19, 1898—10 a. m.

The court met pursuant to the last adjournment.
Present: All the members and the judge-advocate.
The record of last day's proceedings was read over and approved.
The court was then cleared for deliberation.
The doors being opened, the court adjourned to meet to-morrow, Sunday, March 20, 1898, at 10 a. m.

TWENTY-SECOND DAY.

U. S. S. IOWA (1st rate),
Off Key West, Fla., Sunday, March 20, 1898—2 p. m.

The court met pursuant to the last adjournment.
Present: All the members and the judge-advocate.
The record of last day's proceedings was read over and approved.
The court was then cleared for deliberation.

The doors being opened, the court adjourned at 4.30 p. m. to meet to-morrow, Monday, the 21st day of March, 1898.

TWENTY-THIRD DAY.

U. S. S. IOWA (1st rate),
Key West, Fla., Monday, March 21, 1898—10 a. m.

The court met pursuant to the adjournment of yesterday.
Present: All the members and the judge-advocate.
The record of last day's proceedings was read over and approved.
The court was then cleared for deliberation.

After full and mature consideration of all the testimony before it, the court finds as follows:

1. That the United States battle ship *Maine* arrived in the harbor of Habana, Cuba, on the 25th day of January, 1898, and was taken to buoy No. 4, in from $5\frac{1}{2}$ to 6 fathoms of water by the regular Government pilot.

The United States consul-general at Havana had notified the authorities at that place, the previous evening, of the intended arrival of the *Maine*.

2. The state of discipline on board the *Maine* was excellent, and all orders and regulations in regard to the care and safety of the ship were strictly carried out.

All ammunition was stowed in accordance with prescribed instructions, and proper care was taken whenever ammunition was handled.

Nothing was stowed in any one of the magazines or shell rooms which was not permitted to be stowed there.

The magazines and shell rooms were always locked after having been opened, and after the destruction of the *Maine* the keys were found in their proper place in the captain's cabin, everything having been reported secure that evening at 8 p. m.

The temperatures of the magazines and shell rooms were taken daily and reported. The only magazine which had an undue amount of heat was the after 10-inch magazine, and that did not explode at the time the *Maine* was destroyed.

The torpedo war heads were all stowed in the after part of the ship, under the ward room, and neither caused nor participated in the destruction of the *Maine*.

The dry gun-cotton primers and detonators were stowed in the cabin aft, and remote from the scene of the explosion.

Waste was carefully looked after on board the *Maine* to obviate danger. Special orders in regard to this had been given by the commanding officer.

Varnishes, driers, alcohol, and other combustibles of this nature were stowed on or above the main deck and could not have had anything to do with the destruction of the *Maine*.

The medical stores were stowed aft, under the ward room, and remote from the scene of the explosion.

No dangerous stores of any kind were stowed below in any of the other storerooms.

The coal bunkers were inspected daily. Of those bunkers adjacent to the forward magazines and shell rooms four were empty, namely: B3, B4, B5, B6. A15 had been in use that day, and A16 was full of New River coal. This coal had been carefully inspected before receiving it on board. The bunker in which it was stowed was accessible on three sides at all times, and the fourth side at this time on account of bunkers B4 and B6 being empty. This bunker, A16, had been inspected that day by the engineer officer on duty.

The fire alarms in the bunkers were in working order, and there had never been a case of spontaneous combustion of coal on board the *Maine*.

The two after boilers of the ship were in use at the time of the disaster, but for auxiliary purposes only, with a comparatively low pressure of steam, and being tended by a reliable watch.

These boilers could not have caused the explosion of the ship. The four forward boilers have since been found by the divers, and are in a fair condition.

On the night of the destruction of the *Maine* everything had been reported secure for the night at 8 p. m. by reliable persons, through the proper authorities, to the commanding officer. At the time the *Maine* was destroyed the ship was quiet, and, therefore, least liable to accident caused by movements from those on board.

EXPLOSIONS.

3. The destruction of the *Maine* occurred at 9.40 p. m. on the 15th day of February, 1898, in the harbor of Havana, Cuba, she being at the time moored to the same buoy to which she had been taken upon her arrival. There were two explosions of a distinctly different character, with a very short but distinct interval between them, and the forward part of the ship was lifted to a marked degree at the time of the first explosion. The first explosion was more in the nature of a report like that of a gun, while the second explosion was more open, prolonged, and of greater volume. This second explosion was, in the opinion of the court, caused by the partial explosion of two or more of the forward magazines of the *Maine*.

CONDITION OF THE WRECK.

4. The evidence bearing upon this, being principally obtained from divers, did not enable the court to form a definite conclusion as to the condition of the wreck, although it was established that the after part of the ship was practically intact, and sank in that condition a very few minutes after the destruction of the forward part.

The following facts in regard to the forward part of the ship are, however, established by the testimony:

A portion of the port side of the protective deck, which extends from about frame 30 to about frame 41, was blown up, aft, and over to port. The main deck, from about frame 30 to about frame 41, was blown up, aft, and slightly over to starboard, folding the forward part of the middle superstructure over and on top of the after part.

This was, in the opinion of the court, caused by the partial explosion of two or more of the forward magazines of the *Maine*.

5. At frame 17 the outer shell of the ship, from a point 11½ feet from the middle line of the ship, and 6 feet above the keel when in its normal position, has been forced up so as to be now about 4 feet above the surface of the water, therefore about 34 feet above where it would be had the ship sunk uninjured.

The outside bottom plating is bent into a reversed V shape (Λ), the after wing of which, about 15 feet broad and 32 feet in length (from frame 17 to frame 25), is doubled back upon itself against the continuation of the same plating, extending forward.

At frame 18 the vertical keel is broken in two, and the flat keel bent into an angle similar to the angle formed by the outside bottom plating. This break is now about 6 feet below the surface of the water, and about 30 feet above its normal position.

In the opinion of the court this effect could have been produced only by the explosion of a mine situated under the bottom of the ship at about frame 18 and somewhat on the port side of the ship.

6. The court finds that the loss of the *Maine* on the occasion named was not in any respect due to fault or negligence on the part of any of the officers or members of the crew of said vessel.

7. In the opinion of the court the *Maine* was destroyed by the explosion of a submarine mine, which caused the partial explosion of two or more of the forward magazines.

8. The court has been unable to obtain evidence fixing the responsibility for the destruction of the *Maine* upon any person or persons.

W. T. SAMPSON,
Captain, U. S. N., President.
A. MARIX,
Lieut. Com., U. S. N., Judge-Advocate.

The court having finished the inquiry it was ordered to make, adjourned at 11 a. m., to await the action of the convening authority.

W. T. SAMPSON,
Captain, U. S. N., President.
A. MARIX,
Lieut.-Com., U. S. N., Judge-Advocate.

U. S. FLAGSHIP NEW YORK,
Off Key West, Fla., March 22, 1898.

The proceedings and findings of the court of inquiry in the above case are approved.

M. SICARD,
*Rear Admiral, Commander in Chief of the
United States Naval force on the North Atlantic Station.*

INDEX TO EXHIBITS.

A.—Precept, with telegrams forming part of it.
B.—Letter from convening authority, permitting certain officers to be present during the inquiry.
C.—Letter from the convening authority upon the same subject.
D.—Sketch of portions of underside of protective deck.
E.—Sketch of protective deck where it shows above water.
F.—Translation of an anonymous letter in regard to a plot.
G.—Letter showing the amount of ammunition on board the *Maine* June 30, 1897.
H.—Sketch showing forward part of the ship under water; keel about as far aft as frame 28, and two plates bent into a V shape.
I.—Photographs of wreck.
K.—Survey of soundings around the wreck of the *Maine*.
L.—Plans of the keel and other permanent points of the wreck.
M.—Plan made by diver of break of vertical and flat keel of the *Maine*, frame 18.

EXHIBITS.

A.

U. S. FLAGSHIP NEW YORK (1st rate),
Key West, Fla., February 19, 1898.

Capt. WILLIAM T. SAMPSON, U. S. N.,
Commanding U. S. S. Iowa, Key West, Fla.

SIR: A court of inquiry, consisting of yourself as president, and of Capt. French E. Chadwick and Lieut. Commander William P. Potter, United States Navy, as additional members, and of Lieut. Commander Adolph Marix, United States Navy, as judge-advocate, is hereby ordered to convene at noon on Monday, February 21, 1898, or as soon thereafter as practicable, for the purpose of inquiring into the circumstances connected with the loss by explosion of the United States battle ship *Maine*, in the harbor of Havana, Cuba, on the night of Tuesday, February 15, 1898.

The court is authorized to hold its sessions on board any ship of the North Atlantic Squadron, or in the city of Key West, Fla., or in the harbor of the city of Havana, Cuba.

The attention of the court is invited to the instructions, concerning the particulars to be investigated in the case of the loss or grounding of a ship of the Navy, contained in the United States Navy Regulations.

The following-described papers relating to the loss of the U. S. S. *Maine* on the occasion referred to are attached to and made part of this precept:

1. The copy of a telegram sent by Capt. C. D. Sigsbee, United States Navy, at Havana, Cuba, to Commander James M. Forsyth, United States Navy, at Key West, Fla., without date, but probably sent on the night of February 15, as it was received at Key West, Fla., by Lieut. Commander William S. Cowles, United States Navy, at 1 a. m. of February 16, 1898, and by the commander in chief at 5.30 a. m. of February 16, at Dry Tortugas, Fla.

2. A telegram sent by Capt. C. D. Sigsbee, United States Navy, to the commander in chief at Key West, Fla., dated Havana, Cuba, February 16, 1898.

The court will diligently and thoroughly inquire into all the circumstances attending the loss of said vessel on the date named, and upon the conclusion of the investigation will report to the commander in chief its proceedings, all the testimony taken, and the facts which it may deem established by the evidence adduced, together with its opinion as to what further proceedings, if any, should be had in the matter.

The court will also report whether or not the loss of said vessel was, on the occasion named, in any respect due to fault or negligence on the part of any of the officers or members of the crew of said vessel, and if so, the names of such officers or members of the crew, and in what respect and to what extent any or either of them were so at fault or negligent.

If the court shall be of opinion that further proceedings should be had in the matter, it will include in its report a succinct statement as to the person or persons against whom, and the specific matter upon which, such proceedings should be had.

The court will also report its opinion as to the cause or causes of the explosion, or other incidents that bore directly or indirectly upon the loss of the *Maine*.

It will also record any information that it may be able to obtain by testimony and evidence, as to any person or persons not connected with the Navy of the United States, who are, in its opinion, responsible, in part or wholly, directly or indirectly, for the explosion and loss of the *Maine*, and will include their names, in its opinion, together with the degree of responsibility in each case.

            M. SICARD,
      Rear-Admiral, Commander in Chief,
    U. S. Naval Force on North Atlantic Station.

I certify the above to be a true copy.

             A. MARIX,
      Lieut.-Com., U. S. N., Judge-Advocate.

No. 1.

FORSYTH, *Key West:*

Tell admiral *Maine* blown up and destroyed. Send light-house tenders. Many killed and wounded. Don't send war vessels if others available.

               SIGSBEE.

I certify the above to be a true copy.

             A. MARIX,
      Lieut. Com., U. S. N., Judge-Advocate.

No. 2.

              FEBRUARY 16.

COMMANDER IN CHIEF, *Key West:*

Maine blown up in Habana harbor at 9.40 last night and destroyed. Many wounded and doubtless more killed or drowned. Wounded and others on board Spanish man-of-war and Ward Line steamers. Send light-house tender from Key West for crew and the few pieces of equipment above water. None has clothing other than that upon him. Public opinion should be suspended until further report. All officers believed to be saved; Jenkins and Merritt not yet accounted for. Many Spanish officers, including representatives of General Blanco, now with me to express sympathy.

               SIGSBEE.

I certify the above to be a true copy.

             A. MARIX,
      Lieut. Com., U. S. N., Judge-Advocate.

B.

U. S. FLAGSHIP NEW YORK (1st rate),
Key West, Fla., February 19, 1898.

SIR: Referring to my order of this date convening a court of inquiry, of which you are president, to meet at such place as the president of the court may deem proper, on Monday, February 21, 1898, at noon, for the purpose of inquiring into the circumstances connected with the loss of the U. S. battle ship *Maine* in the harbor of Havana, Cuba, on the night of Tuesday, February 15, 1898, I have to inform you that Capt. Charles D. Sigsbee, United States Navy, commanding the U. S. S. *Maine*, and Lieut. Commander Richard Wainwright, United States Navy, the executive officer, and Lieut. George F. W. Holman, United States Navy, the navigator, and Chief Engineer Charles P. Howell, United States Navy, the chief engineer of that vessel, have been informed of their right to be present during the investigation, to cross examine witnesses, and offer evidence before the court should they desire to do so.

As the court has been directed to report whether or not the loss of the U. S. S. *Maine* was in any respect due to fault or negligence on the part of any of the officers or crew of said vessel, etc., you will inform the officers and such of the crew as may have filled positions of special responsibility upon the occasion referred to that they have the same right to be present during the sessions of the court, to offer evidence, and to cross-examine witnesses, if they so desire.

Very respectfully,

M. SICARD,
Rear-Admiral, Commander in Chief,
U. S. Naval Force on North Atlantic Station.

Capt. WILLIAM T. SAMPSON, U. S. N.,
Commanding U. S. S. Iowa, Key West, Fla.

I certify the above to be a true copy.

A. MARIX,
Lieut. Com., U. S. N., Judge-Advocate.

C.

U. S. FLAGSHIP NEW YORK (1st rate),
          Key West, Fla., February 19, 1898.

SIR: Referring to my communication of this date informing you that Capt. Charles D. Sigsbee, United States Navy; Lieut. Commander Richard Wainwright, United States Navy; Lieut. George F. W. Holman, United States Navy, and Chief Engineer Charles P. Howell, United States Navy, have been informed of their right to be present during the investigation to cross-examine witnesses and offer evidence before the court should they desire to do so, I have to inform you that if, during the progress of the investigation it shall appear that others than those above mentioned should be entitled to appear as defendants, they will be called before the court and informed of their right to be present and cross-examine witnesses and offer such evidence as they may desire.

Very respectfully,   M. SICARD,
          Rear-Admiral, Commander in Chief
          U. S. Naval Force on North Atlantic Station.

Capt. WILLIAM T. SAMPSON, U. S. N.,
  Commanding U. S. S. Iowa, Key West, Fla.

I certify the above to be a true copy.

                              A. MARIX,
          Lieut. Com., U. S. N., Judge-Advocate.

DESTRUCTION OF THE U. S. BATTLE SHIP MAINE.

D.

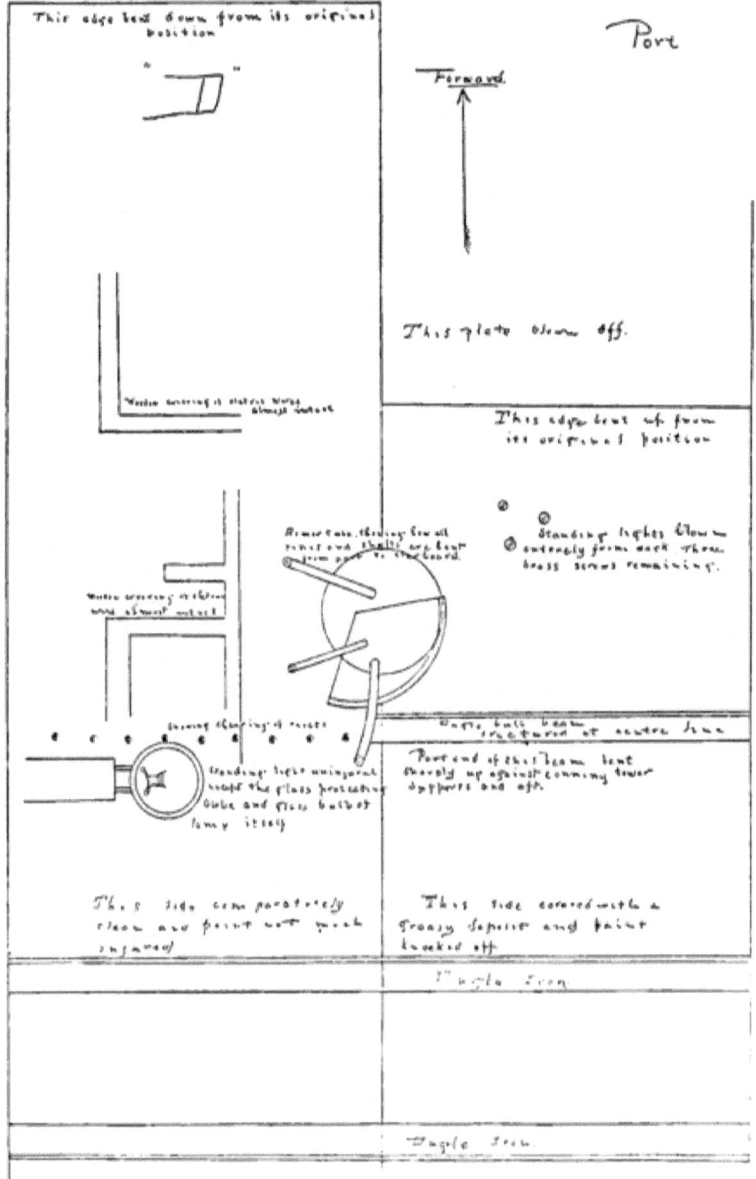

E.

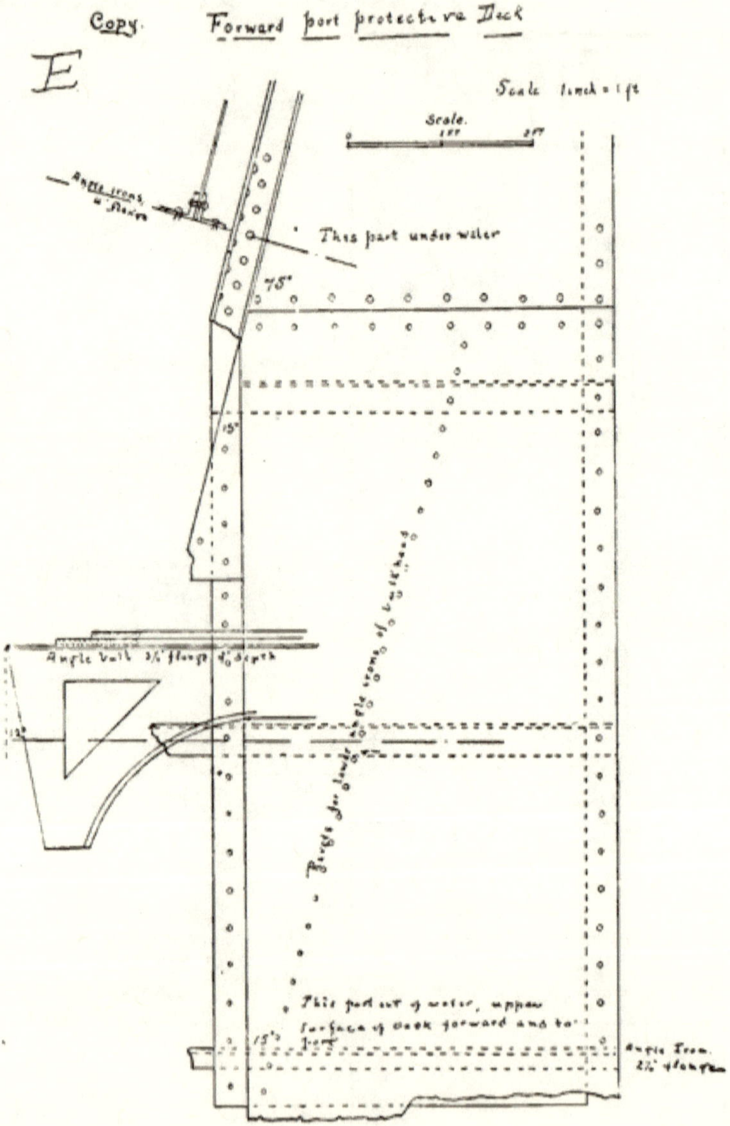
Copy. Forward port protective Deck
E
Scale 1 inch = 1 ft
Scale.
0 1 ft 2 ft
This part under water
75°
15°
This part out of water, upper surface of deck forward and to port
15°

F.

It should be remembered that at dawn of the day of the terrible catastrophe an individual was killed in a small boat, together with another, who is to be found wounded and a prisoner. They were going about the cruisers *Maine* and *Alfonso XII*, and as the said individuals are the worst antecedents as harbor thieves, I have interested myself in investigating what connection this occurrence could have with the explosion of the *Maine*, and I have discovered that those two men, together with another, who is called Pepe Taco, had bought in a hardware store in Mercaderes street, called La Marina, a hose such as is used by divers, and that the three left Regla in a small boat, which they placed under the wharves of Sta. Catalina, and they were loitering more than an hour and a half, while Pepe Taco, who is a calker and diver, probably the best in these parts, did the work to bring about the explosion of the *Maine*. With this data I went to Regla and discovered that the family of the dead man, who lived in the utmost misery in a house in Rodriguez Batista street, had moved to a well-furnished one in Gelabert street. There I learned that they had agreed with some merchants of Muralla street for the work of blowing up the ship for the sum of $6,000—$2,000 in advance, the other $4,000 after seeing the result. But as they did not come out of the adventure very well, having been attacked when they were retiring, the result of which was the death of one, who left his teeth in the boat, and another one wounded, the third one has not presented himself to collect the rest of the money, and it could probably be secretly done that, by paying him the rest that the others will not now pay him, he would declare the truth of all this. The one whom I call the third is the diver Pepe Taco, who was unwounded, who no doubt is afraid to present himself to collect the rest. In Muralla street they tell me was the place where the business was arranged with Messrs. Garcia Corujedo, Villasuso, Maribona, and others, whom I do not remember. The man arrested is being administered morphine constantly to see if he will die and not give evidence, so as not, as they express it, to spoil the affair after it has come off so much to their taste.

HAVANA, *Feb. 11th, 1898.*

I certify the above to be a true copy.

A. MARIX,
Lieut. Com. U. S. Navy, Judge-Advocate.

G.

U. S. S. MAINE (1st rate),
Hampton Roads, Va., June 30, 1897.

SIR: In compliance with the commandant's indorsement of the Bureau of Construction letter, No. 1096–E3, of June 23, 1897, directing that a statement of the amount of ammunition of each size stowed in the various ammunition rooms be given, I make the following report, which gives the amount stowed in the ammunition rooms as well as that stowed outside in the handling and passing rooms.

The amount given is the full allowance of ammunition.

Very respectfully,

C. D. SIGSBEE,
Captain, U. S. N., Commanding U. S. S. Maine.

The COMMANDANT, NAVY-YARD AND STATION.

U. S. FLAGSHIP NEW YORK,
Fortress Monroe, Va., June 30, 1897.

Forwarded by direction of commander in chief.

C. H. WEST,
Commander, U. S. N., Chief of Staff.

[Second Indorsement.]

NAVY-YARD, NEW YORK, *July 2, 1897.*

1. Respectfully referred to the Bureau of Construction and Repair.
2. This letter is in reply to the Bureau's No. 1096–E3 of the 23d ultimo.

F. M. BUNCE,
Commodore, U. S. Navy, Commandant Navy-Yard and Station.

Forward magazine (Compartment A 6M).—99 full charges for 6-inch B. L. R.; 164 reduced charges for 6-inch B. L. R.; 146 common shell, in slings, for 6-inch B. L. R.; 100 armor-piercing shells, in slings, for 6-inch B. L. R.; 24 shrapnel, in slings, for 6-inch B. L. R.

Forward fixed ammunition room (A 9M).—152 chests 6-pounder steel shell (1,672 rounds); 112 chests 6-pounder common shell (1,232 rounds); 27 chests 6-pounder blank (297 rounds); 17 chests 1-pounder steel shell (1,020 rounds); 11 chests 1-pounder common shell (660 rounds); 10 chests 6mm. cartridge, ball (10,000 rounds); 3 chests .38-caliber cartridges, ball (9,000 rounds).

Forward 10-inch shell room (A 12M).—90 common shell for 10-inch B. L. R.; 74 armor-piercing shell for 10-inch B. L. R.

Forward 10-inch magazine (A 13M).—92 full charges for 10-inch B. L. R.; 88 reduced charges for 10-inch B. L. R.

Reserve magazine (A 14M).—113 full charges for 6-inch B. L. R; 51 reduced charges for 6-inch B. L. R.; 3,400 pounds of spare saluting powder (19 tanks); 100 pounds of shrapnel and impulse powder.

10-inch shell room amidships (C 3M).—90 armor-piercing shell for 10-inch B. L. R.; 90 common shell, loaded and fused, for 10-inch B. L. R.

10-inch magazine amidships (C 4M).—88 full charges for 10-inch B. L. R.; 91 reduced charges for 10-inch B. L. R.

6-inch magazine amidships (C 5M).—101 full charges for 6-inch B. L. R.; 131 reduced charges for 6-inch B. L. R.; 208 common shell, loaded and fused, for 6-inch B. L. R.; 100 armor-piercing shell for 6-inch B. L. R.; 23 shrapnel, in slings, for 6-inch B. L. R.

After torpedo head and fixed ammunition room (D 1M).—8 Whitehead torpedo warheads, filled; 8 Whitehead torpedo wet primer cases, filled; 76 chests of 6-pounder steel shell (836 rounds); 32 chests of 6-pounder common shell (396 rounds); 32 chests of 1-pounder steel shell (1,920 rounds); 20 chests of 1-pounder common shell (1,200 rounds); 20 chests of .45-caliber cartridges, ball (20,000 rounds); 7 chests of .3'-caliber cartridges, ball (21,000 rounds); 100 chests of 6 mm. cartridges, ball (100,000 rounds); 10 chests of .22 caliber cartridges, ball (93,000 rounds); 11 chests of 6 mm. cartridges, blank (11,000 rounds); 7 chests of United States cannon primers, 3,700 rounds; 8 boat ammunition tanks, small arm, 7,000 rounds.

In addition to the shell stowed in the shell rooms there are stowed 10-inch shells as follows:

Forward 10-inch loading room (A55).—2 common shell for 10-inch B. L. R.; 2 armor-piercing shells for 10-inch B. L. R.

Forward 10-inch passing room.—2 drill shells for 10-inch B. L. R.

Midship 10-inch loading room (C1').—1 armor-piercing shell for 10-inch B. L. R.; 2 drill shells for 10-inch B. L. R.

Midship 10-inch passing room.—15 armor-piercing shells for 10-inch B. L. R.

I certify the above to be a true copy.

A. MARIX,
Lieut. Com., U. S. N., Judge-Advocate.

EXHIBIT H.

SKETCH SHOWING FORWARD PART OF THE SHIP UNDER WATER, KEEL ABOUT AS FAR AFT AS FRAME 28, AND TWO PLATES BENT INTO A V SHAPE.

EXHIBIT I.

PHOTOGRAPHS OF WRECK.

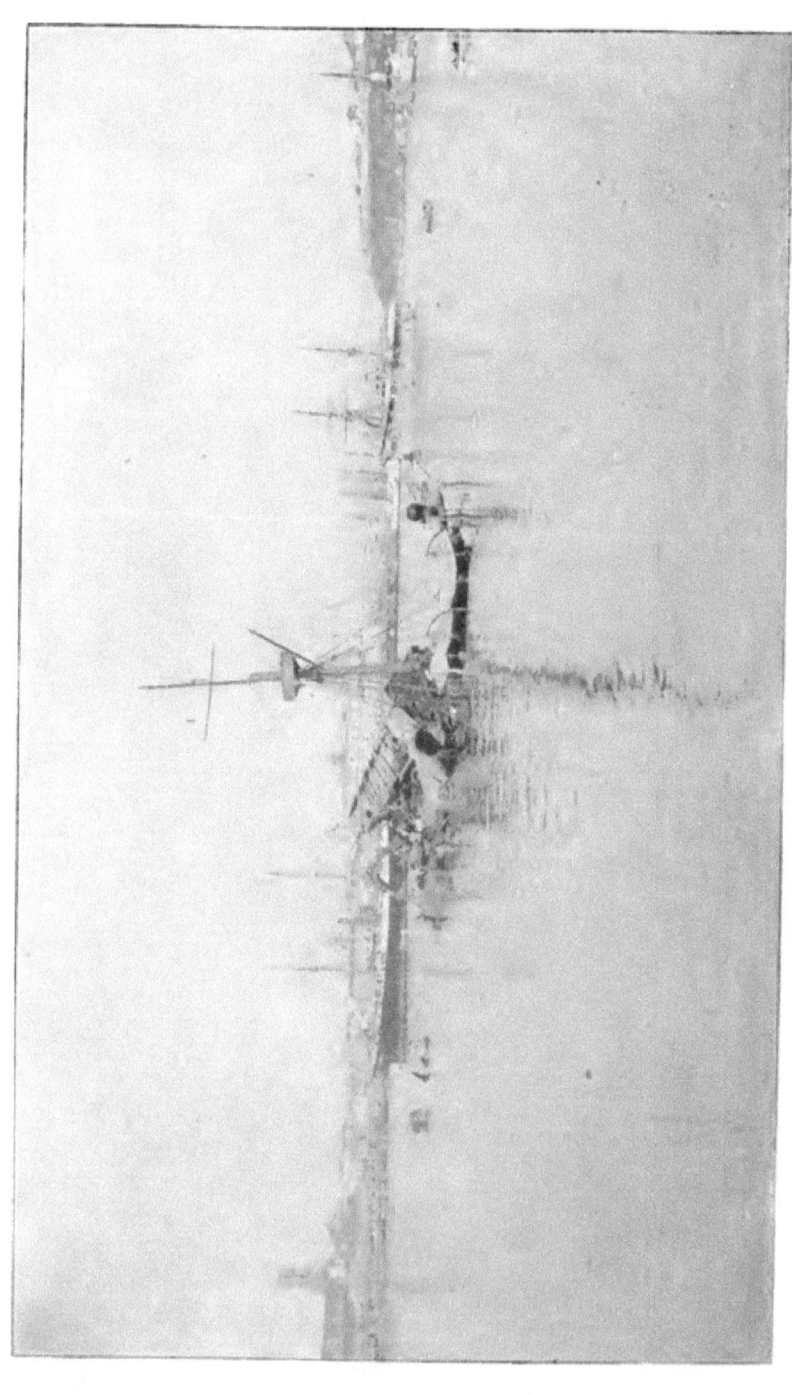

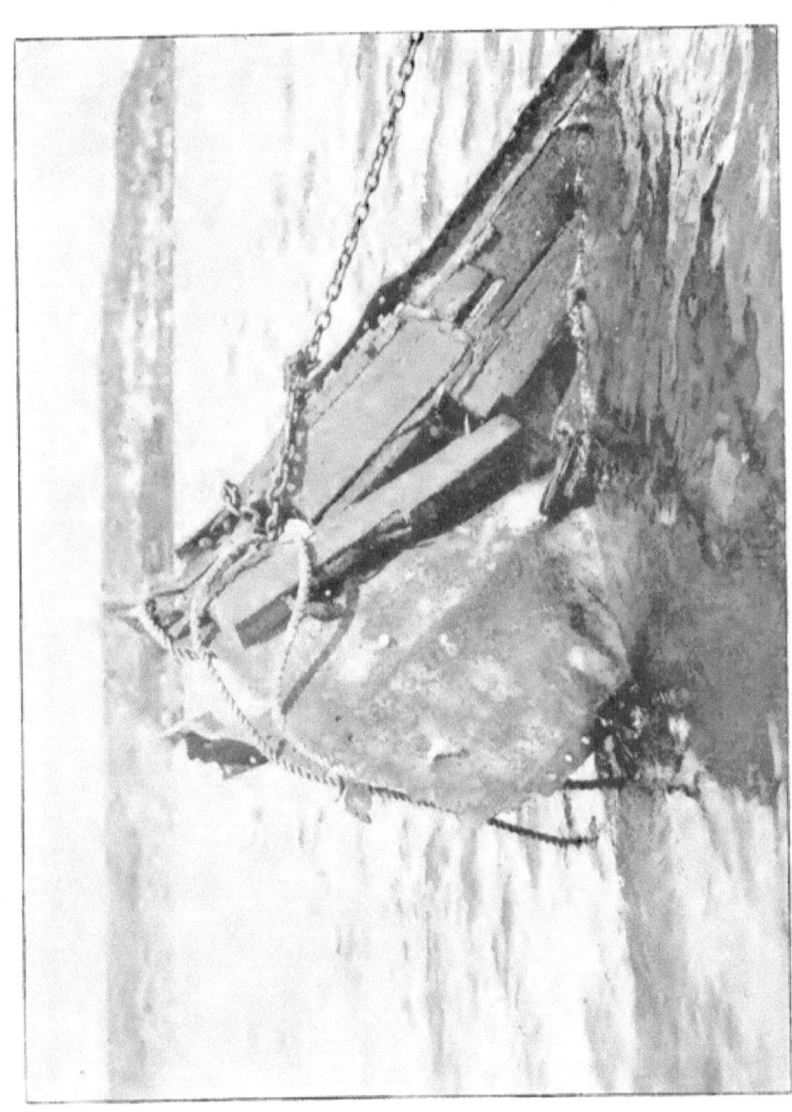

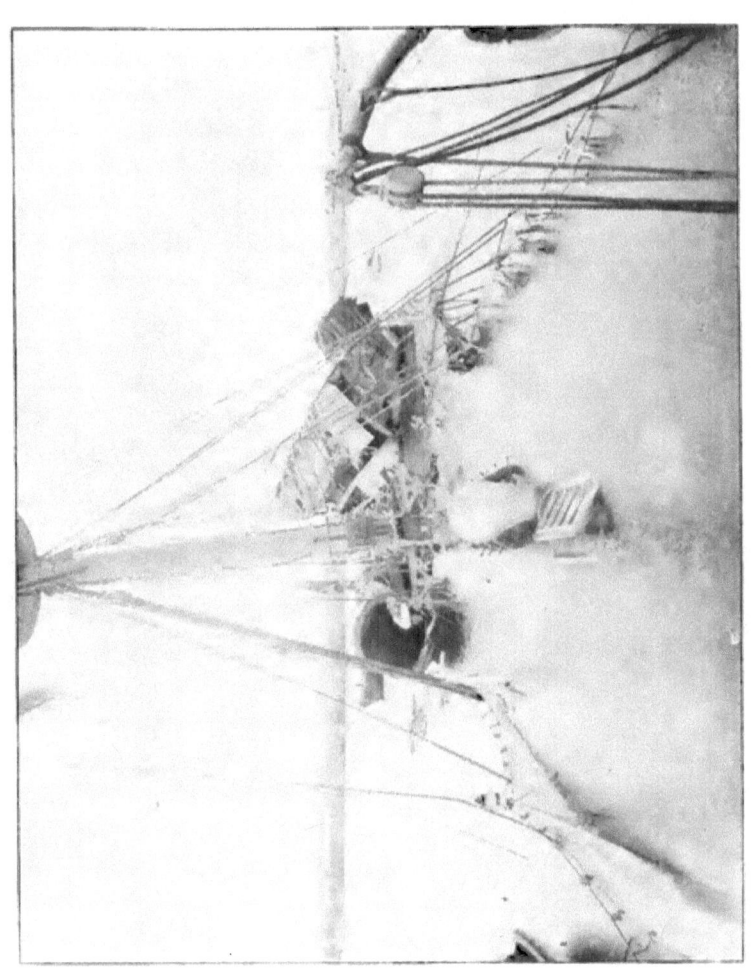

EXHIBIT K.

SURVEY OF SOUNDINGS AROUND THE WRECK OF THE MAINE.

FOLDOUT

FOLDOUT

EXHIBIT L.

PLANS OF THE KEEL AND OTHER PROMINENT POINTS OF THE WRECK.

FOLDO

FOLDOUT

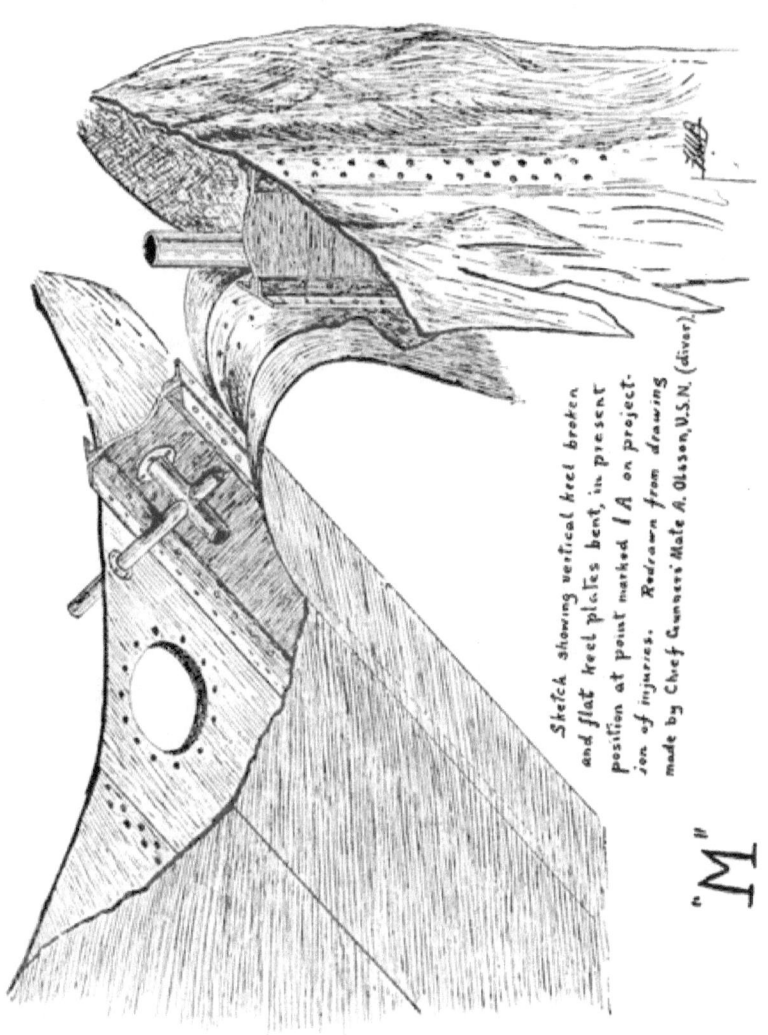

Sketch showing vertical keel broken and flat keel plates bent, in present position at point marked 1A on projection of injuries. Redrawn from drawing made by Chief Gunner's Mate A. Olesen, U.S.N. (diver).

"M"

EXHIBIT M.

PLAN MADE BY DIVER OF BREAK OF VERTICAL AN FLAT KEEL OF THE MAINE, FRAME 18.

INDEX TO TESTIMONY.

	Page.
First day:	
Capt. Charles D. Sigsbee, U. S. Navy	10–19
Second day:	
Lieut. F. M. G. Holman, U. S. Navy	20–24
Lieut. Commander Richard Wainwright, U. S. Navy	25–29
Naval Cadet W. T. Cluverius, U. S. Navy	29, 30
Naval Cadet J. H. Holden, U. S. Navy	30, 31
Third day:	
Chief Engineer Charles P. Howell, U. S. Navy	32–36
Lieut. F. M. G. Holman (recalled)	36, 37
Paymaster Charles M. Ray, U. S. Navy	38
Surg. L. G. Henneberger, U. S. Navy	39, 40
Private William Anthony, U. S. Navy	40, 41
Capt. Charles D. Sigsbee (recalled)	41–43
Ensign W. V. N. Powelson, U. S. Navy	43–49
Fourth day:	
William H. Van Syckel	49–51
Chief Engineer Charles P. Howell, U. S. Navy	51, 52
Capt. Frederick G. Teasdale	52–55
Chaplain John P. Chidwick, U. S. Navy	55, 56
Sigmond Rothschild	57–62
Louis Wertheimer	62–66
Gunner Charles Morgan, U. S. Navy	66–69
Chief Gunner's Mate Andrew Olsen, U. S. Navy	69–76
Fifth day:	
Gunner's Mate Thomas Smith, U. S. Navy	76–83
Seaman Martin Reden, U. S. Navy	83–87
Gunner's Mate W. H. F. Schluter, U. S. Navy	88
Gunner's Mate Carl Rundquist, U. S. Navy	89–93
Witness, name not given. (See testimony)	93–95
Ensign W. V. N. Powelson (recalled)	96–100
Sixth day:	
Henry Drain	100–102
Capt. Charles D. Sigsbee (recalled)	102, 103
Lieut. Commander Richard Wainwright (recalled)	103–105
Ensign W. V. N. Powelson (recalled)	105–112
Gunner's Mate Olsen (recalled)	112
Seventh day:	
Lieut. John J. Blandin, U. S. Navy	113–116
Lieut. John Hood, U. S. Navy	116–126
Lieut. George P. Blow, U. S. Navy	126–130
Lieut. Carl W. Jungen, U. S. Navy	130–136
Naval Cadet Amon Bronson, jr., U. S. Navy	136–138
Naval Cadet D. F. Boyd, jr., U. S. Navy	138–141
Lieut. George F. W. Holman, U. S. Navy (recalled)	141
Lieut. A. W. Catlin, U. S. Marine Corps	142, 143
Gunner Joseph Hill, U. S. Navy	143–146
Boatswain Francis E. Larkin, U. S. Navy	146, 147
Carpenter George Helm, U. S. Navy	147–150
Eighth day:	
Past Asst. Engineer Frederick C. Bowers	151–154
Asst. Engineer John R. Morris	154–156
Naval Cadet Pope Washington	156
Naval Cadet Arthur Crenshaw	156–158
Private Edward McKay, U. S. Marine Corps	160–162

                                                                          Page.
Eighth day—Continued.
    Apprentice Ambrose Ham, U. S. Navy............................. 162, 163
    Lieutenant Blow, recalled.. 164
    Apprentice C. J. Dressler, U. S. Navy............................. 164–166
    Sergeant Michael Mehan, U. S. Marine Corps....................... 166, 167
    Corporal Frank G. Thompson, U. S. Marine Corps................... 167–169
    Lieut. C. W. Jungen, recalled.................................... 170
    Master at Arms John B. Load, U. S. Navy.......................... 170–173
    Seaman Peter Larsen, U. S. Navy.................................. 173–175
    Seaman Louis Moriniere, U. S. Navy............................... 175, 176
    Boatswain's Mate Charles Bergman................................. 176–178
    Landsman George Fox, U. S. Navy.................................. 178–180
    Landsman Michael Lanahan, U. S. Navy............................. 180, 181
    Coalpasser Thomas Melville, U. S. Navy........................... 181–184
    Coxswain Benjamin R. Wilber, U. S. Navy.......................... 184, 185
    Fireman John H. Pank, U. S. Navy................................. 185, 186
    Seaman Otto Rau, U. S. Navy...................................... 186, 187
    Fireman William Gartrell, U. S. Navy............................. 187–189
    Seaman Edward Mattson, U. S. Navy................................ 189–191
    Mess Attendant John H. Turpin, U. S. Navy........................ 191–193
    Seaman Martin Larsen, U. S. Navy................................. 193
Ninth day:
    Passed Assistant Engineer Bowers (recalled)...................... 194
    Seaman Harry S. McCann, U. S. Navy............................... 199, 200
    Landsman Kane, U. S. Navy.. 200, 201
    Commander James M. Forsyth, U. S. Navy........................... 201–203
    Machinist Charles Goodwin.. 203, 20.
    Interrogation of survivors, officers and men, of the Maine, at military
      barracks, Key West... 204
Tenth day:
    Ensign W. V. N. Powelson (recalled).............................. 205–218
    George Cornell... 218–220
    Capt. Frank Stevens.. 220, 221
Eleventh day:
    Chief Engineer Howell (recalled)................................. 221, 222
    Ensign Powelson (recalled)....................................... 222
    Chief Engineer Howell (recalled)................................. 224
    Gunner's Mate Rundquist (recalled)............................... 224–229
    Gunner's Mate Schluter (recalled)................................ 229–231
    Chief Gunner's Mate Olsen (recalled)............................. 232–238
    Naval Cadet Cluverius (recalled)................................. 238, 239
Twelfth day:
    Gunner's Mate Smith.. 239–242
    Naval Constructor J. B. Hoover................................... 242–244
    Carpenter Helm (recalled).. 244–246
    Consul-General Fitzhugh Lee...................................... 246, 247
Thirteenth and fourteenth days:
    Naval Constructor Hoover... 247
    Carpenter Helm, U. S. Navy....................................... 247
    Ensign Powelson, U. S. Navy...................................... 248
    Chief Gunner's Mate Olsen, U. S. Navy............................ 249–252
    Gunner's Mate T. Smith, U. S. Navy............................... 252
    Gunner's Mate Schluter, U. S. Navy............................... 252, 253
    Gunner's Mate Rundquist, U. S. Navy.............................. 253–256
Fifteenth day:
    Commander G. A. Converse, U. S. Navy............................. 257–260
Sixteenth day:
    Capt. John Haggerty.. 261, 262
    William Henry Dwyer, submarine diver............................. 262–264
    Ensign Powelson (recalled)....................................... 264, 265
    Andrew Olsen, chief gunner's mate (recalled)..................... 265–267
    T. Smith, gunner's mate (recalled)............................... 267, 268
    Carl Rundquist, gunner's mate (recalled)......................... 268, 269
    Gunner's Mate Schluter (recalled)................................ 270
    Lieutenant-Commander Wainwright (recalled)....................... 270, 271
    Naval Constructor Hoover (recalled).............................. 271
Seventeenth day:
    Lieut. H. Hutchins... 272
    Chief Engineer Howell (recalled)................................. 272, 273
    Commander Converse (recalled).................................... 273, 274

	Page.
Eighteenth day:	
Submarine Diver Dwyer (recalled)	274–277
Lieutenant Hutchins (recalled)	277
Ensign Powelson (recalled)	277
Nineteenth day	278
Twentieth day	278
Twenty-first day	278
Twenty-second day	279
Twenty-third day:	
Findings of the court	279–281
Adjournment	281
Exhibits:	
A	285
B	287
C	288
D	289
E	290
F	291
G	292
H	295
I	297
K	299
L	301
M	303

www.ingramcontent.com/pod-product-compliance
Lightning Source LLC
Chambersburg PA
CBHW030259240426
43673CB00040B/1002